THE VERBAL TENSE SYSTEM
IN LATE BIBLICAL HEBREW PROSE

HARVARD SEMITIC MUSEUM PUBLICATIONS

Lawrence E. Stager, General Editor
Michael D. Coogan, Director of Publications

HARVARD SEMITIC STUDIES

W. Randall Garr, Jo Ann Hackett, and John Huehnergard, editors

THE VERBAL TENSE SYSTEM
IN
LATE BIBLICAL HEBREW PROSE

by
Ohad Cohen

Translated by
Avi Aronsky

Eisenbrauns
Winona Lake, Indiana
2013

THE VERBAL SYSTEM
IN LATE BIBLICAL HEBREW PROSE
by
Ohad Cohen

Printed in the United States of America

www.eisenbrauns.com

Library of Congress Cataloging-in-Publication Data

Cohen, Ohad, 1971– author.
  [Ma'arekhet ha-zemanim shel ha-po'al ba-'Ivrit ha-mikra'it ha-me'uheret.
  English]
  The verbal tense system in late Biblical Hebrew prose / by Ohad Cohen ;
  translated by Avi Aronsky.
        pages cm. — (Harvard Semitic studies ; 63)
        Revised and expanded version of the author's thesis (doctoral)—
        Universitah ha-'Ivrit bi-Yerushalayim, 2008.
        Includes bibliographical references and index.
        ISBN 978-1-57506-943-2 (hardback : alk. paper)
        1. Hebrew language—Tense.   2. Bible. Old Testament—Language,
  style.   I. Title.
        PJ4659.C64 2013
        492.4′562—dc23
                                                          2013015991

The paper used in this publication meets the minimum requirements of the American
National Standard for Information Sciences—Permanence of Paper for Printed Library
Materials, ANSI Z39.48-1984.⊗™

For my parents, Karlo and Naomi

Contents

Acknowledgments

Rarely, a person raised in one country, with its language, meets a person from another country, with its other language, and the two share a mutual sense of home. I met Avi Aronsky at the National Library, in a moment of grace that blossomed into friendship and collaboration. I thank Avi for his careful and dedicated translation of this book. Without his work, I may never have completed this intense and intensive journey. I would like to thank my supervisor Steven Fassberg for his patient encouragement and advice throughout my entire time as his student. I also owe a debt of gratitude to Avi Hurvitz, the co-supervisor of my thesis with Prof. Fassberg, for essentially introducing me to the field of Second Temple Hebrew.

At many stages of this project, I benefited from the intellectual inspiration of Gideon Goldenberg. His guidance, erudition, and encouragement pushed me to dig deeper and enhance my understanding of the verbal tense system. Dana Taube read multiple drafts of this book and commented on every chapter. I appreciate Dana's friendship, intellectual inspiration, and penetrating constructive criticism— all of which obliged me to constantly reorganize my thoughts and sharpen my findings, arguments, and theory.

I truly appreciate the interest, support, and helpful comments of John Huehnergard, the general editor of the Harvard Semitic Studies Series. I would also like to thank W. Randall Garr and Jo Ann Hackett, the editors of this series, for their insightful and thought-provoking suggestions. Moreover, I owe a debt of gratitude to Michael D. Coogan, the director of publications, for his copyediting and review of the entire manuscript.

Between 2001 and 2002, a group of scholars met at The Hebrew University's Institute for Advanced Studies to discuss Biblical Hebrew in its Northwest Semitic setting. At this forum, I had the privilege of building relationships with Jan Joosten, Edward L. Greenstein, and Elisha Qimron. I would like to thank them for the scholarly conversations, which elicited an abundance of helpful comments and suggestions.

I owe a debt of gratitude to my Akkadian teacher and friend Elnathan Weissert for suffusing me with his passion for ancient languages. I cherish our long friendship, gastronomic adventures, and German football odysseys. I would also like to thank Ronnie Goldstein for our discussions on the complex nature of biblical texts. His experience, knowledge, and uncompromising insistence on detailed analysis have contributed immensely to my research. Throughout our shared trek through the various strata of the academy, Ronnie's friendship was and remains a precious resource.

I gratefully acknowledge the pre-press services of Miriam Nisim and the assiduous verification of scriptural references on the part of my research assistant, Aure Ben-Zevi. The same can be said for the guidance and sage advice that was offered by Shukki (Yehoshua) Weiss and Sonia Blubstein.

This book was published with the generous support of the Israel Science Foundation.

In addition, I would like to express my enduring gratitude to my family: my father Karlo and my mother Naomi to whom I dedicate this book; my sisters Orian and Noya (although we all left Yad Mordechai and embarked on separate paths, I still carry with me the special childhood memories from the kibbutz); and to my brother-in-law Nir for instilling some order and logic into the untidy nature of my work.

Last but not least, I am eternally grateful to my wife Shimrit for her love and patience and for taking care of everyday life as I was writing this book; and to my children Yahli, Nevo, and Meitar—the only ones who take my stories seriously.

Ohad Cohen
Jerusalem 2013

Introduction

This book provides a synchronic and diachronic structural account of the Biblical Hebrew verbal tense system during the Second Temple period. More specifically, this analysis covers the books of Esther, Daniel, Ezra and Nehemiah, and some of Chronicles (the non-synoptic parts). The use of the term "tense," which appears in the title of this work, is a mere formality and carries no significance regarding the actual meaning of the verbal system. As such, the "tenses" that have been included in our description comprise the entire range of the verbal usages (or all the "*tiroirs verbaux*"[1]) in the biblical corpus. This structural account is grounded on three fundamental distinctions: between a diachronic and synchronic perspective of the linguistic system; between "langue" and "parole"; and between the syntagmatic and paradigmatic spheres.[2]

In the first part of the book, we will address the inherently complex nature of the biblical text, as well as the ramifications of this complexity for our account of Biblical Hebrew. A major premise of this work is that the Bible contains different styles and was written by different authors over many centuries. For this very reason, we will analyze the system using two different methods: a synchronic approach; and a diachronic comparison with the other strata of the Hebrew language, namely the biblical texts of the First Temple period and the Dead Sea Scrolls, and when necessary the language of the Sages.

From a diachronic standpoint, this structural analysis is based on the assumption that the maintenance and replacement of a linguistic marker are two sides of the same coin (Saussure 1972:104-113). The use of any linguistic marker is likely to erode over time, but the most salient feature of any frayed usage is the staying power of the old material. Regardless of the factors behind the erosion, this process always severs the relationship between the marked and the marker on the diachronic level. In fact, this rupture constitutes no less than the primary interest of this work. Put differently, we will endeavor to delineate the changes that marked the transition from the classical era to the Second Temple period. Moreover, where possible, we will discern the reasons behind these changes by dint of a meticulous synchronic review of the Second Temple period verbal system.

Saussure's schematic outline (ibid.:246) underscores both the continuity and change that informed the transition between these two eras:

---

1. This is the term used by Damourette and Pichon (1932:§806-807).
2. The structuralist approach that we will use is grounded on the works of Saussure (1972) and Hjelmslev (1961), inter alios. These distinctions were introduced by Saussure (1972:97-103, 166-169, 170-175). His seminal work on modern linguistics, *Cours de linguistique générale* (1972), was first published in 1916.

Period A

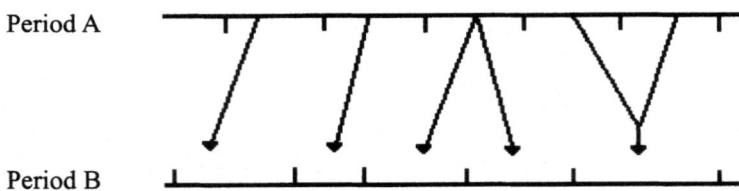

Period B

Another Saussurian idea that underpins our structural account is the distinction between "langue" and "parole." The former is the theoretical structure of a language that is shared by all its speakers, whereas "parole" is the actual use of the "langue" within a given context (ibid.:97-103, 166-169). The first step in this process is to classify and analyze all the verb forms that turn up in our corpus, namely to conduct an exhaustive review of the "parole." The next step is to present the generalizations that derive from the first stage and undergird our account of the system's "langue" elements. Finally, we will elucidate the complex mutual relations between the two spheres. In other words, we will elucidate the manner in which the abstract edifice rests on the foundations of all the occurrences, on the one hand, and how the theoretical meaning is reflected in each and every occurrence, on the other. One of the methodological risks that looms over any account that ignores this distinction is the possibility of confusing the linguistic marker's hypothetical or possible meanings with its concrete expressions in different linguistic environments.

With the objective of shedding some light on the system that stands behind the "parole," the structural analysis will draw on yet another primary distinction—the one between syntagmatic and paradigmatic relationships (ibid.:170-175). In other words, we will differentiate between the manner in which multiple verb forms interact in a succession and how they replace one another within identical or similar contexts. The aim of this undertaking is to evaluate the various alternatives and assess their limitations.

Over the years, myriad efforts have been made to provide an in-depth account of the Hebrew verbal system. Among the most notable routes that scholars have embarked upon are temporal, aspectual, modal, comparative-historical, and, in recent decades, text-linguistic. Our own efforts to formulate a comprehensive description of the verbal system during the Second Temple period using the structural method aspires neither to introduce a new approach nor to reject the established dichotomies. On the contrary, we will avail ourselves of the existing approaches throughout this work for the purpose of illuminating our claims. Moreover, in adopting the structural method, we hope to establish a new overarching framework for the research of the Biblical Hebrew verbal system.

In applying the structural method to the discussion of the biblical verbal system, our primary goal is to cast the long-standing debate between the temporal and aspectual approaches in a new light. Since the early nineteenth century, biblical scholars have argued over the fundamental difference between forms that are inflected with a prefix (*yiqtol*) and those inflected with a suffix (*qatal*). According to the aspectual school of thought, which dates back to the work of Ewald (1827) and reached its apex with the treatise of Driver (1892), the basic distinction between these two forms is a matter of aspect. In contrast, the tense school avers that the distinction is between two different tenses.

Adherents of the structuralist approach undertake to determine the meaning of linguistic markers by contrasting them with the other linguistic markers in a given environment. Therefore, any structuralist would probably consider a theory on the verbal system that is based on but one primary distinction, such as the contrast between *yiqtol* and *qatal*, as arbitrary and inadequate. For example, the distinction between *yiqtol* and *qatal* (known as the imperfect and perfect) presupposes that the contrast between these forms undergirds the entire system. A change in perspective to, say, *wayyiqtol* and the participle is thus likely to lead to different conclusions. Alternatively, the distinction might be the one between *weqatal* and the imperative, and so on. According to the structural analysis, none of these dichotomies outranks the others.

Goldenberg argues that the finite verb is a "predicative complex," which is comprised of three fundamental components: the lexical element; the marking of person; and the nexus (1985). On the morphological level, verbal predication also requires the marking of tense, mode, aspect, and voice. These tasks are accomplished in Hebrew by setting the components of the predicative complex in a particular order (e.g., a prefixed inflection alongside a suffixed inflection) and by using various patterns (i.e., verbal stems). Following in Goldenberg's footsteps, any description of the "predicative complex" must take into account the different axes on which the grammatical contrasts are aligned. This analysis does not seek to subordinate one axis to another, but to evaluate the complex relationships between the various axes. In so doing, we accentuate the interaction between the axes, regardless of whether they bolster or neutralize each other.

In putting together this methodical, structural, and synchronic account, we also hope to provide a philological tool for assaying biblical texts. One hundred years ago, Saussure called upon researchers to isolate the science of linguistics from classical philology (1972:13-22). This measure was important at the time because it helped place the field of linguistics on solid footing. However, over the years, this barrier has had a detrimental effect, for it has frequently prevented a mutually beneficial cross-pollination between these two branches of the humanities. The Bible is a complex, multilayered text that mounts numerous philological challenges to those seeking to enter its gates. With this in mind, the present study undertakes to strike a bond between these two fields of research.

Structure of the Book

The present work is divided into two main parts: a methodological survey and a descriptive analysis of the verbal system in late biblical prose. In the methodological section, we will discuss the eclectic nature of the biblical corpus, including the implications of this heterogeneity on linguistic efforts to formulate a synchronic structural account of its texts. We will then discuss the principal linguistic concepts of this work and the complex nature of the verbal paradigm. This will be followed by a survey of the different solutions that have been broached over the years for interpreting the Hebrew verbal system, with a special emphasis on the debate among the supporters of the tense-based theories, scholars focusing on aspect, and those focusing on mode. Against this background, we will demonstrate the advantages of an approach that stresses the connection between these perspectives over those seeking to impose the view of one camp at the expense of the other.

The second main part will offer a synchronic account of the verbal system from the Second Temple period. This chapter features a categorical breakdown and analysis of all the verbs in the prose texts of our corpus (4,270 in toto). The functions of each form will be evaluated on two different levels: from a syntagmatic standpoint, we will describe the relations between each form and the verbs or other components in a given context; from a paradigmatic standpoint, we will evaluate the significance of alternative elements within the framework of similar sentence patterns. This section is comprised of three chapters, each of which is dedicated to a different group of verb forms: the first chapter discusses the indicative system (*qatal*, *wayyiqtol*, and the participle); the second explores the modal system[3] and arrays the general modal forms (*yiqtol*, *weqatal*, and the infinitive construct) opposite the volitive system (the cohortative, the imperative, and the jussive); and the third chapter discusses the unique predicative roles of the infinitive absolute form. Each chapter is divided into two central parts—the reference time and modal axes.

---

3. For the purposes of this study, the *yiqtol* and *weqatal* forms are considered part of the modal system.

Terminology

The following is a categorization of all the biblical verb forms from the Second Temple period:[4]

Qatal (קטל, עבר, Perfect, Past)

Wayyiqtol (ויקטל, עתיד מהופך, Converted Imperfect, Imperfect with *Waw* Consecutive)

Participle (קוטל, הווה, בינוני, Present)

Yiqtol (יקטל, עתיד, Imperfect, Future)

Infinitive Construct (לקטל, מקור נטוי)

Weqatal (וקטל, עבר מהופך, Converted Perfect, Perfect with *Waw* Consecutive)

Cohortative (אקטלה, עתיד מוארך)

Imperative (ציווי)

Jussive (עתיד מקוצר)

Infinitive Absolute (קטול, מקור מוחלט)

As can be seen, we will be using a general-purpose style of transliteration rather than an academic one (e.g., *weqatal* instead of *wǝqȧṭal*).

---

4. As noted above, the linguistic terminology in this field is weighed down by a surfeit of terms that are ascribed to each and every form. The names are primarily based on elementary inflected forms from the *qatal* root. Every term is essentially an abridgement of all the persons and verbal stems that are likely to appear in that same pattern. For example, the *qatal* form (third person singular) is used to denote all the persons: קטלתי, קטלתָ, קטלתְ, קטלָה, קטלנו etc.

Part I
The Research Methodology of the Biblical Verb System

1. The Text

1.1 The Corpus: The Chronological Facet

In this chapter, we will examine the methodological ramifications of the characteristics of the biblical texts on the linguistic account of this corpus. There is wide consensus among biblical scholars[5] that the Bible is a conglomeration of multifarious texts which were written over many generations. Nevertheless, the literature tends to refer to all the parts of the biblical canon as a coherent unit that can be analyzed from a synchronic standpoint. In consequence, one can find examples in which juridical passages in Leviticus, prose from Genesis, a psalm dated to the Second Temple period, and the wisdom literature in Ecclesiastes are grouped together under the same analytical framework. This approach, which ignores the text's various strata and the different contexts in which it was created, is liable to result in misguided conclusions.

Those wishing to research Biblical Hebrew in adherence to linguistical standards are bound to encounter several methodological obstacles, which may be divided into two categories: the development of modern biblical research and the multilayered nature of the text. Modern research originated with an attempt to break away from the theological approach, which assumes that the Bible's books constitute a harmonious cultural and textual whole. Notwithstanding linguistic attempts to atomize the Bible, theological approaches continue to impact contemporary biblical research. Since linguistic accounts are never free of cultural considerations, the notion of unity and cultural continuity also plays a decisive role in the widespread perception of a united biblical text. Ben-Hayyim (1985:17-18) explains why the link between linguistic continuity and the question of Hebrew's unity is so complex:

> Admitting the historical unity of the Hebrew language is another facet of admitting to the continuity of the literary tradition in all its forms. Only this sort of view can justify the reason why—for example—an historian of the Hebrew language—a grammarian or lexicographer—will not include the inscription of Mesha the king of Moab or the inscriptions of the kings of Byblos within the boundaries of the Hebrew language, but will include . . . the language of the *piyyut* [Hebrew liturgical poetry] or the Rabbinical literature. For there is no doubt that from a purely linguistical standpoint, free of any consideration of a

---

5. I have no intention of discussing the claims of the "minimalist school," according to which the entire Bible was written during a relatively short time span in the Second Temple period. To the best of my knowledge, there is no linguistic evidence to support this theory; see Hurvitz (2000).

bond to society and its literature, the Mesha inscription is closer to a chapter in the book of Kings than the propinquity of *Josippon* to the book of Kings.

Accordingly, the theological and cultural unity that is imputed to the Bible, as well as the canonization process its texts underwent, hinders the formulation of a linguistic account which endeavors to implement a meticulous linguistic methodology.

The difference between a diachronic account—a historical survey that tracks a language's changes over time—and a synchronic account—an examination of every element of a language at a given point in time—did not always fall under the purview of linguistics. In other words, this perspective was not at the forefront of linguistic research until the late nineteenth century. The primary architect and standard bearer of this distinction was the linguist Ferdinand de Saussure (1857-1913), but it took many years for his approach to seep into the field of Bible research,[6] as researchers only began to focus on synchronic accounts of various units of the Hebrew Bible in the 1970s. According to Ben-Hayyim (1977:77, including note 24):

> For some reason, the early Hebrew grammarians did not manage to offer an all-encompassing theory on the uses of the tenses. . . . [T]hey viewed the entire language of the Bible as though it was of the same cloth. . . . It is incumbent upon one that seeks . . . a solution to the Hebrew tenses to attempt to isolate literary and linguistic units and observe them as individual units.[7]

In consequence, those interested in the biblical verbal system must take into account the fact that all the important grammar books in this field—be they from the early[8] or late[9] twentieth century—are lacking in this respect. Furthermore, the absence of a methodological approach that aims to distinguish between the Bible's assorted layers of language is glaring, even in distinguished works other than the comprehensive grammars.[10]

---

6. In all likelihood, the discussions that Driver provided in his introductory book (1891) are the first systematic examination of the differences between classical and Second Temple period Hebrew. He was preceded by Gesenius (1815:28-30), who put together a long list of "late" words and phrases that are characteristic of the Second Temple period. Although these first signs of a diachronic consciousness date back to as early as the nineteenth century, contemporaneous scholars did not fully comprehend the systematic methodology that ultimately germinated from this conception.

7. In the aftermath of Ben-Hayyim's article, many important studies have taken into account the synchronic viewpoint. Among the most distinguished works are Niccacci (1990), Eskhult (1990, 2000), Hatav (1997), Goldfajn (1998), and Heller (2004).

8. E.g., Gesenius, Kautzsch, and Cowley (1910), Joüon (1923), Bergsträsser (1918-1928), and Davidson (1901).

9. Also see Joüon and Muraoka (1996) as well as Waltke and O'Connor (1990).

10. For example, Ewald (1827), Driver (1892), Bauer (1910), Bauer and Leander (1922),

Another obstacle pertains to the multilayered nature of the biblical corpus itself. Not only is the text comprised of many works, but the books themselves are often comprised of various layers of editing. Put differently, even after grappling with the diachronic question, the researcher must still untangle editorial knots, such as the following well-known examples.

The first is the story of the crossing of the Red Sea in Exodus 14 and 15. On the face of things, chapter 15 picks up where the former left off, namely Moses and the Israelites continue to express their gratitude for the miracle. However, a closer look at the two chapters reveals that they diverge in all that concerns their content, theological objective, and language. Scholars basically agree that the song in chapter 15 is one of the oldest texts in the Bible, as its language is representative of Hebrew's archaic corpus.[11] What is more, this change is relatively easy to distinguish because there is a clear transition from prose to poetry.

The second example is more complicated, for it does not involve a transition from one genre to another. The book of Isaiah contains 66 chapters that are attributed to the seer Isaiah son of Amoz, who prophesied concerning Judah and Jerusalem in the reigns of Uzziah, Jotham, Ahaz, and Hezekiah, kings of Judah (Isaiah 1:1). However, most scholars agree that only chapters 1-39 reflect the prophecies of Isaiah son of Amoz, and the rest of the book is attributed to the enterprise of a prophet (or prophets) who is generally referred to as "Deutero-Isaiah."[12] Whereas the "son of Amoz" lived in the eighth century BCE, Deutero-Isaiah is a postexilic prophet. In other words, during the transition from chapter 39 to 40, which usually appear on the same page of the biblical text, the reader unwittingly skips over a swath of about two hundred years.[13] It bears noting that these two examples are merely the tip of the iceberg in all that concerns the editorial complexity of the biblical texts.

Lastly, the extant linguistic information in the biblical texts presents certain difficulties. The phonetic system is uniform due to the fact that most of the phonetic data (i.e., the vowel points and accents) about Biblical Hebrew has reached our hands via the mediation of the Masoretes between the sixth and ninth century

---

Blake (1951), and Andersen (1974). A comprehensive survey of all the important roadmarks from the medieval grammarians until the mid-twentieth century can be found in McFall (1982). All the studies that he enumerates share this handicap.

11. This song is discussed in all the scientific books of commentary, such as Durham (1987:198-210). On pp. 198-199, Durham provides an extensive bibliographical list of works that touch upon this subject.

12. For a discussion of "Deutero-Isaiah" see, among others, the introduction to Baltzer's commentary (1999:1-44).

13. The prophetic material of an anonymous seer was also added to the book of Zechariah. Whereas chapters 1 through 8 are attributed to Zechariah himself, chapters 9 through 14 apparently belong to another prophet or other prophets; see the introduction to Meyers and Meyers (1999:3-84).

ce. For the most part, the same can be said for the morphological system. The vocalization and accentuation of the Hebrew Bible reflect the Masoretic reading tradition of the biblical texts, which in many respects is indicative of an ancient and authentic linguistic reality. That said, can we be sure that this tradition duly reflects the original language and the development from the beginning of the First Temple period to the latter stages of the Second Temple period?

It is almost certain that more than a few linguistic changes occurred over the ages. For example, it is reasonable to assume that by the time of the Masoretes there was no longer a distinction between the pharyngeal and velar ח, for otherwise they would have marked the phonetic difference between these two consonants, just as was done in the case of the *šin* right (שׁ) and *śin* left (שׂ). However, a review of the transliterations of the Hebrew names in the Septuagint, which was rendered in the second century bce, shows that there was once a distinction between these two phonemes. For example, חנה = Avva (1 Sm 1:2), חירה = Ιρας (Gn 38:1), and חמדן = Αμαδα (Gn 36:26) differ from אחיתפל = Αχιτοφελ (2 Sm 15:12), אחימעץ = Αχιμαας (2 Sm 15:36), and חירם = Χιραμ (2 Sm 5:11). Be that as it may, the delicate question of which linguistic reality and time period the Septuagint reflects[14] is beyond the scope of this book.

1.2 The Various Genres and Textemes

In addition to the corpus's aforementioned chronological complexity, the profusion of genres constitutes yet another obstacle for scholars attempting to decipher the Hebrew Scriptures. As cited above, Ben-Hayyim (1977:77, note 24) claims that the early grammarians failed to develop an extensive account of the Hebrew verbal system due to their lack of interest in the corpus's linguistic units (i.e., the diachronic dimension) and literary units: all forms of prose; the language of the law; chronological and genealogical lists; poetry; prophecy; and wisdom literature.

Until the rise of text linguistics in the 1960s, books of grammar and related studies basically turned a blind eye to linguistical approaches that distinguish between the various genres. Starting in the late 1960s, the field's attention shifted away from the lone sentence to larger units of text. One of the leading representatives of this approach is H. Weinrich (1964:19):

> Eine Beschreibung der Tempus-Formen und ihrer Funktionen ist Teil der Grammatik einer Sprache, genauer der Syntax. Die Syntax ist jedoch nur dann ein adäquater Ort für die in Frage stehende Tempus-Theorie, wenn sie der Untersuchung den nötigen Spielraum läßt. . . . Offensichtlich ist der Satz weder die größte noch die kleinste Einheit einer sprachlichen Äußerung,

---

14. For an expansive discussion on this matter, see Blau's seminal article (1983).

sondern allenfalls eine Einheit mittlerer Länge irgendwo—zwischen dem Text und seinen Phonemen oder Merkmalen.

Text linguistics thus paved the way for an approach that places an emphasis on the different textual units and genres. That said, differentiating between genres is not always simple, especially in all that concerns the distinction between prose and poetry. With this in mind, Watson (1984) established linguistic and stylistic criteria for distinguishing between these two genres,[15] such as unique vocabulary, exceptional word order, and the use of tempo, meter, parallelism, and word pairs. The main problem with Watson's list is that most of his criteria apply to prose as well. For instance, Berlin (1985:9-10) claims that,

> Nonpoetic texts not only have parallelism—they have a lot of it! The question is not how much parallelism a text has, but how much of it is effective and meaningful in terms of focusing the message on itself (the poetic function).

Berlin bases her arguments on the work of Roman Jakobson, who had a significant influence on the linguistic research of parallelism. According to Jakobson (1960:358):

> The selection is produced on the base of equivalence, similarity and dissimilarity, synonymity, and antonymity, while the combination, the build up of the sequence, is based on contiguity. *The poetic function projects the principle of equivalence from the axis of selection into the axis of combination.* Equivalence is promoted to the constitutive device of the sequence.

At this point, we have no intention of delving into the complicated distinction between prose and poetry. However, soft-pedaling this distinction is liable to undermine the structural account of the system.[16] Niccacci (1997:92) suggests that,

> Perhaps, as some scholars claim, we are unable to draw a clear-cut distinction between poetry and prose in every case; after all, we face a similar problem with today's texts. However cases of clear, "pure" poetry do exist. . . . My proposal, then, is to begin by carefully studying clear poetry and to try to evaluate it against clear prose.

As per Niccacci's recommendation, let us examine the differences between two separate accounts—prose and poetic—of the parting of the Red Sea in Exodus 14:21-27 (on the right) versus 15:4-8 (left):

---

15. See Watson (1984:44-60), especially the list on pp. 46-47.
16. A prominent example of a researcher ignoring the distinction between prose and poetry is McFall's criticism of the conversive theory (1982:18). In order to substantiate his arguments, McFall cites a long list of *wayyiqtol* forms that intermittently signify the past and future, but he fails to account for the fact that all the past forms are in the field of prose and all the future forms in poetic frameworks.

(2)	(1)
מַרְכְּבֹת פַּרְעֹה וְחֵילוֹ **יָרָה** בַיָּם	**וַיֵּט** מֹשֶׁה אֶת יָדוֹ עַל הַיָּם
וּמִבְחַר שָׁלִשָׁיו **טֻבְּעוּ** בְיַם סוּף	**וַיּוֹלֶךְ** יְהוָה אֶת הַיָּם בְּרוּחַ קָדִים עַזָּה כָּל הַלַּיְלָה
תְּהֹמֹת **יְכַסְיֻמוּ**	**וַיָּשֶׂם** אֶת הַיָּם לֶחָרָבָה
יָרְדוּ בִמְצוֹלֹת כְּמוֹ אָבֶן	**וַיִּבָּקְעוּ** הַמָּיִם
יְמִינְךָ יְהוָה נֶאְדָּרִי בַּכֹּחַ	**וַיָּבֹאוּ** בְנֵי יִשְׂרָאֵל בְּתוֹךְ הַיָּם בַּיַּבָּשָׁה
יְמִינְךָ יְהוָה **תִּרְעַץ** אוֹיֵב	וְהַמַּיִם לָהֶם חוֹמָה מִימִינָם וּמִשְּׂמֹאלָם
וּבְרֹב גְּאוֹנְךָ **תַּהֲרֹס** קָמֶיךָ	**וַיִּרְדְּפוּ** מִצְרַיִם
תְּשַׁלַּח חֲרֹנְךָ	**וַיָּבֹאוּ** אַחֲרֵיהֶם כֹּל סוּס פַּרְעֹה רִכְבּוֹ וּפָרָשָׁיו אֶל תּוֹךְ הַיָּם ...
יֹאכְלֵמוֹ כַּקַּשׁ	**וַיֵּט** מֹשֶׁה אֶת יָדוֹ עַל הַיָּם
וּבְרוּחַ אַפֶּיךָ **נֶעֶרְמוּ** מַיִם	**וַיָּשָׁב** הַיָּם לִפְנוֹת בֹּקֶר לְאֵיתָנוֹ
נִצְּבוּ כְמוֹ נֵד נֹזְלִים	וּמִצְרַיִם **נָסִים** לִקְרָאתוֹ
קָפְאוּ תְהֹמֹת בְּלֶב יָם	**וַיְנַעֵר** יְהוָה אֶת מִצְרַיִם בְּתוֹךְ הַיָּם

Pharaoh's chariots and his army he **has cast (qatal)** into the sea; and the pick of his officers **drowned (qatal)** in the Sea of Reeds. The deeps **covered them (yiqtol)**; they **went down (qatal)** into the depths like a stone. Your right hand, O LORD, glorious in power, your right hand, O LORD, **shattered (yiqtol)** the foe! In your great triumph **you broke (yiqtol)** your opponents; **you sent forth (yiqtol)** your fury, it **consumed (yiqtol)** them like straw. At the blast of your nostrils the waters **piled up (qatal)**, the floods **stood straight (qatal)** like a wall; the deeps **froze (qatal)** in the heart of the sea. (Ex 15:4-8)

Then Moses **held out (wayyiqtol)** his arm over the sea and the LORD **drove back (wayyiqtol)** the sea with a strong east wind all that night, and **turned (wayyiqtol)** the sea into dry ground. The waters **were split (wayyiqtol)**, and the Israelites **went (wayyiqtol)** into the sea on dry ground, the waters forming a wall for them on their right and on their left. The Egyptians **came in pursuit (wayyiqtol)** after them into the sea, all of Pharaoh's horses, chariots, and horsemen. . . . Moses **held out (wayyiqtol)** his arm over the sea, and at daybreak the sea **returned (wayyiqtol)** to its normal state, and the Egyptians **fled (participle)** at its approach. But the LORD **hurled (wayyiqtol)** the Egyptians into the sea. (Ex 14:21-27)

The contrast between the role of the verb forms in each passage jumps out at the eye. Exodus 14 features a string of *wayyiqtol* forms that construct a narrative succession of past actions. The story progresses from one action to the next by concatenating a series of sequential actions. In contrast, the crux of the matter in Exodus 15 is repetition and emphasis, not succession. Although the verb forms therein also represent past events, they comprise a parallelism of two different verb forms *qatal/yiqtol*, for example:

(3) תְּהֹמֹת **יְכַסְיֻמוּ** // **יָרְדוּ** בִמְצוֹלֹת כְּמוֹ אָבֶן

The deeps **covered them**; **they went down** into the depths like a stone (Ex 15:5)

Instead of presenting a new action, the verse refers to the same event. The iterations in the second clause of the parallelism constitute semantic counterparts which expand upon the description of the action in the first part.[17]

It is worth noting that other distinctions, besides the one between prose and poetry, must be grasped in order to attain an in-depth understanding of the biblical verbal system. For instance, Niccacci demonstrates that there are significant differences in the prose corpus between the use of a verb in direct speech and in narrative contexts.[18]

1.3 Research Methods

Following in Niccacci's footsteps, the point of departure of this book is that each genre must be investigated on an individual basis.[19] In the case of the Second Temple period corpus, it is incumbent upon us to base this account on those texts for which there is broad consensus over their genre. Once the preliminary work of demarcating the various genres is behind us, we will refine the distinction between the various textemes within each genre. Only after this taxonomy has been completed will we be able to step back and view the entire system.

We will also draw a chronological distinction between the different units. With this in mind, a linguistic examination will be integrated with the conclusions of critical Bible commentary. This, then, brings us to the question of the appropriate chronological scope for our account of the verbal system. If we consistently apply the logic behind the contention that there is a substantial difference between texts from the ninth century bce and those from the Hellenistic age, then we should also assume a similar gap between a text from the fifth century bce and one from the Hellenistic era. Stretching the logic of chronological differentiation to its limit may very well lead us to the conclusion that it is impossible to compare all the texts of the Bible or to generalize about the entire corpus, for every observation of this sort inevitably entails a degree of conjecture. This kind of purist approach is liable to stand in the way of a comprehensive account and leave us with nothing but loosely connected examples.

---

17. Berlin (1985:12-14) and Niccacci (1997:78-80) offer similar explanations for the different accounts of Sisera's demise in chapter 4 and 5 of the book of Judges. O'Connor (1980), Watson (1984), Zevit (1990), Landy (1992), Niccacci (2001), and Collins (1978) also explore on the linguistic differences between prose and poetry in Biblical Hebrew.
18. Niccacci has published several articles that touch upon this topic. He elaborates on his approach in *The Syntax of the Verb in Classical Hebrew Prose* (1990).
19. See Niccacci (1997:92).

Against this background, the outlook of this work dovetails smoothly with the prevalent view according to which the biblical corpus is divided into three primary historical units of language: archaic poetry, classical Biblical Hebrew from the First Temple period, and Second Temple period Biblical Hebrew.[20] From the outset of modern research, scholars realized that the language of the Bible left numerous signs of diachronic development. The linguistic Rubicon that most standard accounts refer to is the Babylonian exile. In other words, the dividing line is the transition from the language of the First Temple period to that of the Second Temple. For instance, Gesenius, Kautzsch, and Cowley (1910:§2l) noted that:

> Even in the language of the Old Testament, notwithstanding its general uniformity, there is noticeable a certain progress from an earlier to a later stage. Two periods, though with some reservations, may be distinguished: the *first*, down to the end of the Babylonian exile; and the *second*, after the exile.

Notwithstanding these observations, the research of the Second Temple period language did not truly mature until the mid-twentieth century. During the field's nascent stages, scholars distinguished between the various eras by virtue of their linguistic sense and, to some extent, their knowledge of the political changes that were ushered in by the Babylonian exile. The fact that the Babylonian exiles lived in an Aramaic-speaking environment for so long, along with the fact that Aramaic became the administrative language of the Persian Empire, had a profound impact on the Hebrew language. The following passage from Nehemiah attests to the external linguistic influences on Biblical Hebrew during this period:

(4) גַּם בַּיָּמִים הָהֵם רָאִיתִי אֶת הַיְּהוּדִים הֹשִׁיבוּ נָשִׁים אַשְׁדֳּדִיּוֹת עַמֳּנִיּוֹת מוֹאֲבִיּוֹת׃
וּבְנֵיהֶם חֲצִי מְדַבֵּר אַשְׁדּוֹדִית וְאֵינָם מַכִּירִים לְדַבֵּר יְהוּדִית וְכִלְשׁוֹן עַם וָעָם׃

> Also at that time, I saw that Jews had married Ashdodite, Ammonite, and Moabite women; a good number of their children spoke the language of Ashdod and the language of those various peoples, and did not know how to speak Judean. (Neh 13:23-24)

Although it is difficult to ascertain the nature of the Ashdodite language from the existing evidence, it is clear that a new linguistic situation had taken root during the return to Zion.

Notwithstanding these developments, not one linguistic work was fully dedicated to characterizing these two periods from a linguistic standpoint until the beginning of the twentieth century. Kropat produced the first monograph on this topic (a treatise on the syntax of Chronicles) in 1909, but it would take another half century before the publication of a related work. This lack of scholarly interest may have been connected to the discovery of Ugaritic in the late 1920s; for in the aftermath of this finding, researchers devoted themselves to exposing the

---

20. For more on this division, see, e.g., Hurvitz (1997).

links between archaic Biblical Hebrew and the newly discovered language. What is more, scholars lacked the appropriate research methods for drawing a linguistic distinction between the two epochs.

The discovery of the Dead Sea Scrolls in the late 1940s marked a true breakthrough in this field. As soon as the news broke, it was obvious that the scrolls offered a rare opportunity for researchers to familiarize themselves with the period's language on a first-hand basis.

In 1959, Kutscher laid down a central pillar in the field of Second Temple period Hebrew. Kutscher's study, *The Language and Linguistic Background of the Isaiah Scroll*, foreshadowed a major turning point in the methodological research of the Second Temple period language. In 1972, Hurvitz published *The Transition Period in Biblical Hebrew* wherein he continued along Kutscher's path and consolidated the method for evaluating the lines of linguistic antecedence and subsequence. However, unlike his mentor, Hurvitz focused primarily on the field of lexicography.[21]

From both a dialectal and chronological standpoint, the linguistic reality during the biblical era was undoubtedly more complicated than a schematic division into the archaic, classic, and Second Temple period categories. On the other hand, many studies show that there is considerable logic to using these chronological units as the basis of a comparative grammatical analysis. Our decision to view Esther, Daniel, Ezra and Nehemiah, and Chronicles (the non-synoptic parts) as an overarching unit is based on the widely accepted assumption that these books are prose texts from the Second Temple period. As such, this compendium is ample for an expansive comparative structural analysis.

---

21. Also see Polzin's research on the non-synoptic parts of Chronicles (an appreciable part of which is grounded on Kropat's conclusions). Polzin compares the language of Chronicles to the Hebrew of the First Temple (1976).

2. The Linguistic Account

This chapter features our linguistic account of Second Temple period Hebrew. It opens with a short discussion on the terminology that will accompany our linguistic description of the verbal system and serve as the conceptual infrastructure for the entire analysis.

2.1 Key Terms

2.1.1 Reference Time (R-time)

In 1947, Hans Reichenbach introduced the term "reference time" or R-time. Adherents of the traditional approach to the tense system had analyzed the chronological relations that are signified by verb forms exclusively in terms of E(vent) time and S(peech) time.[1] In other words, the chronological relations expressed by the verb illustrate the connection between the times in which the speech and event took place. However, Reichenbach showed that this theoretical system was incapable of fully explaining the many nuances expressed by verb forms in different languages. For example, it is impossible to articulate the difference between the simple past and past perfect in English in this fashion, for in both cases the event [E] transpires before the speech time [S]. Therefore, Reichenbach contended that languages express chronological relations not only by means of a binary system comprised of E-time and S-time, but also by referring to a third point which he dubbed R-time. This concept allows for a more accurate account of the chronological relations between the various forms. For instance, the English sentences below can be differentiated in the following manner:[2]

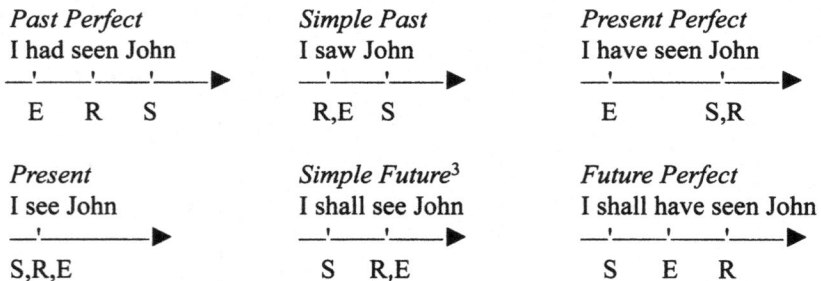

---

1. These are the terms that have been adopted by the adherents of the "tense logic" approach, such as Prior (1967) and Clifford (1969). A focused discussion on this topic, as well as bibliographical references, may be found in Hatav (1997:2-6).
2. The sentences and diagrams are taken from Reichenbach (1947:290).
3. In contrast to this configuration of the simple future, Reichenbach pairs the R with the S, instead of the E (1947:290). That said, see Reichenbach's discussion on pp. 295-296 and 297.

In these diagrams, the arrow signifies the direction of the time axis (from left to right). S stands for speech time (i.e., the present); E for the time of the event; and R for the verb's reference-time point.

Although Reichenbach introduced the concept of "reference time," he did not provide a precise definition for his neologism. Various linguists have adopted Reichenbach's three-pronged distinction, but interpret R-time in different ways. Partee (1984) and Hinrichs (1986) distinguish between verbs that describe an event (E) and those that describe a state (S). In their estimation, R-time is a temporal unit that encompasses the event and is included in the state. For example:

John got up, went to the window, and raised the blind. It was light out.

e_1 e_2 e_3 s_1

He pulled the blind down and went back to bed. He wasn't ready to face the

e_4 e_5 s_2

the day. He was too depressed.[4]

s_3

According to Partee (1984:253-256), the first clause signifies an event (E1) that encompasses an R-time (R0) (Partee assumes that R0 already exists in the discourse). E1 presents a new R-time (R1) in its own right, which contains the event E2 in the next clause. Thereafter, E2 presents a new R-time (R2) that contains E3, which then presents a new R-time (R3). Something different happens during the transition to the fourth clause, as it manifests a state (S) rather than an event. In this case, the state is not included within R3. However, since it coincides with R3, it essentially encompasses it.

Hatav (1997:54-55) offers a different explanation for the relations between the R and E in this case. R, which is represented by a concrete verb form, contains the situation designated by the same verb and not the subsequent one. As a result, there is no need to assume an R0 at the outset of the discourse, so even the verbs that signify a state do not present an R-time. Hence the R of the S(tate) is included in the final R of the succession (i.e., R3).

Kamp and Reyle (1993:§5.2, 5.4) reach a different conclusion, as they claim that there are two distinct referential categories. One category, which they dub "the Reference point (Rpt)," operates as an anaphoric element, namely it connects a given situation and whatever elements were presented earlier in the discourse. In consequence, this category is responsible for advancing the R-time along the time axis, thereby enabling this point of reference to assume a central role in narrative forms (ibid.:594-595). Kamp and Reyle's second category, the "temporal perspec-

---

4.   The sentence is taken from Partee (1984:253) e = event and s = state.

tive point" (TPpt), is charged with marking several chronological relations, such as the past of a past and the future of a past.

Comparing the hypotheses of Partee (1984) and Hatav (1997) to that of Kamp and Reyle (1993) gives rise to the following question: Do narrative forms possesses another category of R-time, as proposed by Kamp and Reyle, or a different sort of relationship between the event (E) and its R-time, as suggested by Partee and Hatav? We assume that the same category of R-time applies to the consecutive forms (*wayyiqtol* and *weqatal*). In light of the above, we can adopt the general contours of Reichenbach's basic distinction whereby the R-time is the temporal unit responsible for a verb's chronological meaning. Put differently, a verb cannot be interpreted from a chronological standpoint without defining its R-time and the nature of the relationship between the R-time and the reported action.

2.1.2 Relative versus Absolute Tense

The distinction between the concepts "relative tense" and "absolute tense" is of utmost importance to understanding the biblical tense system. A useful definition of the term "tense" was put forth by Comrie, who asserted that it is a grammatical expression of a verb form's link to the time axis (1985:9). The existence of a deictic center to which the tense refers is a sine qua non of this grammatical concept.[5] Generally speaking, the deictic axis of an absolute tense form is speech time (S). In other words, actions that come before the S-time point are in the realm of the absolute past, and subsequent elements are in the absolute future. Conversely, the deictic axis of a relative tense form is reference time (R). Therefore, it is the nature of the relationship to the deictic center that distinguishes between relative and absolute tense. Or as Comrie (1985:58, 36) put it:

> The difference between absolute and relative tense is not that between the present moment versus some other point in time as reference point, but rather between a form whose meaning specifies the present moment as reference point and a form whose meaning does not specify that the present moment must be its reference point. Relative tenses thus have the present moment as one of their possible reference points, but this is a problem of interpretation rather than of meaning.
> . . . [T]his should be interpreted to mean a tense [i.e., absolute tense] which includes as part of its meaning the present moment as deictic centre; whereas relative tense refers to a tense which does not include as part of its meaning the present moment as deictic centre.

---

5. According to Comrie, one of the major distinctions between tense and aspect is that the former must have a deictic center, whereas aspect does not even possess such a point of reference. See Comrie (1985:13-18).

In light of the above, the difference between a relative tense system (such as Biblical Hebrew) and an absolute tense system revolves around the deictic center to which the verb form refers. The absolute tenses always maintain two deictic centers. The first is the S-time and the second is the R-time. Take for example the English past perfect:

I had seen John:

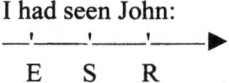

This form simultaneously marks the fact that the action is located on the absolute time axis in the past and that it takes place before its R-time.

Over the course of this research, we have found that Hebrew verbs are indeed full-fledged relative forms,[6] namely their distinct relationship to reference time is the only parameter for determining their chronological meaning. In consequence, the placement of the verb forms on the absolute time axis is always context-dependent and not part of these forms' paradigmatic meaning. In the ensuing pages, we will substantiate these claims with several examples from the Bible.

2.1.2.1   Examples of the Relative Use of *Qatal*

(5) וַיֹּאמֶר אִישׁ הָאֱלֹהִים אֶל הַמֶּלֶךְ אִם תִּתֶּן לִי אֶת חֲצִי בֵיתֶךָ לֹא אָבֹא עִמָּךְ וְלֹא אֹכַל לֶחֶם וְלֹא אֶשְׁתֶּה מַּיִם בַּמָּקוֹם הַזֶּה: כִּי כֵן צִוָּה אֹתִי בִּדְבַר יְהֹוָה לֵאמֹר לֹא תֹאכַל לֶחֶם וְלֹא תִשְׁתֶּה מָּיִם **וְלֹא תָשׁוּב** בַּדֶּרֶךְ אֲשֶׁר **הָלָכְתָּ**:

But the man of God replied to the king, Even if you give me half your wealth, I will not go in with you, nor will I eat bread or drink water in this place; for so I was commanded by the word of the LORD: you shall eat no bread and drink no water, **nor shall you go back** by the road by which you **came** ((S<)E<R). (1 Kgs 13:8-9)

In verse 9, a *qatal* form (הָלָכְתָּ) appears within a relative clause, and its R-time—the verb "תשוב"—is located in the main clause. The prophet relates the instructions that God gave him concerning his stay in Bethel. From the context, it is evident that both the verb "תשוב" and the verb "הלכת" are situated in the future realm because, from the vantage point in which the statement was made, the "man of God" has yet to leave Bethlehem. The *qatal* form expresses the fact that the act of leaving will take place before the return. Consequently, the logical relationship which Reichenbach dubs "the first anterior future" (S-E-R) applies to this case:

---

6.   The only exception to this rule is the volitive forms (the cohortative, the imperative, and the jussive). For more on this particular subject, see §9.2 below.

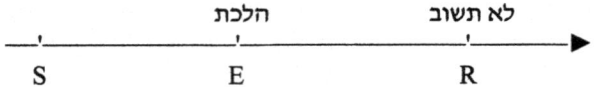

S   E   R

(6) וַיִּחַר אַף יְהֹוָה בְּמֹשֶׁה וַיֹּאמֶר הֲלֹא אַהֲרֹן אָחִיךָ הַלֵּוִי **יָדַעְתִּי** כִּי דַבֵּר **יְדַבֵּר** הוּא

The LORD became angry with Moses, and he said, There is your brother Aaron the Levite. He, **I know ((S)E<R), will speak.** (Ex 4:14)

From a chronological standpoint, the only difference between this verse and example 5 is that the event time (E) runs parallel to the speech time (S). According to Comrie, this scenario is indeed a distinct possibility in relative tense systems (ibid.:58). The essential difference between how this sort of case is interpreted in a relative system and in an absolute one is that in the former the S is a contingent and context-dependent matter, and not a part of the form's deictic axis. As in 1 Kings 13, the action of knowing precedes the action of talking:

E,S   R

(7) וֶאֱלִישָׁע **חָלָה** אֶת חָלְיוֹ אֲשֶׁר יָמוּת בּוֹ **וַיֵּרֶד** אֵלָיו יוֹאָשׁ מֶלֶךְ יִשְׂרָאֵל וַיֵּבְךְ עַל פָּנָיו
וַיֹּאמַר אָבִי אָבִי רֶכֶב יִשְׂרָאֵל וּפָרָשָׁיו:

Elisha **had been stricken (E<R)** with the illness of which he was to die, and King Joash of Israel **went down** to see him. He wept over him and cried, Father, father! Israel's chariots and horsemen! (2 Kgs 13:14)

In this case, the verb "חָלָה" provides the background for a succession of verbs that begins with "וַיֵּרֶד". In other words, "וַיֵּרֶד" is the cataphoric R-time of "חָלָה".

(8) חֲזַק וֶאֱמָץ כִּי אַתָּה **תַּנְחִיל** אֶת הָעָם הַזֶּה אֶת הָאָרֶץ אֲשֶׁר **נִשְׁבַּעְתִּי** לַאֲבוֹתָם
לָתֵת לָהֶם:

Be strong and resolute, for you **shall apportion** to this people the land that **I swore (E<(S<)R)** to their fathers to assign to them. (Josh 1:6)

From a linguistic standpoint, this case is not much different from the first three. Here too, a *qatal* form is arrayed in an embedded clause and its point of reference (R) is in the future. God commands Joshua to bestow (in the future) the land that was promised to Israel's ancestors (in the past). Reichenbach refers to this logical relationship as "the third anterior future" (1947:294). This example also conveys the fact that the *qatal* form ignores S-time:

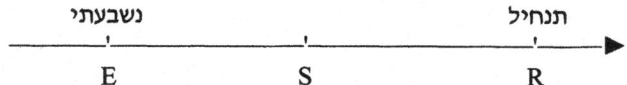

(9) וַתָּקָם הִיא וְכַלֹּתֶיהָ **וַתָּשָׁב** מִשְּׂדֵי מוֹאָב כִּי **שָׁמְעָה** בִּשְׂדֵה מוֹאָב כִּי **פָקַד** יְהוָה
אֶת עַמּוֹ לָתֵת לָהֶם לָחֶם:

She started out with her daughters-in-law and **returned** from the country of Moab; for in the country of Moab **she had heard (E<R(<S))** that the LORD **had taken note (E<R(<S))** of his people and given them food. (Ruth 1:6)

Here too the actions expressed by the *qatal* forms transpire before their reference time. More specifically, God "had taken note of his people" before Naomi got wind of the news; and only upon hearing this turn of events does she head back to Moab. Reichenbach dubs this logical relationship "the anterior past" (E-R-S):

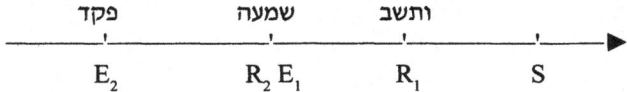

All the occurrences of the *qatal* form that we presented above are characterized by the same chronological relationship E<R.[7] So that *qatal* is an unadulterated relative tense form whose deictic axis is its reference time.

2.1.2.2   Examples of the Relative Use of the Participle

(10) וַיֹּאמֶר לְאַבְרָם יָדֹעַ תֵּדַע כִּי גֵר יִהְיֶה זַרְעֲךָ בְּאֶרֶץ לֹא לָהֶם וַעֲבָדוּם וְעִנּוּ אֹתָם
אַרְבַּע מֵאוֹת שָׁנָה: וְגַם אֶת הַגּוֹי אֲשֶׁר **יַעֲבֹדוּ דָן** אָנֹכִי וְאַחֲרֵי כֵן יֵצְאוּ בִּרְכֻשׁ גָּדוֹל:

And he said to Abram, Know well that your offspring shall be strangers in a land not theirs, and they shall be enslaved and oppressed four hundred years; but **I will execute judgment ((S<) |--E--|)** on the nation **they shall serve**, and
R
in the end they shall go free with great wealth. (Gn 15:13-14)

It is reasonable to assume that God's promise to Abraham did not imply that the taskmasters were judged at the very moment the promise was made. Instead, their day of reckoning would arrive when the Israelites toiled under the Egyptian yoke. In other words, the use of the participle here signifies that the adjudicating would take place in the future:

---

7.   The relationship between the *qatal* form's E and R-time in biblical prose is more complicated than this portrayal, but this general description is basically correct. We will elaborate on the *qatal* form itself in §3.2 below.

דן
יעבדו

S

[———R———]
[———E———]

(11) וַיֹּאמֶר לַמּוֹעֵד הַזֶּה כָּעֵת חַיָּה אַתְּ (אַתְּ) חֹבֶקֶת בֵּן

And Elisha said, **At this season next year**, you **will be embracing** ((S<) |--E--|)
a son. (2 Kgs 4:16)   **R**

This example is identical to 10, except that here the R-time is an adverbial clause
rather than another verb.

למועד הזה כעת חיה
חובקת

S

[———R———]
[———E———]

(12) וַיָּבֹאוּ שְׁנֵי הַמַּלְאָכִים סְדֹמָה בָּעֶרֶב וְלוֹט יֹשֵׁב בְּשַׁעַר סְדֹם

The two angels **arrived** in Sodom in the evening, as Lot **was sitting** (|--E--|
(<S) in the gate of Sodom. (Gn 19:1)   **R**

Here too, the participle form has the same meaning; but unlike the other examples
in this clause, the actions transpire in the past. With respect to its chronological
position, the participle form resembles *qatal* in that it is only characterized relative
to its R-time and ignores the absolute time axis:

ויבאו
ישב

R   S

[———E———]

2.1.2.3   Examples of the Relative Use of *Yiqtol*

(13) וַיֵּ֣לֶךְ הָאִ֗ישׁ מֵהָעִ֛יר מִבֵּ֥ית לֶ֖חֶם יְהוּדָ֑ה לָג֖וּר בַּאֲשֶׁ֣ר יִמְצָ֑א וַיָּבֹ֧א הַר־אֶפְרַ֛יִם עַד־
בֵּ֥ית מִיכָ֖ה לַעֲשֹׂ֥ות דַּרְכּֽוֹ׃

This man **had left** the town of Bethlehem of Judah to take up residence
wherever **he could find (R<E(<S))** a place. On his way, he came to the house
of Micah in the hill country of Ephraim. (Jgs 17:8)

In the context of this particular verse, the language denotes that the act of finding
transpires after the act of leaving. Therefore, this relationship between a posterior
act and an action in the past falls under the category of what Reichenbach terms
"the first posterior past" (R—E—S) (1947:297):

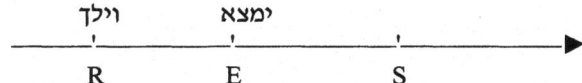

$$R \qquad\qquad E \qquad\qquad S$$

(14) וַיִּפְצַר־בָּ֣ם מְאֹ֔ד וַיָּסֻ֣רוּ אֵלָ֔יו וַיָּבֹ֖אוּ אֶל־בֵּית֑וֹ וַיַּ֤עַשׂ לָהֶם֙ מִשְׁתֶּ֔ה וּמַצּ֥וֹת אָפָ֖ה
וַיֹּאכֵֽלוּ׃ **טֶ֣רֶם** **יִשְׁכָּ֔בוּ** וְאַנְשֵׁ֨י הָעִ֜יר אַנְשֵׁ֤י סְדֹם֙ **נָסַ֣בּוּ** עַל־הַבַּ֔יִת מִנַּ֖עַר וְעַד־זָקֵ֑ן כָּל־הָעָ֖ם
מִקָּצֶֽה׃

But he urged them strongly, so they turned his way and entered his house. He
prepared a feast for them and baked unleavened bread, and they ate. **They had
not yet lain down (R<E(<S))**, when the townspeople, the men of Sodom,
young and old—all the people to the last man—**gathered** about the house.
(Gn 19:3-4)

Here too, a *yiqtol* form signifies that the action it expresses takes place after the R-
time. As opposed to the previous example, however, this relationship is reinforced
by the adverb טֶרֶם.[8]

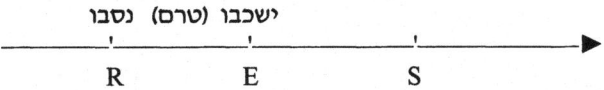

$$R \qquad\qquad E \qquad\qquad S$$

These examples attest to the fact that the basic relationship to reference time expressed by the *yiqtol* form is R<E.

---

8.   See the discussion in §6.2.2.1.3 below on the use of the collocation of the particle אם
     and *yiqtol*.

In sum, comparing *qatal*, the participle, and *yiqtol* shows that each form gener-ally marks its own designated relationship to a deictic axis. The fact that the sole deictic axis of all these forms is their reference time (R), instead of speech time, indicates that they are relative forms.

2.1.3 Consecutive Forms

The definition of the consecutive or sequential forms (*wayyiqtol* and *weqatal*)[9] is of paramount importance to any analysis of the Hebrew verbal tense system. Linguists of the nineteenth and twentieth centuries adopted Schröder's basic ar-gument (1766) according to which *wayyiqtol* forms convey actions that transpire after the preceding verb. Gesenius, Kautzsch, and Cowley formulated this idea in the following manner:

> The *imperfect* with *wāw consecutive* serves to express actions, events, or states, which are to be regarded as the temporal or logical sequel of actions, events, or states mentioned immediately before (1910§111a).
> The perfect, like the imperfect, is used with *wāw consecutive* to express actions, events, or states, which are to be attached to what precedes, in more or less close relation, as its *temporal* or *logical* consequence (§112a).[10]

However, Hatav (2000a) demonstrates that this is a problematic assumption. In her estimation, the forms with proclitic *waw*s (*wayyiqtol* and *weqatal*) can indeed express chronological succession, but these findings necessitate a broader defini-tion. Hatav's definition is predicated on the works of Kamp and Rohrer (1983) and Kamp and Reyle (1993), which are grounded on Reichenbach's concept of reference time. In their analysis, the initial reference time of a narrative unit is presented in the first clause, either explicitly or in an inferred manner, whereas the next clause is likely to use that reference time or exchange it with a new one. By engendering a new R-time, a clause advances the plot and, together with the other clauses, engenders a narrative succession. In various languages, the function of marking succession falls under the "jurisdiction" of the verbal system. Kamp and Rohrer outline the standard verbal successional usage thus:[11]

---

9. On this matter, we adhere to Hatav's definition (1997:56-88). There are cases in clas-sical prose where *qatal* and *yiqtol* serve as consecutive forms, but they are negligible compared to *wayyiqtol* and *weqatal*. A statistical survey by Hatav substantiates these claims: *wayyiqtol* serves as a consecutive form in 94% of its occurrences, *weqatal* 94%, *qatal* 1%, and *yiqtol* 0.65%.
10. Driver (1892:72) expresses the same idea in a different manner: "ויאמר is thus properly not *and he said*, but *and he proceeded to say*."
11. See Kamp and Rohrer (1983:253-254). In these diagrams t_0 = speech time; S = sen-tence; R = reference time; and e = event.

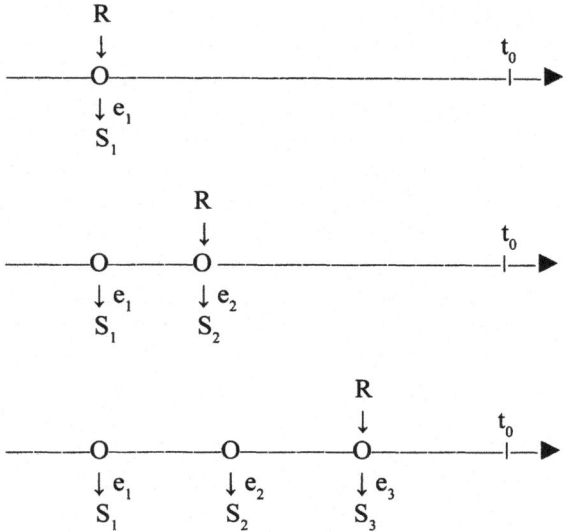

It is important to note that, insofar as Kamp and Rohrer are concerned, the first clause of a succession is considered a sequential clause, even though it is not linked to an anterior form. Following this analysis, one of the crucial features of a verb form that denotes succession is that it contains its own reference time [E,R], and it is this very trait which allows for the construction of the narrative succession. This last point is crucial to understanding the biblical consecutive forms, for *wayyiqtol* and *weqatal* occasionally turn up in the opening slot of verbal chains. For example:

(15) וַיְהִי אַבְרָם בֶּן תִּשְׁעִים שָׁנָה וְתֵשַׁע שָׁנִים וַיֵּרָא יְהֹוָה אֶל אַבְרָם וַיֹּאמֶר אֵלָיו אֲנִי
אֵל שַׁדַּי הִתְהַלֵּךְ לְפָנַי וֶהְיֵה תָמִים:

When Abram **was** ninety-nine years old, the Lᴏʀᴅ appeared to Abram and said to him, I am El Shaddai. Walk in my ways and be blameless. (Gn 17:1)

From the diagrams above, one could conclude that the sequential forms invariably advance the R-time point from a chronological standpoint. However, as Kamp and Rohrer themselves show, this is not always the case.[12]

---

12. E.g.: "L'année dernière Jean escalada le Cervin. Le premier jour il monta jusqu'à la cabane H. Il y passa la nuit. Ensuite il attaqua la face nord. Douze heures plus tard il arriva au sommet." (Kamp-Rohrer 1983:260). This sentence features chronological relations that differ from those in the diagram. In this sentence, the first verb (the *passé simple "escalda"*) basically constitutes a recap of the subsequent chain of actions, so that the transition from the first to the second verb form does not advance the refer-

In light of the above, the R-time's advancement along the time axis should not be considered part of the meaning of Hebrew consecutive forms. Washburn argues that the "*waw*-consecutive should be understood as a morpheme, signaling a separate thought not syntactically connected with what precedes it" (1994:27).

Against this background, it is incumbent upon us to scale back the meaning of consecutive forms to the signification of their own reference time [E,R].[13] In consequence, these forms' chronological relations must be discerned from the context and do not fall under the purview of their meaning. This analysis draws on the terms that were formulated by Reichenbach (1947) and Kamp and Rohrer (1983). Moreover, it develops Washburn's basic assumption whereby each consecutive form conveys a separate thought which is not connected to that which precedes it from a chronological standpoint.[14]

Classical biblical prose reinforces this claim:

(16) וַיַּרְא שָׁם יְהוּדָה בַּת אִישׁ כְּנַעֲנִי וּשְׁמוֹ שׁוּעַ וַיִּקָּחֶהָ וַיָּבֹא אֵלֶיהָ: וַתַּהַר וַתֵּלֶד בֵּן וַיִּקְרָא אֶת שְׁמוֹ עֵר:

There Judah **saw [R,E]** the daughter of a certain Canaanite whose name was Shua, **and he married [R,E]** her **and cohabited [R,E]** with her. **She conceived [R,E]** and **bore [R,E]** a son, **and he named [R,E]** him Er. (Gn 38:2-3)

(17) וְיַעֲקֹב נָתַן לְעֵשָׂו לֶחֶם וּנְזִיד עֲדָשִׁים וַיֹּאכַל וַיֵּשְׁתְּ וַיָּקָם וַיֵּלַךְ וַיִּבֶז עֵשָׂו אֶת הַבְּכֹרָה:

Jacob then gave Esau bread and lentil stew; **he ate [R,E] and drank [R,E], and he rose [R,E] and went [R,E] away.** Thus did Esau **spurn [R,E]** the birthright. (Gn 25:34)

(18) וַיָּסֹבּוּ וַיֶּאֶרְבוּ לוֹ כָל הַלַּיְלָה בְּשַׁעַר הָעִיר וַיִּתְחָרְשׁוּ כָל הַלַּיְלָה. . . . וַיִּשְׁכַּב שִׁמְשׁוֹן עַד חֲצִי הַלַּיְלָה וַיָּקָם בַּחֲצִי הַלַּיְלָה וַיַּאֲחֹז בְּדַלְתוֹת שַׁעַר הָעִיר וּבִשְׁתֵּי הַמְּזוּזֹת

[T]hey **surrounded [R,E]** the place **and lay in wait [R,E]** for him all night at the gate of the city **and whispered [R,E]** through the night. . . . Now Samson **lay [R,E]** until midnight, and at midnight **he arose [R,E] and took [R,E]** hold of the doors of the city gate and the two posts. (Jgs 16:2-3)

---

ence time along the time axis. According to Hatav, the sequential clause "moves the reference time forward" (2000a:63). This definition acccords with the traditional one whereby sequential forms are signifiers of an action that transpires after the previous one, but Hatav adds Reichenbach's and Kamp and Rohrer's terminology.

13. Brackets are used to signify that the event (E) and reference time (R) merge into a single unit—[R,E].
14. For more on the role of these forms, see the discussion on the complex nature of the verbal paradigm in §2.2.4 below.

In example 16, the verbs engender a linear succession that corresponds to the chronological order of the events. Put differently, each new form pushes the reference time forward along the time axis, in accordance with Kamp and Rohrer's diagram. However, something different happens in examples 17 and 18. In Genesis 25:34, it is obvious that Esau got up before he started to walk away and that he ate and drank before getting up. However, did he quench his thirst only after eating, or did he engage in both acts intermittently? The order of these events is not evident from the *wayyiqtol* forms themselves, but may be inferred from the situation at hand. With respect to the verb "ויבז", did Esau despise the birthright as a result of the eating, drinking, rising, and departing? Or did his behavior stem from his preexisting attitude toward the birthright? Alternatively, the argument can be made that "ויבז" summarizes the previous string of actions. The answer to this question, which is the subject of an interpretive debate, is not explicit from the text. In other words, the forms do not mark the chronological relations that they maintain.

The same can be said for Judges 16:2-3. Although some of the forms therein indeed signify a chronological succession, one would be hard pressed to argue that the Philistines whispered through the night only after lying in wait. Furthermore, the verb forms lack so much as a hint of the transition from the Philistines' actions to those of Samson, so that this development must be inferred from the context. These passages demonstrate that *wayyiqtol* forms do not necessarily denote chronological relations. As already noted, the only constant function of these forms is the signification of the R-time and event as one unit [R,E].

To follow are some examples of *weqatal* forms:

(19) וַיִּשָּׂא יַעֲקֹב רַגְלָיו וַיֵּלֶךְ אַרְצָה בְנֵי קֶדֶם: וַיַּרְא וְהִנֵּה בְאֵר בַּשָּׂדֶה וְהִנֵּה שָׁם שְׁלֹשָׁה עֶדְרֵי צֹאן רֹבְצִים עָלֶיהָ כִּי מִן הַבְּאֵר הַהִוא יַשְׁקוּ הָעֲדָרִים וְהָאֶבֶן גְּדֹלָה עַל פִּי הַבְּאֵר: **וְנֶאֶסְפוּ** שָׁמָּה כָל הָעֲדָרִים **וְגָלְלוּ** אֶת הָאֶבֶן מֵעַל פִּי הַבְּאֵר **וְהִשְׁקוּ** אֶת הַצֹּאן **וְהֵשִׁיבוּ** אֶת הָאֶבֶן עַל פִּי הַבְּאֵר לִמְקֹמָהּ:

Jacob resumed his journey and came to the land of the Easterners. There before his eyes was a well in the open. Three flocks of sheep were lying there beside it, for the flocks would water from that well. The stone on the mouth of the well was large. When all the flocks **would gather [R,E]** there, the stone **would be rolled [R,E]** off the mouth of the well and the sheep **would be watered [R,E]**; then the stone **would be put back [R,E]** in its place on the mouth of the well. (Gn 29:1-3)

(20) וַיְהִי גְּבוּל בְּנֵי אֶפְרַיִם לְמִשְׁפְּחֹתָם וַיְהִי גְּבוּל נַחֲלָתָם מִזְרָחָה עַטְרוֹת אַדָּר עַד בֵּית חוֹרֹן עֶלְיוֹן: **וְיָצָא** הַגְּבוּל הַיָּמָּה הַמִּכְמְתָת מִצָּפוֹן **וְנָסַב** הַגְּבוּל מִזְרָחָה תַּאֲנַת שִׁלֹה **וְעָבַר** אוֹתוֹ מִמִּזְרַח יָנוֹחָה: **וְיָרַד** מִיָּנוֹחָה עֲטָרוֹת וְנַעֲרָתָה **וּפָגַע** בִּירִיחוֹ **וְיָצָא** הַיַּרְדֵּן:

The territory of the Ephraimites, by their clans, was as follows: The boundary of their portion ran from Atroth-addar on the east to Upper Beth-horon, and the boundary **ran [R,E]** on to the Sea. And on the north, the boundary **proceeded [R,E]** from Michmethath to the east of Taanath-shiloh and **passed [R,E]** beyond it up to the east of Janoah; from Janoah it **descended [R,E]** to Ataroth and Naarath, and **touched [R,E]** on Jericho, and **ran [R,E]** on to the Jordan. (Josh 16:5-7)

Hatav (2000:70) avers that the *weqatal* forms in Genesis 29:1-3 signify a chrono-logical succession in which the R-time is forwarded along the time axis.[15] Accord-ingly, the argument can be made that, every time the shepherds gathered by the well, they rolled the stone off its "mouth" and watered the flock, before returning the cover to its place.

However, there are also cases devoid of any chronological progression, such as the second example, which is taken from the list of tribal allotments in Joshua 16. The argument can naturally be made that the list genre is different than the narra-tive one, but in practice the forms in both frameworks operate in a similar fashion, as they all advance a "narrative" by virtue of the fact that they contain their own reference time. Example 20 constitutes a progressive, point-by-point description of the borderline without any movement along the time axis. Although the situ-ation differs in examples 17 and 18 from the discussion on *wayyiqtol* forms, this passage also bolsters the claim that the chronological relations of sequential forms must be discerned from the context and are not part of their meaning.[16]

2.2 The Complex Nature of the Verbal Paradigm

2.2.1 Background

One of the main points of contention that has accompanied the research virtually from the beginning is the debate between the adherents of "tense" and "aspect" theory, wherein both sides have endeavored to promote their views and impose them on the other camp. This state of affairs gives rise to the following questions: Is the notion that researchers must establish a one-dimensional perspective ac-cording to which a single dichotomy spans the entire length of the verbal system tenable? And is there an objective reason to eschew a complex categorical system, which does not endeavor to find an internal hierarchy that is indicative of "Die Sukzessivität des dichotomistischen Prinzips?"[17]

The linguistic assumption that language is a collection of binary scales is one of the cornerstones of Roman Jakobson's phonological analysis of language.[18] Ja-kobson asserted that drawing distinctions between various strata of dichotomous

---

15. For the purpose of this discussion, we ignore the habitual meaning of these forms.
16. For more on the meaning of the sequential forms in Biblical Hebrew, see Cohen (2011).
17. This is the expression used by Rundgren (1961:44-45).
18. See Jakobson and Halle (1971:44-49) and Jakobson (1952:9), inter alios.

pairs allows researchers to accurately judge the attributes that set apart one pho-
neme from the next. However, Chao (1954-1955) challenged this principle. While
in certain linguistic systems the dichotomous hierarchy is an important theoretical
tool, Chao argued that it would be a mistake to apply it to all systems. Goldenberg
(1966:81) questions Rundgren's use (1961:44-45) of this hierarchy. In Rundgren's
phonological model of the system of contrasts, n//d/t, it is unclear according to
which parameter the standing of the nasal/non-nasal contrast was deemed to be
higher than the voiced/voiceless contrast. The account t//n/d (voiceless/voiced as
well as nasal voiced/not nasal) for example is just as good. Rundgren (1961:45)
extends the use of this principle from the phonological field to the verbal system,
thereby drawing yet another of Goldenberg's critical daggers:

> The structural hierarchy is devoid of meaning if it depends on a random,
> or unwarranted, order of actions. A hierarchy of this sort of "dichotomous
> contrasts" in the verbal system, wherein the same verb form appears in more
> than one place, is even less comprehensible. . . . For other considerations are
> likely to give rise to a different outlook, according to which the "opposition"
> of the jussive to anything that is not a jussive is indeed the most prominent.
> From another vantage point, the primary distinction can turn out to be the one
> between the perfect and the jussive, on the one hand, and the gerund and the
> imperfect, on the other, and so forth. None of these possible classifications
> outranks its counterpart. (1966:81)

Goldenberg's insights lead to two principal questions about the traditional means
for describing the Hebrew verb. First, why should the dichotomy between the
qatal and *yiqtol* form be considered the basis for the general depiction of the entire system? Similar to Goldenberg's account of the Amharic verbal system, the
distinctions between, say, *wayyiqtol* and *yiqtol*, *wayyiqtol* and the participle, or
weqatal and the jussive are neither more nor less important than the distinction
between *qatal* and *yiqtol*. Second, even if we were to focus on a single dichotomy,
such as *qatal/yiqtol*, does a one-dimensional presentation of the categories suffice?
In other words, is it reasonable to assume that one dominant contrast between
these forms, such as past/future, prevails over all their interactions? Perhaps it is
best to assume that under certain circumstances, the verbal paradigm can simultaneously contain more than one semantic contrast (e.g., the distinction between the
indicative and modal form in the *qatal-yiqtol* dichotomy), and that it is a system
that possesses mutual relations between various perspectives which simultaneously apply to different forms.

Over the next few pages, we will present the various theories on the dichoto-
mization of the Hebrew verbal system that emerged in the research literature. This
will be followed by a discussion of the ramifications of the verbal paradigm's
complex nature for our theoretical approach to this system.

2.2.2 Tense-based Theories

The idea that the biblical verbal system consists of three tenses dates as far back as the medieval philosopher and grammarian Saadia Gaon (882-942). Although the medieval grammarians considered the *waw* in *wayyiqtol* and *weqatal* an element that converts the forms to the future and past, respectively, it was Elias Levita—popularly known as "Eliahu the Bachelor" (1468-1549)—who coined the familiar term וי׳ו ההיפוך (the *waw* conversive).[19] Levita's work (דקדוק) was directly influenced by the Kimhi dynasty.[20]

Levita's grammar—along with that of the humanist Johann Reuchlin (1455-1522), which was published in 1506 and also drew heavily on the thought of D. Kimhi[21]—is widely considered to have served as the bridge between the medieval Jewish grammarians and Christian Hebraists and humanists. From that point on, the reins of biblical tense research were in Christian hands. However, the Jewish grammarians' three-tense system (past, present, and future) and their position that the *waw*-prefixed forms are convertive were fully adopted by the Christian Hebraists,[22] who replaced the terms וי׳ו ההיפוך and וי׳ו החיבור with their Latin counterparts: *waw conversivum* and *waw conjunctivum*.[23]

The first to challenge the assumption that the *waw* "converts" the tenses was N.W. Schröder (1721-1798), who claimed that the proclitic signifies that a given *wayyiqtol* form serves as the relative future of the anterior form. For example, in the opening verse of Genesis, "ברא" places the subsequent chain of verbs in the realm of the past, and the ensuing *wayyiqtol* forms signify the future (i.e., they take place in the future relative to "ברא"). In promulgating this view, Schröder and his followers deemed the concept of the "relative future" to be an alternative to the *waw conversium* theory.[24] Consequently, they did not reject the traditional

---

19. Levita (1767: iii, 2): "And the most important is the *waw*, and its uses are twofold. One is known as the *waw* conjunctive and it connects a verb to a verb or a nomen to a nomen etc. . . The second is called the *waw* consecutive, and it converts pasts to futures and futures to pasts."
20. For further reading on the medival traditions that served as the basis for Levita's work, see the following works: for more on Saadia Gaon (882-942), see Dotan (1997, vol. II); Judah ben David Hayyuj (tenth to eleventh century), see Basal (1992); Jonah Ibn Janah (990?-1050?), see Ibn Janah (1964); Abraham Ibn Ezra (1090-1165?), see Ibn Ezra (1791 and 1827) and Charlap (1999:220-232); and R. David Kimhi (RaDaK, 1160-1235), see Kimhi (1793) and McFall (1984:7-9).
21. See McFall (1982:11).
22. Ibid (11-14).
23. These terms would endure for quite some time, as even Gesenius used them in the first thirteen editions of his grammar (1813-1842). It was only with the publication of the updated version of Gesenius's grammar, on the part of his student E. Rödiger, that the terminology was changed to conform to Ewald (1827).
24. McFall surveys the prominent scholars that advocated this view (1982:21-24, 177-179).

view on the Biblical Hebrew tenses, but sought to provide an alternative explanation for the grammatical relationship between forms with a proclitic *waw* and those without.

In his Hebrew grammars (1827 and 1828), Heinrich Ewald was the first to broach the possibility that the verbal system should not be depicted in terms of tense. This hypothesis, which is known as the aspectual approach, gained momentum over the rest of the nineteenth century, culminating in 1892 with the work of Driver. The rising influence of this outlook notwithstanding, there were several attempts throughout the twentieth century to get tense theory back on track. For instance, the steady increase in knowledge about Semitic languages, first and foremost Akkadian, in the early twentieth century prompted Hans Bauer to return to the tense approach from a new direction. In *Die Tempora im Semitschen* (1910), Bauer embraced a comparative historical approach for the sake of contending with the question of the tenses. He claimed that not only did Driver (1892) fail to offer a solution to the problem of the Hebrew verbal tense system, but mounted new difficulties (Bauer 1910:23-24). In essence, Bauer opined that, unlike Akkadian, Hebrew is not a uniform language, but consists of two separate historical tense systems (*Mischsprache*).[25] Therefore, he proposed the term "*waw conservativum*"—a *waw* that preserves the ancient form (ibid.:39).

In many respects, Bauer's hypothesis that there is a chronological difference between *qatal/weqatal* and *yiqtol/wayyiqtol* marked an abrupt return to the medieval grammarians' perspective, albeit from a completely new angle. With the emergence of the comparative Semitic research, appreciable portions of Bauer's account were indeed refuted. However, his pioneering comparative work still constitutes an important blueprint for understanding the Hebrew verbal system, especially his insights on the disparate historical origins of the *yiqtol* and *wayyiqtol* forms.[26]

The most serious methodological flaw in Bauer's theory is his heavy emphasis on the comparative diachronic account, which came at the expense of a synchronic analysis. Riveting as they may be, the morphological analogies from one language's tense system to another *cannot* serve as the basis for an account of any system. A structural depiction must be grounded on a study of the contrasts between the various categories that derive from the linguistic findings. While the comparative data can enhance this sort of account, it cannot undergird the conclusions.

---

25. See McFall for references to other scholars who support this view (1982:95, note 1).
26. There is a consensus that the distinction between the Northwest Semitic **yaqtul* and **yaqtulu* forms was preserved by Biblical Hebrew in three different categories: 1. the עו״י verb type וַיָּקׇם/יָקוּם ; 2. the ל״י verb type וַיִּבֶן/יִבְנֶה ; 3. the הפעיל verb stem וַיַּכְבֵּד/יַכְבִּיד. See Lambert (1893:49-50) and Waltke and O'Connor (1990:469), inter alios.

The Semitist Gotthelf Bergsträsser[27] may be included among Bauer's followers. Although the former accepted his mentor's basic chronological account, he objected to Bauer's notion of *Mischsprache*. More specifically, Bergsträsser believed that it is inconceivable that the earlier meanings of any given language can exist alongside later ones without limitations on their distribution (1929:§3a). However, this claim is less than precise because every linguistic system contains vestiges of earlier periods along with the first signs of new developments. In any event, Bergsträsser's desire to shift the center of gravity from a diachronic to a synchronic vantage point gave his theory an important methodological advantage over Bauer's. [28]

An important contribution to the tense-oriented school is Kuryłowicz's works on, inter alia, the theoretical question of aspect in Biblical Hebrew (1973a, b). Although the *perfective-imperfective* distinction plays a significant role in Slavic linguistics, Kuryłowicz contends that these terms are inappropriate for Semitic languages, Hebrew included.[29] Instead, he posits that the principal distinction in Biblical Hebrew is between tenses. In this respect, the importance of Kuryłowicz's work (1973a:87) is tied to the replacement of the terms past and future with anteriority and non-anteriority: "[M]eanings rendered in other languages by tense or aspect appears in Sem. (West Sem.) as *context conditioned functions* of the only pertinent opposition *non-anteriority (simultaneity):anteriority* referred to the moment of speaking."[30] Put differently, Kuryłowicz places an emphasis on two ideas: the fact that the forms' chronological meanings are context-dependent; and the use of relative concepts instead of "past" and "present."[31]

---

27. See Bergsträsser (1929:§3-§13). The principles of his outlook are explicated in §3.
28. Other attempts to defend Bauer's tense theory were put forth by G. R. Driver (1936); Blake (1951); and Barnes (1965).
29. For an in-depth discussion on this topic, see §2.23 below.
30. The italics appear in the original.
31. Revell examines the dominant role that context plays in determining an action's position on the time axis (1989). Context also stands at the heart of the "discourse language" (*Textlinguistik*) approach, which was established by Harris (1952) and Weinrich (1964), among others. The preeminent representatives of this approach in all that concerns the research of the Hebrew verb are Schneider (1974), Andersen (1974), Niccacci (1990), and Longacre (1983, 1992). In the 1970s, the impact of general linguistics, whose adherents had shifted the discipline's center of gravity from the narrow confines of the lone sentence to larger units of text, began to penetrate the field of the Hebrew verb (and indeed underpins the present study). According to this approach, a systematic analysis of the verbal system must include a reference to textual units that are greater than the lone sentence. Both Schneider (1974) and Niccacci (1990) have predicated their works on Weinrich's fundamental distinction between discourse and narrative (1964). Another important criterion is the matter of foregrounding. This category, which was introduced by Schneider (1974) and further developed by Niccacci,

Despite his use of relative terms, Kuryłowicz (1973a:90) subsequently claims that these concepts refer to the moment of speech: "To regard aspect as the *fundamental* conjugational category of the Sem. verb (and of any other verb) means overlooking the fact that the relation of the action expressed by the verbal form to the *moment of speaking* is the natural basis of every verbal system." By continuing to view speech time as the primary reference point of Hebrew verb forms, Kuryłowicz obfuscates their relative attributes. Although the forms can indeed refer to speech time [S], he ignores the fact that this is entirely dependent on the context and is not a part of their essential meaning.[32]

In many respects, Goldfajn (1998:39-44, esp. 43) expands upon Kuryłowicz's position. Although the former seldom uses the term "relative time," her book is the most comprehensive account of this topic in all that concerns the biblical tense system. From a theoretical standpoint, Goldfajn's most important contribution to the Hebrew verbal system is the inclusion of the Reichenbachian categories event, reference, and speech in the scholarly discussion as well as her emphasis on Kamp and Rohrer's discourse representation theory (DRT).[33] The crux of this theory is that many of the chronological meanings that are attributed to a given verb form stem directly from its relations with the rest of the forms in its context. These insights shed light on the chronological relations between different forms and provide a conceptual framework that allows for a systematic interpretation of these differences.[34]

This survey of the research literature gives rise to the question whether Biblical Hebrew's verb forms indeed express tense. The answer to this question is tied, above all, to which of the particular definitions of the term "tense" we adopt. However there is no consensus among scholars as to its definition. One of the most prevalent definitions views tense as a grammatical category that expresses position in time on a linear axis in which the "absolute zero" (i.e., the present) is S-time. According to this definition, everything to the left of the "0" is the past, and everything to its right is the future (i.e., absolute time):

---

draws a distinction between foreground information and information that sits in the background; see Niccacci (1990:20), inter alios.

32. Hughes offers a more precise analysis of relative tense in his criticism (1993) of Waltke and O'Connor's grammar (1990): "The Hebrew verbal system cannot be an absolute tense system, in which events are related to the time of speaking, but it can be analyzed in terms of relative tense, in which events are related to the time of speaking or some other time, such as the time at which another event occurred."

33. See Kamp (1979) and Kamp and Rohrer (1983).

34. As we will see, Goldfajn's Achilles' heel is not her description of the chronological relations, but her attempt to force this perspective on all the other components of the paradigm; Goldfajn (1998:53-72, 139-140).

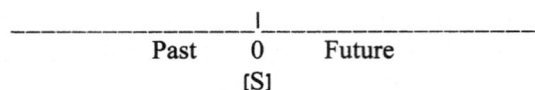

Past   0   Future
[S]

If we adopt this meaning, then the tense system in the Bible does not express tenses! As we have seen, this state of affairs is a product of the relative nature of the biblical verb forms. The quintessential relative attribute of these forms is the fact that an action's placement along the absolute time axis is always context-dependent and thus cannot be marked by the form itself. In other words, location along the absolute time axis is not an integral part of the verb forms and is merely implied from the context.

Nevertheless, this is not the only possible meaning of tense, as a broader definition can be formulated in accordance with Comrie's observation:

> [T]ense is grammaticalised expression of location in time. . . . [T]here are very heavy constraints that language imposes on the range of expressions of location in time that can be grammaticalised. In fact all clear instances of tense cross-linguistically can be represented in terms of the notions of deictic centre (1985:9).

Comrie's words suggest that the category of tense expresses a wide array of chronological relations in multifarious languages. Moreover, it appears as though every tense must have a deictic center. As we have seen, the difference between absolute and relative tense is not whether there is a deictic center, as both categories maintain such a center. Instead, the difference rests on the fact that absolute time simultaneously maintains two deictic centers (S and R), whereas relative time has only one (R). Therefore, if we expand the definition of tense to include cases where the only deictic center is R-time, then the biblical tense system would certainly fit the bill.

2.2.3 A Disquisition on Aspect and Mood

2.2.3.1 The Research on Aspect and Mood

The view according to which the Hebrew verb forms *qatal* and *yiqtol* essentially denote a non-temporal meaning was first put forth in a straight forward manner by Heinrich Ewald (1803-1875). The concepts that Ewald utilized in his first Hebrew grammar (1827) were influenced by the terminology of Johann Jahn (1750-1816), who was the first to replace the terms past and present with first and second aorist.[35]

---

35. See McFall (1982:43-44). The term *aorist* derives from the Greek grammar (αοριστος— not defined, borderless). However, its precise definition is subject to debate, not least because of the complex nature of the Greek aorist, which signifies (in its capacity as an indicative) both tense and aspect.

Jahn availed himself of these terms in order to contend that these forms serve in the realm of the past, present, and future alike.[36] Ewald (1827:219) presented the forms as two moods:

> Zwei Formen hat die Sprache, die mehr den Unterschied des Modus als des Tempus haben; sie werden hier der erste und zweite Modus genannt.

He thus equated the first aorist with "our" indicative and the second with the conjunctive (ibid.:1827:219).

In his second Hebrew grammar, Ewald described the two moods as "aorists from the standpoint of time," which are devoid of all reference to any of the tenses. Whereas the first aorist signifies "Des Vollendente, das Bestimmte und Gewisse," the second signifies "das Unvollendete, das Unbestimmte, von den Umständen Abhängige" (1828:223).

The symbiosis between the first pair of aspectual terms—Vollendente and Unvollendente (complete and incomplete)—and the second pair of modal terms—Bestimmte and Unbestimmte (certain and uncertain)—indicates that Ewald wavered between the two options. Only in his Arabic grammar of 1831 did Ewald introduce the terms perfectum and imperfectum, which soon became the most prevalent terms in Semitic linguistics and are still in use today (1831:112). In contrast to Latin and Greek grammars, Ewald was referring to these terms' etymology. In other words, his intention was that Vollendente and Unvollendente, for example, are signifiers of complete and incomplete actions, respectively.

Over the course of the nineteenth-century debates on yiqtol and qatal, scholars gradually neglected the modal dimension of the distinction between the two forms, which Ewald had stressed in his earlier books. What is more, this topic was excluded from the scholarly discourse for most of the 1900s, but reemerged toward the end of the twentieth century, especially in the works of Hatav (1997) and Joosten (2002).

The interest in the non-temporal facets of Semitic verbal systems in general and Hebrew in particular reached its highpoint in the latter half of the nineteenth century. Accordingly, the grammar books of this period presented a wide range of terms for defining the qatal and yiqtol forms, such as factitive-cogitative (Dietrich 1846:119), perfect-fiens (Böttcher 1866:§587), factum-präsens (Knudtzon 1889), and perfectum-infectum (König 1897).

The lively discussion surrounding the non-temporal uses of the Hebrew forms did not take place in a vacuum, but emanated from the general linguistical discussion in Europe at the time.[37] The origin of the method for describing the relations

---

36. According to Ewald, the main purpose of each category is: "Aoristus primus sistit rem perfectam, jam praesentem, jam praeteritam, jam futuram. Aoristus secundus sisit rem imperfectam, jam praesentem, jam praeteritam, jam futuram." The citation is taken from McFall (1982:44).
37. In this context, see Goldenberg's summary (1966:89).

between the temporal and non-temporal functions dates back to classical grammar, especially the work of the Stoics. According to the proponents of this approach, different verbal categories stem from a combination of tense-oriented distinctions and distinctions that mark whether an action is at its preliminary, middle, or final stages, or has reached its conclusion. In the late eighteenth and nineteenth centuries, the classical verb theory was revived by Harris (1771), Humboldt (1836), and Heyse (1856).[38] Moreover, Curtius's Greek grammar (1863) evidently had a pivotal role in the dissemination of these ideas,[39] as the terms he used entered the parlance of the era's grammarians. Curtius drew a distinction between "*Zeitstufe*," which he considered a signifier of the past, present and future, and "*Zeitart*" (kind of time),[40] which differentiates between *dauernd*, *eintretend*, and *vollendet*.

Samuel Rolles Driver unveiled his seminal work on the Hebrew tenses in 1874 (third edition, 1892). Besides its being the era's most methodical and comprehensive summary of the topic, the pertinence of Driver's treatise rests in the fact that it "imported" prevalent terms from general linguistics to Hebrew. As Brockelmann (1956:38) and Goldenberg (1966:90) have pointed out, Driver's work can largely be viewed as a Hebrew adaptation of Curtius's account of the Greek system. Driver's affinity for Curtius's distinctions led him to conclude that the imperfect (*yiqtol*) always signifies an action in its nascent stages, unlike Ewald who claimed that this meaning is optional. Accordingly, Driver noted that:

> It is . . . of the utmost consequence to understand and bear constantly in mind the fundamental and primary facts . . . (1) that the Hebrew verb notifies the character without fixing the date of an action, and (2) that . . . one [form] is calculated to describe an action as *nascent* and so as imperfect; [and] the other to describe it as *completed* and so as perfect (1892:5).

Driver's work became the most popular and influential work in the field of Hebrew verbal research. Over the course of the twentieth century, many scholars continued along the road that Ewald and Driver had laid down.[41]

For instance, Rundgren's works (1959 and 1961) are recognized as an important theoretical contribution to Ewald and Driver's approach. Rundgren viewed the dichotomous aspectual structure as the main axis of all Semitic verbal systems, to include the ancient variety:[42]

---

38. See Goldenberg (1966:90-91).
39. The first edition of his book came out in 1852.
40. *Zeitart* was subsequently replaced with "*Aktionsart*."
41. A compendium of references to these studies may be found in Joosten (2002:49, note 2).
42. See Rundgren (1961:71-72), inter alios. He adopted the terms *kursiv* and *konstativ* on account of Brockelmann.

Stative   :   Fines
            ┌─┴─┐
       Kursiv : Konstativ

In Akkadian, the first opposition is represented by the difference between the stative (*kašid*) and the prefixed forms, and the second by the distinction between *iprus* and *iparras*. Alternatively, the dichotomy in West Semitic languages is marked by the perfect and imperfect.

In the early 1970s, Kuryłowicz threw down the gauntlet against researchers who underscored the aspectual nature of Semitic verbal systems (1973a, b). Kuryłowicz claimed that the distinction between the perfective and imperfective is an integral part of the Greek and Slavic complex of forms. Moreover, he asserted that the aspectual dichotomy also leans on these languages' lexical differentiation. Furthermore this dichotomy is manifested as an opposition not only in the realm of the past, but in modal (e.g., the imperative) and even nominal verb forms (the participle and infinitive). According to Kuryłowicz's approach, a morphological expression of aspect exists only in languages that contain a pair of antithetical verb forms within the same framework of absolute tenses[43]—a distinction which does not apply to Biblical Hebrew. In fact, Kuryłowicz's basic argument concerning the significance of the perfective-imperfective dichotomy in the Greek and Slavic grammar as opposed to their Semitic counterparts is all the more persuasive when taking into account the link between Driver's terminology (1892) and Curtius's Greek grammar.

The modal element of the distinction between *qatal* and *yiqtol*, which Ewald stressed in his first Hebrew grammars and was subsequently neglected throughout the nineteenth and twentieth century, has been swept back into the limelight by Hatav and Joosten. Similar to Ewald's first impression, Hatav shows that aspect and modality indeed interact (1997:161). Hatav, who predicates her study of the Hebrew verbal system on general linguistic research, avers that the common denominator between the different functions marked by *yiqtol*—the future, generic and habitual actions, iterative actions in the past, and conditional and question clauses—is that they are all part of the modal semantic field. In her estimation, the concept of modality should be expanded to include not only the cohortative, imperative, and jussive, which are traditionally perceived as modal forms (or what Hatav dubs "directive" forms, in contrast to the unmarked modal variety), but the *yiqtol* and *qatal* forms as well (1997:142-162).

Joosten claims that the primary weakness of the aspectual perspective is tied to the roles of the *yiqtol* form (2002). Like Hatav, he shows that *yiqtol*'s assorted uses can be interpreted as part of the general modal meaning. However, Joosten

---

43. In contrast, Joosten believes that it is theoretically possible for a language with a binary system to have all the perfective roles filled by one form and all the imperfective roles filled by another (2002:52).

takes this idea one step further by claiming that in Biblical Hebrew the real present and attendant circumstances, which are two of the most common meanings in languages where the imperfective is considered to be a grammatical category, are marked with the participle, rather than *yiqtol*.

The real present:

(21) וַיֹּאמֶר מֶה עָשִׂיתָ קוֹל דְּמֵי אָחִיךָ **צֹעֲקִים** אֵלַי מִן הָאֲדָמָה:

Then he said, What have you done? Hark, your brother's blood
cries (|----E----|) out to me from the ground! (Gn 4:10)
    R(S)

(22) וַתֹּאמֶר מִפְּנֵי שָׂרַי גְּבִרְתִּי אָנֹכִי **בֹּרַחַת** :

And she said, **I am running** (|----E----|) away from my mistress Sarai.
(Gn 16:8)   **R(S)**

Attendant circumstances:

(23) וַיַּעַל מַלְאַךְ יְהֹוָה בְּלַהַב הַמִּזְבֵּחַ וּמָנוֹחַ וְאִשְׁתּוֹ **רֹאִים**

[T]he angel of the LORD ascended in the flames of the altar, while Manoah and his wife **looked on;** (|----E----|) (Jgs 13:20)
    R(<S)

(24) וַיָּבֹאוּ שְׁנֵי הַמַּלְאָכִים סְדֹמָה בָּעֶרֶב וְלוֹט **יֹשֵׁב** בְּשַׁעַר סְדֹם

The two angels arrived in Sodom in the evening, as Lot **was sitting**
(|----E----|) in the gate of Sodom. (Gn 19:1)
    R(<S)

According to Joosten (2002:66-67), a modal dichotomy is preferable to an aspectual one for the following principal reasons:

1. The typical functions of the imperfective (the real present and attendant circumstances) are not expressed by *yiqtol*.

2. By its very nature, the most dominant use of this form—modality/futurity—is not aspectual.

3. All the functions that were described as signifiers of aspect (the habitual, general present, and iterative actions in the past) can also be considered modal uses.

Like the field of tense, the aspectual and modal accounts of the Biblical Hebrew verbal system are dependent, first and foremost, on the definition that is adopted for these terms. If we trace the traditional linguistic account of these two terms, it turns out that the ostensibly sharp distinction between aspect and mood contains numerous gray areas in which their definitions occasionally overlap. Among the most ambiguous points is the classification of the generic and habitual meanings (in Biblical Hebrew, both *yiqtol* and *weqatal* can signify the habitual present, general truth, iterative actions in the past, and the language of the law). In some languages, these meanings are classified under the aspectual system, [44] while in other languages these functions are considered to be modal.[45]

This state of affairs is liable to lead us to the conclusion that some degree of categorical obfuscation between mood and aspect is unavoidable. However, two points bear noting in all that concerns Biblical Hebrew. One is tied to the work of Kuryłowicz (1973a, b), who calls upon scholars to reserve the distinction between the perfective and imperfective for certain languages.[46]

The second point concerns the conceptual development of the terms perfect and imperfect in the research of the Hebrew verbal system. The two leading representatives of the aspectual approach, Ewald and Driver, leaned on an analogy to non-Hebrew verbal systems. As noted above, Ewald originally used the terms perfect and imperfect in his Arabic grammar (1831) before introducing them to the Hebrew research literature. In this respect, Joosten points to the fact that the Arabic *yaktubu* form signifies both the real present and the attendant circumstance (two meanings that assume a dominant role under the heading of the imperfect in languages that maintain an aspectual category). Therefore, as noted, unlike Hebrew in which these meanings are denoted by the participle, the aspectual approach can be applied to classical Arabic (2002:67).

In his conclusion, Joosten stresses the obfuscation between the two different perspectives, but claims that the linguistic findings, which are the ultimate criteria for evaluating this question, favor the modal approach:

> Perhaps it is fair to sum up the discussion as follows. If one starts out from the supposition that YIQTOL expresses imperfective aspect, it will be possible to account for all or most of the uses of YIQTOL in prose. However, if one focuses on the uses of the form, one does not develop a picture of imperfective function. (2002:66)

---

44. See Comrie (1976:26-32), inter alios.
45. For example, see Hatav (1997:131-138) and Palmer (2001:179).
46. These terms, Kuryłowicz opined, are appropriate for languages, such as the Greek and Slavic languages, which maintain a full oppositional system of forms that belong to either category and engender not only a methodical aspectual distinction between the two oppositions, but frequently give rise to semantic contrasts between verbs of the same root. Conversely, these terms are inappropriate for languages such as Biblical Hebrew that lack this sort of distinction.

The ambiguity that Joosten points to is a requisite part of the verbal research. That said, he claims that the nature of any language's system must be determined on the basis of the pertinent linguistic findings. Following in the footsteps of Hatav and Joosten, we also view the modal meaning to be a prime factor in the construction of the verbal system that informs classical biblical prose.

2.2.3.2   The Concept of Modality

Linguists approach the concept of modality from different vantage points: philosophical,[47] semantic,[48] diachronic-typological,[49] and formal synchronic-typological.[50] The adherents of the purely philosophical approach and, to some extent, the semantic viewpoint have a hard time implementing their ideas within the framework of a particular language and encounter even greater difficulties with typological comparisons between languages. With respect to Biblical Hebrew, the main drawback of the diachronic-typological approach is that it forces us to enter the dubious realm of prehistory. Palmer illustrates the potential drawbacks of predicating an account of the Hebrew verbal system on other languages, such as Arabic (Ewald 1831), Akkadian (Bauer 1910; Bauer and Leander 1922), or Greek (Driver 1892). According to Palmer, the only way to put together a comprehensive account of the modal system is via the synchronic-typological linguistic findings, for otherwise researchers are liable to find themselves mired in a never-ending theoretical discussion over which of the meanings a specific category belongs to. Therefore, in order to ascertain the true nature of a given form in the Biblical Hebrew verbal system, it is incumbent upon us to explicate the mutual relations of *all* its designated meanings. For this very reason, the synchronic-typological approach constitutes the foundation of this book.

Another problem concerning the link to the modal axis is that a single form, *yiqtol*, bears various modal meanings, and the distinction between these meanings is not always obvious from the context. In fact, the signification of disparate modal meanings by the same form is a prevalent phenomenon in quite a few languages. For example, Palmer notes that (2001:15):

> Indeed many languages have the same forms for epistemic and deontic modality. . . . CAN, for instance, may be used as epistemic, deontic or dynamic:
>
> He can't be in his office now (epistemic)
> He can come in now (deontic, permission)
> He can run a mile in four minutes (dynamic, ability)

---

47. Keifer (1987), among others, presents this approach.
48. Lyons (1977) is the primary representative of this approach; also see Keifer (1987).
49. Both Bybee (1994) and Givón (1994) take this route.
50. Palmer is the architect of this approach (2001), and it also turns up in Givón (1994).

The vast majority of the terms in this book are based on Palmer's terminology (2001). One of the fundamental distinctions that Palmer, among others, draws is between propositional and event modality (the second of which includes deontic modality).[51] Propositional modality concerns the speaker's judgment regarding the extent of a proposition's veracity [+probability], while event modality refers to the speaker's attitude [+desire] toward the event.

Propositional modality thus pertains to the value of the truth or the extent of factuality and actuality that speakers attribute to a proposition. Within this category, Palmer claims that quite a few languages draw a secondary distinction between epistemic and evidential modality: in the first category, the speaker appraises the factuality of a certain action, while evidential modality is concerned with the quality of the evidence by which the action has come to the speaker's attention.[52] We will lean on the distinction between epistemic and evidential modality in our effort to characterize the various types of propositional modality that inform late Biblical Hebrew. Epistemic modality refers to the speaker's judgment concerning the veracity of a specific action or the extent of its factuality. Put differently, this category measures the speaker's level of confidence on a "probability axis," which ranges from full certainty to absolute uncertainty.

In Biblical Hebrew, *yiqtol* forms that denote the future can be viewed as signifiers of epistemic modality. In many languages, the future, as opposed to the past, can express chronological relationships and various modal meanings at one and the same time. In certain languages, there is a connection between future forms and the signification of various gradients of epistemic instruction. Furthermore, epistemic modality gauges the confidence a speaker has that a certain event will come to fruition.[53]

Evidential modality also falls under the heading of propositional modality. In contrast to the epistemic variety, which concentrates on the speaker's judgment of a proposition's veracity, the focus of evidential modality is on the nature of the evidence from which the speaker learned about the proposition.

The meaning of habitual or iterative actions that are borne by *yiqtol* forms is a complex topic and, not surprisingly, the subject of a protracted debate.[54]

---

51. Insofar as Palmer is concerned, event modality is a principal category that consists of deontic and dynamic modality. Be that as it may, we do not see the need to include the nuances of this distinction herein, and our main contrast to propositional modality is the deontic variety.

52. In certain languages, there is a clear distinction between actions that the speakers learn about from a secondary source or was already part of their general knowledge and an action that comes to speakers' attention directly through their senses; see Palmer (2001:35-52).

53. See Bybee (1994:247-248).

54. According to Givón, "The status of the *habitual*, a swing modal category par excellence, is murky for good reasons. From a communicative perspective, habitual-marked clauses

Determining the habitual meaning's standing vis-à-vis *yiqtol*'s other meanings necessitates an in-depth comparison of all the meanings that this form signifies throughout the biblical texts, especially since *yiqtol* expresses both propositional (epistemic) and deontic modality in the corpus under examination. In the linguistic tradition, the semantic fields of the terms aspect and modus ovarlap in some spheres. For example, the habitual and the iterative are among the overlaping spheres that these terms have wrought. In every particular language these two meanings should be evaluated according to the other uses of a given form. With this in mind, we have chosen to place habitual and iterative actions in Biblical Hebrew within the framework of evidential modality. These distinctions constitute the building blocks of our research on modality.

2.2.4 The Complexity of the Verbal Paradigm

In many respects, the two-hundred-year-old debate between the supporters of the tense approach and the supporters of the aspect/mode approach is being waged over two simplifications, on the basis of which each camp endeavors to bend the entire system to a single perspective. One of the reasons that this debate has persisted for so long is tied to the verb's essence. Since the verb is a "predicative complex," any attempt to describe it by dint of, and relegate all its meanings to, but one simplification is bound to be lacking. Among the principal assumptions of this work is that a comprehensive description of the verbal system must take into account the fact that there is more than one perspective with which to describe the system.

In light of the previous sections, it appears as though the biblical verbal system's two central axes are the *modal axis*, which is underpinned by the indicative-modal contrast, and the *reference-time axis*, wherein every form is defined according to the chronological relation that it maintains with the deictic center R. Not only do these two axes not contradict one another, they may be viewed as complementary.

---

tend to be strongly asserted, i.e. pragmatically like realis. Semantically, however, they resemble irrealis. . . . [U]nlike realis, which typically signals that an event has occurred at some specific time, a habitual-marked assertion does not refer to any particular event that occurred at any specific time. . . . Given the *habitual*'s mixed functional properties, it is not surprising that it has been grouped in some languages with realis and in others with irrealis." Givón then dubs the habitual field a "hybrid modality," namely a group that is comprised of several contradictory attributes (1994:270-271).

The Verbal Paradigm of First Temple Period Prose

		Mood					
		Indicative		Modal			
		(+realis, -habitual, -iterative)		General (+irrealis, +future, +habitual, +iterative, +directive)		Volitive (+directive)	
R-time	[R,E]	*Wayyiqtol*	[R,E]	*Weqatal*	[R,E]	*Vol. Forms +* ו	
	R≥E	*Qatal*	R≤E	*Yiqtol*	S,R<E	*Volitive Forms*	
	|----E----| R	*Participle*					

This chart outlines the functions of the various forms that comprise the biblical verbal system from the standpoint of the two principal vantage points: the reference-time and modal axes. As already noted, it is only proper that a full accounting of the roles assumed by the various forms comprising the Hebrew verbal system should reflect the fact that every form is connected to both these axes. With respect to langue, every form has a two-part meaning, both of which take effect in unison. For example, *qatal* and *wayyiqtol* are indicative forms that simultaneously denote the chronological relationship R≥E and [R,E], respectively. In contrast, *yiqtol* is a modal form that also signifies the chronological relationship R≤E. A langue-oriented account of the verbal system is insufficient on its own, for it entails a high level of simplification that inevitably neglects many of the gradients and subgradients that turn up in certain contexts. Consequently, a full exposition of the verbal system must be grounded on a survey of its multifarious forms in different contexts, namely its "parole." As demonstrated herein, a parole-based inquiry attests to the fact that the R-time and modal axes are engaged in an intricate game, wherein one of the axes is liable to be neutralized under certain circumstances. An inkling of this complexity may be grasped by visualizing a line whose left side represents the R-time axis and whose right side represents the modal axis:

R-time   Mode

In any given occurrence, the verb is situated at some point along the line. The closer it is to one of the edges, the stronger the link to the related axis and the weaker it is to the other axis. If the verb form is positioned in the middle of the line, then the strength of the links to each axis is equal. In this respect, there are no essential differences between the Hebrew of the First and Second Temple periods, so that the examples below have been taken from both corpuses:[55]

(25) וַיֹּאמְרוּ **נָקוּם** וּבָנִינוּ   **RM**

Then they said, **Let us arise** and build. (Neh 2:18)

(26) וַיֹּאמֶר הַמֶּלֶךְ לְאֶסְתֵּר הַמַּלְכָּה בְּשׁוּשַׁן הַבִּירָה **הָרְגוּ** הַיְּהוּדִים וְאַבֵּד חֲמֵשׁ מֵאוֹת
אִישׁ וְאֵת עֲשֶׂרֶת בְּנֵי הָמָן   **RM**

[T]he king said to Queen Esther, In the fortress Shushan the Jews **have killed** a total of five hundred men, as well as the ten sons of Haman. (Est 9:12)

Examples 25 and 26 feature verb forms that simultaneously refer to both the R-time and modal axes within the context of direct speech. In Nehemiah 2:18, a *yiqtol* form denotes a relation of subsequence (S=R<E) that has yet to occur, namely it is an irrealis action and thus belongs to the modal field. Conversely, the *qatal* form in Esther 9:12 denotes a relation of antecedence (E<R=S) as well as a concrete, indicative action that took place at a specific time and place (realis). Notwithstanding the differences, the links to the modal and reference-time axes are of equal strength in both cases. In consequence, both verses have received the same RM score and are located at the center of the imaginary line:

נקום, הרגו

R-time   Mode

(27) וֶאֱלִישָׁע חָלָה אֶת חָלְיוֹ אֲשֶׁר **יָמוּת** בּוֹ   **Rm**

Elisha had been stricken with the illness of which **he was to die** (2 Kgs 13:14)

(28) כִּי כֵן צִוָּה אֹתִי בִּדְבַר יְהֹוָה לֵאמֹר לֹא תֹאכַל לֶחֶם וְלֹא תִשְׁתֶּה מָּיִם וְלֹא תָשׁוּב
בַּדֶּרֶךְ אֲשֶׁר **הָלָכְתָּ** :   **Rm**

[F]or so I was commanded by the word of the LORD: You shall eat no bread and drink no water, nor shall you go back by the road by which **you will have come**. (1 Kgs 13:9)

---

55. Different-sized fonts are used in order to characterize the intensity of the link: the stronger the link, the larger the font; and vice versa. The Ø in example 31 signifies that the reference-time axis has been neutralized.

(29) בִּשְׁנַת הַיּוֹבֵל יָשׁוּב הַשָּׂדֶה לַאֲשֶׁר **קָנָהוּ** מֵאִתּוֹ **R**m

In the jubilee year the land shall revert to the person whom he **bought** it from.
(Lv 27:24)

(30) כִּי לוּלֵא הִתְמַהְמָהְנוּ כִּי עַתָּה **שַׁבְנוּ** זֶה פַעֲמָיִם: **R**m

If we had not dawdled, we could have **returned** twice. (Gn 43:10)

Unlike the first two examples, the R-time link in this group is stronger than the
modal one. In 2 Kings 13, the *yiqtol* form is situated in the absolute past. By articulating the semantic connotation to some degree (Elisha dies at a specific time
and place), the modal meaning of "ימות" is attenuated to some degree. A similar
swing toward the R-time side informs the next three examples, as the *qatal* forms
serve in unequivocally modal contexts—the future, the language of the law, and
irrealis conditional sentences—and thus induce a modicum of de-actualization. On
the face of things, the processes that unfold in these verses are the exact opposite
of what transpires in the first example, but the outcomes are similar in that they all
involve a weakening of the modal link. In all four examples, the attenuation results
from a "collision" between these forms' semantic field (*qatal* = [+actuality, +con-
creteness]; *yiqtol* = [-actuality, -concreteness]) and the process of de-actualization
and actualization that each form undergoes.

The use of *yiqtol* and *qatal* forms in contexts that seemingly run counter to
their main definition largely stems from the morphological paucity of the Hebrew
verbal system. In other words, due to the fact that Hebrew has only one form capable of expressing a relationship of antecedence and only one capable of expressing
a relationship of subsequence in either the modal or indicative field, the *qatal* and
yiqtol forms serve within the framework of both modal and indicative contexts,
even if this contravenes their inherent nature.[56]

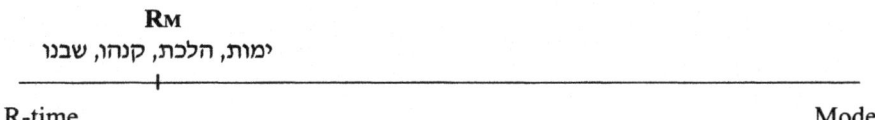

Rm
ימות, הלכת, קנהו, שבנו

R-time   Mode

---

56. Due to the distribution of these verbs, we have placed examples 27 to 30 near the left
end of the line, but not on its very edge. More specifically, relations of antecedence
in Biblical Hebrew are widespread primarily within the framework of the indicative
field, whereas relations of subsequence tend toward the modal sphere. In our estimation, this distribution gives off an echo of the regular meaning even in cases where
the modal aspect is ostensibly nullified, so that there is still a slight connection to the
modal axis.

(31) וְשֹׁחַד לֹא תִקָּח כִּי הַשֹּׁחַד **יְעַוֵּר** פִּקְחִים   **ØM**

Do not take bribes, for bribes **blind** the clear-sighted. (Ex 23:8)

Unlike the previous examples, the *yiqtol* form in Exodus 23:8 bears a generic meaning that signifies a general truth. Consequently, we are unable to determine the form's relationship to the R-time axis. As a result, there is an abrupt shift (rightward) in the direction of the modal side, and the balance between the two sides of our scale is ØM, namely a strong link to the modal axis and a completely neutralized connection to the reference-time axis.

יעור

R-time   Mode

(32) וְיָצָא מִבֵּית אֵל לוּזָה **וְעָבַר** אֶל גְּבוּל הָאַרְכִּי עֲטָרוֹת: **וְיָרַד** יָמָּה אֶל גְּבוּל הַיַּפְלֵטִי
עַד גְּבוּל בֵּית חוֹרֹן תַּחְתּוֹן וְעַד גָּזֶר **וְהָיוּ** תֹצְאֹתָו יָמָּה: **rM**

From Bethel it **runs** to Luz and **passes** on to the territory of the Archites at Ataroth, **descends** westward to the territory of the Japhletites as far as the border of Lower Beth-horon and Gezer, and **runs** on to the Sea. (Josh 16:2-3)

This example is taken from the list of tribal allotments in the book of Joshua. The shift therein resembles the one in example 31; however, it does not go quite so far, as it retains a faint echo of the link to the reference-time axis. The passage's *weqatal* forms delineate the Josephites' border, thereby lugging the semantic weight of one of this form's modal meanings—the habitual present/general truth. As in example 31, the argument could be made that the reference-time link is neutralized because the generic meaning largely negates the relation to the R-time axis. However, this case is somewhat different. From a chronological standpoint, the meaning of *weqatal* is [R,E]. In other words, this form encompasses its own reference time and can thus construct a chain of events. Unlike the salient link to the R-time axis in realis contexts, the link in example 32 is relatively vague. However, the neutralization is incomplete, for the same attribute (the relation [R,E]) that allowed for this chain of events also paved the way for the succession, except that here the string is geographic instead of chronological. Put differently, the recurrence of the attribute [R,E] is what enabled the author to compose a running account of geographical markers that reads as a succession. In light of the above, we have designated the relationship as **rM**:

ויצא, ועבר, וירד. . .

R-time   Mode

All the above cited examples may be summarized in the following manner:

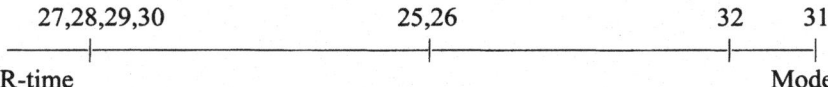

These examples are part of a more complicated network of cases that are informed by mutual relations between the modal and reference-time axes. The complexity can be ascribed to the fact that the verb is not a nuclear unit, but an intricate system that possesses the wherewithal to denote multiple contrasts at one and the same time.[57]

Earlier, we defined consecutive forms as signifiers of their own reference time. Given that the R-time and E-time of consecutive forms merge into one unit [R,E], every occurrence of these forms produces a new reference time, and none of the forms maintain a chronological connection with the other forms in the shared context. On the other hand, the reference time of *qatal*, the participle, and *yiqtol* forms are entirely dependent on their contexts, for they do not encompass their own chronological R-time.

For the sake of illustrating the role of biblical consecutive forms and contrasting them with those of *qatal*, the participle, and *yiqtol*, we will avail ourselves of the image of a slide presentation in which slides are a metaphor of consecutive forms.[58] Since the latter always engender a new R-time, each sequential form in a context is represented by a new slide. Likewise, a narrative continuum is simulated by either passing slides in succession or stopping on a particular slide and elaborating on the form and attendant action. Although each slide in the first scenario constitutes a distinct unit, the "story" is fashioned by concatenating the slides. If a certain slide is singled out, as per the second scenario, we can expand upon and delve deeper into the "story" by adding background information (tasks that are filled by *qatal*, the participle, and *yiqtol*).[59]

Classical Biblical Hebrew features two full-fledged sequential forms: *wayyiqtol* for indicative successions and *weqatal* for modal successions.[60] Every appearance of these forms mounts a new reference time (even when they open a narrative unit). If necessary, the relative tense forms that share the same context can

---

57. For example, Palmer notes that "Mood in the European languages is a morphosyntactic category closely integrated with person, number, tense and voice. The four categories are not independently marked, the form being simultaneously the marker of all the grammatical categories" (2001:185).

58. I would like to thank Prof. Goldenberg for bringing this idea to my attention.

59. Similarly, "discourse grammar" theoreticians define consecutive forms as signifiers of foreground and the relative forms as signifiers of background; see Niccacci (1990).

60. See Hatav (1997:56-82). Even the volitive forms (the cohortative, the imperative, and the jussive) can be used, alongside *weqatal* forms, to denote a succession.

organize themselves around the R-time. As explained above, even though *qatal* and the participle are indicative forms, they can serve in other frameworks when the speaker has to express their singular chronological relations, namely a relation of antecedence and a relation of inclusion in the future (which by its very nature is a modal category). In addition, the *yiqtol* form can denote relations of posteriority in the past. Likewise, the signification of simultaneity is divided between *yiqtol* and *qatal*, with each form marking the relationship in its domain—*yiqtol* in the modal field (the future, habitual actions, and the language of the law) and *qatal* in the indicative field (the past). The charts below outline this division of labor:[61]

The Relation between Consecutive Forms and
Qatal, the Participle, and *Yiqtol* Forms in the Indicative Field:

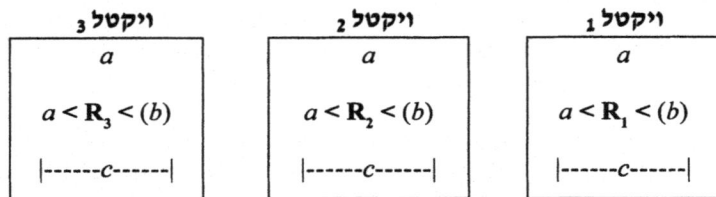

The Relation between Consecutive Forms and
Qatal, the Participle, and *Yiqtol* Forms in the Modal Field:

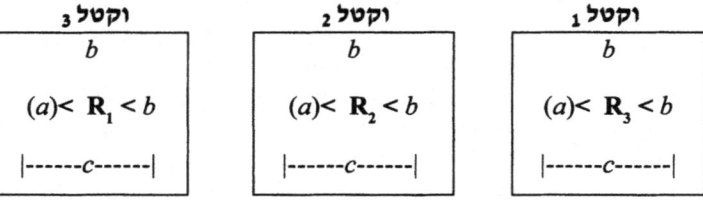

The following examples demonstrate how these relationships come to expression in biblical texts:

---

61. Every rectangle stands for a new "slide," each of which presents a new R-time. The Latin letters represent the various forms: a = *qatal*; b = *yiqtol*; and c = the participle. The parentheses signify an exception with respect to the modal or indicative field.

(33) וַיִּשָּׂא יַעֲקֹב רַגְלָיו וַיֵּלֶךְ אַרְצָה בְנֵי־קֶדֶם: וַיַּרְא וְהִנֵּה בְאֵר בַּשָּׂדֶה וְהִנֵּה־שָׁם
שְׁלֹשָׁה עֶדְרֵי־צֹאן רֹבְצִים עָלֶיהָ כִּי מִן־הַבְּאֵר הַהִוא יַשְׁקוּ הָעֲדָרִים וְהָאֶבֶן גְּדֹלָה
עַל־פִּי הַבְּאֵר: וְנֶאֶסְפוּ שָׁמָּה כָל־הָעֲדָרִים וְגָלֲלוּ אֶת־הָאֶבֶן מֵעַל פִּי הַבְּאֵר וְהִשְׁקוּ אֶת־
הַצֹּאן וְהֵשִׁיבוּ אֶת־הָאֶבֶן עַל־פִּי הַבְּאֵר לִמְקֹמָהּ: וַיֹּאמֶר לָהֶם יַעֲקֹב . . . .

Jacob **resumed [R,E]** his journey and **came [R,E]** to the land of the Easterners,
and there **he saw [R,E]** a well in the open. Three flocks of sheep **were lying**
(|---E---|) there beside it, for from that well **they used to water** the flocks. The
      R(<S)
stone on the mouth of the well was large. When all the flocks **used to gather**
[R,E] there, the stone **would be rolled [R,E]** off the mouth of the well and **they**
used to water [R,E] the sheep; then the stone **would be put [R,E]** back in its
place on the mouth of the well. And Jacob **said [R,E]** to them. . . . (Gn 29:1-4)

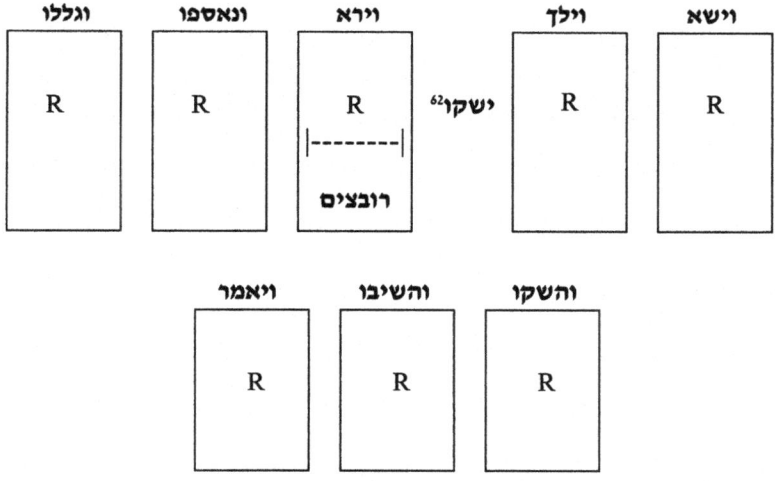

(34) וַתָּקָם הִיא וְכַלֹּתֶיהָ וַתָּשָׁב מִשְּׂדֵי מוֹאָב כִּי שָׁמְעָה בִּשְׂדֵה מוֹאָב כִּי־פָקַד יְהֹוָה
אֶת־עַמּוֹ לָתֵת לָהֶם לָחֶם: וַתֵּצֵא מִן־הַמָּקוֹם אֲשֶׁר הָיְתָה־שָּׁמָּה וּשְׁתֵּי כַלֹּתֶיהָ עִמָּהּ
וַתֵּלַכְנָה בַדֶּרֶךְ לָשׁוּב אֶל־אֶרֶץ יְהוּדָה:

---

62. "יַשְׁקוּ" is an example of a verb that inaugurates a chain of habitual actions and neutralizes the reference-time axis. In consequence, we have placed it outside the framework
of the R-time axis.

She started out [R,E] with her daughters-in-law and **returned [R,E]** from the country of Moab; for in the country of Moab **she had heard (E<R(<S))** that the LORD **had taken note (E<R(<S))** of his people and given them food. Accompanied by her two daughters-in-law, **she left [R,E]** the place where **she had been living (E<R(<S))**; and **they set out [R,E]** on the road back to the land of Judah. (Ru 1:6-7)

ותלכנה	ותצא	ותשב	ותקם
פקד > שמעה > **R**	**R**	היתה > **R**	R

These two examples illustrate the relations between sequential forms that construct a new reference time whenever they appear and all other forms that are connected to these reference times.

Part II
The Verbal Tense System in the Biblical Hebrew of the Second Temple Period

A. The Indicative System

3. Usages of the *Qatal* Form in the Hebrew of the Second Temple Period

3.1 Introduction

Two central axes—reference-time and modality—characterize the functions of the *qatal* form in Biblical Hebrew texts. From the standpoint of reference time, the form's classical Hebrew usages are closely linked to those of the Second Temple period. In other words, it is a relative tense form that denotes the chronological relationship $R \geq E$. However, during this same period, there are evident signs of a breach in the classical pattern, as *qatal* serves, inter alia, as a consecutive form that expresses the relation [R,E]. This breach is relatively minor and tends to be restricted to specific contexts. That said, since the rigid classical framework of consecutive forms begins to erode during this period, it also influences *qatal* and other forms, such as *yiqtol* and the infinitive absolute.[1] Therefore, it should be considered a wide-ranging phenomenon. With respect to the modal axis, *qatal* constitutes a sort of mirror image of the modal *yiqtol* form; In other words, it signifies that an action is actual rather than habitual [+realis, -iterative, -habitual]. Therefore, in all that concerns the *qatal* form's modal usage, its classical roles remained firmly intact.

3.2 The *Qatal* Form's Link to Reference Time

3.2.1 The Relation of Antecedence—$E < R$

3.2.1.1 Antecedence in the Past—$E < R < S$

Locating the reference-time point to which the *qatal* form refers in the past is likely to create a situation in which the form denotes the past of the past, namely the past perfect or plus-que-parfait. Within this framework, R-time is usually signified by means of the following: *wayyiqtol* or *qatal* forms (as well as *yiqtol*, the participle, and infinitive construct forms when expressing an iterative action in the past) or adverbial phrases. The syntactic status of the *qatal* form is of utmost importance in these contexts. There is almost always an $R > E$ relationship[2] when *qatal* appears in a clause that is subordinated to a main one, which contains another form placed in the past. Put differently, in these circumstances, *qatal* constitutes the background for the primary form that stands at the foreground of this discourse:

---

1. See §6.2.4; §10.1.2 below.
2. As we will soon see, there are exceptions to this rule.

(35) וְכִשְׁמֹעַ אָסָא אֶת הַדְּבָרִים הָאֵלֶּה וְהַנְּבוּאָה עֹדֵד הַנָּבִיא הִתְחַזַּק **וַיַּעֲבֵר** הַשִּׁקּוּצִים
מִכָּל אֶרֶץ יְהוּדָה וּבִנְיָמִן וּמִן הֶעָרִים **אֲשֶׁר לָכַד** מֵהַר אֶפְרָיִם

When Asa heard these words, the prophecy of Oded the prophet, he took
courage and **removed** the abominations from the entire land of Judah and
Benjamin and from the cities **that he had captured (E<R(<S))** in the hill
country of Ephraim. (2 Chr 15:8)

(36) וַיִּחַר אַף יְהֹוָה בַּאֲמַצְיָהוּ וַיִּשְׁלַח אֵלָיו נָבִיא וַיֹּאמֶר לוֹ לָמָה **דָרַשְׁתָּ** אֶת אֱלֹהֵי
הָעָם **אֲשֶׁר** לֹא **הִצִּילוּ** אֶת עַמָּם מִיָּדֶךָ:

The LORD was enraged at Amaziah, and sent a prophet to him who said to
him, "Why **are you worshiping** the gods of a people **who could not save
(E<R(<S))** their people from you? (2 Chr 25:15)

(37) וּבְכָל מְדִינָה וּמְדִינָה וּבְכָל עִיר וָעִיר מְקוֹם אֲשֶׁר דְּבַר הַמֶּלֶךְ וְדָתוֹ מַגִּיעַ שִׂמְחָה
וְשָׂשׂוֹן לַיְּהוּדִים מִשְׁתֶּה וְיוֹם טוֹב וְרַבִּים מֵעַמֵּי הָאָרֶץ **מִתְיַהֲדִים כִּי נָפַל** פַּחַד
הַיְּהוּדִים עֲלֵיהֶם:

And in every province and ine very city, when the king's command and decree
arrived, there was gladness and joy among the Jews, a feast and a holiday. And
many of the people of the land **professed to be Jews,** for the fear of the Jews
had fallen (E<R(<S)) upon them. (Est 8:17)

(38) וְרַבִּים מֵהַכֹּהֲנִים וְהַלְוִיִּם וְרָאשֵׁי הָאָבוֹת הַזְּקֵנִים **אֲשֶׁר רָאוּ** אֶת הַבַּיִת הָרִאשׁוֹן
בְּיָסְדוֹ זֶה הַבַּיִת בְּעֵינֵיהֶם **בֹּכִים** בְּקוֹל גָּדוֹל וְרַבִּים בִּתְרוּעָה בְשִׂמְחָה לְהָרִים קוֹל:

Many of the priests and Levites and the chiefs of the clans, the old men **who
had seen (E<R(<S))** the first house, **wept** loudly at the sight of the founding of
this house. Many others shouted joyously at the top of their voices. (Ezr 3:12)

The chronological relationship between the event and the reference time in examples 35 and 36 can be illustrated thus:

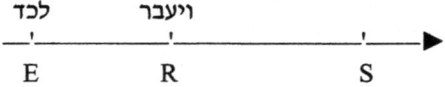

However, in examples 37 and 38, the relationship is more complicated because the
reference time is marked by participle forms that express an iterative action in the
past. The *qatal* form in example 37 signifies antecedence vis-à-vis each and every
action that is expressed by the iterative participle form.[3]

_____

3. A similar relationship may be found when the reference time is the habitual present
    or a form within the language of the law (see §3.3.2). In these instances, the *qatal*

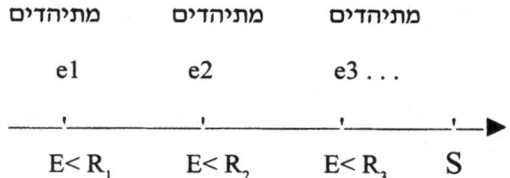

Although the reference time is positioned before the verb in the vast majority of cases, example 38 attests to the fact that it may also come after the verb. In this case, the reference time of the verb "ראו" is the particple "בכים".

If the main sentence has more than one sub-clause, then there are mutual relations within the succession of forms. The fundamental distinction is between cases where a subordinated clause is embedded within another subordinated clause and those in which a clause is followed by a consecutive clause. However, this distinction is not always in force, as there are instances where two clauses appear in succession, but each of them returns to the reference time on an individual basis. For example:

(39) וּפְלִשְׁתִּים פָּשְׁטוּ בְּעָרֵי הַשְּׁפֵלָה וְהַנֶּגֶב לִיהוּדָה . . . **וַיֵּשְׁבוּ** שָׁם: **כִּי הִכְנִיעַ** יְהוָה אֶת יְהוּדָה בַּעֲבוּר אָחָז מֶלֶךְ יִשְׂרָאֵל **כִּי הִפְרִיעַ** בִּיהוּדָה וּמָעוֹל מַעַל בַּיהוָה:[4]

And the Philistines made forays against the cities of the Shephelah and the Negeb of Judah . . . **and they settled** there. Thus the Lord **brought (E<R(<S))** Judah low on account of King Ahaz of Israel, for **he threw (E<R(<S))** off restraint in Judah and trespassed against the Lord. (2 Chr 28:18-19)

This passage is informed by a pair of successive causal clauses. Since the second clause is subordinated to the first, the act of conquest precedes the settlement and the disturbance precedes the conquest. The chronological relationship between the actions is thus:

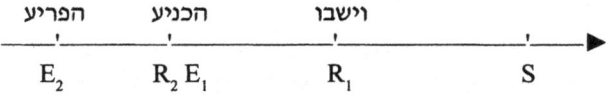

Conversely, example 6 features a casual clause that is comprised of two coordinated sentences:

---

form also possesses multiple reference times due to the habitual usage of these forms. In the first diagram on p. 89, "e" stands for iterative events in the past.

4.   Also see Esther 7:7, 9; Ezra 8:22; Nehemiah 9:10; 1 Chronicles 15:13.

(40) וְאֹמְרָה אֱלֹהַי **בֹּשְׁתִּי וְנִכְלַמְתִּי** לְהָרִים אֱלֹהַי פָּנַי אֵלֶיךָ **כִּי** עֲוֹנֹתֵינוּ **רָבוּ** לְמַעְלָה רֹאשׁ וְאַשְׁמָתֵנוּ **גָדְלָה** עַד לַשָּׁמָיִם:[5]

[A]nd said, O my God, **I am too ashamed and mortified** to lift my face to you, O my God, **for** our iniquities **are overwhelming (E<R(<S))** and our guilt **has grown (E<R(<S))** high as heaven. (Ezr 9:6)

The chronological relation between the main verb "נכלמתי" and "רבו" and "גדלה" is modified as R=E:

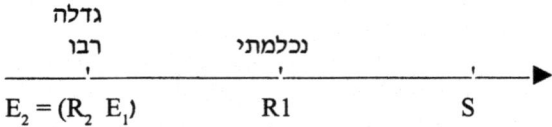

(41) וַיְהִי כַאֲשֶׁר **שָׁמַע** סַנְבַלַּט וְטוֹבִיָּה וְהָעַרְבִים וְהָעַמֹּנִים וְהָאַשְׁדּוֹדִים **כִּי עָלְתָה** אֲרוּכָה לְחֹמוֹת יְרוּשָׁלַ͏ִם **כִּי הֵחֵלּוּ** הַפְּרֻצִים לְהִסָּתֵם וַיִּחַר לָהֶם מְאֹד:[6]

When Sanballat and Tobiah, and the Arabs, the Ammonites, and the Ashdodites **heard** that healing **had come (E<R(<S))** to the walls of Jerusalem, that the breached parts **had begun (E<R(<S))** to be filled, it angered them very much. (Neh 4:1)

This example demonstrates that a pair of successive clauses need not maintain the same chronological relation as in example 39. In this case, the two content clauses return to the act of hearing and thus share the same reference time:

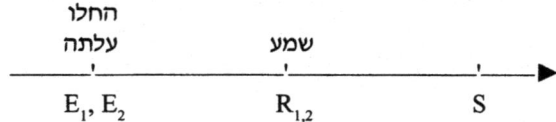

(42) וַיְהִי לִתְקוּפַת הַשָּׁנָה עָלָה עָלָיו חֵיל אֲרָם וַיָּבֹאוּ אֶל יְהוּדָה וִירוּשָׁלַ͏ִם. . . . **כִּי** בְמִצְעָר אֲנָשִׁים **בָּאוּ** חֵיל אֲרָם וַיהוָה **נָתַן** בְּיָדָם חַיִל לָרֹב מְאֹד **כִּי עָזְבוּ** אֶת יְהוָה אֱלֹהֵי אֲבוֹתֵיהֶם וְאֶת יוֹאָשׁ **עָשׂוּ** שְׁפָטִים:

At the turn of the year, the army of Aram marched against him; they invaded Judah and Jerusalem. . . . The invading army of Aram **had come with** but a few men, but the LORD **delivered** a very large army into their hands, **because they had forsaken** the LORD God of their fathers. They **inflicted** punishments on Joash. (2 Chr 24:23-24)

---

5.   Also see 2 Chronicles 15:15; 17:3-4; 19:3; 30:23-24; 35:22.
6.   Also see Esther 2:1; 4:7; 5:11; 2 Chronicles 14:5; 25:16.

This passage underscores the chronological complexity that is likely to be caused by extending a chain of clauses. The passage consists of two casual sentences, both of which are compound sentences. The chronological relationship between the two clauses is similar to the one in example 39, as the act of forsaking God preceded the arrival of Aram's army. However, the relationship between the verbs in the second clause resembles that of example 40, namely the punishment that is meted out to Yoash is part of the nation's abandonment of God.[7]

3.2.1.2. Antecedence to Speech Time—E<R=S

On account of the fact that it is a relative form, *qatal* does not refer to S-time (speech time) as a deictic axis. Nevertheless, it can serve as one of the form's points of reference when the R-time is synchronous to S-time. The natural environment for this sort of chronological relation (E<R=S) is direct speech.[8] Niccacci (1990), whose point of departure is the vantage point of discursive linguistics, claims that the rules which apply to the usage of Hebrew verbs within the context of biblical discourse are substantively different from those that apply to narrative texts. Therefore, a distinction must be drawn between the role of *wayyiqtol* and *qatal* forms in each of these categories. In Niccacci's estimation, the time line of direct speech opens with a *qatal* form, while its narrative counterpart opens with *wayyiqtol* (1990:41-15). In contrast, Hatav contends that direct speech is a special type of sub-narrative text wherein the verb in the first clause is assigned the textual function of marking the transition from the primary narrative continuum to the subordinate dialogical one (1997:181-184).

Following Hatav's view, the only exception to *qatal*'s standard usage is when the form occupies the first verbal slot of a citation. Therefore, within the context of, say, a succession of verbs in direct speech, a *qatal* form is usually relegated to the lead position, whereas the ensuing succession is denoted by *wayyiqtol* forms (the rest of the functions within subordinated clauses are not different from those in narratives). For example:[9]

(43) וַיֹּאמֶר הַנַּעַר הַמַּגִּיד לוֹ נִקְרֹא **נִקְרֵיתִי** בְּהַר הַגִּלְבֹּעַ וְהִנֵּה שָׁאוּל נִשְׁעָן עַל חֲנִיתוֹ וְהִנֵּה הָרֶכֶב וּבַעֲלֵי הַפָּרָשִׁים הִדְבִּקֻהוּ: **וַיִּפֶן** אַחֲרָיו **וַיִּרְאֵנִי וַיִּקְרָא** אֵלַי **וָאֹמַר** הִנֵּנִי: **וַיֹּאמֶר** לִי מִי אָתָּה ויאמר (**וָאֹמַר**) אֵלָיו עֲמָלֵקִי אָנֹכִי: **וַיֹּאמֶר** אֵלַי עֲמָד נָא עָלַי וּמֹתְתֵנִי כִּי אֲחָזַנִי הַשָּׁבָץ כִּי כָל עוֹד נַפְשִׁי בִּי: **וָאֶעֱמֹד** עָלָיו **וַאֲמֹתְתֵהוּ** כִּי יָדַעְתִּי כִּי לֹא יִחְיֶה אַחֲרֵי נִפְלוֹ **וָאֶקַּח** הַנֵּזֶר אֲשֶׁר עַל רֹאשׁוֹ וְאֶצְעָדָה אֲשֶׁר עַל זְרֹעוֹ **וָאֲבִיאֵם** אֶל אֲדֹנִי הֵנָּה:

---

7. In the first clause, "באו" and "נתן" are immersed in an oppositional, R=E relationship.
8. See Hatav (1997:177-184).
9. This sample is cited by Hatav (1997:181-182).

The young man who brought him the news answered, **I happened (*qatal*)** to be at Mount Gilboa, and I saw Saul leaning on his spear, and the chariots and horsemen closing in on him. **He looked (*wayyiqtol*)** around and **saw (*wayyiqtol*)** me, and **he called (*wayyiqtol*)** to me. When **I responded (*wayyiqtol*)**, At your service, **he asked (*wayyiqtol*)** me, Who are you? And **I told (*wayyiqtol*)** him that I was an Amalekite. Then **he said (*wayyiqtol*)** to me, stand over me, and finish me off, for I am in agony and am barely alive. So **I stood (*wayyiqtol*)** over him and **finished (*wayyiqtol*)** him off, for I knew that he would never rise from where he was lying. Then **I took (*wayyiqtol*)** the crown from his head and the armlet from his arm, and **I have brought (*wayyiqtol*)** them here to my lord. (2 Sm 1:6-10)

Unlike the other direct-speech verbs, this example appears to indicate that *qatal* is used differently at the outset of a passage of direct speech than in narrative contexts. With respect to contexts other than direct speech, this case does not deviate from the form's other usages, even from the standpoint of *qatal*'s relation to reference time.

As noted, cases in which the S- and R-time of a *qatal* form are synchronous are exceptional and naturally stem from the relationship between a declarative verb and the content of an instance of direct speech. The declarative verb ויאמר, which usually frames the beginning of a direct-speech passage,[10] is also used to denote the R-time of a *qatal* form that opens a direct speech. This also explains why the reference and speech times in these cases are identical from a chronological standpoint. For example:

(44) וַיֹּאמֶר הַמֶּלֶךְ לְאֶסְתֵּר הַמַּלְכָּה בְּשׁוּשַׁן הַבִּירָה הָרְגוּ הַיְּהוּדִים וְאַבֵּד חֲמֵשׁ מֵאוֹת אִישׁ וְאֵת עֲשֶׂרֶת בְּנֵי הָמָן

[T]he king said to Queen Esther, In the fortress Shushan alone the Jews **have killed (E<R(=S))** a total of five hundred men, as well as the ten sons of Haman. (Est 9:12)

(45) וַיַּעַן שְׁכַנְיָה בֶן יְחִיאֵל מִבְּנֵי עוֹלָם (עֵילָם) וַיֹּאמֶר לְעֶזְרָא אֲנַחְנוּ **מָעַלְנוּ** בֵאלֹהֵינוּ וַנֹּשֶׁב נָשִׁים נָכְרִיּוֹת מֵעַמֵּי הָאָרֶץ

Then Shecaniah son of Jehiel of the family of Elam spoke up and said to Ezra, We **have trespassed (E<R(=S))** against our God by bringing into our homes foreign women from the peoples of the land. (Ezr 10:2)

Other syntactic contexts, such as conditional sentences, display a similar chronological relation within the framework of direct speech:

(46) וַיֵּצֵא דָוִיד לִפְנֵיהֶם וַיַּעַן וַיֹּאמֶר לָהֶם אִם לְשָׁלוֹם **בָּאתֶם** אֵלַי לְעָזְרֵנִי יִהְיֶה לִּי עֲלֵיכֶם לֵבָב לְיָחַד

---

10. See Goldenberg (1991).

[A]nd David went out to meet them, saying to them, If you **come (E<R(=S))**
on a peaceful errand, to support me, then I will make common cause with you.
(1 Chr 12:18)

Here too, the chronological relation E<R=S pertains to the nature of the connection between "ויאמר" and "באתם".

3.2.1.3 Antecedence to a Future Action

When the *qatal* form's R-time is in the future, the action that it expresses precedes
the R-time on the time axis. In these scenarios, the reference time is likely to
be marked by one of the following: *yiqtol* and *weqatal* forms, volitive forms, or
adverbial phrases. Due to the relative attributes of this form, the S-time does not
constitute a deictic axis; hence, the exact location of the E-time along the time axis
is open to contextual interpretation.

3.2.1.3.1 Events Situated in the Past—E<S<R[11]

(47) אָז תַּצְלִיחַ אִם **תִּשְׁמוֹר** לַעֲשׂוֹת אֶת הַחֻקִּים וְאֶת הַמִּשְׁפָּטִים אֲשֶׁר **צִוָּה** יְהֹוָה
אֶת מֹשֶׁה עַל יִשְׂרָאֵל

Then you shall succeed, if you observantly **carry out** the laws and
the rules that the LORD **charged (E(<S)<R)** Moses to lay upon Israel.
(1 Chr 22:13)

(48) וַיֹּאמֶר לָהֶם אַתֶּם רָאשֵׁי הָאָבוֹת לַלְוִיִּם הִתְקַדְּשׁוּ אַתֶּם וַאֲחֵיכֶם **וְהַעֲלִיתֶם** אֵת
אֲרוֹן יְהֹוָה אֱלֹהֵי יִשְׂרָאֵל אֶל **הֲכִינוֹתִי** לוֹ:

He said to them, You are the heads of the clans of the Levites; sanctify
yourselves, you and your kinsmen, **and bring up** the Ark of the LORD God of
Israel to *the place* **I have prepared (E(<S)<R)** for it. (1 Chr 15:12)

(49) **זְכָר** נָא אֶת הַדָּבָר אֲשֶׁר **צִוִּיתָ** אֶת מֹשֶׁה עַבְדֶּךָ

Be mindful of the promise you gave **(E(<S)<R)** to your servant Moses.
(Neh 1:8)

In these examples, R-time is denoted by means of *yiqtol*, *weqatal*, and an imperative, while the *qatal* form's E-time antecedes the S-time:

---

11. Esther 1:15, 18; 3:4; 6:8 (thrice), 10 (twice), 13; 7:4 (twice); 8:5; 9:22 (twice), 25,
31 (twice); Ezra 4:3; 9:11; 10:14; Nehemiah 1:8; 5:19; 13:2, 14; Daniel 10:12, 19; 1
Chronicles 15:12; 22:8, 13, 14 (twice); 24:19; 28:3; 29:19; 2 Chronicles 2:14; 12:7;
20:15; 25:9; 26:18; 29:11; 30:7, 8, 19; 35:3.

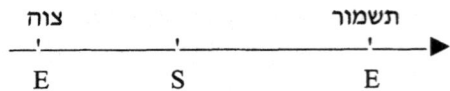

Lexemes that signify R-time usually preceed the *qatal* form, but there are also cases where the R-time is located after the lexeme:

(50) וַיֹּאמְרוּ לוֹ חֲכָמָיו וְזֶרֶשׁ אִשְׁתּוֹ אִם מִזֶּרַע הַיְּהוּדִים מָרְדֳּכַי אֲשֶׁר **הַחִלּוֹתָ** לִנְפֹּל לְפָנָיו לֹא **תוּכַל** לוֹ כִּי נָפוֹל תִּפּוֹל לְפָנָיו:

His advisers and his wife Zeresh said to him, If Mordecai, before whom you **have begun (E(<S)<R)** to fall, is of Jewish stock, you will not **overcome** him; you will fall before him to your ruin. (Est 6:13)

(51) יַעַמְדוּ נָא שָׂרֵינוּ לְכָל הַקָּהָל וְכֹל אֲשֶׁר בֶּעָרֵינוּ **הַהֹשִׁיב**[12] נָשִׁים נׇכְרִיּוֹת **יָבֹא** לְעִתִּים מְזֻמָּנִים וְעִמָּהֶם זִקְנֵי עִיר וָעִיר וְשֹׁפְטֶיהָ עַד לְהָשִׁיב חֲרוֹן אַף אֱלֹהֵינוּ מִמֶּנּוּ עַד לַדָּבָר הַזֶּה:

Let our officers remain on behalf of the entire congregation, and all our townspeople who **have brought (E(<S)<R)** home foreign women **shall appear** before them at scheduled times, together with the elders and judges of each town, in order to avert the burning anger of our God from us on this account. (Ezr 10:14)

3.2.1.3.2 Events Situated in the Future—S<E<R[13]

(52) עַתָּה בְנִי יְהִי יְהֹוָה עִמָּךְ וְהִצְלַחְתָּ **וּבָנִיתָ**[14] בֵּית יְהֹוָה אֱלֹהֶיךָ כַּאֲשֶׁר **דִּבֶּר** עָלֶיךָ:

Now, my son, may the LORD be with you, and may you succeed **in building** the House of the LORD your God as **he ordered ((S<)E<R)** you to do. (1 Chr 22:11)

(53) **וְעָמַד** עַל כַּנּוֹ נִבְזֶה **וְלֹא נָתְנוּ** עָלָיו הוֹד מַלְכוּת וּבָא בְשַׁלְוָה וְהֶחֱזִיק מַלְכוּת בַּחֲלַקְלַקּוֹת:

His place **will be taken** by a contemptible man, on whom royal majesty **was not conferred (E(<S)<R)**; he will come in unawares and seize the kingdom through trickery. (Dn 11:21)

---

12. In the Hebrew of the Second Temple period, the definite article could serve as a relative pronoun of *qatal* forms, such as "וְכֹל **הַהַקְדִּישׁ** שְׁמוּאֵל הָרֹאֶה" (1 Chr 26:28); see Joüon and Muraoka (1996:§145d-e).
13. Esther 4:16? (twice); Daniel 11:4, 21, 36, 39; 1 Chronicles 22:11.
14. "ובנית" and the verbs that signify the reference time in examples 2 and 3 are *weqatal* forms, which express the future rather than *waw + qatal*.

(54) וְעָשָׂה כִרְצֹנוֹ הַמֶּלֶךְ וְיִתְרוֹמֵם וְיִתְגַּדֵּל עַל כָּל אֵל וְעַל אֵל אֵלִים יְדַבֵּר נִפְלָאוֹת וְ**הִצְלִיחַ** עַד כָּלָה זַעַם כִּי נֶחֱרָצָה **נֶעֱשָׂתָה** :

The king will do as he pleases; he will exalt and magnify himself above every God, and he will speak awful things against the God of gods. **He will prosper** until wrath is spent, and what has been decreed **is accomplished (E(<S)<R)**. (Dn 11:36)

The difference between these examples and the previous set is that here the event expressed by the *qatal* form is situated to the right of the S-time:

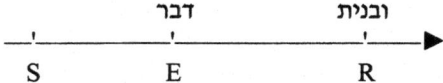

A more complicated instance is to be found in Esther 4:16:

(55) לֵךְ כְּנוֹס אֶת כָּל הַיְּהוּדִים הַנִּמְצְאִים בְּשׁוּשָׁן וְצוּמוּ עָלַי וְאַל תֹּאכְלוּ וְאַל תִּשְׁתּוּ שְׁלֹשֶׁת יָמִים לַיְלָה וָיוֹם גַּם אֲנִי וְנַעֲרֹתַי אָצוּם כֵּן וּבְכֵן **אָבוֹא** אֶל הַמֶּלֶךְ אֲשֶׁר לֹא כַדָּת וְ**כַאֲשֶׁר אָבַדְתִּי אָבָדְתִּי** :

Go, assemble all the Jews who live in Shushan, and fast on my behalf; do not eat or drink for three days, night or day. I and my maidens will observe the same fast. Then **I shall go** to the king, though it is contrary to the law; and if **I am to perish, I shall perish (?(E(<S)<R)?)**

The verbs "אבדתי אבדתי" appear within the framework of a conditional sentence. In principle, one can interpret these actions as being anomalously situated after the reference time (אבוא = R); that is, they are the presumed result of appearing before the king without being summoned. If this is indeed the case, then this is a highly deviant usage of the *qatal* form, as it signifies R<E. Given the *qatal* form's standard usage, Esther may have intended to say that the very thought of preparing for and executing the aforementioned act signals her end; in other words, the queen's demise has already been put into motion before she actually approaches the king. Therefore, it can also be considered an expression of antecedence in the future:

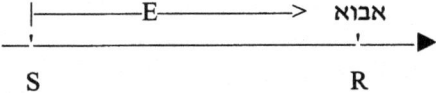

3.2.1.3.3 Events Aligned Parallel to Speech Time—S=E<R

(56) וּשְׁלַח לִי עֲצֵי אֲרָזִים בְּרוֹשִׁים וְאַלְגּוּמִּים מֵהַלְּבָנוֹן כִּי אֲנִי **יָדַעְתִּי** אֲשֶׁר עֲבָדֶיךָ
יוֹדְעִים לִכְרוֹת עֲצֵי לְבָנוֹן

Send me cedars, cypress, and algum wood from the Lebanon, for **I know ((S=)
E<R)** that your servants are skilled at cutting the trees of Lebanon. (2 Chr 2:7)

It appears as if the event that is represented herein by "ידעתי" runs parallel to the
S-time.[15] In Biblical Hebrew, this scenario is not essentially different from the
previous cases that we have discussed, for here too the event takes place before
the R-time and the S-time is ignored. As already noted, the "problem" with this
alignment is not connected to Hebrew itself, but tends to arise when Hebrew is
rendered into a language that maintains an absolute tense system, for in these cases
translators are likely to avail themselves of present forms.[16]

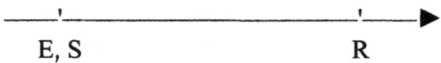

E, S   R

---

15. The semantic content of the verb "ידעתי" deviates from the accepted semantic purview of what is referred to in the grammatical literature as "performative verbs," for
these verbs ordinarily entail an utterance. However, from a chronological standpoint,
"ידעתי" is tantamount to performative verbs, for the chronological relation also signifies concurrence with speech time. For example, Joüon and Muraoka contend that
the "The *qatal* is used for an instantaneous action which, being performed at the very
moment of the utterance, is assumed to belong to the past" (1996:§112f). On the
other hand, Kropat (1909:16) asserts that "Für das Perfekt bei Verheißungen läßt sich
in unsern Büchern kein sichres Beispiel anführen." Nevertheless, since *qatal* was
utilized during this period as a relative tense form, which in all likelihood paved the
way for this sort of syntactic alignment, it is preferable to assume that the fact that
we found only one example articulating this relationship does not necessarily mean it
did not exist. Instead, I would like to suggest that the situation never presented itself
in our limited corpus.
16. Some of the theoretical confusion that these cases begot are discussed by grammarians.
For example, Joüon and Muraoka opine that these actions are perceived as occurring
in the past, even though they are concomitant to speech time: "The *qatal* is used for
an instantaneous action which, being performed at the very moment of the utterance,
is assumed to belong to the past" (1996:§112f). Alternatively Driver (1892:§13) attributes this attribute to the speaker's frame of mind: "The perfect is employed to
indicate actions the accomplishment of which lies indeed in the future, but is regarded
as dependent upon such an unalterable determination of the will that it may be spoken
of as having actually taken place."

3.2.1.3.4 Cases in which the Event Time Begins in the Past and Extends to the Reference Time[17]

(57) וַיְהִי כַּאֲשֶׁר שָׁמַע סַנְבַלַּט כִּי־אֲנַחְנוּ בוֹנִים אֶת־הַחוֹמָה וַיִּחַר לוֹ וַיִּכְעַס הַרְבֵּה וַיַּלְעֵג עַל־הַיְּהוּדִים: . . . **שְׁמַע** אֱלֹהֵינוּ כִּי־**הָיִינוּ** בוּזָה וְהָשֵׁב חֶרְפָּתָם אֶל־רֹאשָׁם וּתְנֵם לְבִזָּה בְּאֶרֶץ שִׁבְיָה:

When Sanballat heard that we were rebuilding the wall, it angered him, and he was extremely vexed. He mocked the Jews. . . . **Hear**, our God, how **we have become** a mockery, and return their taunts upon their heads! Let them be taken as spoil to a land of captivity! (Neh 3:33, 36)

(58) וּבָעֵת הַהִיא יַעֲמֹד מִיכָאֵל הַשַּׂר הַגָּדוֹל הָעֹמֵד עַל־בְּנֵי עַמֶּךָ וְהָיְתָה עֵת צָרָה אֲשֶׁר **לֹא נִהְיְתָה** מִהְיוֹת גּוֹי עַד הָעֵת הַהִיא

At that time, the great prince, Michael, who stands beside the sons of your people, will appear. It will be a time of trouble, the like of which **has never been** since the nation came into being. (Dn 12:1)

(59) וְעַתָּה אֱלֹהֵינוּ הָאֵל הַגָּדוֹל הַגִּבּוֹר וְהַנּוֹרָא שׁוֹמֵר הַבְּרִית וְהַחֶסֶד אַל־יִמְעַט לְפָנֶיךָ אֵת כָּל־הַתְּלָאָה אֲשֶׁר **מְצָאַתְנוּ** לִמְלָכֵינוּ לְשָׂרֵינוּ וּלְכֹהֲנֵינוּ וְלִנְבִיאֵינוּ וְלַאֲבֹתֵינוּ וּלְכָל־עַמֶּךָ מִימֵי מַלְכֵי אַשּׁוּר עַד הַיּוֹם הַזֶּה:

And now, our God, great, mighty, and awesome God, who stays faithful to his covenant, do not treat lightly all the suffering that **has overtaken us**—our kings, our officers, our priests, our prophets, our fathers, and all your people —from the time of the Assyrian kings to this day. (Neh 9:32)

In these examples, the R-time is also situated in the future. However, these passages stand out for the fact that the action evinced by the *qatal* form is not a one-time, fleeting act, but a protracted action that begins at a certain point in the past and lasts until the reference time. These actions generally denote a situation that is either delineated in an express manner or discerned from its temporal context. In these cases, the *qatal* form signifies the relation R>E, rather than the duration of the action:

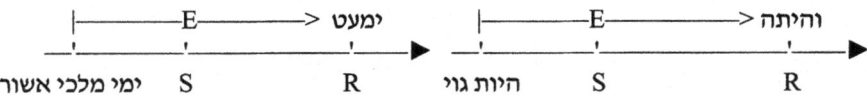

---

17. Ezra 9:10; Nehemiah 3:36; 9:32; Daniel 11:24?, 38?; 1 Chronicles 29:14; 2 Chronicles 14:10; 35:23.

3.2.1.4 Antecedence to a Habitual Present or Iterative Event in the Past

(60) בָּעֶרֶב הִיא בָאָה וּבַבֹּקֶר הִיא שָׁבָה אֶל בֵּית הַנָּשִׁים שֵׁנִי אֶל יַד שַׁעַשְׁגַז סְרִיס הַמֶּלֶךְ שֹׁמֵר הַפִּילַגְשִׁים *לֹא תָבוֹא* עוֹד אֶל הַמֶּלֶךְ כִּי אִם **חָפֵץ** בָּהּ הַמֶּלֶךְ **וְנִקְרְאָה** בְשֵׁם:

She would go in the evening and leave in the morning for a second harem
in charge of Shaashgaz, the king's eunuch, guardian of the concubines. She
would not go again to the king unless the king **wanted her (E<R)**, when **she
would be summoned (E<R)** by name. (Est 2:14)

Given that the only way to denote antecedence is via *qatal* (Hatav 1997:1889), this
form must also be used in modal contexts. The habitual present is one of the *yiqtol*
form's modal usages. In order to express antecedence within this framework, the
author is obliged to resort to the *qatal* form. In these cases, the *qatal* draws its
iterative meaning exclusively from the *yiqtol* form that serves as its R-time.

The next two diagrams map out the chronological alignment in these sorts
of cases:[18]

Put into words, any habitual action is invariably preceded by an action that is
expressed by *qatal*.

3.2.1.5 Antecedence within the Language of the Law

(61) *לְקַיֵּם* עֲלֵיהֶם לִהְיוֹת עֹשִׂים אֵת יוֹם אַרְבָּעָה עָשָׂר לְחֹדֶשׁ אֲדָר וְאֵת יוֹם חֲמִשָּׁה עָשָׂר בּוֹ בְּכָל שָׁנָה וְשָׁנָה: כַּיָּמִים אֲשֶׁר **נָחוּ** בָהֶם הַיְּהוּדִים מֵאֹיְבֵיהֶם וְהַחֹדֶשׁ אֲשֶׁר **נֶהְפַּךְ** לָהֶם מִיָּגוֹן לְשִׂמְחָה וּמֵאֵבֶל לְיוֹם טוֹב

[C]harging them to observe the fourteenth and fifteenth days of Adar, every
year, the same days on which the Jews **enjoyed (E<R)** relief from their foes
and the same month which **had been transformed (E<R)** for them from one
of grief and mourning to one of festive joy. (Est 9:21-22)

---

18. The letter "e" signifies the iterative action that transpires within the framework of the
habitual present/iterative action in the past.

(62) לְקַיֵּם אֵת יְמֵי הַפֻּרִים הָאֵלֶּה בִּזְמַנֵּיהֶם כַּאֲשֶׁר **קִיַּם** עֲלֵיהֶם מָרְדֳּכַי הַיְּהוּדִי וְאֶסְתֵּר הַמַּלְכָּה וְכַאֲשֶׁר **קִיְּמוּ** עַל נַפְשָׁם וְעַל זַרְעָם דִּבְרֵי הַצֹּמוֹת וְזַעֲקָתָם:

These days of Purim shall be observed at their proper time, as Mordecai the Jew—and now Queen Esther—**has obligated (E<R)** them to do, and just as they **have assumed (E<R)** for themselves and their descendants the obligation of the fasts with their lamentations. (Est 9:31)

(63) בַּיּוֹם הַהוּא נִקְרָא בְּסֵפֶר מֹשֶׁה בְּאָזְנֵי הָעָם וְנִמְצָא כָּתוּב בּוֹ אֲשֶׁר לֹא יָבוֹא עַמֹּנִי וּמוֹאָבִי בִּקְהַל הָאֱלֹהִים עַד עוֹלָם: כִּי לֹא **קִדְּמוּ** אֶת בְּנֵי יִשְׂרָאֵל בַּלֶּחֶם וּבַמָּיִם

At that time they read to the people from the book of Moses, and it was found written that no Ammonite or Moabite might ever enter the congregation of God, since they **did not meet (E<R)** Israel with bread and water. (Neh 13:1-2)

(64) אֵלֶּה פְקֻדָּתָם לַעֲבֹדָתָם לָבוֹא לְבֵית יְהוָה כְּמִשְׁפָּטָם בְּיַד אַהֲרֹן אֲבִיהֶם כַּאֲשֶׁר **צִוָּהוּ** יְהוָה אֱלֹהֵי יִשְׂרָאֵל:

According to this allocation of offices by tasks, they were to enter the House of the LORD as was laid down for them by Aaron their father, as the LORD God of Israel **had commanded (E<R)** him. (1 Chr 24:19)

From a chronological standpoint, an action that is expressed within the language of the law is similar to the habitual present or an iterative action in the past, for all three contexts involve an action that potentially recurs along the time axis.[19] As opposed to the verse in the previous section (Est 2:14), the actions expressed herein by *qatal* forms do not derive their habitual meaning from the forms that signify the language of the law. Instead, the event constitutes a quasi-anchor to the past, which the habitual actions inevitably invoke every time they transpire; in other words, every individual action (e.g., "צוהו") has numerous reference times:

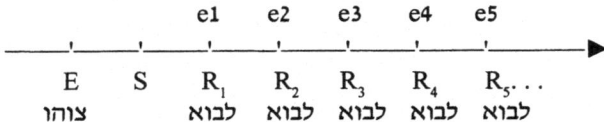

In all likelihood, the disparities between the current examples and the verse in the preceding section are coincidental and not essential to distinguishing the habitual present from the language of the law with respect to the point of antecedence. This argument is bolstered by the fact that the number of legal texts in the given corpus is rather meager. As a result, it is reasonable to assume that the Second Temple period

---

19. The difference between them is that the habitual present is atemporal, namely the action within the language of the law takes effect from the moment the law is given or formulated, whereas the iterative action is restricted to the past.

texts did not exhaust the full range of possibilities. A comparison with similar passages from the First Temple period further strengthens this argument. For example:

(65) בִּשְׁנַת הַיּוֹבֵל **יָשׁוּב** הַשָּׂדֶה לַאֲשֶׁר **קָנָהוּ** מֵאִתּוֹ לַאֲשֶׁר לוֹ אֲחֻזַּת הָאָרֶץ :

In the jubilee year the land **shall revert** to him from whom it **was bought** (E<R), whose holding the land is. (Lv 27:24)

This commandment from Leviticus proclaims that any purchased field must be returned to its previous owners upon the arrival of the jubilee year. The example is highly reminiscent of Esther 2:14. Here too, the *qatal* form ("קנהו") draws its habitual meaning from a posterior verb ("ישוב"), which also serves as its reference time.

3.2.1.6 The Outset of a Narrative Unit as a Background for Consecutive Forms

On occasion, a narrative unit is inaugurated by a *qatal* form that is preceded by a temporal adverbial phrase. An examination of the relationship between *qatal* forms and R-time in these cases reveals an ostensible contradiction to the R>E rule: this is the only syntactical situation[20] where an event expressed by *qatal* trails its reference time (E<R):

(66) **וּכְכַלּוֹת כָּל זֹאת יָצְאוּ** כָל יִשְׂרָאֵל הַנִּמְצְאִים לְעָרֵי יְהוּדָה וַיְשַׁבְּרוּ הַמַּצֵּבוֹת וַיְגַדְּעוּ הָאֲשֵׁרִים וַיְנַתְּצוּ אֶת הַבָּמוֹת וְאֶת הַמִּזְבְּחֹת מִכָּל יְהוּדָה וּבִנְיָמִן וּבְאֶפְרַיִם וּמְנַשֶּׁה עַד לְכַלֵּה וַיָּשׁוּבוּ כָּל בְּנֵי יִשְׂרָאֵל אִישׁ לַאֲחֻזָּתוֹ לְעָרֵיהֶם :

When all this was finished, all Israel who were present **went out** into the towns of Judah and smashed the pillars, cut down the sacred posts, demolished the shrines and altars throughout Judah and Benjamin, and throughout Ephraim and Manasseh, to the very last one. Then all the Israelites returned to their towns, each to his possession. (2 Chr 31:1)

(67) **אַחֲרֵי הַדְּבָרִים וְהָאֱמֶת הָאֵלֶּה בָּא** סַנְחֵרִיב מֶלֶךְ אַשּׁוּר וַיָּבֹא בִיהוּדָה וַיִּחַן עַל הֶעָרִים הַבְּצֻרוֹת וַיֹּאמֶר לְבִקְעָם אֵלָיו :

After these faithful deeds, King Sennacherib of Assyria **invaded** Judah and encamped against its fortified towns with the aim of taking them over. (2 Chr 32:1)

---

20. The Hebrew of the First Temple period is similar in this respect; see Genesis 23:19 and Exodus 34:32, inter alia. Genesis 18:12 constitutes an interesting case, as this structure does not appear in the opening position of a narrative unit, but within a passage of direct speech:

"וַתִּצְחַק שָׂרָה בְּקִרְבָּהּ לֵאמֹר **אַחֲרֵי בְלֹתִי הָיְתָה** לִּי עֶדְנָה וַאדֹנִי זָקֵן :"

Faced with the sudden prospect of bearing a child at a rather advanced age, Sarah responds with a rhetorical question teeming with irony. It could very well be that the decision to apply an unconventional usage—whereby a *qatal* form, instead of the standard *wayyiqtol*, denotes the relation E>R—is meant to accentuate the question's irony.

(68) אַחַר הַדְּבָרִים הָאֵלֶּה גִּדַּל הַמֶּלֶךְ אֲחַשְׁוֵרוֹשׁ אֶת הָמָן בֶּן הַמְּדָתָא הָאֲגָגִי וַיְנַשְּׂאֵהוּ
וַיָּשֶׂם אֶת כִּסְאוֹ מֵעַל כָּל הַשָּׂרִים אֲשֶׁר אִתּוֹ:[21]

Some time afterward, King Ahasuerus **promoted** Haman son of Hammedatha
the Agagite; he advanced him and seated him higher than any of his fellow
officials. (Est 3:1)

The immediate reference time in these examples is noted in adverbial phrases.
Therefore, it would appear as if the actions represented by *qatal* forms transpire
after their reference time (R<E):

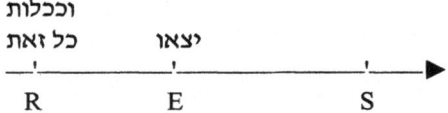

Do these cases indeed contradict the *qatal* form's R>E relationship? Or does this
perhaps constitute a special usage—the signification of a new narrative unit—that
warrants an analysis of its own? This usage indeed characterizes the beginning
of narrative units which pick up where other units off. In other words, it stands at
the confluence of two narrative units. As a result of this intermediary role, these
qatal forms are entrusted with a dual function or a two-pronged link to the reference time. In consequence, they express an action that refers to the anterior textual
unit, while simultaneously serving as a prefatory signifier that sets the stage for
a string of narrative verbs. Additionally, the new group of actions is denoted by
means of *wayyiqtol* forms, which comprise the bulk of the new narrative unit that
was introduced by *qatal*.

The diagram below illustrates the relationship to the reference time that informs these cases:

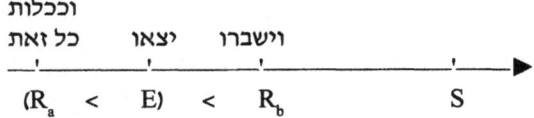

This diagram is predicated on the assumption that there are two R-time foci. To
begin with (inside the parenthesis), the event "יצאו" takes place after the R-time
"וככלות כל זאת". However, the verb "יצאו" is also working on another level (outside the parenthesis), as it simultaneously serves as the background for a chain of
narrative forms that commences with "וישברו". In consequence, "יצאו" marks the
standard relationship of *qatal* forms: R>E.

---

21. Also see Esther 2:1; Ezra 9:1; 2 Chronicles 20:35; 21:18; 24:17; 33:14; 35:14.

The next passage is constructed in a somewhat similar fashion:

(69) **וּכְכַלּוֹת אֵלֶּה נִגְּשׁוּ** אֵלַי הַשָּׂרִים לֵאמֹר לֹא נִבְדְּלוּ הָעָם יִשְׂרָאֵל וְהַכֹּהֲנִים וְהַלְוִיִּם
מֵעַמֵּי הָאֲרָצוֹת כְּתוֹעֲבֹתֵיהֶם לַכְּנַעֲנִי הַחִתִּי הַפְּרִזִּי הַיְבוּסִי הָעַמֹּנִי הַמֹּאָבִי הַמִּצְרִי
וְהָאֱמֹרִי: כִּי נָשְׂאוּ מִבְּנֹתֵיהֶם לָהֶם וְלִבְנֵיהֶם וְהִתְעָרְבוּ זֶרַע הַקֹּדֶשׁ בְּעַמֵּי הָאֲרָצוֹת
וְיַד הַשָּׂרִים וְהַסְּגָנִים הָיְתָה בַּמַּעַל הַזֶּה רִאשׁוֹנָה: וּכְשָׁמְעִי אֶת הַדָּבָר הַזֶּה קָרַעְתִּי
אֶת בִּגְדִי וּמְעִילִי וָאֶמְרְטָה מִשְּׂעַר רֹאשִׁי וּזְקָנִי וָאֵשְׁבָה מְשׁוֹמֵם:

When this was over, the officers **approached** me, saying, The people of Israel
and the priests and Levites have not separated themselves from the peoples of
the land whose abhorrent practices are like those of the Canaanites, the Hittites,
the Perizzites, the Jebusites, the Ammonites, the Moabites, the Egyptians, and
the Amorites. They have taken their daughters as wives for themselves and
for their sons, so that the holy seed has become intermingled with the peoples
of the land; and it is the officers and prefects who have taken the lead in this
trespass. When I heard this, I rent my garment and robe, I tore hair out of my
head and beard, and I sat desolate. (Ezr 9:1-3)

While the link between the *qatal* form and the narrative chain of *wayyiqtol* forms
in examples 66 to 68 is clear and immediate, the connection between "נגשו" and
"ואמרטה" in Ezra 9:1-3 is camouflaged by a protracted excursus (comprised of a
quotation of the officers and additional background activity—"קרעתי"). Nonetheless, the chronological relationships in all these cases are identical.

The relationship R_a=E informs the following passages:[22]

(70) **בִּשְׁנַת אַחַת לְמָלְכוֹ אֲנִי דָנִיֵּאל בִּינֹתִי** בַּסְּפָרִים מִסְפַּר הַשָּׁנִים אֲשֶׁר הָיָה דְבַר
יְהוָה אֶל יִרְמְיָה הַנָּבִיא לְמַלֹּאות לְחָרְבוֹת יְרוּשָׁלַם שִׁבְעִים שָׁנָה: **וָאֶתְּנָה** אֶת פָּנַי אֶל
אֲדֹנָי הָאֱלֹהִים

In the first year of his reign, I, Daniel, consulted the books concerning the
number of years that, according to the word of the LORD that had come to
Jeremiah the prophet, were to be the term of Jerusalem's desolation—seventy
years. I turned my face to the Lord God . . . (Dn 9:2-3)

(71) **וּבִימֵי שָׁאוּל עָשׂוּ** מִלְחָמָה עִם הַהַגְרִאִים וַיִּפְּלוּ בְּיָדָם וַיֵּשְׁבוּ בְּאָהֳלֵיהֶם עַל כָּל
פְּנֵי מִזְרָח לַגִּלְעָד:

And in the days of Saul they made war on the Hagrites, who fell by their
hand; and they occupied their tents throughout all the region east of Gilead.
(1 Chr 5:10)

In these instances, the *qatal* form's link to the reference time may be outlined
thus:

---

22. Also see Daniel 10:1; 2 Chronicles 31:5; 34:3, 14.

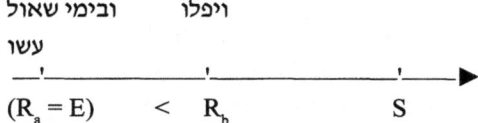

Examples 66 to 69 may be compared to another structure that marks the border between two textual units: the structure אז + יקטל, which signifies a relationship of temporal posteriority in the past.[23] For example:

(72) וַיִּתֵּן יְהוָה לְיִשְׂרָאֵל אֶת כָּל הָאָרֶץ אֲשֶׁר נִשְׁבַּע לָתֵת לַאֲבוֹתָם וַיִּרָשׁוּהָ וַיֵּשְׁבוּ
בָהּ׃ וַיָּנַח יְהוָה לָהֶם מִסָּבִיב כְּכֹל אֲשֶׁר נִשְׁבַּע לַאֲבוֹתָם וְלֹא עָמַד אִישׁ בִּפְנֵיהֶם מִכָּל
אֹיְבֵיהֶם אֵת כָּל אֹיְבֵיהֶם נָתַן יְהוָה בְּיָדָם׃ לֹא נָפַל דָּבָר מִכֹּל הַדָּבָר הַטּוֹב אֲשֶׁר דִּבֶּר
יְהוָה אֶל בֵּית יִשְׂרָאֵל הַכֹּל בָּא׃ **אָז יִקְרָא** יְהוֹשֻׁעַ לָראוּבֵנִי וְלַגָּדִי וְלַחֲצִי מַטֵּה מְנַשֶּׁה׃
וַיֹּאמֶר אֲלֵיהֶם

The LORD gave to Israel the whole country which he had sworn to their fathers that he would assign to them; they took possession of it and settled in it. The LORD gave them rest on all sides, just as he had promised to their fathers on oath. Not one man of all their enemies withstood them; the LORD delivered all their enemies into their hands. Not one of the good things which the LORD had promised to the House of Israel was lacking. Everything was fulfilled. **Then Joshua summoned (R<E(<S))** the Reubenites, the Gadites, and the half-tribe of Manasseh, and said to them . . . (Josh 21:41-22:2)

The chronological relationship herein is very similar to the one noted above:

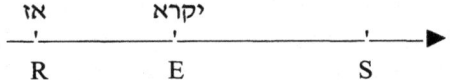

Given the evident lack of a pragmatic difference between the structures in examples 66 to 69 and the phrase אז + יקטל, the two patterns appear to have gradually become interchangeable.

3.2.2 Relationships of Simultaneity—R=E

In the previous section, we examined cases where *qatal* is informed by the relation R>E. At this juncture, we will turn our attention to instances where the *qatal* form and its reference time maintain an R=E relationship, namely a relation of simultaneity. In the context of classical Hebrew, Hatav (1997:103-116, 163-165, 175-177) draws a distinction between simultaneity that signifies the fact that the R-time

---

23. See the discussion on this structure in §3.2.2.1.3 below.

and event (E) transpired at the same point in time (i.e., the relationship expressed by means of the *qatal* form) and simultaneity wherein the reference time is included within the event (a relationship of inclusion, that is expressed in Biblical Hebrew by the participle form). The difference between these relations may be illustrated by the following example:

(73) וַיְהִי כִרְאוֹת הַמֶּלֶךְ אֶת אֶסְתֵּר הַמַּלְכָּה עֹמֶדֶת בֶּחָצֵר **נָשְׂאָה** חֵן בְּעֵינָיו

As soon as the king saw Queen Esther standing in the court, **she won (E=R(<S))** his favor. (Est 5:2)

In this verse, the reference time of both "עמדת" and "נשאה" is "כראות המלך", and both verbs maintain a relation of simultaneity with that phrase. However, *qatal* does not share the same chronological relationship with the participle, as the act of standing encompasses the R-time, whereas the endearment ("נשאה חן") merely runs parallel to the R-time:

```
(עומדת)      |------E1------|
(נשאה חן)          E2
_____▶
   (כראות המלך)  R
```

From the standpoint of the time axis, the relationship R=E is limited to the realm of the past. In contrast, an R>E relation can be situated in any of the tenses (past, present, and future) due to the relative nature of the *qatal* form. There are two reasons for this limitation: First, the *yiqtol* form situates this relationship in the future. Secondly, on account of the real present's circumscribed nature, the S-time is almost always included within the action that signifies the real present. Since the relationship of inclusion is one of the quintessential functions of the participle form, it is the designated choice for these scenarios.

3.2.2.1 Simultaneity with an Adverbial Phrase in the Past

One instance of a *qatal* form maintaining an R=E relationship is when its R-time is an adverbial construction that denotes the past.[24]

(74) **וּבְדַבְּרוֹ** עִמִּי כַּדְּבָרִים הָאֵלֶּה **נָתַתִּי** פָנַי אָרְצָה

While he was saying these things to me, **I looked (E=R(<S))** down. (Dn 10:15)

---

24. Also see Esther 9:25; Ezra 7:9; 9:3, 5; Nehemiah 8:5; Daniel 10:11; 1 Chronicles 12:21, inter alia.

‫(75) וּבִרְאוֹת יְהוָה כִּי נִכְנָעוּ הָיָה דְבַר יְהוָה אֶל שְׁמַעְיָה לֵאמֹר נִכְנָעוּ לֹא אַשְׁחִיתֵם‬

When the LORD **saw** that they had submitted, the word of the LORD **came (E=R(<S))** to Shemaiah, saying, Since they have humbled themselves, I will not destroy them. (2 Chr 12:7)

‫(76) וּמֵאֱלֹהִים הָיְתָה תְּבוּסַת אֲחַזְיָהוּ לָבוֹא אֶל יוֹרָם **וּבְבֹאוֹ יָצָא** עִם יְהוֹרָם אֶל‬
‫יֵהוּא בֶּן נִמְשִׁי אֲשֶׁר מְשָׁחוֹ יְהוָה לְהַכְרִית אֶת בֵּית אַחְאָב:‬

The Lord caused the downfall of Ahaziah because he visited Joram. **During his visit he went out (E=R(<S))** with Jehoram to Jehu son of Nimshi, whom the LORD had anointed to cut off the house of Ahab. (2 Chr 22:7)

In these cases, the chronological relation is thus:

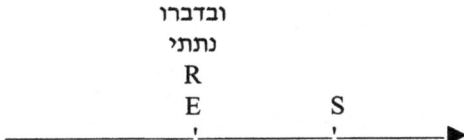

The adverbial construction is usually situated in the clause before the verb form, but it may also be arrayed after the verb:

‫(77) וִיהוֹצָדָק הָלַךְ **בְּהַגְלוֹת יְהוָה אֶת יְהוּדָה וִירוּשָׁלִַם** בְּיַד נְבֻכַדְנֶאצַּר:‬

[A]nd Jehozadak **went (E=R(<S))** into exile **when the LORD exiled Judah and Jerusalem** by the hand of Nebuchadnezzar. (1 Chr 5:41)

3.2.2.2   Simultaneity at the Outset of a Narrative Succession

3.2.2.2.1   Simultaneity with an Adverbial Phrase

Among the means for marking the opening of a narrative succession is a *qatal* form that expresses simultaneity with an adverbial phrase in the past. These cases are akin to those in the previous section, save for the fact that here the verb form is also assigned the textual role of denoting the start of a narrative unit and/or a narrative succession:

‫(78) **בִּשְׁנַת שָׁלוֹשׁ לְמַלְכוּת יְהוֹיָקִים מֶלֶךְ יְהוּדָה בָּא** נְבוּכַדְנֶאצַּר מֶלֶךְ בָּבֶל יְרוּשָׁלִַם‬
‫וַיָּצַר עָלֶיהָ: וַיִּתֵּן אֲדֹנָי בְּיָדוֹ אֶת יְהוֹיָקִים מֶלֶךְ יְהוּדָה וּמִקְצָת כְּלֵי בֵית הָאֱלֹהִים‬
‫וַיְבִיאֵם אֶרֶץ שִׁנְעָר בֵּית אֱלֹהָיו‬

In the third year of the reign of King Jehoiakim of Judah, King Nebuchadnezzar of Babylon **came (E=R(<S))** to Jerusalem and laid siege to

it. The Lord delivered King Jehoiakim of Judah into his power, together with some of the vessels of the House of God, and he brought them to the land of Shinar to the house of his god. (Dn 1:1-2)

(79) **בַּיּוֹם הַהוּא בָּא** מִסְפַּר הַהֲרוּגִים בְּשׁוּשַׁן הַבִּירָה לִפְנֵי הַמֶּלֶךְ: וַיֹּאמֶר הַמֶּלֶךְ
לְאֶסְתֵּר הַמַּלְכָּה

On that same day the number of those slain in the fortress Shushan **was reported (E=R(<S))** to the king, and the king said to Queen Esther . . . (Est 9:11-12)

This structure is likely to appear at the outset of both a major narrative unit, as in Daniel 1:1, and a smaller narrative unit that elicits some sort of change in perspective within the narrative continuum, as in Esther 9:11-12.

3.2.2.2.2 ויהי + an Adverbial Construction + *Qatal*

Another structure that marks the opening of a narrative continuum is the combination of ויהי + an adverbial construction + *qatal* in succession. According to Hatav, the function of ויהי (and והיה) at the outset of narrative successions is to signify that the unit is new or to denote a chronological leap in R-time (1997:76-83, esp. 78). One of the characteristics of this form's usage in this particular context is a lack of agreement between the verb and its subject with respect to both gender and number. Hatav claims that in these situations *qatal* assumes the third person singular. Following in the footsteps of Schneider (1974), Partee (1984), and others,[25] she claims that in these circumstances ויהי is relegated to a purely segmental role, while the adverbial construction determines the reference time, as in the passage below:[26]

(80) **וַיְהִי כְּהָכִין** מַלְכוּת רְחַבְעָם וּכְחֶזְקָתוֹ **עָזַב** אֶת תּוֹרַת יְהוָה וְכָל יִשְׂרָאֵל עִמּוֹ:
וַיְהִי בַּשָּׁנָה הַחֲמִישִׁית לַמֶּלֶךְ רְחַבְעָם **עָלָה** שִׁישַׁק מֶלֶךְ מִצְרַיִם עַל יְרוּשָׁלַם כִּי מָעֲלוּ
בַּיהוָה:

When the kingship of Rehoboam **was firmly established**, and he grew strong, **he abandoned (E=R(<S))** the Teaching of the LORD, he and all Israel with him. **In the fifth year** of King Rehoboam, King Shishak of Egypt **marched (E=R(<S))** against Jerusalem, for they had trespassed against the LORD. (2 Chr 12:1-2)

This example resembles cases wherein ויהי is followed by the particle כאשר:[27]

---

25. See the discussion on the usages of ויהי at the outset of textual units in §4.2.3.2.1 below.
26. Also see Nehemiah 1:1; 2 Chronicles 13:15; 21:19; 24:23.
27. Also see Nehemiah 3:33; 4:6, 9; 6:1; 7:1; 13:19.

(81) וַיְהִי כַאֲשֶׁר שָׁמַע סַנְבַלַּט וְטוֹבִיָּה וְהָעַרְבִים וְהָעַמֹּנִים וְהָאַשְׁדּוֹדִים כִּי עָלְתָה
אֲרוּכָה לְחֹמוֹת יְרוּשָׁלַ͏ִם כִּי הֵחֵלּוּ הַפְּרֻצִים לְהִסָּתֵם וַיִּחַר לָהֶם מְאֹד:

When Sanballat and Tobiah, and the Arabs, the Ammonites, and the Ashdodites
heard (E=R(<S)) that healing had come to the walls of Jerusalem, that the
breached parts had begun to be filled, it angered them very much. (Neh 4:1)

Whereas the previous examples commence with an adverbial construction and a
qatal verb—both of which essentially serve as the background for the start of a
subsequent narrative chain that begins with a *wayyiqtol* form—the narrative unit
of Nehemiah 4:1 starts with a narrative chain that is introduced by a form (וַיְהִי)
carrying its own reference time.

3.2.2.3 Simultaneity that Is Tied to the Relationship between Qatal and Other Verb Forms

Qatal forms that putatively stand on the same plane as *wayyiqtol*, such as instances where the former denote a contrast or negation, are also informed by
an R=E relationship. In these scenarios, one would be hard pressed to establish
whether *qatal* serves as the background for other forms. However, if we somewhat broaden our definition of a background action, then this role can indeed
be ascribed to *qatal*. This leeway is justifiable by dint of *qatal*'s characteristic
feature of not representing its own R-time. In other words, even though these
actions appear to be on equal footing, *qatal* forms basically lean on other verb
forms in these instances too.

3.2.2.3.1 Opposition to the Action Represented by *Wayyiqtol*

In cases informed by a contrast between the action represented by *qatal* and the
action represented by *wayyiqtol*, the *qatal* form's event and reference time are also
synchronous on account of a link to the *wayyiqtol* form. The contrasting relationship
between these verbs places them on the same point along the time axis. Among the
examples of this syntactical phenomenon in classical Hebrew is Genesis 1:5:

(82) וַיִּקְרָא אֱלֹהִים לָאוֹר יוֹם וְלַחֹשֶׁךְ קָרָא לָיְלָה

God **called** the light Day, and the darkness he **called (E=R(<S))** Night. (Gn 1:5)

Instead of underscoring the fact that the creator willed a pair of consecutive actions, this verse emphasizes the contrast between the names that are given to day
and night. The following passages can be understood in a similar fashion:[28]

---

28. Also see 2 Chronicles 3:5; 13:3, 7; 20:18; 21:3; 25:11-12; 27:5; 28:25; 30:15; 35:7-8;
36:17.

(83) וַיָּ֣שָׁב מָרְדֳּכַ֗י אֶל־שַׁ֣עַר הַמֶּ֑לֶךְ וְהָמָן֙ **נִדְחַף֙** אֶל־בֵּית֔וֹ אָבֵ֖ל וַחֲפ֥וּי רֹֽאשׁ׃

Then Mordecai **returned** to the king's gate, while Haman **hurried (E=R(<S))** home, his head covered in mourning. (Est 6:12)

(84) וּבִימֵ֣י שָׁא֗וּל עָשׂ֤וּ מִלְחָמָה֙ עִם־הַֽהַגְרִאִ֔ים וַיִּפְּל֖וּ בְּיָדָ֑ם **וַיֵּשְׁבוּ֙** בְּאָ֣הֳלֵיהֶ֔ם עַ֖ל כָּל־פְּנֵ֥י מִזְרָ֖ח לַגִּלְעָֽד׃ וּבְנֵי־גָ֗ד לְנֶגְדָּ֞ם **יָֽשְׁבוּ֙** בְּאֶ֣רֶץ הַבָּשָׁ֔ן עַד־סַלְכָֽה׃

And in the days of Saul they made war on the Hagrites, who fell by their hand; **and they occupied** their tents throughout all the region east of Gilead. The sons of Gad **dwelt (E=R(<S))** facing them in the land of Bashan as far as Salcah. (1 Chr 5:10)

(85) וַיַּבְדִּילֵ֣ם אֲמַצְיָ֡הוּ לְהַגְּד֣וּד אֲשֶׁר־בָּ֣א אֵלָיו֩ מֵֽאֶפְרַ֨יִם לָלֶ֜כֶת לִמְקוֹמָ֗ם וַיִּ֤חַר אַפָּם֙ מְאֹד֙ בִּֽיהוּדָ֔ה **וַיָּשׁ֥וּבוּ** לִמְקוֹמָ֖ם בׇּחֳרִי־אָֽף׃ וַאֲמַצְיָ֙הוּ֙ **הִתְחַזַּ֔ק**

So Amaziah detached the force that came to him from Ephraim, ordering them to go back to their place. They were greatly enraged against Judah **and returned** to their place in a rage. Amaziah **took courage (E=R(<S))** (2 Chr 25:10-11)

As in the verse from Genesis, these passages accentuate the contrast between the actions that are signified by *wayyiqtol* and *qatal*. For instance, Mordecai's return to the king's gate transpires at the same time as and stands in contradistinction to Haman's disgrace. Likewise, the dwelling of the tribe of Gad is distinguished from that of Reuben. The contrast between these verbs precludes the creation of a new R-time, for the contrast could not have been rendered if another reference time had taken form. Accordingly, this is probably why the authors availed themselves of *qatal* in these cases. In any event, the relationship can be illustrated thus:

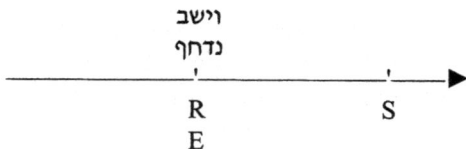

3.2.2.3.2 Negation

E- and R-times may also be synchronous in cases where they are linked to an adjacent verb form when *qatal* forms are arrayed after a negative particle. In these cases, the argument can be made that the negative particle's position at the head of a clause rules out the use of the *wayyiqtol* form because the latter can only occupy the sentence's opening slot. As a result, *qatal* is deemed to be the form of last resort. Alternatively we can also suggest that the reason for using *qatal* after a negative particle is perhaps intrinsically linked to the fact that this form does not bear its own R-time. In other words, negating an action within the framework of the narrative past, as in the above noted cases featuring contrasts,[29] is connected to a positive sentence. Therefore, an action that is expressed by a negative preposition does not bear its own R-time, but draws it from an affiliated positive action. For example:

(86) וּרְאִיתִיו מַגִּיעַ אֵצֶל הָאַיִל וַיִּתְמַרְמַר אֵלָיו וַיַּךְ אֶת הָאַיִל וַיְשַׁבֵּר אֶת שְׁתֵּי קַרְנָיו
וְלֹא הָיָה כֹחַ בָּאַיִל לַעֲמֹד לְפָנָיו:

I saw him reach the ram and rage at him; he struck the ram and broke its two horns, and the ram **has no power (E=R(<S))** to withstand him. (Dn 8:7)

(87) וָאֶהִי עֹלֶה בַנַּחַל לַיְלָה וָאֱהִי שֹׁבֵר בַּחוֹמָה וָאָשׁוּב וָאָבוֹא בְּשַׁעַר הַגַּיְא וָאָשׁוּב:
וְהַסְּגָנִים **לֹא יָדְעוּ** אָנָה הָלַכְתִּי

So I went up the wadi by night, surveying the wall, and, entering again by the Valley Gate, I returned. The prefects **didn't know (E=R(<S))** where I had gone (Neh 2:15-16)

(88) וַיַּעֲמֵד כְּמִשְׁפַּט דָּוִיד אָבִיו אֶת מַחְלְקוֹת הַכֹּהֲנִים עַל עֲבֹדָתָם וְהַלְוִיִּם עַל
מִשְׁמְרוֹתָם לְהַלֵּל וּלְשָׁרֵת נֶגֶד הַכֹּהֲנִים לִדְבַר יוֹם בְּיוֹמוֹ וְהַשּׁוֹעֲרִים בְּמַחְלְקוֹתָם
לְשַׁעַר וָשָׁעַר כִּי כֵן מִצְוַת דָּוִיד אִישׁ הָאֱלֹהִים: **וְלֹא סָרוּ** מִצְוַת הַמֶּלֶךְ עַל הַכֹּהֲנִים
וְהַלְוִיִּם לְכָל דָּבָר [30]

Following the prescription of his father David, he set up the divisions of the priests for their duties, and the Levites for their watches, to praise and to serve alongside the priests, according to each day's requirement, and the gatekeepers in their watches, gate by gate, for such was the commandment of David, the man of God. **They did not depart (E=R(<S))** from the commandment of the king relating to the priests and the Levites in all these matters. (2 Chr 8:14-15)

The diagram from §3.2.2.3.1 befits these passages as well:

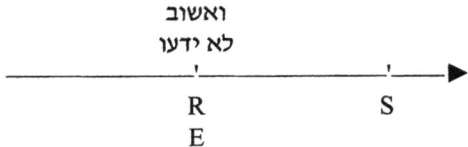

---

29. And in contrast to a negation or prohibition within the language of the law, where the directive may very well be a sentence that stands on its own, such as "לֹא תִרְצָח".
30. Also see Esther 2:10; 3:4; Ezra 8:15; 10:6 (twice); Nehemiah 2:1, 12; 5:8; Daniel 1:19; 9:14; 10:8; 1 Chronicles 23:11, 17, 22; 2 Chronicles 13:7, 10, 20; 17:10; 21:17, 19; 24:19, 22, 25; 28:20; 29:7.

A positive sentence that is invoked by and constitutes the reference time of a *qatal* form preceded by a negative particle can also host forms other than *wayyiqtol*:

(89) וּבִשְׁנֵים עָשָׂר חֹדֶשׁ הוּא חֹדֶשׁ אֲדָר בִּשְׁלוֹשָׁה עָשָׂר יוֹם בּוֹ אֲשֶׁר הִגִּיעַ דְּבַר הַמֶּלֶךְ וְדָתוֹ לְהֵעָשׂוֹת בַּיּוֹם אֲשֶׁר שִׂבְּרוּ אֹיְבֵי הַיְּהוּדִים לִשְׁלוֹט בָּהֶם וְנַהֲפוֹךְ הוּא אֲשֶׁר יִשְׁלְטוּ הַיְּהוּדִים הֵמָּה בְּשׂנְאֵיהֶם: **נִקְהֲלוּ** הַיְּהוּדִים בְּעָרֵיהֶם בְּכָל מְדִינוֹת הַמֶּלֶךְ אֲחַשְׁוֵרוֹשׁ לִשְׁלֹחַ יָד בִּמְבַקְשֵׁי רָעָתָם וְאִישׁ **לֹא עָמַד** לִפְנֵיהֶם[31]

And so, on the thirteenth day of the twelfth month—that is, the month of Adar — when the king's command and decree were to be executed, the very day on which the enemies of the Jews had expected to get them in their power, the opposite happened, and the Jews got their enemies in their power. Throughout the provinces of King Ahasuerus, the Jews **mustered** in their cities to attack those who sought their hurt; and **no one could withstand (E=R(<S))** them. (Est 9:1-2)

(90) בַּיָּמִים הָהֵם אֲנִי דָנִיֵּאל **הָיִיתִי מִתְאַבֵּל** שְׁלֹשָׁה שָׁבֻעִים יָמִים: לֶחֶם חֲמֻדוֹת **לֹא אָכַלְתִּי** וּבָשָׂר וָיַיִן **לֹא בָא** אֶל פִּי וְסוֹךְ **לֹא סָכְתִּי**

At that time, I, Daniel, **kept** three full weeks **of mourning. I ate no (E=R(<S))** tasty food, **nor did (E=R(<S))** any meat or wine **enter** my mouth. **I did not (E=R(<S))** anoint myself. (Dn 10:2-3)

In example 89, the reference time of the verb "עמד" is the event portrayed by "נקהלו", and the relationship between the E- and R-time of "עמד" is the same as in the first three examples. However, the relationship in example 90 is somewhat different, for its reference time is an action (denoted by the structure היה + the participle) that spans over an extended period of time:

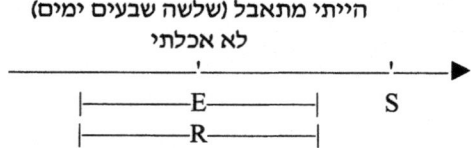

31. Also see Esther 9:10, 16; Ezra 2:62; 3:6; Nehemiah 1:7; 3:5; 5:16, 18; 6:1; 13:26; Daniel 9:6, 10, 13; 10:7, 8; 1 Chronicles 12:20; 27:24; 2 Chronicles 7:2; 17:3; 20:10; 25:16; 29:34.

3.2.2.3.3 Recurrence of an Action Previously Mentioned by a *Wayyiqtol* Form

Scenarios containing a verb that was already introduced by a *wayyiqtol* form are analogous to the above noted contrast and negation patterns, for here too the *qatal* form's reference time is the *wayyiqtol* verb. In these cases, the verb is repeated in order to provide an explanation or expand upon the first instance of the verb, and not to engender a new reference time:

(91) **וַיַּפִּילוּ** גוֹרָלוֹת כַּקָּטֹן כַּגָּדוֹל לְבֵית אֲבוֹתָם לְשַׁעַר וָשָׁעַר׃ וַיִּפֹּל הַגּוֹרָל מִזְרָחָה לְשֶׁלֶמְיָהוּ וּזְכַרְיָהוּ בְנוֹ יוֹעֵץ בְּשֶׂכֶל **הִפִּילוּ** גוֹרָלוֹת וַיֵּצֵא גוֹרָלוֹ צָפוֹנָה׃

They cast lots, small and great alike, by clans, for each gate. The lot for the east gate fell to Shelemiah. Then **they cast (E=R(<S))** lots for Zechariah his son, a prudent counselor, and his lot came out to be the north gate. (1 Chr 26:13-14)

(92) וַיָּקֻמוּ **וַיָּסִירוּ** אֶת הַמִּזְבְּחוֹת אֲשֶׁר בִּירוּשָׁלָם וְאֵת כָּל הַמְקַטְּרוֹת **הֵסִירוּ** וַיַּשְׁלִיכוּ לְנַחַל קִדְרוֹן׃

They set to **and removed** the altars that were in Jerusalem, and **they removed (E=R(<S))** all the incense stands and threw them into Wadi Kidron. (2 Chr 30:14)

(93) וַיַּעַשׂ כָּזֹאת יְחִזְקִיָּהוּ בְּכָל יְהוּדָה **וַיַּעַשׂ** הַטּוֹב וְהַיָּשָׁר וְהָאֱמֶת לִפְנֵי יְהוָה אֱלֹהָיו׃ וּבְכָל מַעֲשֶׂה אֲשֶׁר הֵחֵל בַּעֲבוֹדַת בֵּית הָאֱלֹהִים וּבַתּוֹרָה וּבַמִּצְוָה לִדְרֹשׁ לֵאלֹהָיו בְּכָל לְבָבוֹ **עָשָׂה**

Hezekiah did this throughout Judah. He **acted in a way** that was good, upright, and faithful before the LORD his God. Every work he undertook in the service of the House of God or in the Teaching and the Commandment, to worship his God, **he did (E=R(<S))** with all his heart. (2 Chr 31:20-21)

The same diagram that was used to chart the chronological relations in the two previous sections is applicable here as well.

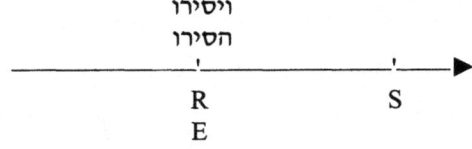

3.2.2.4 Simultaneity following the Particles גם, אז, עוד, and אך

The E=R relationship can also be found in clauses that open with the conjunctions גם, אז, עוד, and אך. Here too, one could argue that situating the verb in a position other than the head of the clause compelled the author to eschew *wayyiqtol* in favor of *qatal*. However, as we have seen, this choice may have also been influenced by the fact that these particles create a situation in which the reference time is located in the previous clause.

(94) וַיַּכּוּ אֵת כָּל־הֶעָרִים סְבִיבוֹת גְּרָר כִּי־הָיָה פַחַד־יְהוָה עֲלֵיהֶם וַיָּבֹזּוּ אֶת־כָּל־הֶעָרִים כִּי־בִזָּה רַבָּה הָיְתָה בָהֶם: **וְגַם־אָהֳלֵי מִקְנֶה הִכּוּ** וַיִּשְׁבּוּ צֹאן לָרֹב וּגְמַלִּים וַיָּשֻׁבוּ יְרוּשָׁלָ͏ִם:[32]

All the cities in the vicinity of Gerar were ravaged, for a terror of the LORD seized them. All the cities were plundered, and they yielded much booty. **They also ravaged (E=R(<S)) the encampment of herdsmen**, capturing much sheep and camels. Then they returned to Jerusalem. (2 Chr 14:13-14)

(95) וַיִּקָּבְצוּ יְהוּדָה לְבַקֵּשׁ מֵיְהוָה **גַּם מִכָּל־עָרֵי יְהוּדָה בָּאוּ** לְבַקֵּשׁ אֶת־יְהוָה:

Judah assembled to beseech the LORD. **They also came (E=R(<S)) from all the towns of Judah** to seek the LORD. (2 Chr 20:4)

(96) וַיַּעַשׂ־לוֹ בָתִּים בְּעִיר דָּוִיד וַיָּכֶן מָקוֹם לַאֲרוֹן הָאֱלֹהִים וַיֶּט־לוֹ אֹהֶל: **אָז אָמַר** דָּוִיד לֹא לָשֵׂאת אֶת־אֲרוֹן הָאֱלֹהִים כִּי אִם־הַלְוִיִּם כִּי־בָם בָּחַר יְהוָה לָשֵׂאת אֶת־אֲרוֹן יְהוָה וּלְשָׁרְתוֹ עַד־עוֹלָם:

He had houses made for himself in the City of David, and he prepared a place for the Ark of God, and pitched a tent for it. **Then David gave orders (E=R(<S))** that none but the Levites were to carry the Ark of God, for the LORD had chosen them to carry the Ark of the LORD and to minister to him forever. (1 Chr 15:1-2)

(97) בַּיּוֹם הַהוּא **אָז נָתַן** דָּוִיד בָּרֹאשׁ לְהֹדוֹת לַיהוָה בְּיַד־אָסָף וְאֶחָיו:

Then, on that day, David first commissioned (E=R(<S)) Asaph and his kinsmen to give praise to the LORD: (1 Chr 16:7)

(98) וַיִּגְבַּהּ לִבּוֹ בְּדַרְכֵי יְהוָה **וְעוֹד הֵסִיר** אֶת־הַבָּמוֹת וְאֶת־הָאֲשֵׁרִים מִיהוּדָה:[33]

His mind was elevated in the ways of the LORD. **Moreover, he abolished (E=R(<S))** the shrines and the sacred posts from Judah. (2 Chr 17:6)

---

32. Also see Esther 1:9; Nehemiah 4:16; 5:14; 2 Chronicles 19:8; 24:7; 26:20; 28:5, 8, 9; 29:7 30:1; 36:14.
33. Also see 2 Chronicles 32:16.

(99) וַיִּהְיוּ הָרָצִים עֹבְרִים מֵעִיר לָעִיר בְּאֶרֶץ אֶפְרַיִם וּמְנַשֶּׁה וְעַד זְבֻלוּן וַיִּהְיוּ מַשְׂחִיקִים עֲלֵיהֶם וּמַלְעִגִים בָּם: **אַךְ** אֲנָשִׁים מֵאָשֵׁר וּמְנַשֶּׁה וּמִזְּבֻלוּן **נִכְנָעוּ** וַיָּבֹאוּ לִירוּשָׁלָם:

As the couriers passed from town to town in the land of Ephraim and Manasseh till they reached Zebulun, they were laughed at and mocked. Some of the people of Asher and Manasseh and Zebulun, **however, were contrite (E=R(<S))**, and came to Jerusalem. (2 Chr 30:10)

Once again, the outline of the chronological relations resembles that of the previous sections:

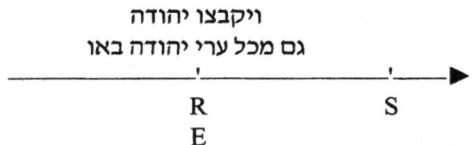

ויקבצו יהודה
גם מכל ערי יהודה באו

R   S
E

3.2.3 Consecutive Forms [R,E]

3.2.3.1 Consecutive Forms—A General View

As per our definition in the first chapter, consecutive forms in Biblical Hebrew are characterized by the relation [R,E], namely every event bears its own reference time. This attribute is what enables these forms to concatenate R-time continuums. In the indicative field of classical Biblical Hebrew, this function is the exclusive domain of the *wayyiqtol* form.[34] However, in the corpus under examination, 230 occurrences of *qatal*—20.7% of 1,107—were found to signify the relationship [R,E]. Compared to the First Temple period, this would appear to be the most dramatic change that the *qatal* form underwent during the Second Temple period. That said, this transformation must be qualified to some extent, for 175 of these occurrences appear within the framework of genealogical lists (15.8% of all). Although the remaining 55 occurrences bearing this relationship (4.9%) do constitute an increase vis-à-vis the First Temple era, the rise is not as dramatic as initially thought.

Be that as it may, the statistical data is liable to be misleading. Even if the presence of narrative sequential chains denoted by *qatal* forms is relatively rare, there are enough occurrences to point to a trend that has significant implications for our understanding of the verbal system of Second Temple period Biblical Hebrew.[35] In addition, the obligatory comparison with Mishnaic Hebrew—an era in which the

---

34. Hatav (1997:57) claims that only 1% of the total number of occurrences of *qatal* in classical Hebrew signifies a succession.

35. Driver already referred to this phenomenon toward the end of the nineteenth century (1892:131).

classic consecutive forms (*wayyiqtol* and *weqatal*) fell out of use—markedly bolsters this claim. Finally, the categorical blurring of *qatal* and *wayyiqtol* was hardly an isolated incident during the Second Temple period—the *yiqtol* form and the modal consecutive form *weqatal* underwent similar processes[36]—and may have been tied to the development of the consecutive infinitive absolute form as well.[37] Therefore, the study of this phenomenon should not be limited to the statistical realm and deserves to be examined within a broader context.

3.2.3.2   Inserting Reference Time in Lists

As already noted, Chronicles and the books of Ezra and Nehemiah are among the largest repositories of *qatal* forms expressing the relation [R,E]. For example,

(100) וּבְנֵי יוֹנָתָן פֶּלֶת וְזָזָא אֵלֶּה הָיוּ בְּנֵי יְרַחְמְאֵל: וְלֹא הָיָה לְשֵׁשָׁן בָּנִים כִּי אִם בָּנוֹת וּלְשֵׁשָׁן עֶבֶד מִצְרִי וּשְׁמוֹ יַרְחָע: *וַיִּתֵּן* שֵׁשָׁן אֶת בִּתּוֹ לְיַרְחָע עַבְדּוֹ לְאִשָּׁה **וַתֵּלֶד** לוֹ אֶת עַתָּי: וְעַתַּי **הֹלִיד** אֶת נָתָן וְנָתָן **הֹלִיד** אֶת זָבָד: וְזָבָד **הֹלִיד** אֶת אֶפְלָל וְאֶפְלָל **הֹלִיד** אֶת עוֹבֵד: וְעוֹבֵד **הֹלִיד** אֶת יֵהוּא וְיֵהוּא **הֹלִיד** אֶת עֲזַרְיָה: וַעֲזַרְיָה **הֹלִיד** אֶת חֶלֶץ וְחֶלֶץ **הֹלִיד** אֶת אֶלְעָשָׂה: וְאֶלְעָשָׂה **הֹלִיד** אֶת סִסְמָי וְסִסְמָי **הֹלִיד** אֶת שַׁלּוּם: וְשַׁלּוּם **הֹלִיד** אֶת יְקַמְיָה וִיקַמְיָה **הֹלִיד** אֶת אֱלִישָׁמָע: וּבְנֵי כָלֵב אֲחִי יְרַחְמְאֵל מֵישָׁע בְּכֹרוֹ הוּא אֲבִי זִיף וּבְנֵי מָרֵשָׁה אֲבִי חֶבְרוֹן: וּבְנֵי חֶבְרוֹן קֹרַח וְתַפֻּחַ וְרֶקֶם וָשָׁמַע: וְשֶׁמַע **הֹלִיד** אֶת רַחַם אֲבִי יָרְקְעָם וְרֶקֶם **הֹלִיד** אֶת שַׁמָּי: וּבֶן שַׁמַּי מָעוֹן וּמָעוֹן אֲבִי בֵית צוּר: וְעֵיפָה פִּילֶגֶשׁ כָּלֵב **יָלְדָה** אֶת חָרָן וְאֶת מוֹצָא וְאֶת גָּזֵז וְחָרָן **הֹלִיד** אֶת גָּזֵז: וּבְנֵי יָהְדָּי רֶגֶם וְיוֹתָם וְגֵישָׁן וָפֶלֶט וְעֵיפָה וָשָׁעַף: פִּילֶגֶשׁ כָּלֵב מַעֲכָה **יָלַד**(ה את) שֶׁבֶר וְאֶת תִּרְחֲנָה: *וַתֵּלֶד* שַׁעַף אֲבִי מַדְמַנָּה אֶת שְׁוָא אֲבִי מַכְבֵּנָה וַאֲבִי גִבְעָא וּבַת כָּלֵב עַכְסָה:[38]

The sons of Jonathan: Peleth and Zaza. These were the descendants of Jerahmeel. Sheshan had no sons, only daughters; Sheshan had an Egyptian slave, whose name was Jarha. So Sheshan gave his daughter in marriage to Jarha his slave; and she **bore** him Attai. Attai **begot [R,E]** Nathan and Nathan **begot [R,E]** Zabad. Zabad **begot [R,E]** Ephlal, and Ephlal **begot [R,E]** Obed. Obed **begot [R,E]** Jehu, and Jehu **begot [R,E]** Azariah. Azariah **begot [R,E]** Helez, and Helez **begot [R,E]** Eleasah. Eleasah **begot [R,E]** Sisamai, and Sisamai **begot [R,E]** Shallum. Shallum **begot [R,E]** Jekamiah, and Jekamiah **begot [R,E]** Elishama. The sons of Caleb brother of Jerahmeel: Meshah his first-born, who was the father of Ziph. The sons of Mareshah father of Hebron. The sons of Hebron: Korah, Tappuah, Rekem, and Shema. Shema **begot [R,E]** Raham the father of Jorkeam, and Rekem **begot [R,E]** Shammai. The son of Shammai: Maon, and Maon was the father of Beit Tzur. Ephah, Caleb's concubine, bore Haran, Moza, and Gazez; Haran **begot [R,E]** Gazez. The

---

36. See §6.2.4 below.
37. See §10.1.2 below.
38. Also see 1 Chronicles 2:3-32; 4:2-23; 5:2-40; 7:14-32; 8:7-37; 9:1-43; Nehemiah 3:1-32; 7:69-71; 12:10-11.

sons of Jahdai: Regem, Jotham, Geshan, Pelet, Ephah, and Shaaph. Maacah, Caleb's concubine, **bore [R,E]** Sheber and Tirhanah. She also bore Shaaph father of Madmannah, Sheva father of Machbenah and father of Gibea; the daughter of Caleb was Achsah. (1 Chr 2:33-49)

It appears as though the *qatal* forms in this chain bear their own reference time, instead of drawing it from the context. This allows the verbs to concatenate the actions and generate a sort of chronological succession within the genealogical list. The beginning of this list can be said to be denoted by the verb "ותלד", and only after do the *qatal* forms engender an elaborative chain. However, as evidenced by the first verse of this same chapter, a string need not begin with *wayyiqtol*.

(101) אֵלֶּה בְּנֵי יִשְׂרָאֵל רְאוּבֵן שִׁמְעוֹן לֵוִי וִיהוּדָה יִשָּׂשכָר וּזְבֻלוּן דָּן יוֹסֵף וּבִנְיָמִן נַפְתָּלִי גָד וְאָשֵׁר: בְּנֵי יְהוּדָה עֵר וְאוֹנָן וְשֵׁלָה שְׁלוֹשָׁה **נוֹלַד** לוֹ מִבַּת שׁוּעַ הַכְּנַעֲנִית נִיְהִי עֵר בְּכוֹר יְהוּדָה רַע בְּעֵינֵי יְהֹוָה נַיְמִיתֵהוּ : וְתָמָר כַּלָּתוֹ **יָלְדָה** לּוֹ אֶת פֶּרֶץ וְאֶת זָרַח כָּל בְּנֵי יְהוּדָה חֲמִשָּׁה: בְּנֵי פֶרֶץ חֶצְרוֹן וְחָמוּל: וּבְנֵי זֶרַח זִמְרִי וְאֵיתָן וְהֵימָן וְכַלְכֹּל וָדָרַע כֻּלָּם חֲמִשָּׁה: וּבְנֵי כַּרְמִי עָכָר עוֹכֵר יִשְׂרָאֵל אֲשֶׁר מָעַל בַּחֵרֶם: וּבְנֵי אֵיתָן עֲזַרְיָה: וּבְנֵי חֶצְרוֹן אֲשֶׁר נוֹלַד לוֹ אֶת יְרַחְמְאֵל וְאֶת רָם וְאֶת כְּלוּבָי: וְרָם **הוֹלִיד** אֶת עַמִּינָדָב וְעַמִּינָדָב **הוֹלִיד** אֶת נַחְשׁוֹן נְשִׂיא בְּנֵי יְהוּדָה: וְנַחְשׁוֹן **הוֹלִיד** אֶת שַׂלְמָא וְשַׂלְמָא **הוֹלִיד** אֶת בֹּעַז: וּבֹעַז **הוֹלִיד** אֶת עוֹבֵד וְעוֹבֵד **הוֹלִיד** אֶת יִשָׁי: וְאִישַׁי **הוֹלִיד** אֶת בְּכֹרוֹ אֶת אֱלִיאָב וַאֲבִינָדָב הַשֵּׁנִי וְשִׁמְעָא הַשְּׁלִשִׁי: נְתַנְאֵל הָרְבִיעִי רַדַּי הַחֲמִישִׁי: אֹצֶם הַשִּׁשִּׁי דָּוִיד הַשְּׁבִעִי: וְאַחְיֹתֵיהֶם צְרוּיָה וַאֲבִיגָיִל וּבְנֵי צְרוּיָה אַבְשַׁי וְיוֹאָב וַעֲשָׂהאֵל שְׁלֹשָׁה: וַאֲבִיגַיִל **יָלְדָה** אֶת עֲמָשָׂא וַאֲבִי עֲמָשָׂא יֶתֶר הַיִּשְׁמְעֵאלִי: וְכָלֵב בֶּן חֶצְרוֹן **הוֹלִיד** אֶת עֲזוּבָה אִשָּׁה וְאֶת יְרִיעוֹת וְאֵלֶּה בָנֶיהָ יֵשֶׁר וְשׁוֹבָב וְאַרְדּוֹן: וַתָּמָת עֲזוּבָה נַיִּקַּח לוֹ כָלֵב אֶת אֶפְרָת נַתֵּלֶד לוֹ אֶת חוּר: וְחוּר **הוֹלִיד** אֶת אוּרִי וְאוּרִי **הוֹלִיד** אֶת בְּצַלְאֵל:

These are the sons of Israel: Reuben, Simeon, Levi, Judah, Issachar, Zebulun, Dan, Joseph, Benjamin, Naphtali, Gad, and Asher. The sons of Judah: Er, Onan, and Shelah; these three, Bath-shua the Canaanite woman **bore [R,E]** to him. But Er, Judah's first-born, was displeasing to the LORD, and he took his life. His daughter-in-law Tamar also **bore [R,E]** him Perez and Zerah. Judah's sons were five in all. The sons of Perez: Hezron and Hamul. The sons of Zerah: Zimri, Ethan, Heman, Calcol, and Dara, five in all. The sons of Carmi: Achar, the troubler of Israel, who committed a trespass against the proscribed thing; and Ethan's son was Azariah. The sons of Hezron that were born to him: Jerahmeel, Ram, and Chelubai. Ram **begot [R,E]** Amminadab, and Amminadab **begot [R,E]** Nahshon, prince of the sons of Judah. Nahshon **begot [R,E]** Salma, and Salma **begot [R,E]** Boaz, and Boaz **begot [R,E]** Obed, and Obed **begot [R,E]** Jesse. Jesse **begot [R,E]** Eliab his first-born, Abinadab the second, Shimea the third, Nethanel the fourth, Raddai the fifth, Ozem the sixth, David the seventh; their sisters were Zeruiah and Abigail. The sons of Zeruiah: Abishai, Joab, and Asahel, three. Abigail **bore [R,E]** Amasa, and the father of Amasa was Jether the Ishmaelite. Caleb son of Hezron **had [R,E]** children by his wife Azubah, and by Jerioth; these were her sons: Jesher, Shobab, and Ardon. When Azubah

died, Caleb married Ephrath, who bore him Hur. Hur **begot [R,E]** Uri, and Uri
begot [R,E] Bezalel. (1 Chr 2:1-20)

From a pragmatic standpoint, it is not always easy to discern the relationship between the two forms in these sorts of lists. Nevertheless, the *wayyiqtol* form is
predominantly used in the sentence's lead position, whereas the *qatal* is ordinarily
situated in other slots.[39]

In addition, this period contains other lists that paint a similar picture with respect to the usage of *qatal*, such as the list from Nehemiah enumerating the people
who took part in the construction of Jerusalem's wall:

(102) וַיָּקָם אֶלְיָשִׁיב הַכֹּהֵן הַגָּדוֹל וְאֶחָיו הַכֹּהֲנִים וַיִּבְנוּ אֶת שַׁעַר הַצֹּאן הֵמָּה
קִדְּשׁוּהוּ וַיַּעֲמִידוּ דַּלְתֹתָיו וְעַד מִגְדַּל הַמֵּאָה **קִדְּשׁוּהוּ** עַד מִגְדַּל חֲנַנְאֵל: וְעַל יָדוֹ
בָּנוּ אַנְשֵׁי יְרֵחוֹ וְעַל יָדוֹ **בָנָה** זַכּוּר בֶּן אִמְרִי: וְאֵת שַׁעַר הַדָּגִים **בָּנוּ** בְּנֵי הַסְּנָאָה הֵמָּה
קֵרוּהוּ וַיַּעֲמִידוּ דַּלְתֹתָיו מַנְעוּלָיו וּבְרִיחָיו: וְעַל יָדָם **הֶחֱזִיק** מְרֵמוֹת בֶּן אוּרִיָּה בֶּן
הַקּוֹץ וְעַל יָדָם **הֶחֱזִיק** מְשֻׁלָּם בֶּן בֶּרֶכְיָה בֶּן מְשֵׁיזַבְאֵל וְעַל יָדָם **הֶחֱזִיק** צָדוֹק בֶּן
בַּעֲנָא: וְעַל יָדָם **הֶחֱזִיקוּ** הַתְּקוֹעִים וְאַדִּירֵיהֶם לֹא הֵבִיאוּ צַוָּרָם בַּעֲבֹדַת אֲדֹנֵיהֶם:
וְאֵת שַׁעַר הַיְשָׁנָה **הֶחֱזִיקוּ** יוֹיָדָע בֶּן פָּסֵחַ וּמְשֻׁלָּם בֶּן בְּסוֹדְיָה הֵמָּה **קֵרוּהוּ** וַיַּעֲמִידוּ
דַּלְתֹתָיו וּמַנְעֻלָיו וּבְרִיחָיו: וְעַל יָדָם **הֶחֱזִיק** מְלַטְיָה הַגִּבְעֹנִי וְיָדוֹן הַמֵּרֹנֹתִי אַנְשֵׁי
גִבְעוֹן וְהַמִּצְפָּה לְכִסֵּא פַּחַת עֵבֶר הַנָּהָר: עַל יָדוֹ **הֶחֱזִיק** עֻזִּיאֵל בֶּן חַרְהֲיָה צוֹרְפִים וְעַל
יָדוֹ **הֶחֱזִיק** חֲנַנְיָה בֶּן הָרַקָּחִים וַיַּעַזְבוּ יְרוּשָׁלַ͏ִם עַד הַחוֹמָה הָרְחָבָה: וְעַל יָדָם **הֶחֱזִיק**
רְפָיָה בֶּן חוּר שַׂר חֲצִי פֶּלֶךְ יְרוּשָׁלָ͏ִם: וְעַל יָדָם **הֶחֱזִיק** יְדָיָה בֶּן חֲרוּמַף וְנֶגֶד בֵּיתוֹ וְעַל
יָדוֹ **הֶחֱזִיק** חַטּוּשׁ בֶּן חֲשַׁבְנְיָה: מִדָּה שֵׁנִית **הֶחֱזִיק** מַלְכִּיָּה בֶן חָרִם וְחַשּׁוּב בֶּן פַּחַת
מוֹאָב וְאֵת מִגְדַּל הַתַּנּוּרִים: וְעַל יָדוֹ **הֶחֱזִיק** שַׁלּוּם בֶּן הַלּוֹחֵשׁ שַׂר חֲצִי פֶּלֶךְ יְרוּשָׁלַ͏ִם
הוּא וּבְנוֹתָיו: אֵת שַׁעַר הַגַּיְא **הֶחֱזִיק** חָנוּן וְיֹשְׁבֵי זָנוֹחַ הֵמָּה **בָנוּהוּ** וַיַּעֲמִידוּ דַּלְתֹתָיו
מַנְעֻלָיו וּבְרִיחָיו וְאֶלֶף אַמָּה בַּחוֹמָה עַד שַׁעַר הַשְּׁפוֹת: וְאֵת שַׁעַר הָאַשְׁפּוֹת **הֶחֱזִיק**
מַלְכִּיָּה בֶן רֵכָב שַׂר פֶּלֶךְ בֵּית הַכָּרֶם[40]

Then Eliashib the high priest and his fellow priests set to and rebuilt the Sheep
Gate; they **consecrated [R,E]** it and set up its doors, **consecrating [R,E]** it
as far as the Hundred's Tower, as far as the Tower of Hananel. Next to him,
the men of Jericho **built [R,E]**. Next to them, Zaccur son of Imri **built [R,E]**.
The sons of Hassenaah rebuilt **[R,E]** the Fish Gate; they **roofed [R,E]** it and
set up its doors, locks, and bars. Next to them, Meremoth son of Uriah son of
Hakkoz **repaired [R,E]**; and next to him, Meshullam son of Berechiah son
of Meshezabel **repaired [R,E]**. Next to him, Zadok son of Baana **repaired
[R,E]**. Next to him, the Tekoites **repaired [R,E]**, though their nobles would
not take upon their shoulders the work of their Lord. Joiada son of Paseah
and Meshullam son of Besodeiah **repaired [R,E]** the Jeshanah Gate; they
roofed [R,E] it and **set up** its doors, locks, and bars. Next to them, Melatiah
the Gibeonite and Jadon the Meronothite **repaired [R,E]**, with the men of

---

39. This rule was not compulsory throughout this period. As we will see below, the "lead
spot" is also filled by *waw* + *qatal*.
40. This list continues until verse 32.

Gibeon and Mizpah, under the jurisdiction of the governor of the province of Beyond the River. Next to them, Uzziel son of Harhaiah, of the smiths, **repaired [R,E]**. Next to him, Hananiah, of the perfumers **repaired [R,E]**. They restored Jerusalem as far as the Broad Wall. Next to them, Rephaiah son of Hur, chief of half the district of Jerusalem, **repaired [R,E]**. Next to him, Jedaiah son of Harumaph **repaired [R,E]** in front of his house. Next to him, Hattush son of Hashabneiah **repaired [R,E]**. Malchijah son of Harim and Hasshub son of Pahath-moab **repaired [R,E]** a second stretch, including the Tower of Ovens. Next to them, Shallum son of Hallohesh, chief of half the district of Jerusalem, **repaired [R,E]**—he and his daughters. Hanun and the inhabitants of Zanoah **repaired [R,E]** the Valley Gate; **they rebuilt [R,E]** it and **set up** its doors, locks, and bars. And *they also repaired* a thousand cubits of wall to the Dung Gate. Malchijah son of Rechab, chief of the district of Beth-haccherem, **repaired [R,E]** the Dung Gate. (Neh 3:1-14)

The repeated use of the prepositional phrase "על יד" (next to) heightens the sense of geographic contiguity that this list seeks to impart.[41]

Comparing this state of affairs to the language of the First Temple period reveals a complex picture, as in this corpus the task of concatenating successions is filled almost exclusively by the *wayyiqtol* form.[42] Nevertheless, there are also a couple of cases where *qatal* forms are cast in this role.[43]

Lists in Chronicles that correspond to ones in Genesis usually feature the same *wayyiqtol* form as the original,[44] but there is one instance where the classical *wayyiqtol* form has been replaced with *qatal*:

(103) וַיֹּסֶף אַבְרָהָם וַיִּקַּח אִשָּׁה וּשְׁמָהּ קְטוּרָה: **וַתֵּלֶד** לוֹ אֶת זִמְרָן וְאֶת יָקְשָׁן

Abraham took another wife, whose name was Keturah. She **bore [R,E]** him Zimran, Jokshan (Gn 25:1-2)

(104) וּבְנֵי קְטוּרָה פִּילֶגֶשׁ אַבְרָהָם **יָלְדָה** אֶת זִמְרָן וְיָקְשָׁן

The sons of Keturah, Abraham's concubine: she **bore** Zimran, Jokshan (1 Chr 1:32)

---

41. It is worth comparing this list to Joshua 15:2-4:
וַיְהִי לָהֶם גְּבוּל נֶגֶב מִקְצֵה יָם הַמֶּלַח מִן הַלָּשֹׁן הַפֹּנֶה נֶגְבָּה: **וְיָצָא** אֶל מִנֶּגֶב לְמַעֲלֵה עַקְרַבִּים **וְעָבַר** צִנָה
וְעָלָה מִנֶּגֶב לְקָדֵשׁ בַּרְנֵעַ **וְעָבַר** חֶצְרוֹן **וְעָלָה** אַדָּרָה וְנָסַב הַקַּרְקָעָה: **וְעָבַר** עַצְמוֹנָה **וְיָצָא** נַחַל מִצְרַיִם
והיה (**וְהָיוּ**) תֹצְאוֹת הַגְּבוּל יָמָּה.
This description of Judah's borders consists of *weqatal* forms and does not denote succession via prepositional particles (see page 90 above).
42. Also see Genesis 4:17-21; 5:1-14,15-32; 11:10-26; 22:20-24; 36:1-43; 46:8-27; Exodus 6:14-25.
43. Also see Genesis 4:18; 10:1-12, 13-32; 11:27; 22:20-23.
44. For instance, compare Genesis 36:31-43 to 1 Chronicles 1:43-54.

From a diachronic standpoint, these findings can be understood in one of two ways.[45] First, on the basis of our recognition of the entire verbal system of both periods, we may conclude that the passages from Genesis containing *qatal* were added or revised at a later date. The second, more cautious approach is to suggest that there were already two different conventions in First Temple period Hebrew—a more widespread *wayyiqtol* model and a less popular *qatal* one—and that the *qatal* paradigm rose to the ascendancy at some point during the Second Temple period.[46]

With respect to the lists in our corpus, the use of *qatal* is the most commonplace method for signifying the relation [R,E]. The claim that the lists constitute a separate texteme vis-à-vis narrative texts is indeed an important argument, but other contexts indicate that there is indeed an occasional connection between the usage of the verb forms in both of these frameworks.[47]

3.2.3.3   Inserting Reference Time in Narrative Contexts

Signifying the relation [R,E] by means of a *qatal* form is less pervasive in narratives than in lists (44 occurrences). Compared to other usages in the Second Temple period texts, the percentage of this function is not much greater than the First Temple period aggregate—3.4% compared to 1% in the First Temple period.[48] However, as noted earlier, the quantitative aspects are not the primary consideration in this context, for these cases must be evaluated within the broader picture of the blurring of roles that neutralized the differences between the classical consecutive forms (*wayyiqtol* and *weqatal*) and *qatal* and *yiqtol* during this era.

We have located four passages in the Second Temple period corpus featuring *qatal* forms that create a sequence of verbs in the narrative past:

(105) וַתֹּאמֶר אֶסְתֵּר אִישׁ צַר וְאוֹיֵב הָמָן הָרָע הַזֶּה וְהָמָן **נִבְעַת** מִלִּפְנֵי הַמֶּלֶךְ
וְהַמַּלְכָּה׃ וְהַמֶּלֶךְ **קָם** בַּחֲמָתוֹ מִמִּשְׁתֵּה הַיַּיִן אֶל גִּנַּת הַבִּיתָן וְהָמָן **עָמַד** לְבַקֵּשׁ עַל
נַפְשׁוֹ מֵאֶסְתֵּר הַמַּלְכָּה כִּי רָאָה כִּי כָלְתָה אֵלָיו הָרָעָה מֵאֵת הַמֶּלֶךְ׃ וְהַמֶּלֶךְ **שָׁב** מִגִּנַּת

---

45. Andersen (1974:87-88) attempts to provide a syntactic explanation for the anomalous appearance of *qatal* forms in Genesis lists, which he has dubbed "pseudocircumstantial sequential clauses." That said, a diachronic comparison with the lineages from the Second Temple period indicates that *qatal* can indeed be used to mark a succession. As a result, Andersen's ad hoc description is superfluous.

46. The research literature on the compilation of these pedigrees leans in a couple of mutually exclusive directions. An inkling of this issue's complexity may be gleaned from the scholarly discourse on the origins of the Pentateuch. For example, Skinner avers that Genesis 9 was penned by two different authors (J and P) (1930:187-195).

47. See the section on consecutive forms (§2.1.3), especially the discussion on the usage of *weqatal* forms within the list that traces the courses of the Land of Israel's brooks.

48. The data on the First Temple period prose is taken from Hatav (1997:57)

הַבִּיתָן אֶל בֵּית מִשְׁתֵּה הַיַּיִן וְהָמָן נֹפֵל עַל הַמִּטָּה אֲשֶׁר אֶסְתֵּר עָלֶיהָ וַיֹּאמֶר הַמֶּלֶךְ הֲגַם לִכְבּוֹשׁ אֶת הַמַּלְכָּה עִמִּי בַּבָּיִת הַדָּבָר **יָצָא** מִפִּי הַמֶּלֶךְ וּפְנֵי הָמָן חָפוּ׃

The adversary and enemy, replied Esther, is this evil Haman! And Haman
cringed [R,E] in terror before the king and the queen. The king, in his fury,
left [R,E] the wine feast for the palace garden, while Haman **remained [R,E]**
to plead with Queen Esther for his life; for he saw that the king had resolved
to destroy him. When the king **returned [R,E]** from the palace garden to
the banquet room, Haman was lying prostrate on the couch on which Esther
reclined. Does he mean, cried the king, to ravish the queen in my own palace?
No sooner did these words **leave [R,E]** the king's lips than Haman's face was
covered. (Est 7:6-8)

(106) וַיִּכְתֹּב בְּשֵׁם הַמֶּלֶךְ אֲחַשְׁוֵרֹשׁ וַיַּחְתֹּם בְּטַבַּעַת הַמֶּלֶךְ וַיִּשְׁלַח סְפָרִים בְּיַד
הָרָצִים בַּסּוּסִים רֹכְבֵי הָרֶכֶשׁ הָאֲחַשְׁתְּרָנִים בְּנֵי הָרַמָּכִים׃ אֲשֶׁר נָתַן הַמֶּלֶךְ לַיְּהוּדִים
אֲשֶׁר בְּכָל עִיר וָעִיר . . . . הָרָצִים רֹכְבֵי הָרֶכֶשׁ הָאֲחַשְׁתְּרָנִים **יָצְאוּ** מְבֹהָלִים וּדְחוּפִים
בִּדְבַר הַמֶּלֶךְ וְהַדָּת **נִתְּנָה** בְּשׁוּשַׁן הַבִּירָה׃ וּמָרְדֳּכַי **יָצָא** מִלִּפְנֵי הַמֶּלֶךְ בִּלְבוּשׁ מַלְכוּת
תְּכֵלֶת וָחוּר וַעֲטֶרֶת זָהָב גְּדוֹלָה וְתַכְרִיךְ בּוּץ וְאַרְגָּמָן וְהָעִיר שׁוּשָׁן **צָהֲלָה וְשָׂמֵחָה**׃
לַיְּהוּדִים **הָיְתָה** אוֹרָה וְשִׂמְחָה וְשָׂשֹׂן וִיקָר׃[49]

He had them written in the name of King Ahasuerus and sealed with the king's
signet. Letters were dispatched by mounted couriers, riding steeds used in the
king's service, bred of the royal stud, to this effect: The king has permitted the
Jews of every city. . . . The couriers, mounted on royal steeds, **went out [R,E]**
in urgent haste at the king's command; and the decree was **proclaimed [R,E]**
in the fortress Shushan. Mordecai **left [R,E]** the king's presence in royal robes
of blue and white, with a magnificent crown of gold and a mantle of fine linen
and purple wool. And the city of Shushan **rang [R,E]** with joyous cries. The
Jews **enjoyed [R,E]** light and gladness, happiness and honor. (Est 8:10-16)

(107) בֶּן עֶשְׂרִים וְחָמֵשׁ שָׁנָה יוֹתָם בְּמָלְכוֹ וְשֵׁשׁ עֶשְׂרֵה שָׁנָה מָלַךְ בִּירוּשָׁלַםִ וְשֵׁם אִמּוֹ
יְרוּשָׁה בַּת צָדוֹק׃ וַיַּעַשׂ הַיָּשָׁר בְּעֵינֵי יְהוָה כְּכֹל אֲשֶׁר עָשָׂה עֻזִּיָּהוּ אָבִיו רַק לֹא בָא
אֶל הֵיכַל יְהוָה וְעוֹד הָעָם מַשְׁחִיתִים׃ הוּא **בָּנָה** אֶת שַׁעַר בֵּית יְהוָה הָעֶלְיוֹן וּבְחוֹמַת
הָעֹפֶל **בָּנָה** לָרֹב׃ וְעָרִים **בָּנָה** בְּהַר יְהוּדָה וּבֶחֳרָשִׁים **בָּנָה** בִּירָנִיּוֹת וּמִגְדָּלִים׃ וְהוּא
נִלְחַם עִם מֶלֶךְ בְּנֵי עַמּוֹן וַיֶּחֱזַק עֲלֵיהֶם וַיִּתְּנוּ לוֹ בְנֵי עַמּוֹן בַּשָּׁנָה הַהִיא מֵאָה כִּכַּר
כֶּסֶף וַעֲשֶׂרֶת אֲלָפִים כֹּרִים חִטִּים וּשְׂעוֹרִים עֲשֶׂרֶת אֲלָפִים

Jotham was twenty-five years old when he became king, and he reigned sixteen
years in Jerusalem; his mother's name was Jerushah daughter of Zadok. He did
what was pleasing to the LORD just as his father Uzziah had done, but he did
not enter the Temple of the LORD; however, the people still acted corruptly.
It was **he** who **built [R,E]** the Upper Gate of the House of the LORD; **he** also
built [R,E] extensively on the wall of Ophel. **He built [R,E]** towns in the hill
country of Judah, and in the woods **he built** fortresses and towers. Moreover,

---

49. Also see Esther 3:15.

he **fought [R,E]** with the king of the Ammonites and overcame them; the
Ammonites gave him that year 100 talents of silver and 10000 kor of wheat
and another 10000 of barley (2 Chr 27:1-5)

(108) וַיָּקוּמוּ רָאשֵׁי הָאָבוֹת לִיהוּדָה וּבִנְיָמִן וְהַכֹּהֲנִים וְהַלְוִיִּם לְכֹל הֵעִיר הָאֱלֹהִים
אֵת רוּחוֹ לַעֲלוֹת לִבְנוֹת אֶת בֵּית יְהוָה אֲשֶׁר בִּירוּשָׁלָם׃ וְכָל סְבִיבֹתֵיהֶם **חִזְּקוּ**
בִידֵיהֶם בִּכְלֵי כֶסֶף בַּזָּהָב בָּרְכוּשׁ וּבַבְּהֵמָה וּבַמִּגְדָּנוֹת לְבַד עַל כָּל הִתְנַדֵּב׃ וְהַמֶּלֶךְ
כּוֹרֶשׁ **הוֹצִיא** אֶת כְּלֵי בֵית יְהוָה אֲשֶׁר הוֹצִיא נְבוּכַדְנֶצַּר מִירוּשָׁלַם וַיִּתְּנֵם בְּבֵית
אֱלֹהָיו׃ . . . כָּל כֵּלִים לַזָּהָב וְלַכֶּסֶף חֲמֵשֶׁת אֲלָפִים וְאַרְבַּע מֵאוֹת הַכֹּל **הֶעֱלָה** שֵׁשְׁבַּצַּר
עִם הֵעָלוֹת הַגּוֹלָה מִבָּבֶל לִירוּשָׁלָם׃[50]

So the chiefs of the clans of Judah and Benjamin, and the priests and Levites,
all whose spirit had been roused by God, got ready to go up to build the House
of the LORD that is in Jerusalem. All their neighbors **supported [R,E]** them
with silver vessels, with gold, with goods, with livestock, and with precious
objects, besides what had been given as a freewill offering. King Cyrus of
Persia **released [R,E]** the vessels of the LORD's house which Nebuchadnezzar
had taken away from Jerusalem and had put in the house of his god. . . . [I]n all,
5400 gold and silver vessels. Sheshbazzar **brought [R,E]** all these back when
the exiles came back from Babylon to Jerusalem. (Ezr 1:5-11)

The forms that are highlighted in these sentences bear their own reference time.
Therefore, despite the fact that they are neither inflected with *waws*[51] nor arrayed
in the sentence's lead position, they maintain an [R,E] relationship. All the verbs
in examples 105 to 108 signify a causal relationship with the prior action. For instance, the king and Haman react to Esther's words (example 105). Similarly the
actions of the couriers, Mordecai, and the Jews in the second passage are the result
of orders that were issued in the name of Ahasuerus. In all likelihood, the line
of development from the classical usage to the consecutive form passes through
cases that put an emphasis on signifying the result.[52]

The following examples, all of which showcase a *waw* + *qatal* construction in
the lead position, underscore the fact that the *qatal* form can be used as a consecutive form:

(109) הַבָּאִים מֵהַשְּׁבִי בְנֵי הַגּוֹלָה **הִקְרִיבוּ** עֹלוֹת לֵאלֹהֵי יִשְׂרָאֵל פָּרִים שְׁנֵים עָשָׂר עַל
כָּל יִשְׂרָאֵל אֵילִים תִּשְׁעִים וְשִׁשָּׁה כְּבָשִׂים שִׁבְעִים וְשִׁבְעָה צְפִירֵי חַטָּאת שְׁנֵים עָשָׂר
הַכֹּל עוֹלָה לַיהוָה׃ וַיִּתְּנוּ אֶת דָּתֵי הַמֶּלֶךְ לַאֲחַשְׁדַּרְפְּנֵי הַמֶּלֶךְ וּפַחֲווֹת עֵבֶר הַנָּהָר
וְנִשְׂאוּ אֶת הָעָם וְאֶת בֵּית הָאֱלֹהִים׃

---

50. Also see Esther 4:8; 9:6?, 10?, 14; Nehemiah 5:15; Daniel 12:8; 1 Chronicles 12:19,
22; 27:24; 29:2-3; 2 Chronicles 20:35 (in these passages, *qatal* forms are used to signify the relationship [R,E], but they do not appear within strings).
51. Save for "ושמחה" in Esther 8:15.
52. I am indebted to Dr. Dana Taube for bringing this matter to my attention.

The returning exiles who arrived from captivity **made [R,E]** burnt offerings to the God of Israel: twelve bulls for all Israel, ninety-six rams, seventy-seven lambs and twelve he-goats as a purification offering, all this a burnt offering to the LORD. They handed the royal orders to the king's satraps and the governors of the province of Beyond the River who **gave [R,E]** support to the people and the House of God. (Ezr 8:35-36)

(110) נָאמְרָה אֲלֵהֶם אַתֶּם קֹדֶשׁ לַיהוה וְהַכֵּלִים קֹדֶשׁ וְהַכֶּסֶף וְהַזָּהָב נְדָבָה לַיהוה אֱלֹהֵי אֲבֹתֵיכֶם: שִׁקְדוּ וְשִׁמְרוּ עַד תִּשְׁקְלוּ לִפְנֵי שָׂרֵי הַכֹּהֲנִים וְהַלְוִיִּם וְשָׂרֵי הָאָבוֹת לְיִשְׂרָאֵל בִּירוּשָׁלָ͏ִם הַלִּשְׁכוֹת בֵּית יְהוָה: **וְקִבְּלוּ** הַכֹּהֲנִים וְהַלְוִיִּם מִשְׁקַל הַכֶּסֶף וְהַזָּהָב וְהַכֵּלִים לְהָבִיא לִירוּשָׁלַ͏ִם לְבֵית אֱלֹהֵינוּ:

I said to them, you are consecrated to the LORD, and the vessels are consecrated, and the silver and gold are a freewill offering to the LORD God of your fathers. Guard them diligently until such time as you weigh them out in the presence of the officers of the priests and the Levites and the officers of the clans of Israel in Jerusalem in the chambers of the House of the LORD. So the priests and the Levites **received [R,E]** the cargo of silver and gold and vessels by weight, to bring them to Jerusalem to the House of our God. (Ezr 8:28-30)

(111) וּמִבְּנֵי יוֹיָדָע בֶּן אֶלְיָשִׁיב הַכֹּהֵן הַגָּדוֹל חָתָן לְסַנְבַלַּט הַחֹרֹנִי *וָאַבְרִיחֵהוּ* מֵעָלָי. . . . **וְטִהַרְתִּים** מִכָּל נֵכָר *וָאַעֲמִידָה* מִשְׁמָרוֹת לַכֹּהֲנִים וְלַלְוִיִּם אִישׁ בִּמְלַאכְתּוֹ:

One of the sons of Joiada son of the high priest Eliashib was a son-in-law of Sanballat the Horonite; I drove him away from me. . . . **I purged [R,E]** them of every foreign element, and arranged for the priests and the Levites to work each at his task by shifts (Neh 13:28-30)

(112) *וַתִּגְדַּל* עַד צְבָא הַשָּׁמָיִם *וַתַּפֵּל* אַרְצָה מִן הַצָּבָא וּמִן הַכּוֹכָבִים *וַתִּרְמְסֵם*: וְעַד שַׂר הַצָּבָא **הִגְדִּיל** וּמִמֶּנּוּ הֵרִים **(הוּרַם)** הַתָּמִיד **וְהֻשְׁלַךְ** מְכוֹן מִקְדָּשׁוֹ:

It grew as high as the host of heaven and it hurled some stars of the heavenly host to the ground and trampled them. **It vaunted [R,E]** itself against the very chief of the host; on its account the regular offering **was suspended [R,E]**, and his holy place **was abandoned [R,E]**. (Dn 8:10-11)

(113) וְאַתָּה דָנִיֵּאל סְתֹם הַדְּבָרִים וַחֲתֹם הַסֵּפֶר עַד עֵת קֵץ יְשֹׁטְטוּ רַבִּים וְתִרְבֶּה הַדָּעַת: **וְרָאִיתִי** אֲנִי דָנִיֵּאל וְהִנֵּה שְׁנַיִם אֲחֵרִים עֹמְדִים אֶחָד הֵנָּה לִשְׂפַת הַיְאֹר וְאֶחָד הֵנָּה לִשְׂפַת הַיְאֹר:

But you, Daniel, keep the words secret, and seal the book until the time of the end. Many will range far and wide and knowledge will increase. Then **I, Daniel, looked [R,E]** and saw two others standing, one on one bank of the river, the other on the other bank of the river. (Dn 12:4-5)

Examples 109, 110, and 111 are essential because they show that it is possible for *qatal* forms to "co-habitate" in a continuum with *wayyiqtol* forms, thereby rein-

forcing the contention that the differences between the two forms were categori-
cally obfuscated. To this may be added the verses in Chronicles that correspond
to verses in Samuel and Kings, wherein constructions made up of *waw* + *qatal*
replace the classical *wayyiqtol* forms:[53]

(114) וַיַּעַל סֹפֵר הַמֶּלֶךְ

[T]he royal scribe . . . **ascended [R,E].** (2 Kgs 12:11)

(115) וּבָא סוֹפֵר הַמֶּלֶךְ

[T]he royal scribe . . . **came [R,E]** (2 Chr 24:11)

3.2.3.4   Inserting Reference Time in Direct Speech and Prayer

There is but one example of *qatal* forms serving as consecutive forms in direct
speech:

(116) וַיֹּאמֶר דָּוִיד הַמֶּלֶךְ לְכָל הַקָּהָל שְׁלֹמֹה בְנִי אֶחָד בָּחַר בּוֹ אֱלֹהִים נַעַר וָרָךְ
וְהַמְּלָאכָה גְדוֹלָה כִּי לֹא לְאָדָם הַבִּירָה כִּי לַיהוָה אֱלֹהִים: וּכְכָל כֹּחִי הֲכִינוֹתִי
לְבֵית אֱלֹהַי הַזָּהָב לַזָּהָב וְהַכֶּסֶף לַכֶּסֶף וְהַנְּחֹשֶׁת לַנְּחֹשֶׁת הַבַּרְזֶל לַבַּרְזֶל וְהָעֵצִים
לָעֵצִים אַבְנֵי שֹׁהַם וּמִלּוּאִים אַבְנֵי פוּךְ וְרִקְמָה וְכֹל אֶבֶן יְקָרָה וְאַבְנֵי שַׁיִשׁ לָרֹב:
וְעוֹד בִּרְצוֹתִי בְּבֵית אֱלֹהַי יֶשׁ לִי סְגֻלָּה זָהָב וָכָסֶף נָתַתִּי לְבֵית אֱלֹהַי לְמַעְלָה מִכָּל
הֲכִינוֹתִי לְבֵית הַקֹּדֶשׁ:

King David said to the entire assemblage, God has chosen my son Solomon
alone, an untried lad, although the work to be done is vast—for the temple
is not for a man but for the LORD God. **I have spared [R,E]** no effort to lay
up for the house of my God gold for golden objects, silver for silver, copper
for copper, iron for iron, wood for wooden, onyx-stone and inlay-stone, stone
of antimony and variegated colors—every kind of precious stone and much
marble. Besides, out of my solicitude for the house of my God, **I gave [R,E]**
over my private hoard of gold and silver to the house of my God—in addition
to all that I laid aside for the holy House. (1 Chr 29:1-3)

As in the narrative examples cited above, the verbs "הכינותי" and "נתתי" signify the
relation [R,E]. However, the verb "בחר" has not been highlighted because it is cus-
tomary to align *qatal* forms in the opening of direct speech.[54]

In the research literature, the following passage from Nehemiah 9:5b-37 is
considered a unique genre of confessional prayer because, on the one hand, it is

---

53. For more examples of this phenomenon, see Rooker (1990:100-101).
54. See Hatav's discussion on the difference between a *qatal* form at the beginning of
    a passage of direct speech and the rest of the passage, which in classical Hebrew is
    marked by *wayyiqtol* (1997:181-184).

endowed with certain poetic qualities, while on the other it is similar to prose, especially with regard to direct speech:[55]

(117) אַתָּה הוּא יְהוָה הָאֱלֹהִים אֲשֶׁר בָּחַרְתָּ בְּאַבְרָם **וְהוֹצֵאתוֹ** מֵאוּר כַּשְׂדִּים **וְשַׂמְתָּ** שְׁמוֹ אַבְרָהָם: **וּמָצָאתָ** אֶת לְבָבוֹ נֶאֱמָן לְפָנֶיךָ **וְכָרוֹת** עִמּוֹ הַבְּרִית לָתֵת אֶת אֶרֶץ הַכְּנַעֲנִי הַחִתִּי הָאֱמֹרִי וְהַפְּרִזִּי וְהַיְבוּסִי וְהַגִּרְגָּשִׁי לָתֵת לְזַרְעוֹ **וַתָּקֶם** אֶת דְּבָרֶיךָ כִּי צַדִּיק אָתָּה: **וַתֵּרֶא** אֶת עֳנִי אֲבֹתֵינוּ בְּמִצְרָיִם וְאֶת זַעֲקָתָם שָׁמַעְתָּ[56] עַל יַם סוּף: **וַתִּתֵּן** אֹתֹת וּמֹפְתִים בְּפַרְעֹה וּבְכָל עֲבָדָיו וּבְכָל עַם אַרְצוֹ כִּי יָדַעְתָּ כִּי הֵזִידוּ עֲלֵיהֶם **וַתַּעַשׂ** לְךָ שֵׁם כְּהַיּוֹם הַזֶּה: וְהַיָּם **בָּקַעְתָּ** לִפְנֵיהֶם, **וַיַּעַבְרוּ** בְתוֹךְ הַיָּם בַּיַּבָּשָׁה וְאֶת רֹדְפֵיהֶם הִשְׁלַכְתָּ בִמְצוֹלֹת כְּמוֹ אֶבֶן בְּמַיִם עַזִּים: וּבְעַמּוּד עָנָן **הִנְחִיתָם** יוֹמָם וּבְעַמּוּד אֵשׁ לַיְלָה לְהָאִיר לָהֶם אֶת הַדֶּרֶךְ אֲשֶׁר יֵלְכוּ בָהּ: וְעַל הַר סִינַי **יָרַדְתָּ** **וְדַבֵּר** עִמָּהֶם מִשָּׁמָיִם **וַתִּתֵּן** לָהֶם מִשְׁפָּטִים יְשָׁרִים וְתוֹרוֹת אֱמֶת חֻקִּים וּמִצְוֹת טוֹבִים: וְאֶת שַׁבַּת קָדְשְׁךָ **הוֹדַעְתָּ** לָהֶם וּמִצְוֹת וְחֻקִּים וְתוֹרָה **צִוִּיתָ** לָהֶם בְּיַד מֹשֶׁה עַבְדֶּךָ: וְלֶחֶם מִשָּׁמַיִם **נָתַתָּה** לָהֶם לִרְעָבָם וּמַיִם מִסֶּלַע **הוֹצֵאתָ** לָהֶם לִצְמָאָם **וַתֹּאמֶר** לָהֶם לָבוֹא לָרֶשֶׁת אֶת הָאָרֶץ אֲשֶׁר נָשָׂאתָ אֶת יָדְךָ לָתֵת לָהֶם: וְהֵם וַאֲבֹתֵינוּ **הֵזִידוּ** **וַיַּקְשׁוּ** אֶת עָרְפָּם וְלֹא שָׁמְעוּ אֶל מִצְוֹתֶיךָ:

You are the LORD God, who chose Abram, who **brought [R,E]** him out of Ur of the Chaldeans and **changed [R,E]** his name to Abraham. **Finding [R,E]** his heart true to you, you made a covenant with him to give the land of the Canaanite, the Hittite, the Amorite, the Perizzite, the Jebusite, and the Girgashite—to give it to his descendants. And you kept your word, for you are righteous. You took note of our fathers' affliction in Egypt, and heard their cry at the Sea of Reeds. You performed signs and wonders against Pharaoh, all his servants, and all the people of his land, for you knew that they acted presumptuously toward them. You made a name for yourself that endures to this day. **You split [R,E]** the sea before them; they passed through the sea on dry land, but you threw their pursuers into the depths, like a stone into the raging waters. **You led [R,E]** them by day with a pillar of cloud, and by night with a pillar of fire, to give them light in the way they were to go. **You came down [R,E]** on Mount Sinai and spoke to them from heaven; you gave them right rules and true teachings, good laws and commandments. **You made known [R,E]** to them your holy sabbath, and **you ordained [R,E]** for them laws, commandments and Teaching, through Moses your servant. **You gave [R,E]** them bread from heaven when they were hungry, and **produced [R,E]** water from a rock when they were thirsty. You told them to go and possess the land that you swore to give them. But they— our fathers—**acted [R,E]** presumptuously; they stiffened their necks and did not obey your commandments. (Neh 9:7-16)

---

55. For a discussion of this genre, see Williamson (1985:305-310).

56. This verb ("שמעת") and "השלכת" in verse 11 are not highlighted because they can be interpreted as expressing a contrast to the action that is presented by *wayyiqtol* (see §3.2.2.3.1 above).

The role assumed by this passage's *qatal* forms, both in the opening slot of sentences and in the middle of clauses, is similar to its use in the previous examples.

3.3 The *Qatal* Form's Position on the Modal Axis

3.3.1 [+Indicative, +Actual, -Modal, -Habitual, and -Iterative]

From the standpoint of modality, *qatal* serves as an indicative form, which by definition portrays an action as a given fact. In this context, one can characterize the *qatal* form as a sort of mirror image of the *yiqtol* form: Whereas *yiqtol* denotes an action that is not actual [-actual] within the framework of both future (i.e., an action that has yet to transpire) and habitual actions [+habitual, and +iterative] (an iterative action in the past, the habitual present, or the language of the law), *qatal* signifies an actual action [+actual]; in other words, the act has indeed transpired at a given time and place, so that it is neither habitual nor iterative [-habitual, -iterative].[57] This trait is especially prominent in instances where *qatal*'s indicative attributes can be contrasted with modal (habitual) characteristics of the *yiqtol* form:

(118) וּבְהַגִּיעַ תֹּר נַעֲרָה וְנַעֲרָה לָבוֹא אֶל הַמֶּלֶךְ אֲחַשְׁוֵרוֹשׁ מִקֵּץ הֱיוֹת לָהּ כְּדָת הַנָּשִׁים שְׁנֵים עָשָׂר חֹדֶשׁ כִּי כֵּן יִמְלְאוּ יְמֵי מְרוּקֵיהֶן שִׁשָּׁה חֳדָשִׁים בְּשֶׁמֶן הַמֹּר וְשִׁשָּׁה חֳדָשִׁים בַּבְּשָׂמִים וּבְתַמְרוּקֵי הַנָּשִׁים: וּבָזֶה הַנַּעֲרָה בָּאָה אֶל הַמֶּלֶךְ אֵת כָּל אֲשֶׁר תֹּאמַר יִנָּתֵן לָהּ לָבוֹא עִמָּהּ מִבֵּית הַנָּשִׁים עַד בֵּית הַמֶּלֶךְ: בָּעֶרֶב הִיא בָאָה וּבַבֹּקֶר הִיא שָׁבָה אֶל בֵּית הַנָּשִׁים שֵׁנִי אֶל יַד שַׁעַשְׁגַז סְרִיס הַמֶּלֶךְ שֹׁמֵר הַפִּילַגְשִׁים... וּבְהַגִּיעַ תֹּר אֶסְתֵּר בַּת אֲבִיחַיִל דֹּד מָרְדֳּכַי אֲשֶׁר **לָקַח** לוֹ לְבַת לָבוֹא אֶל הַמֶּלֶךְ **לֹא בִקְשָׁה**[58] דָּבָר כִּי אִם אֶת אֲשֶׁר יֹאמַר הֵגַי סְרִיס הַמֶּלֶךְ שֹׁמֵר הַנָּשִׁים

When each girl's turn came to go to King Ahasuerus at the end of the twelve months' treatment prescribed for women (for that was the period spent on beautifying them: six months with oil of myrrh and six months with perfumes and women's cosmetics, and it was after that that the girl would go to the king), whatever she asked for would be given her to take with her from the harem to the king's palace. She would go in the evening and leave in the morning for a second harem in charge of Shaashgaz, the king's eunuch, guardian of the concubines . . . When the turn came for Esther daughter of Abihail—the uncle of Mordecai, who **had adopted [+indicative]** her as his own daughter—to go to the king, **she did not ask [+indicative]** for anything but what Hegai, the king's eunuch, guardian of the women, advised (Est 2:12-15)

---

57. The next section consists of an in-depth examination of the use of *qatal* for expressing a relation of antecedence within modal contexts.

58. See the ensuing discussion for more on negation.

119) נָאֹמְרָה הַאִישׁ כָּמוֹנִי יִבְרָח. . . . וָאַכִּירָה וְהִנֵּה לֹא אֱלֹהִים **שְׁלָחוֹ**

I replied, Will a man like me take flight? . . . Then I realized that it was not God who **sent [+indicative]** him (Neh 6:11-12)

120) אֵין טוֹב בָּאָדָם *שֶׁיֹּאכַל וְשָׁתָה וְהֶרְאָה* אֶת נַפְשׁוֹ טוֹב בַּעֲמָלוֹ גַּם זֹה **רָאִיתִי** אָנִי
כִּי מִיַּד הָאֱלֹהִים הִיא:[59]

There is nothing worthwhile for a man but to eat and drink and afford himself enjoyment with his means. And even that, **I noted [+indicative]**, comes from God. (Eccl 2:24)

In these passages, *yiqtol*, *weqatal*, and participle forms are used to express one of the following moods: an iterative action in the past, the habitual present, or a general truth. The transition from these forms to *qatal* signifies a shift from the habitual mood—wherein the action is not "actual"—to the actual indicative mood. For instance, Esther 2 features a transition from the verbs "תאמר", "באה", "ימלאו", "ינתן", "באה", and "שבה", which depict actions that occur *every time* one of the candidates' preparatory phase comes to an end, to the verb "לקח", which informs us of the fact that Mordecai took responsibility for Esther.

The phenomenon of negation poses a theoretical challenge to the claim that the *qatal* form expresses an actual action. Within the syntactical environment of a negative sentence, the argument can be made that an action affiliated with *qatal* is not actual, for the very purpose of a negation is to signify that an event has *not* transpired. Nevertheless, this point is not as cut and dried as it appears, for there are languages that developed a separate framework of negative verb forms which do not correspond to their system for positive forms. For example, Amharic has a distinct syntactical system for negative verb forms.[60] This system is tied to modal and subordinated forms and stands in contradistinction to the set of forms that Amharic utilizes in positive sentences. In Goldenberg's estimation (1966:88):

> The choice between perfect and imperfect in relative and conjunctional clauses and in negation have been described above as being connected to a distinction between various temporal categories of tense (in reference to some "point-zero"). . . . In a positive independent clause, those same two verb forms denote different modal categories.

On the basis of a comparison with Goldenberg's description of the Amharic, we can assume that Biblical Hebrew did not entail this sort of system. That said, it could very well be that the context of negation should be considered a distinct syntactical environment wherein *qatal* forms are used to mark the chronological

---

59. Although this example is not from our corpus, it was chosen on account of the clear contrast between the habitual forms and the indicative one.
60. See Goldenberg (1966:83-88).

relation R>E.[61] This same point may also pertain to the upcoming section on the function of *qatal* in modal contexts.

3.3.2 *Qatal* as a Signifier of Antecedence (R>E) in Modal Contexts

The relatively limited range of verb forms in Biblical Hebrew generates a certain amount of dissonance between the modal and reference-time axes in all that concerns the *qatal* form. On the one hand, *qatal* is the only form that expresses relations of antecedence (R>E), while on the other it is part of the indicative system. In consequence, how does Biblical Hebrew signify a relation of antecedence within a modal context? The fact that Biblical Hebrew turns to *qatal* in these cases should hardly come as a surprise, for we have already seen that this form is used to expressing relations of antecedence in the following circumstances: the future, the habitual present, iterative actions in the past (all of which are modal usages), and the language of the law. To follow are three different modal contexts in which *qatal* forms denote antecedence:

(121) עַתָּה בְנִי יְהִי יְהוָה עִמָּךְ וְהִצְלַחְתָּ **וּבָנִיתָ** בֵּית יְהוָה אֱלֹהֶיךָ כַּאֲשֶׁר **דִּבֶּר** עָלֶיךָ׃

Now, my son, may the LORD be with you, and may you succeed in **building** the House of the LORD your God as **he promised (E<R)** you would. (1 Chr 22:11)

(122) בָּעֶרֶב הִיא בָאָה וּבַבֹּקֶר הִיא שָׁבָה אֶל בֵּית הַנָּשִׁים שֵׁנִי אֶל יַד שַׁעֲשְׁגַז סְרִיס הַמֶּלֶךְ שֹׁמֵר הַפִּילַגְשִׁים **לֹא תָבוֹא** עוֹד אֶל הַמֶּלֶךְ כִּי אִם **חָפֵץ** בָּהּ הַמֶּלֶךְ **וְנִקְרְאָה** בְשֵׁם׃

She would go in the evening and leave in the morning for a second harem in charge of Shaashgaz, the king's eunuch, guardian of the concubines. **She would not go** again to the king unless the king **wanted (E<R)** her, when she **would be summoned (E<R)** by name. (Est 2:14)

(123) אֵלֶּה פְקֻדָּתָם לַעֲבֹדָתָם **לָבוֹא** לְבֵית יְהוָה כְּמִשְׁפָּטָם בְּיַד אַהֲרֹן אֲבִיהֶם כַּאֲשֶׁר **צִוָּהוּ** יְהוָה אֱלֹהֵי יִשְׂרָאֵל׃

According to this allocation of offices by tasks, they were **to enter** the House of the LORD as was laid down for them by Aaron their father, as the LORD God of Israel **had commanded him (E<R)**. (1 Chr 24:19)

In the first example, the *qatal* form expresses antecedence in the future realm:

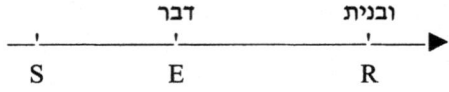

```
                דבר              ובנית
——'————————————'——————————————'———▶
   S             E                R
```

---

61. For an in-depth survey on negation, see §3.2.2.3.2 above.

In the second example, antecedence is established within the framework of the habitual present:[62]

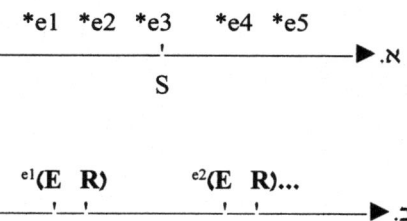

The third example signifies relations of antecedence within the language of the law. In contrast to the second example, the action conveyed by *qatal* therein serves as the background for a chain of optional future actions that are latent in the language of the law:

The most problematic ...

Of the three verses, the most problematic is Esther 2:14 because the action signified by *qatal* recurs time and again, along with the affiliated habitual action. This phenomenon can also be found within the language of the law, as in the following example from the First Temple period:[63]

(124) בִּשְׁנַת הַיּוֹבֵל **יָשׁוּב** הַשָּׂדֶה לַאֲשֶׁר **קָנָהוּ** מֵאִתּוֹ לַאֲשֶׁר לוֹ אֲחֻזַּת הָאָרֶץ:

In the jubilee year the land **shall revert** to him from whom **it was bought** (E<R), whose holding the land is. (Lv 27:24)

These cases give rise to the following question: Do these passages violate the rule according to which *qatal* forms only express actual actions that are neither habitual nor iterative? Given both the relative dearth of these cases and the overall picture that emerges from the aggregate total of the form's occurrences, I am inclined to believe that there is no contradiction here. In the second chapter of this work,[64] the argument was made that these cases epitomize the steady decline in the *qatal* form's relationship to the modal axis. In other words, to some extent,

---

62. In the forthcoming diagrams, the letter "e" denotes a recurrent action that transpires within the framework of the habitual present or an iterative action in the past.

63. See Hatav's disquisition on this particular issue (1997:189–192).

64. See the discussion on the simultaneous links to the modal and time-reference axes in §2.2.4 above.

these forms turned to describing non-actual scenarios, on account of a contextual constraint that is reminiscent of the actualization that the *yiqtol* forms underwent for the purpose of denoting a relation of subsequence in the past.

This argument is buttressed, inter alia, by the fact that researchers have not found any other occurrences of the *qatal* form expressing a habitual mood. Moreover, Hatav claims that relations of simultaneity within modal contexts are articulated by *yiqtol*—not *qatal*—and cites the following verses to bolster her case:

(125) וְהָיָה כִּי יִרְאוּ אֹתָךְ הַמִּצְרִים וְאָמְרוּ אִשְׁתּוֹ זֹאת וְהָרְגוּ אֹתִי וְאֹתָךְ **יְחַיּוּ**:

If the Egyptians see you, and think, She is his wife, they will kill me and **let you live (R=E)**. (Gn 12:12)

(126) וְצִפִּיתָ אֹתוֹ זָהָב טָהוֹר מִבַּיִת וּמִחוּץ **תְּצַפֶּנּוּ**

Overlay it with pure gold—overlay it inside and out—and **make (R=E)** upon it a gold molding round about. (Ex 25:11)

And in our corpus:

(127) וּבְהַגִּיעַ תֹּר נַעֲרָה וְנַעֲרָה לָבוֹא אֶל הַמֶּלֶךְ אֲחַשְׁוֵרוֹשׁ מִקֵּץ הֱיוֹת לָהּ כְּדָת הַנָּשִׁים שְׁנֵים עָשָׂר חֹדֶשׁ כִּי כֵּן **יִמְלְאוּ** יְמֵי מְרוּקֵיהֶן שִׁשָּׁה חֳדָשִׁים בְּשֶׁמֶן הַמֹּר וְשִׁשָּׁה חֳדָשִׁים בַּבְּשָׂמִים וּבְתַמְרוּקֵי הַנָּשִׁים: וּבָזֶה הַנַּעֲרָה בָּאָה אֶל הַמֶּלֶךְ אֵת כָּל אֲשֶׁר **תֹּאמַר** יִנָּתֵן לָהּ לָבוֹא עִמָּהּ מִבֵּית הַנָּשִׁים עַד בֵּית הַמֶּלֶךְ:

When each girl's turn came to go to King Ahasuerus at the end of the twelve months' treatment prescribed for women (for that was the period **spent** on beautifying them: six months with oil of myrrh and six months with perfumes and women's cosmetics, and it was after that that the girl would go to the king), whatever she **asked (R=E)** for would be given her to take with her from the harem to the king's palace. (Est 2:12-13)

The examples below further strengthen the argument that *qatal* receives its habitual meaning from the context and does not mark this mood on its own:

(128) ויאמר (וָאֹמַר) לָהֶם **לֹא יִפָּתְחוּ** שַׁעֲרֵי יְרוּשָׁלַם עַד חֹם הַשֶּׁמֶשׁ

I said to them, The gates of Jerusalem **are not to be opened** until the heat of the day. (Neh 7:3)

(129) וַיֹּאמֶר הַתִּרְשָׁתָא לָהֶם אֲשֶׁר **לֹא יֹאכְלוּ** מִקֹּדֶשׁ הַקֳּדָשִׁים עַד עֲמֹד הַכֹּהֵן לְאוּרִים וְתֻמִּים:

The Tirshatha ordered them **not to eat** of the most holy things until a priest with Urim and Thummim should appear. (Neh 7:65)

The habitual context of these verses is a general commandment or the language of the law. The prohibitions against opening the gates of Jerusalem and eating the consecrated food are not one-time decrees, but general directives, so that the actions are iterative. Accordingly, the prohibition against opening the gates is in force until the "heat of day" and the prohibition against eating expires once the priest assumes his position. As a result, the relationship to the reference time in both cases is R>E. One would have expected the *qatal* form to be used in these situations, for as we have seen it also signifies this relationship in habitual contexts. However, since the forms herein are charged with opening a succession of commands and stand in an independent fashion, there is nothing to mark them as habitual. In light of the above, it can be assumed that the *yiqtol* form was employed in these contexts because *qatal* is unable to articulate the fact that these are commands, much less general directives. The contradiction between the *yiqtol* form's paradigmatic meaning (a relation of subsequence) and its present usage as a signifier of antecedence is somewhat discordant, but the authors favored *yiqtol* over *qatal* because the latter, as above mentioned, is utterly incapable of expressing a modal meaning on its own. So although this phenomenon is indeed an anomaly, it is an exception that attests to the rule.

Another modal context that is amenable to *qatal* forms is real and unreal conditional sentences:

(130) אִם **מָצָאתִי** חֵן בְּעֵינֵי הַמֶּלֶךְ וְאִם עַל הַמֶּלֶךְ טוֹב לָתֵת אֶת שְׁאֵלָתִי וְלַעֲשׂוֹת אֶת בַּקָּשָׁתִי *יָבוֹא* הַמֶּלֶךְ וְהָמָן אֶל הַמִּשְׁתֶּה אֲשֶׁר אֶעֱשֶׂה לָהֶם[65]

[I]f your Majesty **will do me the favor (E<R)**, if it please your Majesty to grant my wish and accede to my request—let your Majesty and Haman come to the feast which I will prepare for them. (Est 5:8)

(131) וַתַּעַן אֶסְתֵּר הַמַּלְכָּה וַתֹּאמַר אִם **מָצָאתִי** חֵן בְּעֵינֶיךָ הַמֶּלֶךְ וְאִם עַל הַמֶּלֶךְ טוֹב תִּנָּתֶן לִי נַפְשִׁי בִּשְׁאֵלָתִי וְעַמִּי בְּבַקָּשָׁתִי: כִּי נִמְכַּרְנוּ אֲנִי וְעַמִּי לְהַשְׁמִיד לַהֲרוֹג וּלְאַבֵּד וְאִלּוּ לַעֲבָדִים וְלִשְׁפָחוֹת **נִמְכַּרְנוּ** הֶחֱרַשְׁתִּי כִּי אֵין הַצָּר שֹׁוֶה בְּנֵזֶק הַמֶּלֶךְ:

Queen Esther replied: If your Majesty **will do me the favor (E<R)**, and if it pleases your Majesty, let my life be granted me as my wish, and my people as my request. For we have been sold, my people and I, to be destroyed, massacred, and exterminated. Had we only **been sold (E<R)** as bondmen and bondwomen, I would have kept silent; for the adversary is not worthy of the king's trouble. (Est 7:3-4)

(132) וַיֵּצֵא דָוִיד לִפְנֵיהֶם וַיַּעַן וַיֹּאמֶר לָהֶם אִם לְשָׁלוֹם **בָּאתֶם** אֵלַי לְעָזְרֵנִי *יִהְיֶה* לִי עֲלֵיכֶם לֵבָב לְיָחַד

---

65. Also see Esther 8:5.

[A]nd David went out to meet them, saying to them, If **you come (E<R)** on
a peaceful errand, to support me, then I will make common cause with you.
(1 Chr 12:18)

In these examples, *qatal* forms appear in the protasis. Here too, they are employed
by virtue of their ability to express antecedence. The second passage from Esther
contains both a real hypothetical clause, wherein the relation of antecedence refers
to a future action, and an unreal one, wherein the relation of antecedence pertains
to an action that is situated in the past.

These instances also cast doubt on the relationship between these forms and
the modal field. As in the previous examples, the irrealis meaning stems from the
context, and *qatal* is used on account of a given morphological reality that lacks a
designated form for expressing relations of antecedence in the modal field.

In sum, the use of *qatal* forms within various modal contexts stems directly
from the relative paucity of verb forms in Biblical Hebrew. Since *qatal* is the only
form that marks relations of antecedence, authors were forced to resort to it even
when characterizing such a relationship in modal contexts. In these cases, *qatal*'s
link to the modal axis [+actual] is attenuated and the form undergoes a certain
degree of de-actualization.

4. The Uses of *Wayyiqtol* in the Hebrew of the Second Temple Period

4.1 Introduction

From a diachronic standpoint, *wayyiqtol* is the most "conservative" form of the Second Temple period verbal system. In evaluating its uses, one would be hard pressed to point to new developments vis-à-vis First Temple period biblical prose, as nearly all its documented classical meanings and functions have been preserved.

That said, this observation warrants some qualification, for the verbal system underwent major changes during the Second Temple period in all that concerns consecutive forms. Besides the classical sequential forms (*wayyiqtol* and *weqatal*), which hitherto enjoyed a monopoly over this role, there was also a marked increase in the use of the other tense forms (*yiqtol*, *qatal*, the participle, and לקטול) for denoting succession. The infinitive absolute was also recast as an unmarked consecutive form with respect to the modal axis. Furthermore, there is one significant morphological distinction between the classical and late eras: the proliferation of the elongated *wa'eqtelah* form in the first person (over 50%) at the expense of the truncated ואקטל form—a phenomenon that, as we will see, is informed by a clear diachronic line of development.[1]

On the synchronic level, the guiding principle of this work is that an understanding of verb forms warrants a comprehensive examination of their usage from the vantage point of both the reference-time and modal axes. With this in mind, we will attempt to explain the difference between *wayyiqtol*'s principal function, namely a narrative form in the past, and its chronological meaning: [R,E]. Moreover, we will explore the combined effects of this chronological relationship and *wayyiqtol*'s indicative role.

4.2 The *Wayyiqtol* Form's Link to Reference Time

4.2.1 A Consecutive Form—Placing the Reference Time [R,E]

As established in the first part of this work,[2] the signature mark of consecutive forms in Biblical Hebrew is that they bear their own reference time [R,E].[3] Because the event (E) and reference time (R) of sequential forms merge in an indistinguishable manner, the addition of every new form engenders a new R-time. To illustrate this phenomenon, we will draw upon the image of a slide presentation in which the consecutive forms constitute the slides and the relative forms are elaborate the situation of each and every "slide." The chronological

---

1. See the discussion on this topic in the morphological addendum to this chapter (§4.4).
2. See the discussion on the meaning of consecutive forms (§2.1.3) and their function vis-à-vis relative forms (§2.2.4).
3. The description herein is a synthesis of the works of Reichenbach (1947), Kamp and Rohrer (1983), Kamp and Reyle (1993), Hatav (1997, 2000, 2004), and Washburn (1994).

relations between the consecutive forms and the other forms in the indicative field can be outlined thus:[4]

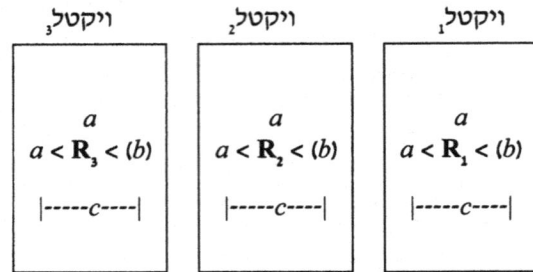

The diagram indicates that the sequential forms themselves bear no mark of their chronological relations with the other forms in the succession. This attribute is a direct result of the nature of *wayyiqtol* forms that contain their own reference time. In contrast the reference time of *qatal*, the participle, and *yiqtol* is always discerned from the context.[5]

In the forthcoming sections, we will discuss the various semantic contexts that host *wayyiqtol* forms. The objective is to discern the various applications of this relationship and their impact on consecutive forms.

4.2.2 Chronological Sequence

4.2.2.1   Advancing the Reference Time along the Time Axis

The *wayyiqtol* form's most prevalent use is to advance its reference time along the time axis:[6]

(133) וְלֹא הֵסֵב יֹאשִׁיָּהוּ פָנָיו מִמֶּנּוּ כִּי לְהִלָּחֵם בּוֹ הִתְחַפֵּשׂ וְלֹא שָׁמַע אֶל דִּבְרֵי נְכוֹ
מִפִּי אֱלֹהִים **וַיָּבֹא** לְהִלָּחֵם בְּבִקְעַת מְגִדּוֹ: **וַיֹּרוּ** הַיֹּרִים לַמֶּלֶךְ יֹאשִׁיָּהוּ **וַיֹּאמֶר** הַמֶּלֶךְ
לַעֲבָדָיו הַעֲבִירוּנִי כִּי הָחֳלֵיתִי מְאֹד: **וַיַּעֲבִירֻהוּ** עֲבָדָיו מִן הַמֶּרְכָּבָה **וַיַּרְכִּיבֻהוּ** עַל
רֶכֶב הַמִּשְׁנֶה אֲשֶׁר לוֹ **וַיּוֹלִיכֻהוּ** יְרוּשָׁלַם **וַיָּמָת וַיִּקָּבֵר** בְּקִבְרוֹת אֲבֹתָיו וְכָל יְהוּדָה
וִירוּשָׁלַם מִתְאַבְּלִים עַל יֹאשִׁיָּהוּ:

---

4. In this diagram, every rectangle represents a new slide, each of which depicts a new *wayyiqtol* form. R stands for the reference time that is encompassed by each consecutive form; a = *qatal*; b = *yiqtol*; and c = the participle. See §2.2.4 above for a discussion on the link between consecutive and relative forms.

5. This description is premised on Washburn's thesis (1994) and avails itself of the terminology of Reichenbach (1947) and Kamp and Rohrer (1983).

6. In contrast to its other functions, I will not cite all the occurrences of this usage, for it is extremely diffuse; out of the 1,200 *wayyiqtol* forms in our corpus, approximately 86% advance the R-time along the time axis.

But Josiah would not let him alone; instead, he donned *his armor* to fight him, heedless of Necho's words from the mouth of God; and **he came [R,E]** to fight in the plain of Megiddo. Archers **shot [R,E]** King Josiah, and the king **said [R,E]** to his servants, Get me away from here, for I am badly wounded. His servants **carried [R,E]** him out of his chariot and **put [R,E]** him in the wagon of his second-in-command, and **conveyed [R,E]** him to Jerusalem. There **he died [R,E]**, and **was buried [R,E]** in the grave of his fathers, and all Judah and Jerusalem went into mourning over Josiah. (2 Chr 35:22-24)

Each of the actions in this textual unit pushes the reference time forward. In other words, the actions and their affiliated verb forms are aligned in a chronological succession: the chain begins with Josiah's arrival to the plain of Megiddo, where-upon the archers shoot him, and so on and so forth.

4.2.2.2 Expressing Resultativity

As a result of the primary meaning of advancing the reference time, the relation-ship between two sequential actions can often be characterized as one of cause and effect.[7]

(134) נָצוּמָה וַנְּבַקְשָׁה מֵאֱלֹהֵינוּ עַל זֹאת **וַיֵּעָתֵר** לָנוּ:

So we fasted and besought our God for this, and **he responded [R,E]** to our plea. (Ezr 8:23)

(135) אֵלֶּה בִּקְשׁוּ כְתָבָם הַמִּתְיַחְשִׂים וְלֹא נִמְצָא **וַיְגֹאֲלוּ** מִן הַכְּהֻנָּה:

[T]hese searched for their genealogical records, but they could not be found, so **they were disqualified [R,E]** for the priesthood. (Neh 7:64)

(136) וַיֹּאמֶר דָּוִיד לְכָל הַקָּהָל בָּרְכוּ נָא אֶת יְהוָה אֱלֹהֵיכֶם **וַיְבָרֲכוּ** כָל הַקָּהָל לַיהוָה אֱלֹהֵי אֲבֹתֵיהֶם[8]

David said to the whole assemblage, Now bless the LORD your God. All the assemblage **blessed [R,E]** the LORD God of their fathers (1 Chr 29:20)

Resultativity does not rule out the expression of a chronological string, but con-stitutes one of its possible ramifications. In the first example, the verb "ויעתר" is a consequence of the anterior chain of *wayyiqtol* forms. The *wayyiqtol* form "ויגאלו" in Nehemiah 7 stands in succession with *qatal* forms and signifies the result of the preceding chain of verbs.

---

7. See Joüon and Muraoka (2006:§118h); Waltke and O'Connor (1990:547-548).
8. Also see 2 Chronicles 13:20; 31:11, inter alia.

4.2.3 Cases Without Chronological Succession

As opposed to the cases in the previous section, there are instances where the arrayal of consecutive forms does not advance the reference time along the time axis. Although the identification of these occurrences is largely grounded on understanding the context, we have chosen to display them as a group on account of the difficulty they pose for those who claim that consecutive forms only express chronological and logical successions. Furthermore, a brief digression on this semantic attribute is likely shed light on the majority of *wayyiqtol* forms, which indeed signify chronological succession, and thus bolster our argument that the only function of consecutive forms is to express the relationship [R,E].

4.2.3.1 A Change in Perspective
4.2.3.1.1 Changing the Perspective of the Same Event
4.2.3.1.1.1 Repetition of the Same Verb[9]

The corpus under examination includes quite a few verbal sequences with a pair of identical *wayyiqtol* forms.[10] In these instances, commentators would be hard pressed to contend that there is a chronological relationship between the two forms, as they both refer to the same action. Moreover, this phenomenon cannot be considered a tautology or extraneous repetitions of the same verb, for the two clauses that host the respective verbs invariably differ from one another. For instance, if the subject of one of the clauses is explicit, then the other is implied (as in the first verse below); if one describes a place, its counterpart refers to an object (example 139):

1. Subject-Object

(137) **וַיֹּאמֶר** הַמֶּלֶךְ אֲחַשְׁוֵרוֹשׁ **וַיֹּאמֶר** לְאֶסְתֵּר הַמַּלְכָּה מִי הוּא זֶה וְאֵי זֶה הוּא אֲשֶׁר מְלָאוֹ לִבּוֹ לַעֲשׂוֹת כֵּן:[11]

Thereupon King Ahasuerus **demanded [R,E]** of Queen Esther and **said [R,E]** Who is he and where is he who dared to do this? (Est 7:5)

An explicit subject (Ahasuerus) is attached to the first clause, while an indirect object and a direct quote appear in the second clause, which refrains from expressly mentioning the subject.

---

9. See Esther 7:5; Daniel 1:7; 8:2-3, 9-10; Ezra 10:2; Nehemiah 2:20; 3:34; 4:7; 7:5; 8:16-17; 2 Chronicles 2:10-11; 11:5-6; 17:9; 31:10, 20.
10. Like the rest of the occurrences of *wayyiqtol*, this phenomenon is not unique to the Hebrew of the Second Temple period. See Blau (1971:234-240).
11. Also see 2 Chronicles 31:10; 34:10-11.

2. Object-Subject

(138) **וַיַּעֲשׂוּ** לָהֶם סֻכּוֹת אִישׁ עַל גַּגּוֹ וּבְחַצְרֹתֵיהֶם וּבְחַצְרוֹת בֵּית הָאֱלֹהִים וּבִרְחוֹב שַׁעַר הַמַּיִם וּבִרְחוֹב שַׁעַר אֶפְרָיִם: **וַיַּעֲשׂוּ** כָל הַקָּהָל הַשָּׁבִים מִן הַשְּׁבִי סֻכּוֹת

So the people went out and brought them, and **made [R,E]** themselves booths on their roofs, in their courtyards, in the courtyards of the House of God, in the square of the Water Gate and in the square of the Ephraim Gate. The whole community that returned from the captivity **made [R,E]** booths (Neh 8:16-17)

This case is similar to example 137, except that the order is reversed: in the first verse, the object is attached to the verb, while in the second the subject is spelled out for the reader ("The whole community that returned from the captivity").

3. Adverb-Object[12]

(139) **וָאַעֲמִיד** מִתַּחְתִּיּוֹת לַמָּקוֹם מֵאַחֲרֵי לַחוֹמָה בצחחיים (בַּצְּחִחִים) **וָאַעֲמִיד** אֶת הָעָם לְמִשְׁפָּחוֹת עִם חַרְבֹתֵיהֶם רָמְחֵיהֶם וְקַשְּׁתֹתֵיהֶם:

I stationed [R,E] on the lower levels of the place, behind the walls, on the bare rock—**I stationed [R,E]** the people by families with their swords, their lances, and their bows. (Neh 4:7)

In this particular verse, the first clause describes a location, whereas a direct object headlines the second.

4. Object-Adverb[13]

(140) **וַיָּחֶל** שְׁלֹמֹה לִבְנוֹת אֶת בֵּית יְהוָה בִּירוּשָׁלַם בְּהַר הַמּוֹרִיָּה אֲשֶׁר נִרְאָה לְדָוִיד אָבִיהוּ אֲשֶׁר הֵכִין בִּמְקוֹם דָּוִיד בְּגֹרֶן אָרְנָן הַיְבוּסִי: **וַיָּחֶל** לִבְנוֹת בַּחֹדֶשׁ הַשֵּׁנִי בַּשֵּׁנִי בִּשְׁנַת אַרְבַּע לְמַלְכוּתוֹ:

Then Solomon **began [R,E]** to build the House of the LORD in Jerusalem on Mount Moriah, where *the LORD* had appeared to his father David, at the place which David had designated, at the threshing floor of Ornan the Jebusite. **He began [R,E]** to build on the second day of the second month of the fourth year of his reign. (2 Chr 3:1-2)

As opposed to the previous example, the complete predicate "ויחל שלמה לבנות" in the first verse is followed by a direct object, while the second verse notes when the event took place.

---

12. Also see Nehemiah 3:34; 2 Chronicles 17:9.
13. Also see 2 Chronicles 31:20.

5. General Object-Specific Object[14]

(141) וַיֵּשֶׁב רְחַבְעָם בִּירוּשָׁלָם **וַיִּבֶן** עָרִים לְמָצוֹר בִּיהוּדָה: **וַיִּבֶן** אֶת בֵּית לֶחֶם וְאֶת עֵיטָם וְאֶת תְּקוֹעַ:

Rehoboam dwelt in Jerusalem and **built [R,E]** fortified towns in Judah. He **built [R,E]** up Bethlehem, and Etam, and Tekoa. (2 Chr 11:5-6)

In this passage, the verb in the first clause is accompanied by a general object (towns), and the subsequent clause fills in the details (Bethlehem, Etam, and Tekoa).

6. Adverb-Adverb—Different Aspects of the Same Description

(142) וּמִן הָאַחַת מֵהֶם יָצָא קֶרֶן אַחַת מִצְּעִירָה **וַתִּגְדַּל** יֶתֶר אֶל הַנֶּגֶב וְאֶל הַמִּזְרָח וְאֶל הַצְּבִי: **וַתִּגְדַּל** עַד צְבָא הַשָּׁמָיִם

From one of them emerged a small horn, which **extended [R,E]** itself greatly toward the south, toward the east, and toward the beautiful land. **It grew [R,E]** as high as the host of heaven (Dn 8:9-10)

Each verse illustrates a different aspect of the same object (a he-goat's horn): its horizontal and vertical protrusion, respectively.

These examples give rise to the following questions: What is the nature of this phenomenon? And how does this tie into what we deem to be the chronological role of consecutive forms—the marking of the relation [R,E]? Comparing these cases to those involving the recurrence of verbs other than *wayyiqtol* may improve our understanding of this construction.

In an article titled "On the Repetition of the Predicate in the Bible," Blau examined verses that adhere to the following construction:

(143) **וְשָׂרַף** אֹתוֹ עַל עֵצִים בָּאֵשׁ עַל שֶׁפֶךְ הַדֶּשֶׁן **יִשָּׂרֵף**:

[A]nd **burn** it up in a wood fire; it **shall be burned** on the ash heap. (Lv 4:12)

Blau offers two different interpretations of this iteration model. The first is to regard it as an example of the prevalent conversive phenomenon known as the "after-thought," whereby the second clause serves as a sort of appendix to the first. Blau (1971:237) even provides a modern example of this model: "אני שם וו עליו—וו קטן עליו" (I put a check mark on him—a small check mark on him). The second interpretation, according to the researcher, is to consider the final clause a "cleft sentence,"[15] a construction in which the language turns part of a segment

---

14. Also see Daniel 1:7; Nehemiah 7:5.
15. The term "cleft sentence," which derives from the Danish grammar, was first used in the linguist Otto Jespersen's English grammar; see Goldenberg (1977:127-128, note 5).

into a logical predicate (usually by means of a nominal clause or copular verb), while the other part, which tends to contain a verb, is designated a nominal clause. Goldenberg (1977:80) phrases the phenomenon thus:

> The formation of the cleft sentence may be described in brief as forming the "logical predicate" into a predicate of a nominal, or a copular, sentence, the rest of the utterance being nominalized so as to become the subject of that nominal or copular sentence. The subject-clause is most often placed in extraposition, and is represented pronominally.[16]

Accordingly, Blau suggests that the verb in the first clause of Leviticus 4:14 serves in the "usual" role as a predicate and rheme. However, insofar as the second clause is concerned, it is difficult to argue that the verb "ישרף" constitutes the sentence's rheme because it is taken from the immediate context. The adverb "על שפך הדשן" should therefore be viewed as the sentence's logical predicate (*vedette*) and the element that bears the primary stress, while "ישרף" serves as the clausal subject (*glose*).

Goldenberg's aforementioned definition is liable to cast doubt on Blau's contention, for there is nothing to suggest that the verb constitutes a subordinated form. On the other hand, many languages, Biblical Hebrew included,[17] feature cleft sentences in which the *glose* is unmarked:

(144) מִי הוּא יַרְשִׁיעֵנִי

Who is the one that can get a verdict against me? (Is 50:9)

or

(145) מַה זֹּאת עָשִׂיתָ

What have you done! (Gn 12:18)

versus

(146) מִי אֲשֶׁר חָטָא לִי אֶמְחֶנּוּ מִסִּפְרִי

He **who** has sinned against me, only him will I erase from my record. (Ex 32:33)

Goldenberg (1977), who dubbed these sorts of cases "imperfectly-transformed cleft sentences," posits that, in the absence of any formal morphological designation of a cleft, the language is likely to turn to other means of signification. For example, in spoken language, mere intonation can lead the reader to the conclusion that a sentence is a cleft (ibid.:132).

---

16. Goldenberg provides the following examples in ibid.:128: "זה אני שהלכתי" (Hebrew); "אנא הוא דאפיקית" (Babylonian Aramaic); "It is he who has done it" (English); and "C'est lui qui l'a fait" (French).

17. See ibid.

Blau's second suggestion is buttressed by Goldenberg's definition. The repetition of the same verb in two adjacent clauses wherein the first hosts a consecutive form and the second *qatal, yiqtol,* or a participle form raises the possibility of another syntactical route (besides the alternatives enumerated by Goldenberg) for linguistically marking inherently rhematic components as non-rhematic. In other words, this construct should also be viewed as an imperfectly transformed cleft sentence.[18]

In his taxonomy of iterations, Blau (1971) files the following constructions under the same category: consecutive forms followed by the forms *qatal* and *yiqtol,* such as the featured verse from Leviticus 4:12; and pairs of successive verbs, like the above noted examples of *wayyiqtol-wayyiqtol.* However, there are doubts as to whether this grouping is indeed justified. Even if the two constructions share an outward resemblance—both contain a repetition of the same verb and a change with respect to the supplement—there is a significant difference between them, which will be discussed below. What is more, this distinction has profound implications on our understanding of the chronological role of these consecutive forms.

For the purpose of underscoring the structural difference between the two models, we will evaluate two cases: a chain consisting of two identical consecutive verbs; and a chain comprised of two different forms sharing the same verb root:[19]

I. Consecutive Form-Consecutive Form
Wayyiqtol-wayyiqtol

(147) וָאַעֲמִיד מִתַּחְתִּיּוֹת לַמָּקוֹם מֵאַחֲרֵי לַחוֹמָה בַּצְּחִחִיים (בַּצְּחִחִים) וָאַעֲמִיד אֶת
הָעָם לְמִשְׁפָּחוֹת עִם חַרְבֹתֵיהֶם רָמְחֵיהֶם וְקַשְׁתֹתֵיהֶם:

I stationed [R,E], on the lower levels of the place, behind the walls, on the bare rock—I stationed [R,E] the people by families with their swords, their lances, and their bows. (Neh 4:7)

Weqatal-weqatal

(148) וְאָכַל אַהֲרֹן וּבָנָיו אֶת בְּשַׂר הָאַיִל וְאֶת הַלֶּחֶם אֲשֶׁר בַּסָּל פֶּתַח אֹהֶל מוֹעֵד:
וְאָכְלוּ אֹתָם אֲשֶׁר כֻּפַּר בָּהֶם לְמַלֵּא אֶת יָדָם לְקַדֵּשׁ אֹתָם וְזָר לֹא יֹאכַל כִּי קֹדֶשׁ הֵם:

[A]nd Aaron and his sons **shall eat [R,E]** the flesh of the ram, and the bread that is in the basket, at the entrance of the Tent of Meeting. These things **shall be eaten [R,E]** only by those for whom expiation was made with them when they were ordained and consecrated; they may not be eaten by a layman, for they are holy. (Ex 29:32-33)

---

18. Taube refers to cleft sentences as "echo patterns." See Taube (1997:397-420). For a look at the origins of this moniker, see ibid.:397 (footnote 1).
19. These are the same examples cited by Blau.

II. Consecutive Form-Other Form
Wayyiqtol » Qatal [20]

(149) וַיַּעַשׂ יְרִיעֹת עִזִּים לְאֹהֶל עַל הַמִּשְׁכָּן עַשְׁתֵּי עֶשְׂרֵה יְרִיעֹת עָשָׂה אֹתָם׃

He made [R,E] cloths of goats' hair for a tent over the tabernacle; **he made** (E=R) the cloths eleven in number. (Ex 36:14)

Weqatal » yiqtol [21]

(150) וְשָׂרַף אֹתוֹ עַל עֵצִים בָּאֵשׁ עַל שֶׁפֶךְ הַדֶּשֶׁן יִשָּׂרֵף׃

[A]nd **burn [R,E]** it up in a wood fire; **it shall be burned (E=R)** on the ash heap. (Lv 4:12)

Insofar as Blau's claim is concerned, the second group is apparently a special example of what Goldenberg refers to as "imperfectly-transformed cleft sentences." Although the cleft in the second clause of examples 149 and 150 is unmarked, it can be deduced from the context. In terms of "theme" and "rheme," it would be more accurate to say that the rhemes of these sentences are verb complements, rather than verbs.[22]

---

20. Also see Genesis 43:15; Exodus 36:17; 37:7, 23-24; 38:3-6; Numbers 31:7-8. There are also cases in which the same *qatal* verb form is repeated. For example, Genesis 1:27:
וַיִּבְרָא אֱלֹהִים אֶת הָאָדָם בְּצַלְמוֹ בְּצֶלֶם אֱלֹהִים בָּרָא אֹתוֹ זָכָר וּנְקֵבָה בָּרָא אֹתָם׃

21. Also see Exodus 30:7; Leviticus 25:29; Numbers 5:17; 30:12; 35:2. There are also cases in which different *yiqtol* forms share the same verb root. For example, Exodus 28:15:
וְעָשִׂיתָ חֹשֶׁן מִשְׁפָּט מַעֲשֵׂה חֹשֵׁב כְּמַעֲשֵׂה אֵפֹד תַּעֲשֶׂנּוּ זָהָב תְּכֵלֶת וְאַרְגָּמָן וְתוֹלַעַת שָׁנִי וְשֵׁשׁ מָשְׁזָר תַּעֲשֶׂה אֹתוֹ׃

22. Blau points to the fact that this phenomenon also exists in other languages, among them classical Arabic, Arabic dialects of Central Asia, the new Aramaic of Ma'aloula, and Modern Hebrew as well. For example, Blau (1971:238-239) cites the following sentence from S. Yizhar's *Days of Ziklag*: "הכל נגמר בשני פגרים, נורא מהר נגמר" (It all ended with two carcasses, terribly fast did it all end).

Azar provides an analysis of a Modern Hebrew syntactical structure in which the recurrence of the same element marks the text that is situated between two occurrences of the same word. He dubs this phenomenon the "sandwiched focus," namely the focus of the information (the logical subject) (1992:96). This model also exists in Yiddish. Taube examines a chain of Yiddish structures, which he refers to as "echo patterns." The Yiddish model, "which at first glance appears to be a mere profusion of extraneous words, is basically a pattern consisting of designated functions in the sphere of the message: an over-characterization of the thematic relations in a sentence. This is accomplished by repeating components that are endowed with "natural" rhemes, such as verb groups and question pronouns, so as to designate them as non-rhemaic and simultaneously designate the unrepeated component as rhematic" (1997:418). In our estimation, Taube's description of Yiddish can be applied to Biblical Hebrew in adjacent sequential form-relative form chains.

To constitute a cleft sentence, a verb must be capable of serving as a subordinated form; in other words, it must undergo a process of nominalization (by means of an explicit marker or otherwise). The final clauses in examples 149 and 150 meet this condition, as the verb forms can be presumed to have been subordinated. In Biblical Hebrew, *qatal* and *yiqtol* tend to abut subordinate particles (e.g., אשר יקטל and אשר קטל are acceptable collocations). Zewi (1992:180-185) provides a long list of biblical cleft sentences (examples 151 to 153 below) and imperfectly transformed cleft sentences (154 to 156), including the following:

(151) וְזֶה אֲשֶׁר **תַּעֲשֶׂה** עַל הַמִּזְבֵּחַ

This is what **you shall do** upon the altar. . . (Ex 29:38)

(152) הוּא אֲשֶׁר **דִּבַּרְתִּי** אֲלֵכֶם

This is what **I have told** you [people] about. . . (Gn 42:14)

(153) נוֹרָא הוּא אֲשֶׁר אֲנִי **עֹשֶׂה** עִמָּךְ׃

[A]wesome is the deed which **I will perform** for you. (Ex 34:10)

(154) מַה זֹּאת **עָשִׂית**

What is this (that) **you have done**! (Gn 3:13)

(155) לָמָּה זֶּה **תִּשְׁאַל** לִשְׁמִי

Why is it (that) **you ask** my name! (Gn 32:30)

(156) יְהוָה אֱלֹהֶיךָ הוּא **עֹבֵר** לְפָנֶיךָ

The LORD your God Himself **is passing** before you (Dt 31:3)

Qatal, yiqtol, and the participle are the only forms in the examples cited by Zewi. As explained below, it is no coincidence that none of these verses contain a consecutive form.

The "consecutive form-consecutive form" sentences (group I) differ from the "consecutive form-other form" variety (group II) in that one cannot assume that the former are cleft sentences. The inability to subordinate the consecutive form is what sets it apart from a syntactic standpoint. On account of the proclitic *waw* in sequential forms, collocations cannot be comprised of a proposed subordinate particle and consecutive form. For instance, the collocations אשר וקטל or אשר ויקטל are impossible. In other words, the basic condition for a cleft sentence—a "subordinable" verb form—does not apply to consecutive forms. This, then, rules out Blau's explanation with respect to this category.

This state of affairs is also directly connected to the temporal meaning of these forms. In essence, our hypothesis continues along the lines of Washburn's position according to which consecutive forms signify independent actions or events that do not maintain a syntactic relation with their surrounding verb forms and thus refrain from designating the nature of their temporal relations with the latter (1994:32-33).

4.2.3.1.1.2 Another Aspect of the Same Event[23]

Another group of *wayyiqtol* verbs is adjacent sequential forms that convey two different aspects of the same action. Unlike the examples in §2.2.3.1.1.1, this group uses different verbs to describe the same event. Together, they express multiple dimensions of the same event:

(157) וַיַּאַסְפוּ אֶת אֲחֵיהֶם וַיִּתְקַדְּשׁוּ וַיָּבֹאוּ כְמִצְוַת הַמֶּלֶךְ בְּדִבְרֵי יְהוָה לְטַהֵר בֵּית יְהוָה: וַיָּבֹאוּ הַכֹּהֲנִים לִפְנִימָה בֵית יְהוָה לְטַהֵר וַיּוֹצִיאוּ אֵת כָּל הַטֻּמְאָה אֲשֶׁר מָצְאוּ בְּהֵיכַל יְהוָה לַחֲצַר בֵּית יְהוָה וַיְקַבְּלוּ הַלְוִיִּם לְהוֹצִיא לְנַחַל קִדְרוֹן חוּצָה: וַיָּחֵלּוּ בְּאֶחָד לַחֹדֶשׁ הָרִאשׁוֹן לְקַדֵּשׁ וּבְיוֹם שְׁמוֹנָה לַחֹדֶשׁ בָּאוּ לְאוּלָם יְהוָה

[A]nd they **gathered [R,E]** their brothers, and **sanctified [R,E]** themselves and **came [R,E]**, by a command of the king concerning the LORD's ordinances, to purify the House of the LORD. The priests **went [R,E]** into the House of the LORD to purify it, and **brought [R,E]** all the unclean things they found in the Temple of the LORD out into the court of the House of the LORD; *there* the Levites **received [R,E]** them, to take them outside to Wadi Kidron. They **began [R,E]** the sanctification on the first day of the first month; on the eighth day of the month they reached the porch of the LORD. (2 Chr 29:15-17)

(158) וַיָּבֹא יְהוֹשָׁפָט וְעַמּוֹ לָבֹז אֶת שְׁלָלָם וַיִּמְצְאוּ בָהֶם לָרֹב וּרְכוּשׁ וּפְגָרִים וּכְלֵי חֲמֻדוֹת וַיְנַצְּלוּ לָהֶם לְאֵין מַשָּׂא וַיִּהְיוּ יָמִים שְׁלוֹשָׁה בֹּזְזִים אֶת הַשָּׁלָל כִּי רַב הוּא:

Jehoshaphat and his army **came [R,E]** to take the booty, and **found [R,E]** an abundance of goods, corpses, and precious objects, which **they pillaged [R,E]**, more than they could carry off. For three days **they were taking [R,E]** booty, there was so much of it. (2 Chr 20:25)

(159) וַיַּעֲשׂוּ כָל הַקָּהָל הַשָּׁבִים מִן הַשְּׁבִי סֻכּוֹת וַיֵּשְׁבוּ בַסֻּכּוֹת כִּי לֹא עָשׂוּ מִימֵי יֵשׁוּעַ בִּן נוּן כֵּן בְּנֵי יִשְׂרָאֵל עַד הַיּוֹם הַהוּא וַתְּהִי שִׂמְחָה גְדוֹלָה מְאֹד:

The whole community that returned from the captivity **made [R,E]** booths and **dwelt [R,E]** in the booths—the Israelites had not done so from the days of Joshua son of Nun to that day—and there **was [R,E]** very great rejoicing. (Neh 8:17)

In example 157, the shift from the series of verb forms to "וַיָּחֵלּוּ" prompts a transition from a description of the events themselves to the time period in which they

---

23. See Esther 3:6; Nehemiah 8:3/4-5, 17/18; 12:43/44; 2 Chronicles 11:17; 14:5/6; 20:25; 26:6; 7; 29:15-16/17; 30:25/26.

were held. Put differently, the final clause refers to the same event from a different angle. Something similar takes place in the second example with the shift from the chain of actions to the verb "ויהיו". Likewise, it stands to reason that the joy that is reported in Nehemiah 8 via the verb "ותהי" did not transpire after the previous actions, but constitutes a different facet of the same event.

4.2.3.1.1.3 Generalization and Specification
A chain of *wayyiqtol* forms can also denote a shift from a general perspective to specific details:

(160) וּבְעֵת הָצֵר לוֹ **וַיּוֹסֶף** לִמְעוֹל בַּיהוָה הוּא הַמֶּלֶךְ אָחָז: **וַיִּזְבַּח** לֵאלֹהֵי דַרְמֶשֶׂק הַמַּכִּים בּוֹ **וַיֹּאמֶר** כִּי אֱלֹהֵי מַלְכֵי אֲרָם הֵם מַעְזְרִים אֹתָם לָהֶם אֲזַבֵּחַ וְיַעְזְרוּנִי וְהֵם הָיוּ לוֹ לְהַכְשִׁילוֹ וּלְכָל יִשְׂרָאֵל: **וַיֶּאֱסֹף** אָחָז אֶת כְּלֵי בֵית הָאֱלֹהִים **וַיְקַצֵּץ** אֶת כְּלֵי בֵית הָאֱלֹהִים **וַיִּסְגֹּר** אֶת דַּלְתוֹת בֵּית יְהוָה **וַיַּעַשׂ** לוֹ מִזְבְּחוֹת בְּכָל פִּנָּה בִּירוּשָׁלָם:

In his time of trouble, this King Ahaz **trespassed [R,E]** even more against the LORD, **he sacrificed [R,E]** to the gods of Damascus which had defeated him, for **he thought [R,E]**, The gods of the kings of Aram help them; I shall sacrifice to them and they will help me; but they were his ruin and that of all Israel. Ahaz **collected [R,E]** the utensils of the House of God, and **cut [R,E]** the utensils of the House of God to pieces. **He shut [R,E]** the doors of the House of the LORD and **made [R,E]** himself altars in every corner of Jerusalem. (2 Chr 28:22-24)

(161) וַיָּקָם יָרָבְעָם בֶּן נְבָט עֶבֶד שְׁלֹמֹה בֶן דָּוִיד **וַיִּמְרֹד** עַל אֲדֹנָיו: **וַיִּקָּבְצוּ** עָלָיו אֲנָשִׁים רֵקִים בְּנֵי בְלִיַּעַל **וַיִּתְאַמְּצוּ** עַל רְחַבְעָם בֶּן שְׁלֹמֹה וּרְחַבְעָם הָיָה נַעַר וְרַךְ לֵבָב וְלֹא הִתְחַזַּק לִפְנֵיהֶם:

Jeroboam son of Nebat had been in the service of Solomon son of David, but he rose up and **rebelled [R,E]** against his master. Riffraff and scoundrels **gathered [R,E]** around him and **pressed [R,E]** hard upon Rehoboam son of Solomon. Rehoboam was inexperienced and fainthearted and could not stand up to them. (2 Chr 13:6-7)

(162) **וַיֵּשֶׁב** רְחַבְעָם בִּירוּשָׁלָם **וַיִּבֶן** עָרִים לְמָצוֹר בִּיהוּדָה: **וַיִּבֶן** אֶת בֵּית לֶחֶם וְאֶת עֵיטָם וְאֶת תְּקוֹעַ: וְאֶת בֵּית צוּר וְאֶת שׂוֹכוֹ וְאֶת עֲדֻלָּם: וְאֶת גַּת וְאֶת מָרֵשָׁה וְאֶת זִיף: וְאֶת אֲדוֹרַיִם וְאֶת לָכִישׁ וְאֶת עֲזֵקָה: וְאֶת צָרְעָה וְאֶת אַיָּלוֹן וְאֶת חֶבְרוֹן אֲשֶׁר בִּיהוּדָה וּבְבִנְיָמִן עָרֵי מְצֻרוֹת: **וַיְחַזֵּק** אֶת הַמְּצֻרוֹת **וַיִּתֵּן** בָּהֶם נְגִידִים וְאֹצְרוֹת מַאֲכָל וְשֶׁמֶן וָיָיִן: וּבְכָל עִיר וָעִיר צִנּוֹת וּרְמָחִים **וַיְחַזְּקֵם** לְהַרְבֵּה מְאֹד **וַיְהִי** לוֹ יְהוּדָה וּבִנְיָמִן:[24]

---

24. Also see Nehemiah 13:11, 25; 2 Chronicles 11:5-12; 13:6-7, 16-17; 17:1-2; 21:4; 28:5, 22-24.

Rehoboam **dwelt [R,E]** in Jerusalem and **built [R,E]** fortified towns in Judah.
He built [R,E] up Bethlehem, and Etam, and Tekoa, and Beth-zur, and Soco,
and Adullam, and Gath, and Mareshah, and Ziph, and Adoraim, and Lachish,
and Azekah, and Zorah, and Aijalon, and Hebron, which are in Judah and in
Benjamin, as fortified towns. **He strengthened [R,E]** the fortified towns and
put [R,E] commanders in them, along with stores of food, oil, and wine, and
shields and spears in every town. **He strengthened [R,E]** them exceedingly;
thus Judah and Benjamin **were [R,E]** his. (2 Chr 11:5-12)

In 2 Chronicles 28:22-24, the verbs "ויזבח" and "ויאמר" provide, inter alia, the
details of the actions that were introduced by the verb "ויוסף", and the same can be
said for the next passage. The verb denoting the generalization in these examples
is situated before the chain that unveils the specifics. Conversely, the verb ויהי
toward the end of example 162 can be viewed as a recap or generalization of the
previous string of actions.

4.2.3.1.1.4 Hendiadys
Hendiadys is a grammatical phenomenon in which a single idea is expressed by
means of two successive words that provide no explicit indication of the hierarchi-
cal relation between them. For example:

(163) וְכִי תַשִּׂיג יַד **גֵּר וְתוֹשָׁב** עִמָּךְ וּמָךְ אָחִיךָ עִמּוֹ וְנִמְכַּר **לְגֵר תּוֹשָׁב** עִמָּךְ אוֹ לְעֵקֶר
מִשְׁפַּחַת גֵּר:

If **a resident alien** among you has prospered, and your kinsman being in
straits, comes under his authority and gives himself over to the **resident alien**
among you, or to an offshoot of an alien's family. . . (Lv 25:47)

The phrase "גר (ו)תושב" refers to but one person. Whereas this particular sample involves nouns, a hendiadys can also consist of verbs. To wit: two verbs can denote
a single, indivisible occurrence (examples 164 to 169 below)[25] or two actions that
are perceived as one event (example 170):

(164) **וַתַּעַן** אֶסְתֵּר **וַתֹּאמַר** שְׁאֵלָתִי וּבַקָּשָׁתִי: אִם מָצָאתִי חֵן בְּעֵינֵי הַמֶּלֶךְ[26]

My wish, **replied [R,E]** Esther and **said [R,E]**, my request—if your Majesty
will do me the favor. . . . (Est 5:7-8)

---

25. In examples 46 to 48, the second verb in the succession is the conversive ויאמר. Despite the fact that on the pragmatic level these verbs mark the beginning of an instance
of direct speech, they have been included in this discussion because there is no fundamental difference between these examples and the others in all that concerns the signification of chronological relations. For more on the role of these verbs as signifiers of
direct speech, see Goldenberg (1991) and Hatav (2000a: 63-84).
26. Also see Esther 7:3; 1 Chronicles 12:18; 2 Chronicles 29:31.

(165) וָאֶשְׁמַע קוֹל אָדָם בֵּין אוּלָי וַיִּקְרָא **וַיֹּאמַר** גַּבְרִיאֵל הָבֵן לְהַלָּז אֶת הַמַּרְאֶה:[27]

I heard a human voice from the middle of Ulai, and the voice **was calling out [R,E]**, **saying [R,E]** Gabriel, make that man understand the vision. (Dn 8:16)

(166) וַיָּבֶן **וַיְדַבֵּר** עִמִּי **וַיֹּאמַר** דָּנִיֵּאל עַתָּה יָצָאתִי לְהַשְׂכִּילְךָ בִינָה:

He made me understand by **speaking [R,E]** to me and **saying [R,E]**, Daniel, I have just come forth to give you understanding. (Dn 9:22)

(167) וַיִּשְׁמַע סַנְבַלַּט הַחֹרֹנִי וְטֹבִיָּה הָעֶבֶד הָעַמּוֹנִי וְגֶשֶׁם הָעַרְבִי **וַיַּלְעִגוּ** לָנוּ **וַיִּבְזוּ** עָלֵינוּ וַיֹּאמְרוּ מָה הַדָּבָר הַזֶּה אֲשֶׁר אַתֶּם עֹשִׂים הַעַל הַמֶּלֶךְ אַתֶּם מֹרְדִים:

When Sanballat the Horonite and Tobiah the Ammonite servant and Geshem the Arab heard, they **mocked [R,E]** us and **held [R,E]** us **in contempt** and said, What is this that you are doing? Are you rebelling against the king? (Neh 2:19)

(168) וַיְהִי כַּאֲשֶׁר שָׁמַע סַנְבַלַּט כִּי אֲנַחְנוּ בוֹנִים אֶת הַחוֹמָה **וַיִּחַר** לוֹ **וַיִּכְעַס** הַרְבֵּה וַיַּלְעֵג עַל הַיְּהוּדִים:

When Sanballat heard that we were rebuilding the wall, it **angered [R,E]** him, and **he was** extremely **vexed [R,E]**. He mocked the Jews, (Neh 3:33)

(169) **וַיִּזְקַן** יְהוֹיָדָע **וַיִּשְׂבַּע** יָמִים וַיָּמָת בֶּן מֵאָה וּשְׁלֹשִׁים שָׁנָה בְּמוֹתוֹ:

Jehoiada **got old [R,E]** and **reached [R,E]** a ripe old age and died; he was one hundred and thirty years old at his death. (2 Chr 24:15)

(170) **וַיֹּאכְלוּ וַיִּשְׁתּוּ** לִפְנֵי יְהֹוָה בַּיּוֹם הַהוּא בְּשִׂמְחָה גְדוֹלָה[28]

[A]nd they **ate [R,E]** and **drank [R,E]** in the presence of the LORD on that day with great joy. (1 Chr 29:22)

The examples in this group are not on an equal footing in all that concerns the similarity between each of their constituent parts. This is bound to have both pragmatic and syntactical implications on each category of hendiadys.[29] In the case

---

27. Also see 2 Chronicles 14:10.
28. For more on the tandem "אכל ושתה", see Waltke and O'Connor (1990:653): "Conjunctive *waw* serves to join two clauses which describe interrelated or overlapping situations not otherwise logically related. Pairs of such clauses may form a *hendiadys*."
29. For example, Kuzar shows that contemporary Hebrew consists of assorted behavioral criteria for distinguishing a pair of actions that are linked in a simple bond from hendiadys, such as omissions. While one of the components in the sentence "Dani sneezed and closed the window" can be omitted ("Dani sneezed and did not close the window"), in the sentence "The Prison Service held negotiations [נשא ונתן] with Deri," it is impossible to erase just one of the verbs, for "The Prison Service נתן לא אבל נשא"

of synonymous verbs, as in examples 167 to 169, it is impossible to interpret the phrase "ויחר ויכעס" as "ויחר" and "ויכעס" (example 168) because the two verbs have identical meanings. In contrast, the phrase "ויאכלו וישתו" (example 170) can be understood as "ויאכלו" and "וישתו", even though they are perceived as denoting the same event.[30] That said, the disparate levels of congruence between the verbs in each passage do not change the fact that none of these examples comprise a chronological succession, but rather two actions representing a single occurrence. Consequently, the hendiadys phenomenon constitutes yet another application of the *wayyiqtol* form. In this sense, "two that are one" is akin to a chronological sequence, for both patterns entail a semantic implication that derives from the context,[31] and none of these categories deal with the meaning of the verb forms themselves.

4.2.3.1.2 Change in Actor

As in the cases featuring a new perspective of the same action, a change in actor is likely to shift the direction of a chronological succession. That said, the *wayyiqtol* form offers no indication of such a change. In other words, a new actor does not denote a break in the succession. Therefore, in order to determine the nature and extent of the continuum, readers rely on their understanding of the context:

(171) **וַיֹּאמֶר** הָמָן לַמֶּלֶךְ אֲחַשְׁוֵרוֹשׁ יֶשְׁנוֹ עַם אֶחָד מְפֻזָּר וּמְפֹרָד בֵּין הָעַמִּים בְּכֹל מְדִינוֹת מַלְכוּתֶךָ. . . . **וַיָּסַר** הַמֶּלֶךְ אֶת טַבַּעְתּוֹ מֵעַל יָדוֹ וַיִּתְּנָהּ לְהָמָן בֶּן הַמְּדָתָא הָאֲגָגִי צֹרֵר הַיְּהוּדִים: וַיֹּאמֶר הַמֶּלֶךְ לְהָמָן הַכֶּסֶף נָתוּן לָךְ וְהָעָם לַעֲשׂוֹת בּוֹ כַּטּוֹב בְּעֵינֶיךָ: **וַיִּקָּרְאוּ** סֹפְרֵי הַמֶּלֶךְ בַּחֹדֶשׁ הָרִאשׁוֹן בִּשְׁלוֹשָׁה עָשָׂר יוֹם בּוֹ **וַיִּכָּתֵב** כְּכָל אֲשֶׁר צִוָּה הָמָן

---

makes no sense. Therefore, the omission can only encompass the entire phrase: "The Prison Authority לא נשא ונתן with Deri." See Kuzar (2006:119-138).

30. A comprehensive exposition of the hendiadys phenomenon must take into account the fact that there are a host of intermediary situations in which the verbs maintain various levels of propinquity between the two outer poles, namely a pair of consecutive verbs that are devoid of any semantic link and two synonymous verbs arrayed in succession and expressing a single unit.

31. From a terminological standpoint, the inability to differentiate between the semantic and syntactical sphere occasionally results in a profusion of terms. For instance, the *waw* is customarily known as a "*waw* consecutive" in chronological successions and a hendiadys is called a "*waw explicativum*." See Baker (1980:129-136); and Waltke and O'Connor (1990:649). These terms refer exclusively to the semantic level because, syntactically speaking, the *waw* fills a similar role in both. According to Joüon and Muraoka, "There is even less sense of succession when the Waw has **explanatory** value. . . . The very frequent occurrence of wayyiqtol in narration brought about an ever-broadening use and misuse of this form." (2006:§118j-k).

Haman then **said [R,E]** to King Ahasuerus, There is a certain people, scattered and dispersed among the other peoples in all the provinces of your realm. . . . Thereupon the king **removed [R,E]** his signet ring from his hand and gave it to Haman son of Hammedatha the Agagite, the foe of the Jews. And the king said, The money and the people are yours to do with as you see fit. On the thirteenth day of the first month, the king's scribes **were summoned [R,E]** and a decree **was issued [R,E]**, as Haman directed (Est 3:8-12)

(172) **וָאָבוֹא** אֶל פַּחֲווֹת עֵבֶר הַנָּהָר **וָאֶתְּנָה** לָהֶם אֵת אִגְּרוֹת הַמֶּלֶךְ **וַיִּשְׁלַח** עִמִּי הַמֶּלֶךְ שָׂרֵי חַיִל וּפָרָשִׁים:

When I **came [R,E]** to the governors of the province of Beyond the River I **gave [R,E]** them the king's letters. The king also **sent [R,E]** army officers and cavalry with me. (Neh 2:9)

(173) **וַיְחַזְּקוּ** אֶת מַלְכוּת יְהוּדָה **וַיְאַמְּצוּ** אֶת רְחַבְעָם בֶּן שְׁלֹמֹה לְשָׁנִים שָׁלוֹשׁ כִּי הָלְכוּ בְּדֶרֶךְ דָּוִיד וּשְׁלֹמֹה לְשָׁנִים שָׁלוֹשׁ: **וַיִּקַּח** לוֹ רְחַבְעָם אִשָּׁה אֶת מָחֲלַת בֶּן (בַּת) יְרִימוֹת בֶּן דָּוִיד אֲבִיחַיִל בַּת אֱלִיאָב בֶּן יִשָׁי: **וַתֵּלֶד** לוֹ בָּנִים אֶת יְעוּשׁ וְאֶת שְׁמַרְיָה וְאֶת זָהַם:

They strengthened [R,E] the kingdom of Judah, and **supported [R,E]** Rehoboam son of Solomon for three years, for they followed the ways of David and Solomon for three years. Rehoboam **married [R,E]** Mahalath daughter of Jerimoth son of David, and Abihail daughter of Eliab son of Jesse. **She bore [R,E]** him sons: Jeush, Shemariah, and Zaham. (2 Chr 11:17-19)

(174) **וַיִּכָּנְעוּ** בְנֵי יִשְׂרָאֵל בָּעֵת הַהִיא **וַיֶּאֶמְצוּ** בְּנֵי יְהוּדָה כִּי נִשְׁעֲנוּ עַל יְהוָה אֱלֹהֵי אֲבוֹתֵיהֶם: **וַיִּרְדֹּף** אֲבִיָּה אַחֲרֵי יָרָבְעָם **וַיִּלְכֹּד** מִמֶּנּוּ עָרִים אֶת בֵּית אֵל וְאֶת בְּנוֹתֶיהָ וְאֶת יְשָׁנָה וְאֶת בְּנוֹתֶיהָ וְאֶת עֶפְרוֹן (עֶפְרַיִן) וּבְנֹתֶיהָ:[32]

The Israelites **were crushed [R,E]** at that time, while the people of Judah **triumphed [R,E]** because they relied on the LORD God of their fathers. Abijah **pursued [R,E]** Jeroboam and **captured [R,E]** some of his cities—Bethel with its dependencies, Jeshanah with its dependencies, and Ephrain with its dependencies. (2 Chr 13:18-19)

Notwithstanding the change in actor, the activities in example 171 are aligned in chronological order. Conversely, the change in example 172 derails the chronological continuum, for the dispatch of army officers and cavalry obviously preceded the letters' arrival. The third passage combines elements of examples 171 and 172, as the shift from the nation ("ויאמצו") to Rehoboam ("ויקח") makes it difficult to pinpoint the chronological relationship between the two forms. In contrast, the transition in the second half of the passage between the individuals that

---

32. Also see Nehemiah 2:9; 4:2/3/4/5; 9:4; 1 Chronicles 10:13/14; 2 Chronicles 11:17/18; 13:18/19; 14:11/12; 15:9/10; 28:6-8; 29:20-30; 30:21/22.

accompany the verbs "ויקח" and "ותלד" maintains a chronological succession. On the other hand, the chronological link in example 174 between the verbs that are attached to the various actors is unclear. Hence, these examples strengthen the argument according to which consecutive forms do not, in and of themselves, determine the nature of the chronological relationship between their respective actions. In certain circumstances, a change in actor might facilitate a chronological succession, while in others it might turn back the clock or induce an ambiguous chronological relationship between two successive actions.

The consequences of this phenomenon are especially prominent in long narrative successions involving several protagonists represented by *wayyiqtol* verbs. The transition between the various actors is likely to engender oscillations back and forth in time. For example:

(175) **וַיַּשְׁכֵּם** יְחִזְקִיָּהוּ הַמֶּלֶךְ **וַיֶּאֱסֹף** אֶת שָׂרֵי הָעִיר **וַיַּעַל** בֵּית יְהוָה: **וַיָּבִיאוּ** פָרִים שִׁבְעָה וְאֵילִים שִׁבְעָה וּכְבָשִׂים שִׁבְעָה וּצְפִירֵי עִזִּים שִׁבְעָה לְחַטָּאת עַל הַמַּמְלָכָה וְעַל הַמִּקְדָּשׁ וְעַל יְהוּדָה **וַיֹּאמֶר** לִבְנֵי אַהֲרֹן הַכֹּהֲנִים לְהַעֲלוֹת עַל מִזְבַּח יְהוָה: **וַיִּשְׁחֲטוּ** הַבָּקָר **וַיְקַבְּלוּ** הַכֹּהֲנִים אֶת הַדָּם **וַיִּזְרְקוּ** הַמִּזְבֵּחָה **וַיִּשְׁחֲטוּ** הָאֵלִים **וַיִּזְרְקוּ** הַדָּם הַמִּזְבֵּחָה **וַיִּשְׁחֲטוּ** הַכְּבָשִׂים **וַיִּזְרְקוּ** הַדָּם הַמִּזְבֵּחָה: **וַיַּגִּישׁוּ** אֶת שְׂעִירֵי הַחַטָּאת לִפְנֵי הַמֶּלֶךְ וְהַקָּהָל **וַיִּסְמְכוּ** יְדֵיהֶם עֲלֵיהֶם: **וַיִּשְׁחָטוּם** הַכֹּהֲנִים **וַיְחַטְּאוּ** אֶת דָּמָם הַמִּזְבֵּחָה לְכַפֵּר עַל כָּל יִשְׂרָאֵל כִּי לְכָל יִשְׂרָאֵל אָמַר הַמֶּלֶךְ הָעוֹלָה וְהַחַטָּאת: **וַיַּעֲמֵד** אֶת הַלְוִיִּם בֵּית יְהוָה בִּמְצִלְתַּיִם בִּנְבָלִים וּבְכִנֹּרוֹת בְּמִצְוַת דָּוִיד וְגָד חֹזֵה הַמֶּלֶךְ וְנָתָן הַנָּבִיא כִּי בְיַד יְהוָה הַמִּצְוָה בְּיַד נְבִיאָיו: **וַיַּעַמְדוּ** הַלְוִיִּם בִּכְלֵי דָוִיד וְהַכֹּהֲנִים בַּחֲצֹצְרוֹת: **וַיֹּאמֶר** חִזְקִיָּהוּ לְהַעֲלוֹת הָעֹלָה לְהַמִּזְבֵּחַ וּבְעֵת הֵחֵל הָעוֹלָה הֵחֵל שִׁיר יְהוָה וְהַחֲצֹצְרוֹת וְעַל יְדֵי כְּלֵי דָּוִיד מֶלֶךְ יִשְׂרָאֵל: וְכָל הַקָּהָל מִשְׁתַּחֲוִים וְהַשִּׁיר מְשׁוֹרֵר וְהַחֲצֹצְרוֹת מַחְצְרִים (מַחְצְרִים) הַכֹּל עַד לִכְלוֹת הָעֹלָה: וּכְכַלּוֹת לְהַעֲלוֹת כָּרְעוּ הַמֶּלֶךְ וְכָל הַנִּמְצְאִים אִתּוֹ **וַיִּשְׁתַּחֲווּ**: **וַיֹּאמֶר** יְחִזְקִיָּהוּ הַמֶּלֶךְ וְהַשָּׂרִים לַלְוִיִּם לְהַלֵּל לַיהוָה בְּדִבְרֵי דָוִיד וְאָסָף הַחֹזֶה **וַיְהַלְלוּ** עַד לְשִׂמְחָה **וַיִּקְּדוּ וַיִּשְׁתַּחֲווּ**:

King Hezekiah **rose [R,E]** early, **gathered** the officers of the city, and **went up [R,E]** to the House of the LORD. **They brought [R,E]** seven bulls and seven rams and seven lambs and seven he-goats as a sin offering for the kingdom and for the Sanctuary and for Judah. **He ordered [R,E]** the Aaronite priests to offer them on the altar of the LORD. The priests **slaughtered [R,E]** the cattle, and **received [R,E]** the blood and **dashed [R,E]** it against the altar; **they slaughtered [R,E]** the rams and **dashed [R,E]** the blood against the altar; **they** also **slaughtered [R,E]** the lambs and **dashed [R,E]** the blood against the altar. **They** also **presented [R,E]** the he-goats for the sin offering to the king and the congregation, who **laid [R,E]** their hands upon them. The priests **slaughtered [R,E]** them and **performed [R,E]** the purgation rite with the blood against the altar, to expiate for all Israel, for the king had designated the burnt offering and the sin offering to be for all Israel. **He stationed [R,E]** the Levites in the House of the LORD with cymbals and harps and lyres, as David and Gad the king's seer and Nathan the prophet had ordained, for the ordinance was by the LORD through his prophets. When the Levites **were [R,E]** in place with the instruments of David, and the priests with their trumpets, Hezekiah **gave [R,E]** the order to offer the burnt offering on the altar. When the burnt offering began, the song of the LORD and the trumpets began also, together with the instruments of King David of Israel. All the congregation prostrated themselves, the song was sung and the trumpets were blown—all this until the end of the burnt offering. When the offering was finished, the king and all who were there with him knelt and **prostrated [R,E]** themselves. King Hezekiah and the officers **ordered [R,E]** the Levites to praise the LORD in the words of David and Asaph the seer; so **they praised [R,E]** rapturously, and **they bowed [R,E]** and **prostrated [R,E]** themselves. (2 Chr 29:20-30)

This narrative unit consists of four different actors (Hezekiah, the city's officers, the priests, and Levites). Upon tracing the chronological link between the sundry actions, it is evident that the actions that are carried out by each of the protagonists are arranged in chronological order. However, this does not apply to the entire passage, as the succession of verbs after changes in actor is informed by shifts back and forth along the time axis. In other words, the passage is comprised of four distinct yet intercrossing time lines.

4.2.3.2 *Wayyiqtol* at the Outset of Narrative Units

As in the previous category, *wayyiqtol* forms do not necessarily denote a chronological succession when opening a narrative unit. Bauer (1910:35-39) cites this particular function upon criticizing Driver (1892) for assuming that the "*waw* consecutive" invariably denotes a chronological or logical continuation of the preceding form(s).[33] According to Bauer, the fact that eleven of the Hebrew Bible's books commence with forms of *wayyiqtol* refutes the argument whereby *wayyiqtol*'s lone function is to signify chronological successions with its anterior counterparts. Our findings, including some of the examples that have been presented earlier, demonstrate that Bauer's criticism of Driver is not without basis.

Unlike Bauer, we accept the term "consecutive forms," but adopt a different definition for "succession." Instead of assuming that a succession expresses a chronological relation between forms, we consider it a concatenation of forms, each of which successively mounts its own reference time [R,E]. As such, this definition readily encompasses consecutive forms that open narrative units.

Returning to the above-mentioned "slides metaphor," the decision to open a unit with a consecutive form can be said to introduce a new "slide." Thereafter, the preliminary information can be expanded upon by means of other forms, and additional R-times can be inserted by concatenating sequential forms.

---

33. For a summary of Bauer's arguments, see McFall (1982:93-94).

4.2.3.2.1 ויהי at the Outset of Textual Units

ויהי frequently stand at the beginning of narrative units:

(176) וַיְהִי בִּימֵי אֲחַשְׁוֵרוֹשׁ הוּא אֲחַשְׁוֵרוֹשׁ הַמֹּלֵךְ מֵהֹדּוּ וְעַד כּוּשׁ שֶׁבַע וְעֶשְׂרִים וּמֵאָה מְדִינָה:

It happened [R,E] in the days of Ahasuerus, that Ahasuerus who reigned over a hundred and twenty-seven provinces from India to Nubia. (Est 1:1)

The contention that the practice of opening a narrative unit with ויהי decreases during the Second Temple period, in comparison to the First Temple period, occasionally rears its head in the research literature.[34] One of the problems of leaning on statistical comparisons is the size disparity between the two corpuses. What is more, researchers do not always emphasize the randomness with which the extant texts have reached our hands. That said, we found 66 occurrences of ויהי in the Second Temple period texts, the largest group of which consists of forms that either open narrative units or mark a transition to a new narrative perspective. Consequently, the reports of the decline of this structure appear to be unwarranted.

One of the most important contributions of discursive linguistics to the study of Biblical Hebrew verb forms has been to turn scholars' attention to the relationship between large textual units. Schneider's work (1974) constitutes the first large-scale effort at writing a grammar of Biblical Hebrew from this perspective. In fact, it was the widespread use of the verb ויהי at the start of textual units (what Schneider coined "*Einleitungsformeln*") that initially caught his eye (ibid.:251). According to Schneider, these verbs function as "macro-syntactical border markers" (*Übergangssignal*) (ibid.:261-262). Put differently, ויהי forms positioned between two textual units are charged with signifying the beginning of the new unit (ibid.). Following in Schneider's footsteps, Talstra claims that, besides demarcating the border between two principal textual units, ויהי can help distinguish a story's main plot from supplementary information (1978:173). To bolster his claim, Talstra points to the following example:

(177) וַיְהִי אַחֲרֵי מוֹת שָׁאוּל וְדָוִד שָׁב מֵהַכּוֹת אֶת הָעֲמָלֵק וַיֵּשֶׁב דָּוִד בְּצִקְלָג יָמִים שְׁנָיִם: וַיְהִי בַּיּוֹם הַשְּׁלִישִׁי וְהִנֵּה אִישׁ בָּא מִן הַמַּחֲנֶה מֵעִם שָׁאוּל וּבְגָדָיו קְרֻעִים, וַאֲדָמָה עַל רֹאשׁוֹ וַיְהִי בְּבֹאוֹ אֶל דָּוִד וַיִּפֹּל אַרְצָה וַיִּשְׁתָּחוּ:

And it happened [R,E] that after the death of Saul—David had already returned from defeating the Amalekites—David stayed two days in Ziklag.

---

34. See Kropat (1909:23) and Driver (1913:538), inter alios. Polzin (1976:56) contends that, although 125 occurrences of ויהי have been found in Kings, there are only 34 in the non-corresponding sections of Chronicles. However, this statistical argument is problematic, for it fails to mention the size disparity between the two corpuses.

And it happened [R,E] that on the third day, a man came from Saul's camp,
with his clothes rent and earth on his head; **and [R,E]** as he approached David,
he flung himself to the ground and bowed low. (2 Sm 1:1-2)

In Talstra's estimation, not only are ויהי forms capable of demarcating the boundary between narrative units, but they can signify a return to the primary storyline
as well.

Though Hatav basically continues along the lines of her predecessors, she
also draws a distinction between the "predicative" and "segmentational" functions of ויהי and והיה. Hatav claims that the predicative function of the two
constitutes an integral part of the verbal tense system, so that in this respect
they digress from the rest of the forms (*qatal*, *yiqtol*, and the participle) of the
verb root היה.

In contrast to the aforementioned scholars, we define consecutive forms as signifiers of the relationship [R,E], namely a form that mounts a new R-time whenever
it (a "new slide") appears. This formulation enables us to classify ויהי's various
functions under the general framework of consecutive forms.

As we have seen, there are many instances in which *wayyiqtol* forms provide
the reader with different perspectives of the same event. Quite a few occurrences
of ויהי can also be interpreted in this fashion, including the following passage:[35]

(178) וַיִּמְלֹךְ יְהוֹשָׁפָט בְּנוֹ תַּחְתָּיו וַיִּתְחַזֵּק עַל יִשְׂרָאֵל: וַיִּתֶּן חַיִל בְּכָל עָרֵי יְהוּדָה
הַבְּצֻרוֹת וַיִּתֵּן נְצִיבִים בְּאֶרֶץ יְהוּדָה וּבְעָרֵי אֶפְרַיִם אֲשֶׁר לָכַד אָסָא אָבִיו: **וַיְהִי** יְהוָה
עִם יְהוֹשָׁפָט. . . . וַיָּכֶן יְהוָה אֶת הַמַּמְלָכָה בְּיָדוֹ וַיִּתְּנוּ כָל יְהוּדָה מִנְחָה לִיהוֹשָׁפָט
וַיְהִי לוֹ עֹשֶׁר וְכָבוֹד לָרֹב. . . . **וַיְהִי** פַּחַד יְהוָה עַל כָּל מַמְלְכוֹת הָאֲרָצוֹת אֲשֶׁר
סְבִיבוֹת יְהוּדָה

His son Jehoshaphat succeeded him as king, and took firm hold of Israel. He
stationed troops in all the fortified towns of Judah, and stationed garrisons
throughout the land of Judah and the cities of Ephraim which his father Asa had
captured. The LORD **was [R,E]** with Jehoshaphat. . . . So the LORD established
the kingdom in his hands, and all Judah gave presents to Jehoshaphat. **He had
[R,E]** wealth and glory in abundance. . . . A terror of the LORD **seized [R,E]** all
the kingdoms of the lands around Judah (2 Chr 17:1-10)

The use of "ויהי" herein contradicts Hatav's claim that it always advances the R-
time along the temporal axis. For instance, "ויהי יהוה עם יהושפט" is not subsequent
to the anterior verbs.

Stressing the correlation between the forms' usage herein and the above-mentioned
wayyiqtol forms, which denote another facet of the same action, is no less convincing
than Schneider's position. For instance, it is worth comparing the way the various occurrences of "ויהי" in example 178 alter the reader's vantage point of the same event
with how this is accomplished by the verb "ויחלו" in the following passage:

---

35. Also see 2 Chronicles 20:29; 29:32; 30:26.

(179) וַיַּאַסְפוּ אֶת אֲחֵיהֶם וַיִּתְקַדְּשׁוּ וַיָּבֹאוּ כְמִצְוַת הַמֶּלֶךְ בְּדִבְרֵי יְהוָה לְטַהֵר בֵּית יְהוָה: וַיָּבֹאוּ הַכֹּהֲנִים לִפְנִימָה בֵית יְהוָה לְטַהֵר וַיּוֹצִיאוּ אֵת כָּל הַטֻּמְאָה אֲשֶׁר מָצְאוּ בְּהֵיכַל יְהוָה לַחֲצַר בֵּית יְהוָה וַיְקַבְּלוּ הַלְוִיִּם לְהוֹצִיא לְנַחַל קִדְרוֹן חוּצָה: **וַיָּחֵלּוּ** בְּאֶחָד לַחֹדֶשׁ הָרִאשׁוֹן לְקַדֵּשׁ וּבְיוֹם שְׁמוֹנָה לַחֹדֶשׁ בָּאוּ לְאוּלָם יְהוָה

[A]nd, gathering their brothers, they sanctified themselves and came, by a command of the king concerning the Lord's ordinances, to purify the House of the Lord. The priests went into the House of the Lord to purify it, and brought all the unclean things they found in the Temple of the Lord out into the court of the House of the Lord; *there* the Levites received them, to take them outside to Wadi Kidron. **They began [R,E]** the sanctification on the first day of the first month; on the eighth day of the month they reached the porch of the Lord. (2 Chr 29:15-17)

Unlike the passage from 2 Chronicles 17, here the context that the emboldened verb refers to is the previous series of actions.

As in the cases above, and in accordance with its standard task, the role of the ויהי forms in the following examples (180 to 182) is to mount a new reference time. What sets apart these instances from other occurrences of *wayyiqtol* is that the verb ויהי serves as a semantically "blank slide" because the chronological context is provided by the adverbial phrase, which is attached to the verb form.

(180) **וַיְהִי בְחֹדֶשׁ כִּסְלֵו שְׁנַת עֶשְׂרִים** וַאֲנִי הָיִיתִי בְּשׁוּשַׁן הַבִּירָה:

It happened **[R,E] in the month of Kislev of the twentieth year,** when I was in the fortress of Shushan. (Neh 1:1)

(181) **וַיְהִי כַּאֲשֶׁר שָׁמַע סַנְבַלַּט כִּי אֲנַחְנוּ בוֹנִים אֶת הַחוֹמָה** וַיִּחַר לוֹ

It happened **[R,E] when Sanballat heard that we were rebuilding the wall,** it angered him. (Neh 3:33)

(182) **וַיְהִי כַּאֲשֶׁר נִבְנְתָה הַחוֹמָה** וָאַעֲמִיד הַדְּלָתוֹת וַיִּפָּקְדוּ הַשּׁוֹעֲרִים וְהַמְשֹׁרְרִים וְהַלְוִיִּם:

It happened **[R,E] when the wall was rebuilt** and I had set up the doors, tasks were assigned to the gatekeepers, the singers, and the Levites. (Neh 7:1)

Since the root הי״ה is a quasi-empty verb form from a semantic standpoint, the argument can be made that insofar as the message is concerned the purpose of this structure is to accentuate the adverbial complement, which signifies when the event transpired. In other words, there is no syntactical difference between the use of ויהי and the rest of the *wayyiqtol* forms, as they both mount a new R-time. However, with respect to the functional sentence perspective, this structure is prevalent in cases where the writer sought to emphasize the action's chronological context. This, then, may very well explain why these verb forms tend to appear within the framework of changes in perspective, be it large or small narrative units, or a change in the vantage point of the same event.

4.2.3.2.2 Opening a New Narrative Unit with *Wayyiqtol* Forms Other than ויהי

Though less prevalent than ויהי, there are other *wayyiqtol* forms that open narrative units:

(183) וַיֵּשְׁבוּ שָׂרֵי הָעָם בִּירוּשָׁלָם וּשְׁאָר הָעָם הִפִּילוּ גוֹרָלוֹת לְהָבִיא אֶחָד מִן הָעֲשָׂרָה לָשֶׁבֶת בִּירוּשָׁלַם עִיר הַקֹּדֶשׁ וְתֵשַׁע הַיָּדוֹת בֶּעָרִים:

The officers of the people **settled [R,E]** in Jerusalem; the rest of the people cast lots for one out of ten to come and settle in the holy city of Jerusalem, and the other nine-tenths to stay in the towns. (Neh 11:1)

(184) וַיַּקְהֵל דָּוִיד אֶת כָּל שָׂרֵי יִשְׂרָאֵל שָׂרֵי הַשְּׁבָטִים וְשָׂרֵי הַמַּחְלְקוֹת הַמְשָׁרְתִים אֶת הַמֶּלֶךְ

David **assembled [R,E]** all the officers of Israel—the tribal officers, the divisional officers who served the king. (1 Chr 28:1)

(185) וַיִּתְחַזֵּק שְׁלֹמֹה בֶן דָּוִיד עַל מַלְכוּתוֹ וַיהוָה אֱלֹהָיו עִמּוֹ וַיְגַדְּלֵהוּ לְמָעְלָה:[36]

Solomon son of David **took [R,E] firm hold** of his kingdom, for the LORD his God was with him and made him exceedingly great. (2 Chr 1:1)

In all three examples, the verse opens a textual unit that presents a new topic. There is no difference between the *wayyiqtol* forms herein and ויהי forms in other cases. More specifically, all these versions of *wayyiqtol* open a narrative unit by establishing a new R-time.

4.2.3.3   Cases of Chronological Ambiguity

There are other sequels of *wayyiqtol* in which the chronological relationship between its constituents is less than clear. Most of these cases involve a string of actions that are somehow linked to one another and embedded in a shared context:

(186) וּכְכַלּוֹת כָּל זֹאת יָצְאוּ כָל יִשְׂרָאֵל הַנִּמְצְאִים לְעָרֵי יְהוּדָה וַיְשַׁבְּרוּ הַמַּצֵּבוֹת וַיְגַדְּעוּ הָאֲשֵׁרִים וַיְנַתְּצוּ אֶת הַבָּמוֹת וְאֶת הַמִּזְבְּחוֹת מִכָּל יְהוּדָה וּבִנְיָמִן וּבְאֶפְרַיִם וּמְנַשֶּׁה עַד לְכַלֵּה

When all this was finished, all Israel who were present went out into the towns of Judah and **smashed [R,E]** the pillars, **cut down [R,E]** the sacred posts,

---

36. Also see Nehemiah 3:1; 1 Chronicles 4:39; 5:25.

demolished [R,E] the shrines and altars throughout Judah and Benjamin, and throughout Ephraim and Manasseh, to the very last one. (2 Chr 31:1)

(187) נַיִּתְחַזַּק **וַיִּבֶן** אֶת כָּל הַחוֹמָה הַפְּרוּצָה **וַיַּעַל** עַל הַמִּגְדָּלוֹת וְלַחוּצָה הַחוֹמָה אַחֶרֶת **וַיְחַזֵּק** אֶת הַמִּלּוֹא עִיר דָּוִיד **וַיַּעַשׂ** שֶׁלַח לָרֹב וּמָגִנִּים: **וַיִּתֵּן** שָׂרֵי מִלְחָמוֹת עַל הָעָם

He acted with vigor, and **rebuilt [R,E]** the whole breached wall, **and raised [R,E]** towers on it, outside the other wall. **He fortified [R,E]** the Millo of the City of David, and **made [R,E]** a great quantity of arms and shields. **He appointed [R,E]** battle officers over the people. (2 Chr 32:5-6)

(188) **וַיֵּלֶךְ** שְׁמוֹ עַד לָבוֹא מִצְרַיִם כִּי הֶחֱזִיק עַד לְמָעְלָה: **וַיִּבֶן** עֻזִּיָּהוּ מִגְדָּלִים בִּירוּשָׁלַם עַל שַׁעַר הַפִּנָּה וְעַל שַׁעַר הַגַּיְא וְעַל הַמִּקְצוֹעַ וַיְחַזְּקֵם: **וַיִּבֶן** מִגְדָּלִים בַּמִּדְבָּר **וַיַּחְצֹב** בֹּרוֹת רַבִּים[37]

[A]nd his fame **spread [R,E]** to the approaches of Egypt, for he grew exceedingly strong. Uzziah **built [R,E]** towers in Jerusalem on the Corner Gate and the Valley Gate and on the Angle, and fortified them. **He built [R,E]** towers in the wilderness and **hewed out** many cisterns. (2 Chr 26:8-10)

In all these passages, it is impossible to determine the exact chronological relationship between the actions. The list-like nature of these chains places the verbs on equal footing and thus precludes a definitive conclusion regarding the chronological order of these events.

4.3 The *Wayyiqtol* Form's Link to the Modal Axis
[+Indicative, +Realis, -Modal, -Habitual, -Iterative]

From the standpoint of the modal axis, *wayyiqtol* is an indicative form [+indicative]. In other words, it is a non-modal form [-modal] that signifies an actual action [+actual], which occurred in a determinate time and place. From this vantage point, *wayyiqtol* belongs to the same category as *qatal* and participle forms and is to be distinguished from the general modal (*yiqtol* and *weqatal*) and volitive (the cohortative, the imperative, and the jussive) forms. Just as *qatal* can be aligned with *yiqtol* in a modal context, *wayyiqtol* can appear alongside *weqatal* and volitive forms that denote succession (*waw* + volitive). The modal consecutive forms designate actions as non-actual [-actual], be it in the framework of the future (the action has yet to occur and thus cannot be actual), deontic modality (as noted above), or habitual actions (a generic action that cannot be pinned to a concrete time and place).

---

37. Also see 2 Chronicles 13:21; 21:1; 26:14-15; 29:6-7; 36:19.

To illustrate the differences between the various uses of the consecutive forms, we will examine a passage in which *wayyiqtol* forms alternate with modal consecutive forms:[38]

(I) = Indicative; (M) = Modal

(189) **וַיְדַבֵּר** יְהוָה אֶל מֹשֶׁה לֵךְ עֲלֵה מִזֶּה אַתָּה וְהָעָם אֲשֶׁר הֶעֱלִיתָ מֵאֶרֶץ מִצְרָיִם אֶל הָאָרֶץ אֲשֶׁר נִשְׁבַּעְתִּי לְאַבְרָהָם לְיִצְחָק וּלְיַעֲקֹב לֵאמֹר לְזַרְעֲךָ אֶתְּנֶנָּה: **וְשָׁלַחְתִּי** לְפָנֶיךָ מַלְאָךְ **וְגֵרַשְׁתִּי** אֶת הַכְּנַעֲנִי הָאֱמֹרִי וְהַחִתִּי וְהַפְּרִזִּי הַחִוִּי וְהַיְבוּסִי: אֶל אֶרֶץ זָבַת חָלָב וּדְבָשׁ כִּי לֹא אֶעֱלֶה בְּקִרְבְּךָ כִּי עַם קְשֵׁה עֹרֶף אַתָּה פֶּן אֲכֶלְךָ בַּדָּרֶךְ: **וַיִּשְׁמַע** הָעָם אֶת הַדָּבָר הָרָע הַזֶּה **וַיִּתְאַבָּלוּ** וְלֹא שָׁתוּ אִישׁ עֶדְיוֹ עָלָיו: **וַיֹּאמֶר** יְהוָה אֶל מֹשֶׁה אֱמֹר אֶל בְּנֵי יִשְׂרָאֵל אַתֶּם עַם קְשֵׁה עֹרֶף רֶגַע אֶחָד אֶעֱלֶה בְקִרְבְּךָ **וְכִלִּיתִיךָ** וְעַתָּה הוֹרֵד עֶדְיְךָ מֵעָלֶיךָ **וְאֵדְעָה** מָה אֶעֱשֶׂה לָּךְ: **וַיִּתְנַצְּלוּ** בְנֵי יִשְׂרָאֵל אֶת עֶדְיָם מֵהַר חוֹרֵב: וּמֹשֶׁה יִקַּח אֶת הָאֹהֶל **וְנָטָה** לוֹ מִחוּץ לַמַּחֲנֶה הַרְחֵק מִן הַמַּחֲנֶה **וְקָרָא** לוֹ אֹהֶל מוֹעֵד **וְהָיָה** כָּל מְבַקֵּשׁ יְהוָה יֵצֵא אֶל אֹהֶל מוֹעֵד אֲשֶׁר מִחוּץ לַמַּחֲנֶה: **וְהָיָה** כְּצֵאת מֹשֶׁה אֶל הָאֹהֶל יָקוּמוּ כָּל הָעָם **וְנִצְּבוּ** אִישׁ פֶּתַח אָהֳלוֹ **וְהִבִּיטוּ** אַחֲרֵי מֹשֶׁה עַד בֹּאוֹ הָאֹהֱלָה: **וְהָיָה** כְּבֹא מֹשֶׁה הָאֹהֱלָה יֵרֵד עַמּוּד הֶעָנָן **וְעָמַד** פֶּתַח הָאֹהֶל **וְדִבֶּר** עִם מֹשֶׁה: **וְרָאָה** כָל הָעָם אֶת עַמּוּד הֶעָנָן עֹמֵד פֶּתַח הָאֹהֶל **וְקָם** כָּל הָעָם **וְהִשְׁתַּחֲווּ** אִישׁ פֶּתַח אָהֳלוֹ: **וְדִבֶּר** יְהוָה אֶל מֹשֶׁה פָּנִים אֶל פָּנִים כַּאֲשֶׁר יְדַבֵּר אִישׁ אֶל רֵעֵהוּ **וְשָׁב** אֶל הַמַּחֲנֶה וּמְשָׁרְתוֹ יְהוֹשֻׁעַ בִּן נוּן נַעַר לֹא יָמִישׁ מִתּוֹךְ הָאֹהֶל: **וַיֹּאמֶר** מֹשֶׁה אֶל יְהוָה

Then the LORD **said [R,E]**[(I)] to Moses, Set out from here, you and the people that you have brought up from the land of Egypt, to the land of which I swore to Abraham, Isaac, and Jacob, saying, To your offspring will I give it—**I will send [R,E]**[(M)] an angel before you, and **I will drive [R,E]**[(M)] out the Canaanites, the Amorites, the Hittites, the Perizzites, the Hivites, and the Jebusites—a land flowing with milk and honey. But I will not go in your midst, since you are a stiffnecked people, lest I destroy you on the way. When the people **heard [R,E]**[(I)] this harsh word, they **went into mourning [R,E]** [(I)], and none put on his finery. The LORD **said [R,E]**[(I)] to Moses, Say to the Israelite people, you are a stiffnecked people. If I were to go in your midst for one moment, **I would destroy [R,E]**[(M)] you. Now, then, leave off your finery, and **I will consider [R,E]**[(M)] what to do to you. So the Israelites **remained [R,E]**[(I)] stripped of the finery from Mount Horeb. Moses would take the Tent and **would pitch [R,E]**[(M)] it outside the camp, at some distance from the camp. He **called [R,E]**[(M)] it the Tent of Meeting, and whoever **sought [R,E]** [(M)] the LORD would go out to the Tent of Meeting that was outside the camp. Whenever Moses **would go [R,E]**[(M)] out to the Tent, all the people would rise and **stand [R,E]**[(M)], each at the entrance of his tent, and **gaze [R,E]**[(M)] at Moses until he had entered the Tent. And when Moses **would enter [R,E]**[(M)] the Tent, the pillar of cloud would descend and **stand [R,E]**[(M)] at the entrance of the Tent, while **he spoke [R,E]**[(M)] with Moses. When all the people **would**

---

38. We are turning to an example from the First Temple period on account of the decline in the use of the *weqatal* form's use in Second Temple period Hebrew from both a contextual and syntactical standpoint (see §7 below).

see [R,E]$^{(M)}$ the pillar of cloud poised at the entrance of the Tent, all the people **would rise [R,E]**$^{(M)}$ and **bow [R,E]**$^{(M)}$ low, each at the entrance of his tent. The LORD **would speak [R,E]**$^{(M)}$ to Moses face to face, as one man speaks to another. And **he would** then **return [R,E]**$^{(M)}$ to the camp; but his attendant, Joshua son of Nun, a youth, would not stir out of the Tent. Moses **said [R,E]**$^{(I)}$ to the LORD (Ex 33:1-12)

This passage includes several transitions between indicative sequential *wayyiqtol* forms and various modal sequential forms. In the opening verse, "וידבר" denotes an actual action that reportedly transpired at a specific time and place. After establishing the fact that God spoke with Moses, verses 1 to 3 reveal the content of his words. The consecutive forms "ושלחתי" and "וגרשתי" mark the events as modal actions that have yet to occur. Verses 4 and 5 revert back to *wayyiqtol* forms: "וישמע", "ויתאבלו", and "ויאמר" inform the reader that the instances of hearing, grieving, and telling are actual actions that transpired in a determinate time and place. The second half of verse 5 fills in the content of God's message. At this juncture, there is another transition to modal consecutive forms that also signify deontic modality: "וכליתיך" is a warning and "ואדעה" is an expression of will. The *wayyiqtol* form resurfaces in the next verse with the objective of denoting an actual action, whereupon the text turns to the signification of iterative actions in the past. For the sake of marking the transition from the actuality of verse 6 to the habituality in verses 7 to 11, the author once again deploys modal consecutive forms, but this time they denote epistemic modality.[39] In other words, the actions in these verses are not actual; although they transpired on an intermittent basis, one cannot point to a definite time or place. Finally, the *wayyiqtol* form in verse 12 marks yet another return to actuality.

One of the phenomena in Biblical Hebrew prose that has long challenged scholars is that, unlike *qatal*, participle, *yiqtol*, and *weqatal* forms which can appear in every one of the absolute time realms (past, present, future), the *wayyiqtol* form express no other realm save for the absolute past.[40] This restriction, as well as the historical connection between *wayyiqtol* and the ancient preterite *yaqtul* form,

---

39. For more on the inclusion of habitual actions under the category of epistemic modality, see the discussion on *yiqtol*'s modal uses in §4.3 above.

40. There are practically no exceptions to this rule throughout the biblical prose of both the First and Second Temple periods. However, there are several instances of *wayyiqtol* forms donning the absolute future in poems and poetic prophecies; see Joüon and Muraoka (2006:§118s) and Waltke and O'Connor (1990:557). The poetic corpus warrants a closer look. One possible route is to examine whether these forms link up to the modal axis, of all things, rather than the R-time axis. If it can be shown that the connection to the modal axis underwent a modicum of obfuscation in these texts, then scholars may be able to account for the existence of these forms in the future.

which Bauer was the first of many to note, is responsible for the fact that many researchers consider *wayyiqtol* to be a past form. Against this background, should *wayyiqtol* be perceived as an exception that signifies the absolute past within a system entirely predicated on the expression of relative time? In accordance with Bauer's observation, the argument can be made that *wayyiqtol* constitutes a remnant of an earlier system. That said, the research would be better served by describing *wayyiqtol*'s synchronic usages within the framework of this system. The fact that *wayyiqtol* always appears, at least throughout biblical prose, in the absolute past is a direct result of its connection to both the reference-time and modal axes.[41] In other words, since *wayyiqtol* is an indicative form that denotes the relationship [R,E], it is limited to the past. This restriction stems from both the function of *wayyiqtol* and the emergence of a corresponding form, *weqatal*, which dominate the modal sphere in the biblical verbal system.

The suppletion that took root in consecutive forms—a pair of morphemes, *wayyiqtol* and *weqatal*, seized the indicative and modal fields, respectively—did not happen to any of the other forms. As a result, Biblical Hebrew writers resorted to using the *yiqtol* and *qatal* forms in a manner that somewhat contradicts their modal functions when expressing subsequence in the past, antecedence in the future, and other modal contexts.[42] The development of two parallel consecutive forms should enable scholars to make a clean break from the Hebrew language's earlier stages and explain why *wayyiqtol* forms only appear in the absolute past. Although the above-noted connection to the preterite (*yaqtul*) form is significant from a diachronic standpoint, focusing exclusively on this particular aspect diverts attention away from *wayyiqtol*'s synchronic function. A comprehensive review of *wayyiqtol*'s synchronic role cannot ignore the fact that, in stark contrast to the historical preterite, it forms a compound with the proclitic *waw* and is arrayed in a complementary distribution with the modal consecutive *weqatal* form.

Like the other verb forms in this system, the claim that *wayyiqtol* does not maintain a link to speech time (S>[E,R]) appears to be a more straightforward solution than the opposite approach due to the following reasons: similar to the rest of the biblical forms, *wayyiqtol* is only linked to one deictic axis—the reference-time axis [E,R]; and the form's "relegation" to the past is a direct corollary of its relation to the modal axis, namely the form's indicative meaning.

---

41. In this regard, we are following Hatav: "The interpretation of *wayyiqtol* in the past sphere only is entailed from the combination of its features [+SEQ] [-MOD]" (1997:84).

42. See §2.2.4 above, for more on the consequences of this constraint on these forms' paradigmatic functions.

4.4 Morphological Addendum—*Wa'eqtelah* as an Analogy of the Volitive System

In contrast to the syntactic sphere, the morphological differences between the Biblical Hebrew verbal system of the First and Second Temple periods are rather modest. Excludeing verb forms that end with the "paragogic *nun*" (e.g., יכתבון), which practically vanished from our corpus,[43] there are virtually no morphological differences between the verbal system of both eras. An exception to this rule is the prevalence of elongated *wayyiqtol* verb forms in the first person (*wa'eqtelah*) within the framework of the Second Temple period texts:

(190) וָאֶקְבְּצֵם אֶל הַנָּהָר הַבָּא אֶל אַהֲוָא וַנַּחֲנֶה שָׁם יָמִים שְׁלֹשָׁה **וָאָבִינָה** בָעָם וּבַכֹּהֲנִים וּמִבְּנֵי לֵוִי לֹא מָצָאתִי שָׁם: **וָאֶשְׁלְחָה** לֶאֱלִיעֶזֶר לַאֲרִיאֵל לִשְׁמַעְיָה וּלְאֶלְנָתָן וּלְיָרִיב וּלְאֶלְנָתָן וּלְנָתָן וְלִזְכַרְיָה וְלִמְשֻׁלָּם רָאשִׁים וּלְיוֹיָרִיב וּלְאֶלְנָתָן מְבִינִים: ואוצאה (**וָאֲצַוֶּה**) אוֹתָם עַל אִדּוֹ הָרֹאשׁ בְּכָסִפְיָא הַמָּקוֹם **וָאָשִׂימָה** בְּפִיהֶם דְּבָרִים לְדַבֵּר אֶל אִדּוֹ אָחִיו הנתונים (הַנְּתִינִים) בְּכָסִפְיָא הַמָּקוֹם לְהָבִיא לָנוּ מְשָׁרְתִים לְבֵית אֱלֹהֵינוּ:

These I assembled by the river that enters Ahava, and we encamped there for three days. **I reviewed [R,E]**(+ה) the people and the priests, but I did not find any Levites there. **I sent [R,E]**(+ה) for Eliezer, Ariel, Shemaiah, Elnathan, Jarib, Elnathan, Nathan, Zechariah, and Meshullam, the leading men, and also for Joiarib and Elnathan, the instructors, and **I gave [R,E]**(+ה) them an order for Iddo, the leader at the place *called* Casiphia. **I gave [R,E]**(+ה) them a message to convey to Iddo *and* his brother, temple-servants at the place *called* Casiphia, that they should bring us attendants for the house of our God. (Ezr 8:15-17)

On the other hand, there are also instances of the normal form:

(191) **וָאַעֲמִיד** מִתַּחְתִּיּוֹת לַמָּקוֹם מֵאַחֲרֵי לַחוֹמָה בצחחיים (בַּצְּחִחִים) **וָאַעֲמִיד** אֶת הָעָם לְמִשְׁפָּחוֹת עִם חַרְבֹתֵיהֶם רָמְחֵיהֶם וְקַשְּׁתֹתֵיהֶם: **וָאֵרֶא וָאָקוּם וָאֹמַר** אֶל הַחֹרִים וְאֶל הַסְּגָנִים וְאֶל יֶתֶר הָעָם אַל תִּירְאוּ מִפְּנֵיהֶם. . . . וַיְהִי כַּאֲשֶׁר שָׁמְעוּ אוֹיְבֵינוּ כִּי נוֹדַע לָנוּ וַיָּפֶר הָאֱלֹהִים אֶת עֲצָתָם **ונשוב (וַנָּשָׁב)** כֻּלָּנוּ אֶל הַחוֹמָה אִישׁ אֶל מְלַאכְתּוֹ. . . . **וָאֹמַר** אֶל הַחֹרִים וְאֶל הַסְּגָנִים

I stationed [R,E] on the lower levels of the place, behind the walls, on the bare rock—**I stationed [R,E]** the people by families with their swords, their lances, and their bows. Then **I beheld [the situation] [R,E] and got up [R,E] and said [R,E]** to the nobles, the prefects, and the rest of the people, Do not be afraid of them! . . . When our enemies learned that it had become known to us, and God had thus frustrated their plan, **we all returned [R,E]** to the wall, each to his work. . . . **I said [R,E]** to the nobles, the prefects . . . (Neh 4:7-13)

In total, we documented 64 occurrences of *wa'eqtelah* forms in the first person as opposed to 59 *wa'eqtol* forms. There is no evident condition or rule that governs

---

43. See Joüon and Muraoka (2006:§44e-f).

the rotation between these forms, as they are apparently substituted in an unregimented fashion. According to Bergsträsser, a bird's-eye view of ancient Hebrew shows that the first and third person were used interchangeably, and the distinct form was merely acquired on a secondary basis due to an analogy from the volitive system (1929:§5d).

Talshir (1987) discusses this phenomenon at length. Building upon Bergsträsser's hypothesis, he claims that the picture that arises from the biblical texts is complex. A few exceptions notwithstanding, he avers that classical Hebrew (especially the Pentateuch) still preserved the morphological distinction between the first and other two persons (ibid.:591).[44] As evidenced from the language on the Mesha Stele, this account probably applies to the archaic state of these forms as well (ibid.:589). By dint of the clear morphological link between the sequential and the jussive forms, the modal system underwent an analogy at a later phase:

יקם: ויקם = אקומה: ? (ואקומה)

Our knowledge of the Second Temple period's elongated forms derives from their relative abundance in the Masoretic texts from the Second Temple period[45] as well as the Samaritan Pentateuch, where there are many elongated forms in the first person. For instance, while the Masoretic version of Deuteronomy 22:14 opts for "ואקרב", the Samaritan version goes with "ואקרבה" (ibid.:590). What was a growing phenomenon in the Second Temple period prose becomes the rule in the Hebrew of Qumran. In all that concerns the sectarian texts, Qimron (1986:45-46) shows that only the elongated forms were conjugated in the first person:

wa'eqtelah // wattiqtol wayyiqtol
(Waw + cohortative // wetiqtol weyiqtol)

In light of the above, we can divide the development of the elongated form into four stages:
1. During the earliest known phase (the Mesha Stele), yiqtol's configuration was the same in all the persons.
2. During the second phase (the Hebrew of the First Temple period), there are sporadic attestations of the wa'eqtelah form.

---

44. The modal system in the pre-biblical stage is beyond the scope of this book. In consequence, Talshir's postulation will not be examined herein. With respect to the question of the plene forms (ואקום) vis-à-vis the defective forms (ואקם), Talshir shows that there is a difference between First and Second Temple period Hebrew, at least with respect to the ketiv (what is written).
45. According to Talshir (1987:589), about two thirds of the elongated form's 90 occurrences in the Hebrew Bible turn up in the Second Temple period prose. Our own survey has indeed confirmed this figure.

3. During the third stage (Biblical Hebrew of the Second Temple period and the Samaritan Pentateuch), the morphological distinction between the first person and the other persons steadily coalesces, to the extent where the truncated and elongated forms are used interchangeably (52% of the former and 48% of the latter in our corpus).

4. In the final phase (Qumran), *wa'eqtelah* becomes the exclusive means for conjugating the first person.

5. Usages of the Participle in the Hebrew of the Second Temple Period

5.1 Introduction

The participle form is associated with more than one paradigm. From a morphological standpoint, the participle is an adjective. Therefore, in contrast to other verb forms, it is not conjugated in accordance to person, but corresponds to the noun with respect to gender, number, and definiteness. As a result, researchers have long tended to discuss the participle within the framework of the nominal sentence rather than the Biblical Hebrew tense system.[1] In contrast, Joosten (1989) and Hatav (1997:89-116) claim that it is impossible to provide an exhaustive synchronic description of the Biblical Hebrew verbal system without including the participle within the framework of the verbal paradigm. The assumption that the participle is part of the biblical verbal tense system constitutes a working hypothesis of this book.

Participles filling predicative usages are a general linguistic phenomenon that has been well documented in many languages. In this context, it is worth enumerating those languages that contain nominal sentences. The family of Semitic languages has multiple examples in which the participle has evolved into a part of the verbal conjugation system. In fact, this process was apparently responsible for the creation of the *qatal* form at a nascent stage in the development of these languages. Moreover, the Akkadian stative as well as the inflexion of the participle in modern Aramaic dialects developed along similar lines.[2] Unlike the Akkadian stative and the participle in modern Aramaic dialects, Biblical Hebrew eschewed a full-fledged conjugational system; yet this does not justify the Hebrew participle's exclusion from the verbal system. The participle's adnominal and predicative usages do not run counter to each other but have mutual links, some of which are illustrated in the following examples:

(192) יְהֹוָה אֲשֶׁר הֶעֱלָה אֶתְכֶם מֵאֶרֶץ מִצְרַיִם

The LORD, who brought (אשר+קטל) you out of the land of Egypt (2 Kgs 17:36)

əgzi"abəher *zä'awṣə'akkəmu* əmmədrä gəbṣ

τῷ κυρίῳ, ὃς ἀνήγαγεν
ὑμᾶς ἐκ γῆς Αἰγύπτου

---

1. See, for example, Gesenius, Kautzsch, and Cowley (1910).
2. See Goldenberg (1983) with respect to new Aramaic, Huehnergard (1987) with respect to Akkadian, and D. Cohen (1984) on the verbalization process in Semitic languages.

(193) יְהוָה הַמַּעֲלֶה אֶתְכֶם מֵאֶרֶץ מִצְרָיִם

For I the LORD am he who **brought (קוטל+ה)** you up from the land of Egypt
(Lv 11:45)

əgzi'abəher zä'awṣə'akkəmu əmmədrä gəbṣ   κύριος ὁ ἀναγαγὼν ὑμᾶς ἐκ
γῆς Αἰγύπτου

(194) אֲנָשִׁים הַהֹשִׁיבוּ נָשִׁים נָכְרִיּוֹת

[M]en who had **brought (קטל+ה)** home foreign women (Ezr 10:17)

In the first example, the adjectival clause hosts a conjugated verb ("העלה"),
whereas the similar clause in example 193 has a participial form that is placed
after a definite article. The difference between an adjectival clause and an adjective is accentuated in the Septuagint. However, these two expressions can easily
be translated into a clause containing an inflected verb in languages where a relative structure is the most prevalent and readily available choice (see Goldenberg
1983:2), such as the Geez translation of the Jewish scriptures. The same process
occurs in example 194, only in the opposite direction: the clause containing an
inflected verb undergoes a process of nominalization or, more precisely, a process of adjectivization,[3] as the verb is headed by a definite article rather than a
relative pronoun.[4]

As early as the Middle Ages, some grammarians opined that the participle is
situated between the *qatal* and *yiqtol* forms and denotes the present.[5] This view is
still supported by scholars today. For example, Joosten (1989) contends that the
fundamental purpose of the participle is to express the real present and that the rest
of its meanings derive from this function.[6] On the other hand, grammarians such
as Gesenius, Kautzsch, and Cowley (1910:§116d) and Bergsträsser (1929:§13b)
have averred that the participle's basic function is to denote a relationship of simultaneity, while its position along the time axis is discerned from the context.
According to Hatav (1997:103-116), the term "simultaneity" (signifying the fact
that an action expressed by, say, the participle form takes place at the same time
as the reference time R=E) is not precise enough for describing the participle's usages in Biblical Hebrew, for *qatal* and *yiqtol* are also likely to express categories

---

3. Goldenberg discusses a similar process in Ethiopian languages (1983b:2).
4. This phenomenon is one of the hallmarks of Second Temple period Hebrew; see Gesenius, Kautzsch, and Cowley (1996:§145d).
5. For example, Saadia Gaon and Abraham ibn Ezra. The latter divides the participle's
   tenses into the past, present (standing present), and future (see our discussion on the
   medieval grammarians in §2.2.2 above).
6. Joosten distinguishes between the subject-participle and participle-subject alignments.
   This distinction elucidates the contrast between the actual and factual. Joosten's contention refers to the subject-participle alignment.

of simultaneity. Instead, Hatav singles out the participle form as a signifier of the relationship of inclusion. As opposed to simultaneity, inclusion refers to an action that encompasses its own reference time. In other words, the action begins before the reference time and will end after it has expired. The diagram below outlines this relationship:

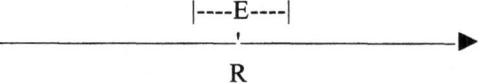

Following Hatav, we demonstrate that inclusion is one of the participle form's basic functions, albeit with one important reservation: Hatav likens the participle's functions in Biblical Hebrew to those of the English progressive ("-ing"). However, this analogy is only partially justified, for the English progressive runs counter to verb forms that are not progressive. For example, the distinction in English between the simple present and present progressive does not exist in Hebrew.[7] As we will see, the participle form's primary task is to express the relationship of inclusion, but in certain contexts it can also signify an "uninclusive" relationship of simultaneity.[8] For instance, expressing a "performative" meaning by means of the participle corresponds to the English simple present and not to the present progressive. Consequently, drawing an analogy between a form in a verbal system that is informed by a clear distinction between progressive and non-progressive paradigms, on the one hand, and a form that serves in a system lacking this sort of differentiation, on the other, is problematic.

In contrast to the First Temple period, one of the most significant innovations that pertain to the Hebrew participle in the Second Temple period is the proliferation of its habitual usage (the habitual present or an iterative action in the past). Hatav (1997:109) has shown that the habitual use of participle forms in classical Biblical Hebrew is scarce (4% of the total occurrences), but that this function becomes rather commonplace in the Second Temple period biblical texts (we found 135 occurrences of this usage in our corpus, comprising 44.12% of the total[9]).

---

7. See Bybee (1994:133-134) for more on the distinction between these two paradigms in English.
8. According to Comrie (1985:36-41), the difference between a relationship of simultaneity and a relationship of inclusion is not very significant with respect to the present tense. In most languages, instances of absolute simultaneity are rare, so that present forms are likely to denote a relationship of simultaneity with the S-time point, while ignoring the question of whether the action is on-going.
9. The statistical breakdown of the 306 predicative occurrences of the participle form in the Second Temple period texts is as follows: 87 habitual present (28.43%); 48 iterative action in the past (15.69%); 49 real present (15.85%); 87 inclusion in the past (28.43%); 16 inclusion in the future (5.22%); 8 near future (2.61%); 5 simultaneity in the past (1.63%); and 6 problematic cases (1.96%).

Joosten (1989) shows that there is a clear distinction between subject-participle and participle-subject sequences in classical Biblical Hebrew. For example:

(195) קוֹל עַנּוֹת **אָנֹכִי שֹׁמֵעַ** :

It is the sound of song that **I hear**! (Ex 32:18)

(196) דַּבֶּר נָא אֶל עֲבָדֶיךָ אֲרָמִית כִּי **שֹׁמְעִים אֲנָחְנוּ** וְאַל תְּדַבֵּר עִמָּנוּ יְהוּדִית

Please, speak to your servants in Aramaic, for **we understand** it; do not speak to us in Judean. (2 Kgs 18:26)

According to Joosten, in the verse from Exodus, the speaker simply expresses what he is hearing at actual present, whereas in the second example the subjects are referring to what they are capable of hearing at that moment should the interlocutor speak. However, this distinction is undermined during the Second Temple period due to the profusion of the habitual usage, as neither the habitual present nor an iterative action in the past can be considered "actual."

The participle's habitual usage constitutes a theoretical challenge in all that concerns its relation with *yiqtol* and the infinitive construct, for all three verb forms essentially vie over the "habitual action slot" during this period. This overlap comes to expression in the way these forms replace one another in habitual contexts:

(197) וּבְכָל מְדִינָה וּמְדִינָה מָקוֹם אֲשֶׁר דְּבַר הַמֶּלֶךְ וְדָתוֹ **מַגִּיעַ** אֵבֶל גָּדוֹל לַיְּהוּדִים
וְצוֹם וּבְכִי וּמִסְפֵּד שַׂק וָאֵפֶר **יֻצַּע** לָרַבִּים :

Also, in every province that the king's command and decree **would reach (participle)**, there was great mourning among the Jews, with fasting, weeping, and wailing, and everybody **used to be offered (*yiqtol*)** a sackcloth and ashes. (Est 4:3)

(198) וַיִּסָּפְרוּ הַלְוִיִּם מִבֶּן שְׁלֹשִׁים שָׁנָה וָמַעְלָה וַיְהִי מִסְפָּרָם לְגֻלְגְּלֹתָם לִגְבָרִים
שְׁלֹשִׁים וּשְׁמוֹנָה אָלֶף : מֵאֵלֶּה **לְנַצֵּחַ** עַל מְלֶאכֶת בֵּית יְהוָה עֶשְׂרִים וְאַרְבָּעָה אָלֶף
וְשֹׁטְרִים וְשֹׁפְטִים שֵׁשֶׁת אֲלָפִים : וְאַרְבַּעַת אֲלָפִים שֹׁעֲרִים וְאַרְבַּעַת אֲלָפִים **מְהַלְלִים**
לַיהוָה בַּכֵּלִים אֲשֶׁר עָשִׂיתִי לְהַלֵּל :

The Levites, from the age of thirty and upward, were counted; the head-count of their males was 38000: of these 24000 **would be charged (infinitive construct)** with the work of the House of the LORD, 6000 officers and magistrates, 4000 gatekeepers, and 4000 **would praise (participle)** the LORD with instruments I devised for singing praises. (1 Chr 23:3-5)

(199) וַיֵּצֵא אֶל פָּנָיו יֵהוּא בֶן חֲנָנִי הַחֹזֶה וַיֹּאמֶר אֶל הַמֶּלֶךְ יְהוֹשָׁפָט הֲלָרָשָׁע **לַעְזֹר**
וּלְשֹׂנְאֵי יְהוָה **תֶּאֱהָב**

Jehu son of Hanani the seer went out to meet King Jehoshaphat and said to him, **Should you give aid (infinitive construct)** to the wicked and **befriend (*yiqtol*)** those who hate the LORD? (2 Chr 19:2)

At first glance, it would appear as though there has been a certain degree of neutralization between the usages of these forms, and this possibility is liable to raise doubts as to the nature of their link to the modal axis. In our discussion on *yiqtol* and infinitive construct forms, the argument was made that their function as signifiers of the habitual present and an iterative action in the past is part of their modal meaning. If this is indeed the case, does the participle assume a modal role in the Hebrew of the Second Temple period? The answer to this question is, in all likelihood, no. The assertion whereby the habitual meaning of *yiqtol* and the infinitive construct constitutes but one of several roles that these forms fill is largely predicated on the fact that the rest of their usages can also be said to fall under the modal category; however, the same cannot be said for the participle.

In his disquisition on habitual actions, Comrie (1985:40) claims that habitual meanings straddle the border between tense, aspectuality, and modality. This argument is predicated on the fact that habituality enables the reader to discern the following elements: the location of the action on the time axis (tense); the internal features of the action (aspect); and the speaker's attitude toward the action (mood). Since various languages use habitual forms in different systems, it can be said that, within the context of Second Temple period Hebrew, habituality comprises part of the link to either the modal (the infinitive construct and *yiqtol*) or reference-time (the participle form) axis.

A survey of the participle's relation to the modal axis reveals that, with the exception of its habitual usage, the form is not connected to any of the other modal meanings, and it is essentially an indicative form.[10] Despite its penetration into the field of habituality, the assumption that the participle is first and foremost an indicative form is bolstered by the fact that it does not signify the language of the law—a category that fills the gap between deontic modality and habituality—throughout the Second Temple era.[11] In this regard, there is an appreciable difference between Biblical Hebrew of the Second Temple period and Mishnaic Hebrew, where the participle form is used in unequivocally modal contexts, such as the future and the language of the law (Azar 1995:20; Mishor 1983:272-274; and Sharvit 1980:117). For example, the participle serves in modal contexts within the framework of the language of the law in the following passages from the *Mishna*:

1. **מַזְכִּירִין** גְּבוּרוֹת גְּשָׁמִים בִּתְחִיַּת הַמֵּתִים **וְשׁוֹאֲלִין** הַגְּשָׁמִים בְּבִרְכַּת הַשָּׁנִים

State (law) the power of the rains in who revives the dead and **ask (law)** for the rains in the Blessing of the Seasons. (Berakhot 5:2)

2. **דָּשִׁים וְזוֹרִין וְדוֹרְכִין וּמְעַמְּרִין** אֲבָל לֹא **קוֹצְרִין** וְלֹא **בּוֹצְרִין** וְלֹא **מוֹסְקִין**

---

10. For an in-depth discussion on this matter, see §5.3 below.
11. See the discussion on the language of the law in the chapter on *yiqtol* in §6.3.2.2 below.

One may thresh (law), winnow (law), tread (law) and **bind (law)**, but not **harvest (law)**, nor **gather (law)** grapes nor **pick (law)** olives. (Shevi'it 6:2)

3. הַמְקַבֵּל עָלָיו לִהְיוֹת חָבֵר אֵינוֹ **מוֹכֵר** לְעַם הָאָרֶץ לַח וְיָבֵשׁ וְאֵינוֹ **לוֹקֵחַ** מִמֶּנּוּ לַח וְאֵינוֹ **מִתְאָרֵחַ** אֵצֶל עַם הָאָרֶץ וְלֹא **מְאָרְחוֹ** אֶצְלוֹ בִּכְסוּתוֹ

Whoever undertakes to become a member **may not sell (law)** to an '*am ha'aretz* anything moist or dry, nor **may he buy (law)** from him anything moist, and he **may not be the guest (law)** of an *am ha'aretz*, nor **may he receive (law)** him as his guest in his garments. (Demai 2:3)

In contrast to *yiqtol* and the infinitive construct, the participle can be viewed as a broadening of the relationship of inclusion. Accordingly, compared to other forms, the participle's usage in this context appears to extend the duration of an action:

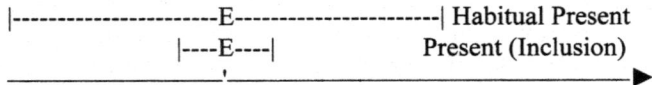

Although the purviews of *yiqtol*, the infinitive construct, and the participle mildly overlap with respect to the expression of habituality, they did not reach this position from the same point of departure. In light of the above, the roles that are filled by the participle in the Second Temple period texts can be said to engender a situation that vastly differs from both the classical Hebrew of the Bible and Mishnaic Hebrew.

5.2 The Participle Link to Reference Time

5.2.1 Inclusion

A relationship of inclusion refers to a situation in which the denoted action's duration contains its own reference time. According to Hatav, the signification of inclusion is the participle form's principal meaning in classical Biblical Hebrew (1997:103-106). Like the *qatal* and *yiqtol* forms, the participle belongs to the relative tense system. In other words, it does not bear its own reference time (unlike the sequential forms) and is capable of expressing a relationship of inclusion with an event that is situated in the present, past, or future. The difference between a verb that signifies either habituality or a situation and a relationship of inclusion is not always crystal clear. As noted above, the transition from inclusion to habituality or a situation involves a broadening of an action's duration. Concomitantly, the habitual present or situation can be interpreted as marking a relationship of inclusion, for the scenario that is depicted also applies to the moment of speech. As we will soon see, the Second Temple period bears witness to a substantial rise in the habitual use of the participle form.

5.2.1.1 Relationships of Inclusion in the Present—the Real Present

One of the participial form's most common tasks in the Hebrew of the Second Temple period is the signification of the real present, and inclusion is indeed the most prevalent temporal relationship in this category. Although there are instances where the real present denotes simultaneity, these are rare and limited to specific contextual frameworks.[12] One natural environment for this particular usage is direct speech:

(200) וָאוֹמַר אֲלֵהֶם אַתֶּם **רֹאִים** הָרָעָה אֲשֶׁר אֲנַחְנוּ בָהּ

Then I said to them, You **see** (|--E--|) the bad state we are in. (Neh 2:17)
R

(201) וָאֶשְׁלְחָה עֲלֵיהֶם מַלְאָכִים לֵאמֹר מְלָאכָה גְדוֹלָה אֲנִי **עֹשֶׂה** וְלֹא אוּכַל לָרֶדֶת

I sent them messengers, saying, I **am engaged** (|--E--|) in a great work and cannot come down. (Neh 6:3)
R

(202) וָאָרִיבָה אֶת חֹרֵי יְהוּדָה וָאֹמְרָה לָהֶם. . . . וְאַתֶּם **מוֹסִיפִים** חָרוֹן עַל יִשְׂרָאֵל
לְחַלֵּל אֶת הַשַּׁבָּת :

I censured the nobles of Judah, saying to them.... [A]nd now you **give** (|--E--|)
R
cause for further wrath against Israel by profaning the sabbath! (Neh 13:17-18)

In these examples, the participle is employed in the main sentence of direct speech,[13] but the form conveys the same meaning in attributive clauses (examples 203-205) and content clauses (206-207) as well:[14]

(203) תְּהִי נָא אָזְנְךָ קַשֶּׁבֶת וְעֵינֶיךָ פְתוּחוֹת לִשְׁמֹעַ אֶל תְּפִלַּת עַבְדְּךָ אֲשֶׁר אָנֹכִי
מִתְפַּלֵּל לְפָנֶיךָ הַיּוֹם

Let your ear be attentive and your eyes open to receive the prayer of your servant that I **am praying** (|--E--|) to you now. (Neh 1:6)
R

---

12. See the discussion on participle forms that express a relationship of simultaneity: §5.2.2 below.
13. Also see Daniel 1:10; 9:18; Nehemiah 2:2; 5:7; 6:6; 2 Chronicles 28:10.
14. For more on the particle הנה in its capacity as the "opening particle" of content clauses, see Kogut (1987).

(204) וַיֹּאמֶר (וָאֹמַר) לֹא טוֹב הַדָּבָר אֲשֶׁר אַתֶּם **עֹשִׂים**

So I continued, What you **are doing** (|--E--|) is not right. (Neh 5:9)

R

(205) וָאָרִיבָה אֵת חֹרֵי יְהוּדָה וָאֹמְרָה לָהֶם מָה הַדָּבָר הָרָע הַזֶּה אֲשֶׁר אַתֶּם **עֹשִׂים**

I censured the nobles of Judah, saying to them, What evil thing is this that you
are doing (|--E--|)? (Neh 13:17)

R

(206) וַיֹּאמְרוּ נַעֲרֵי הַמֶּלֶךְ אֵלָיו הִנֵּה הָמָן **עֹמֵד** בֶּחָצֵר וַיֹּאמֶר הַמֶּלֶךְ יָבוֹא :

Haman **is standing** (|--E--|) in the court, the king's servants answered

R

him. Let him enter, said the king. (Est 6:5)

(207) וַיֹּאמֶר חַרְבוֹנָה אֶחָד מִן הַסָּרִיסִים לִפְנֵי הַמֶּלֶךְ גַּם הִנֵּה הָעֵץ . . . **עֹמֵד** בְּבֵית
הָמָן גָּבֹהַּ חֲמִשִּׁים אַמָּה

Then Harbonah, one of the eunuchs in attendance on the king, said . . . a stake
is standing (|--E--|) at Haman's house, fifty cubits high. (Est 7:9)

R

Another context in which the participle form is used to denote the present is interrogative sentences:

(208) וַיֹּאמְרוּ עַבְדֵי הַמֶּלֶךְ אֲשֶׁר בְּשַׁעַר הַמֶּלֶךְ לְמָרְדֳּכָי מַדּוּעַ אַתָּה **עוֹבֵר** אֵת מִצְוַת
הַמֶּלֶךְ :

Then the king's courtiers who were in the palace gate said to Mordecai, Why
do you **disobey** (|--E--|) the king's order? (Est 3:3)

R

(209) וַיֹּאמֶר לִי הַמֶּלֶךְ עַל מַה זֶּה אַתָּה **מְבַקֵּשׁ**

The king said to me, What are you **asking** (|--E--|) for? (Neh 2:4)

R

(210) וַיֹּאמְרוּ מָה הַדָּבָר הַזֶּה אֲשֶׁר אַתֶּם **עֹשִׂים** הַעַל הַמֶּלֶךְ אַתֶּם **מֹרְדִים** :

[A]nd they said, What is this that you **are doing** (|--E--|)? **Are** you
rebelling (|--E--|) against the king? (Neh 2:19)   R

R

To enhance our understanding of this phenomenon, it is worth comparing the use of the participle form in question sentences within the framework of our corpus to the use of *yiqtol* in classical Hebrew:[15]

(211) וַיִּמְצָאֵהוּ אִישׁ וְהִנֵּה תֹעֶה בַּשָּׂדֶה וַיִּשְׁאָלֵהוּ הָאִישׁ לֵאמֹר מַה **תְּבַקֵּשׁ** :

[A] man came upon him wandering in the fields. The man asked him, What **are you looking ((S=)E=R)** for? (Gn 37:15)

(212) וַיֹּאמֶר בּוֹא בְּרוּךְ יְהֹוָה לָמָּה **תַעֲמֹד** בַּחוּץ וְאָנֹכִי פִּנִּיתִי הַבַּיִת וּמָקוֹם לַגְּמַלִּים :

Come in, O blessed of the LORD, he said, why **do you remain ((S=)E=R)** outside, when I have made ready the house and a place for the camels? (Gn 24:31)

(213) וַתִּבְכֶּה וְלֹא תֹאכַל : וַיֹּאמֶר לָהּ אֶלְקָנָה אִישָׁהּ חַנָּה לָמֶה **תִבְכִּי** וְלָמֶה **לֹא תֹאכְלִי**

[A]nd she wept and would not eat. Her husband Elkanah said to her, Hannah, why **are you crying ((S=)E=R)** and why **aren't you eating ((S=)E=R)**? (1 Sm 1:7-8)

Most grammarians realized that the role of *yiqtol* in these instances is anomalous, for they can be understood as expressing the present. What, then, is the difference between *yiqtol* and participle forms in these scenarios? The answer is reminiscent of the one we proposed for the question concerning the difference between *yiqtol* and participle forms that denote habitual actions in the Second Temple period, as these cases also entail a certain degree of neutralization between the usages of these two forms. However, here too, each form reached this usage via a unique path: The use of *yiqtol* in question sentences,[16] which can be interpreted as running parallel to speech time, constitutes an extension of the form's latent modal meaning, namely the signification of the chronological relation R=E. On the other hand, the use of participle forms in similar contexts has widened the relationship of inclusion with speech time (i.e., the real present) to the modal field of question sentences, which have undergone a fair share of de-actualization.

5.2.1.2 Relationships of Inclusion in the Past

Similar to the relative functions of *qatal* and *yiqtol* forms, the participle form is not limited to expressing the real present (in which the reference time runs parallel to speech time), but can also be situated in the realm of the past or future. Hatav (1997:103-116) asserts that the participle's main function in classical Biblical He-

---

15. We have not found an exact parallel to this usage in our corpus. In questions, *yiqtol* forms are used to mark feasibility/unviability; see §6.3.1.1.1 below.
16. Grammarians tend to classify question sentences in the modal field; see Palmer (2001:11-12), inter alios.

brew is to signify relationships of inclusion. This usage is rather commonplace in our corpus too (87 occurrences), where it appears in several contexts: main sentences (examples 214-215 below),[17] content clauses (examples 216-217),[18] causal clauses (218),[19] circumstantial clauses (219),[20] and attributive clauses (220-221):[21]

(214) וַיֹּאמֶר לִי הַמֶּלֶךְ וְהַשֵּׁגַל **יוֹשֶׁבֶת** אֶצְלוֹ עַד מָתַי יִהְיֶה מַהֲלָכְךָ וּמָתַי תָּשׁוּב

[T]he king said to me while his concubine **was sitting** (|--E--|) with him, How
                                                                    R
long will you be gone and when will you return? (Neh 2:6)

(215) וַיִּשְׁלַח סַנְבַלַּט וְגֶשֶׁם אֵלַי לֵאמֹר לְכָה וְנִוָּעֲדָה יַחְדָּו בַּכְּפִירִים בְּבִקְעַת אוֹנוֹ
וְהֵמָּה **חֹשְׁבִים** לַעֲשׂוֹת לִי רָעָה׃

Sanballat and Geshem sent a message to me, saying, Come, let us get together in Kephirim in the Ono valley; while at the same time they **were planning** (|--E--|) to do me harm. (Neh 6:2)
                                                      R

(216) וַיִּשְׁמְעוּ צָרֵי יְהוּדָה וּבִנְיָמִן כִּי בְנֵי הַגּוֹלָה **בּוֹנִים** הֵיכָל לַיהוָה אֱלֹהֵי יִשְׂרָאֵל׃

When the adversaries of Judah and Benjamin heard that the returned exiles **were building** (|--E--|) a temple to the LORD God of Israel. (Ezr 4:1)
                                                                    R

(217) וָאֶשּׁוֹב וָאָבוֹא בְּשַׁעַר הַגַּיְא וָאָשׁוּב׃ וְהַסְּגָנִים לֹא יָדְעוּ אָנָה הָלַכְתִּי וּמָה אֲנִי **עֹשֶׂה**

So I went up the wadi by night, surveying the wall, and, entering again by the Valley Gate, I returned. The prefects knew nothing of where I had gone or what I **was doing** (|--E--|). (Neh 2:15-16)
                                                                    R

(218) וַיָּקָם עֶזְרָא מִלִּפְנֵי בֵּית הָאֱלֹהִים וַיֵּלֶךְ אֶל לִשְׁכַּת יְהוֹחָנָן בֶּן אֶלְיָשִׁיב וַיֵּלֶךְ שָׁם
לֶחֶם לֹא אָכַל וּמַיִם לֹא שָׁתָה כִּי **מִתְאַבֵּל** עַל מַעַל הַגּוֹלָה׃

---

17. Also see Esther 2:19, 20, 21; 5:1; Ezra 9:4; Nehemiah 8:7; 1 Chronicles 15:27; 2 Chronicles 5:12; 7:3, 6; 13:14; 20:13; 29:28; 30:16, 22; 33:17; 35:11, 24.
18. Also see Esther 3:5; Daniel 8:6; 12:5; Nehemiah 3:33.
19. Also see Esther 9:4; Ezra 3:13; Nehemiah 8:9.
20. Also see Daniel 9:20, 21; Ezra 10:1.
21. The appearance of a participle form after a definite article that serves as a relative pronoun strengthens the connection to the form's original function—an adjective. However, this fact does not obfuscate the inclusion, which constitutes the fundamental chronological relationship that this form signifies. Also see Esther 1:10; Daniel 8:13; Ezra 8:25; Nehemiah 12:44; 1 Chronicles 4:40; 2 Chronicles 20:22; 21:17; 26:7; 28:9, 12, 23; 30:21.

Then Ezra rose from his place in front of the House of God and went into the chamber of Jehohanan son of Eliashib; there, he ate no bread and drank no water, for he **was in mourning** (|--E--|) over the trespass of those who had returned from exile. (Ezr 10:6)   **R**

(219) עוֹדָם **מְדַבְּרִים** עִמּוֹ וְסָרִיסֵי הַמֶּלֶךְ הִגִּיעוּ וַיַּבְהִלוּ לְהָבִיא אֶת הָמָן

While **they were** still **speaking** (|--E--|) with him, the king's eunuchs arrived
R
and hurriedly brought Haman (Est 6:14)

(220) וּבִמְלוֹאת הַיָּמִים הָאֵלֶּה עָשָׂה הַמֶּלֶךְ לְכָל הָעָם **הַנִּמְצְאִים** בְּשׁוּשַׁן הַבִּירָה לְמִגָּדוֹל וְעַד קָטָן מִשְׁתֶּה שִׁבְעַת יָמִים

At the end of this period, the king gave a banquet for seven days for all the people who **lived** (|--E--|) in the fortress Shushan, high and low alike. (Est 1:5)
R

(221) וַיְהִי בְּצֵאת הַכֹּהֲנִים מִן הַקֹּדֶשׁ כִּי כָּל הַכֹּהֲנִים **הַנִּמְצְאִים** הִתְקַדָּשׁוּ אֵין לִשְׁמוֹר לְמַחְלְקוֹת:

When the priests came out of the Sanctuary—all the priests who **were present** (|--E--|) had sanctified themselves, without keeping to the set divisions.
R   (2 Chr 5:11)

The chronological relationship in all these passages can be outlined thus:

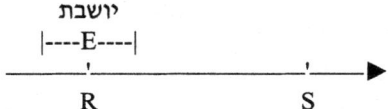

Joosten discusses cases in which the participle denotes the historic present (1989:142-144). This phenomenon is tied to the particular outlook of the text's author. Within a narrative succession, the author may refer to what are essentially past events as if they are currently in progress. For example:[22]

(222) וַיְהִי בִּרְאֹתִי אֲנִי דָנִיֵּאל אֶת הֶחָזוֹן וָאֲבַקְשָׁה בִינָה וְהִנֵּה **עֹמֵד** לְנֶגְדִּי כְּמַרְאֵה גָבֶר:

While I, Daniel, was seeing the vision, and trying to understand it, there **appeared** (|--E--|) before me one who looked like a man. (Dn 8:15)
R

---

22. In principle, this usage can be classified under either the real present or past realm.

5.2.1.3   Relationships of Inclusion in the Future

As argued above, the participle can maintain a relationship of inclusion in the future on account of its relative characteristics:[23]

(223) וְיַעַשׂ הַבָּא אֵלָיו כִּרְצוֹנוֹ וְאֵין **עוֹמֵד** לְפָנָיו

His opponent will do as he pleases, for none **will hold** (|--E--|) out against him. (Dn 11:16)   **R**

(224) וְיִטַּע אָהֳלֵי אַפַּדְנוֹ בֵּין יַמִּים לְהַר צְבִי קֹדֶשׁ וּבָא עַד קִצּוֹ וְאֵין **עוֹזֵר** לוֹ:

He will pitch his royal pavilion between the sea and the beautiful holy mountain, and he will meet his doom and no one **will help** (|--E--|) him. (Dn 11:45)   **R**

(225) וַיֹּאמֶר נִוָּעֵד אֶל בֵּית הָאֱלֹהִים אֶל תּוֹךְ הַהֵיכָל וְנִסְגְּרָה דַּלְתוֹת הַהֵיכָל כִּי **בָאִים**
לְהָרְגֶךָ וְלַיְלָה בָּאִים לְהָרְגֶךָ:

[A]nd he said, Let us meet in the House of God, inside the sanctuary, And let us shut the doors of the sanctuary, for they **are coming** (|--E--|) to kill you—by night they are coming to kill you. (Neh 6:10)   **R**

(226) מָחָר רְדוּ עֲלֵיהֶם הִנָּם **עֹלִים** בְּמַעֲלֵה הַצִּיץ וּמְצָאתֶם אֹתָם בְּסוֹף הַנַּחַל פְּנֵי
מִדְבַּר יְרוּאֵל:

March down against them tomorrow as they **will come up** (|--E--|) by the
                                                                        R
Ascent of Ziz; you will find them at the end of the wadi in the direction of the wilderness of Jeruel. (2 Chr 20:16)

(227) וְכָל הַנִּשְׁאָר מִכָּל הַמְּקֹמוֹת אֲשֶׁר הוּא **גָר** שָׁם יְנַשְּׂאוּהוּ אַנְשֵׁי מְקֹמוֹ

[A]nd all who stay behind, wherever he **may be living** (|--E--|), let the people of his place assist him. (Ezr 1:4)   **R**

These verses indicate that the reference time of participle forms can be the verb forms *yiqtol*, *weqatal*, the cohortative, the jussive, or an imperative. In general, the reference time appears before the participle, but example 227 attests to the fact that it can also be situated thereafter. The diagram plots out the chronological relationship in these sorts of instances:

---

23. Although these cases are infrequent, they are well-documented. Also see Ezra 1:4; 1 Chronicles 15:16; 22:19; 2 Chronicles 19:10.

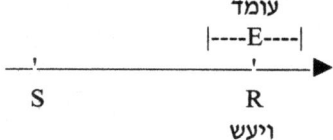

5.2.1.4　The Habitual Present

The rise in the participial form's use as a signifier of habitual actions is among the most prominent features of the Second Temple period. Hatav demonstrates (1997:109) that the participle's habitual usage in the First Temple period is comparatively sparse, if not negligible (4%). Conversely, the number of occurrences in the Second Temple period is almost on par with those of the relationship of inclusion.

The habitual present can express either an iterative action (a) or a state of affairs (b).

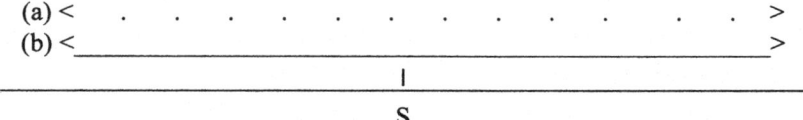

The first three verses are examples of situations; in the remaining examples, the participle signifies an iterative action:

(228) וְהָעֹשֶׁר וְהַכָּבוֹד מִלְּפָנֶיךָ וְאַתָּה **מוֹשֵׁל** בַּכֹּל וּבְיָדְךָ כֹּחַ וּגְבוּרָה

Riches and honor are yours to dispense; you **have dominion** over all; with you are strength and might. (1 Chr 29:12)

(229) וְיָדַעְתִּי אֱלֹהַי כִּי אַתָּה **בֹּחֵן** לֵבָב וּמֵישָׁרִים תִּרְצֶה[24]

I know, God, that **you search** the heart and desire uprightness. (1 Chr 29:17)

(230) וְאַתָּה שְׁלֹמֹה בְנִי דַּע אֶת אֱלֹהֵי אָבִיךָ וְעָבְדֵהוּ בְּלֵב שָׁלֵם וּבְנֶפֶשׁ חֲפֵצָה כִּי כָל לְבָבוֹת **דּוֹרֵשׁ** יְהוָה וְכָל יֵצֶר מַחֲשָׁבוֹת **מֵבִין**

And you, my son Solomon, know the God of your father, and serve him with single mind and fervent heart, for the LORD **searches** all minds and **discerns** the design of every thought. (1 Chr 28:9)

---

24. Compare the substitution of "בחן" for "תרצה" herein and "דורש" for "מבין" in example 230. Similar cases may be found in Esther 3:2; 4:3, inter alia. As argued above, these substitutions stem, at least in part, from the gradual neutralization or overlap of these forms in all that concerns the expression of habituality.

(231) וְכָל זֶה אֵינֶנּוּ שֹׁוֶה לִי בְּכָל עֵת אֲשֶׁר אֲנִי **רֹאֶה** אֶת מָרְדֳּכַי הַיְּהוּדִי יוֹשֵׁב בְּשַׁעַר הַמֶּלֶךְ:

Yet all this means nothing to me every time I **see** that Jew Mordecai sitting in the palace gate. (Est 5:13)

(232) עַל כֵּן הַיְּהוּדִים הפרוזים (הַפְּרָזִים) הַיֹּשְׁבִים בְּעָרֵי הַפְּרָזוֹת **עֹשִׂים** אֵת יוֹם אַרְבָּעָה עָשָׂר לְחֹדֶשׁ אֲדָר שִׂמְחָה וּמִשְׁתֶּה וְיוֹם טוֹב

That is why village Jews who live in unwalled towns **observe** the fourteenth day of the month of Adar and make it a day of merrymaking and feasting. (Est 9:19)

(233) וַיִּגְּשׁוּ אֶל זְרֻבָּבֶל וְאֶל רָאשֵׁי הָאָבוֹת וַיֹּאמְרוּ לָהֶם נִבְנֶה עִמָּכֶם כִּי כָכֶם נִדְרוֹשׁ לֵאלֹהֵיכֶם ולא (וְלוֹ) אֲנַחְנוּ **זֹבְחִים** מִימֵי אֵסַר חַדֹּן מֶלֶךְ אַשּׁוּר הַמַּעֲלֶה אֹתָנוּ פֹּה:

[T]hey approached Zerubbabel and the chiefs of the clans and said to them, Let us build with you, since we too worship your God, **having offered sacrifices** to him since the time of King Esarhaddon of Assyria, who brought us here. (Ezr 4:2)

5.2.1.5   An Iterative Action in the Past

Here too, the case can be made that upon the transition from the classical era to the Second Temple period, tehre was a semantic expansion of the chronological borders of the action signified by the participle. More specifically, the participle is restricted to marking the relationship of inclusion in all that concerns its habitual usage.

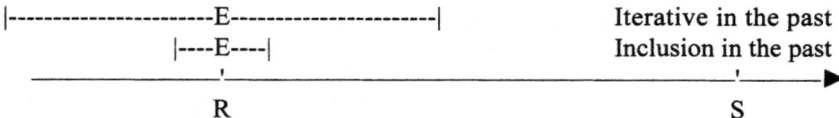

|----------------------E----------------------| Iterative in the past
     |----E----| Inclusion in the past
         R   S

In First Temple period Hebrew, the transition from a narrative succession to a habitual field is likely to be denoted by a shift from *wayyiqtol* to either *yiqtol* or *weqatal* forms:

(432) **וַיִּתְנַצְּלוּ** בְנֵי יִשְׂרָאֵל אֶת עֶדְיָם מֵהַר חוֹרֵב: וּמֹשֶׁה **יִקַּח** אֶת הָאֹהֶל **וְנָטָה** לוֹ מִחוּץ לַמַּחֲנֶה הַרְחֵק מִן הַמַּחֲנֶה **וְקָרָא** לוֹ אֹהֶל מוֹעֵד **וְהָיָה** כָּל מְבַקֵּשׁ יְהוָה **יֵצֵא** אֶל אֹהֶל מוֹעֵד אֲשֶׁר מִחוּץ לַמַּחֲנֶה: **וְהָיָה** כְּצֵאת מֹשֶׁה אֶל הָאֹהֶל **יָקוּמוּ** כָּל הָעָם **וְנִצְּבוּ** אִישׁ פֶּתַח אָהֳלוֹ **וְהִבִּיטוּ** אַחֲרֵי מֹשֶׁה

So the Israelites **remained stripped** (*wayyiqtol*) of the finery from Mount Horeb on. Now Moses **would take** (*yiqtol*) the Tent **and pitch** (*weqatal*) it outside the camp, at some distance from the camp. **And he would call** (*weqatal*) it the Tent of Meeting, **and whoever sought** (*weqatal*) the LORD would go out (*yiqtol*) to the Tent of Meeting that was outside the camp. Whenever Moses **would go out** (*weqatal*) to the Tent, all the people **would rise** (*yiqtol*) and **stand** (*weqatal*), each at the entrance of his tent, and **gaze** (*weqatal*) after Moses. (Ex 33:6-8)

Likewise, in the Second Temple period, this transition is often marked by a shift from *wayyiqtol* forms to a participle:

(235) **וַיּוֹשַׁע** יְהֹוָה אֶת יְחִזְקִיָּהוּ וְאֵת יֹשְׁבֵי יְרוּשָׁלַם מִיַּד סַנְחֵרִיב מֶלֶךְ אַשּׁוּר וּמִיַּד כֹּל **וַיְנַהֲלֵם** מִסָּבִיב: וְרַבִּים **מְבִיאִים** מִנְחָה לַיהֹוָה לִירוּשָׁלַם וּמִגְדָּנוֹת לִיחִזְקִיָּהוּ מֶלֶךְ יְהוּדָה **וַיִּנַּשֵּׂא** לְעֵינֵי כָל הַגּוֹיִם מֵאַחֲרֵי כֵן:

Thus the LORD **delivered** (*wayyiqtol*) Hezekiah and the inhabitants of Jerusalem from King Sennacherib of Assyria, and from everyone; **he provided** (*wayyiqtol*) for them on all sides. Many **would bring (participle)** tribute to the LORD to Jerusalem, and gifts to King Hezekiah of Judah; thereafter **he was exalted** (*wayyiqtol*) in the eyes of all the nations. (2 Chr 32:22-23)

(236) **וַיַּעֲשׂוּ** בְנֵי יִשְׂרָאֵל הַנִּמְצָאִים בִּירוּשָׁלַם אֶת חַג הַמַּצּוֹת שִׁבְעַת יָמִים בְּשִׂמְחָה גְדוֹלָה **וּמְהַלְלִים** לַיהֹוָה יוֹם בְּיוֹם הַלְוִיִּם וְהַכֹּהֲנִים בִּכְלֵי עֹז לַיהֹוָה:

The Israelites who were in Jerusalem **kept** (*wayyiqtol*) the Feast of Unleavened Bread seven days; with great rejoicing, the Levites and the priests **would praise (participle)** the LORD daily with powerful instruments for the LORD. (2 Chr 30:21)

The transition in example 235 is signified exclusively by the shift to the participle, whereas in the verse from 2 Chronicles 30 the habitual nature of the glorification is underscored by the adverbial clause "יוֹם בְּיוֹם".

In most cases, the action is iterative (examples 237-238),[25] but there are also participles that denote a state of affairs (239):

(237) וּבְכָל מְדִינָה וּמְדִינָה וּבְכָל עִיר וָעִיר מְקוֹם אֲשֶׁר דְּבַר הַמֶּלֶךְ וְדָתוֹ **מַגִּיעַ** שִׂמְחָה וְשָׂשׂוֹן לַיְּהוּדִים מִשְׁתֶּה וְיוֹם טוֹב וְרַבִּים מֵעַמֵּי הָאָרֶץ **מִתְיַהֲדִים** כִּי נָפַל פַּחַד הַיְּהוּדִים עֲלֵיהֶם:

And in every province and in every city, when the king's command and decree **would arrive**, there was gladness and joy among the Jews, a feast and a holiday. And many of the people of the land **would profess to be Jews**, for the fear of the Jews had fallen upon them. (Est 8:17)

(238) וַיְהִי מִן הַיּוֹם הַהוּא חֲצִי נְעָרַי **עֹשִׂים** בַּמְּלָאכָה וְחֶצְיָם **מַחֲזִיקִים** וְהָרְמָחִים הַמָּגִנִּים וְהַקְּשָׁתוֹת וְהַשִּׁרְיֹנִים וְהַשָּׂרִים אַחֲרֵי כָּל בֵּית יְהוּדָה: הַבּוֹנִים בַּחוֹמָה וְהַנֹּשְׂאִים בַּסֵּבֶל **עֹמְשִׂים** בְּאַחַת יָדוֹ **עֹשֶׂה** בַמְּלָאכָה וְאַחַת **מַחֲזֶקֶת** הַשָּׁלַח: וְהַבּוֹנִים אִישׁ חַרְבּוֹ אֲסוּרִים עַל מָתְנָיו **וּבוֹנִים** וְהַתּוֹקֵעַ בַּשּׁוֹפָר אֶצְלִי:

---

25. Also see Esther 3:2; 4:3; 9:3; Nehemiah 4:15, 17; 5:2, 3, 4; 13:24; 1 Chronicles 12:40, 41; 15:24; 16:5; 23:5; 2 Chronicles 17:11; 35:3.

From that day on, half my servants **would do** the work and half **would hold** lances and shields, bows and armor. And the officers stood behind the whole house of Judah who were rebuilding the wall. The basket-carriers **would toil, doing** work with one hand while the other **holding** a weapon. As for the builders, each had his sword girded at his side as he **was building**. The trumpeter stood beside me. (Neh 4:10-12)

(239) גַּם בַּיָּמִים הָהֵם רָאִיתִי אֶת הַיְּהוּדִים הֹשִׁיבוּ נָשִׁים אשדודיות (אַשְׁדָּדִיּוֹת) עמוניות (עַמֳּנִיּוֹת) מוֹאֲבִיּוֹת וּבְנֵיהֶם חֲצִי **מְדַבֵּר** אַשְׁדּוֹדִית וְאֵינָם **מַכִּירִים** לְדַבֵּר יְהוּדִית וְכִלְשׁוֹן עַם וָעָם :

Also at that time, I saw that Jews had married Ashdodite, Ammonite, and Moabite women; a good number of their children **used to speak** the language of Ashdod and the language of those various peoples, and **did not know** how to speak Judean. (Neh 13:23-24)

5.2.2 Relations of Simultaneity—R=E

Alongside the participle's regular function of marking relationships of inclusion, there are also several cases where it is used to denote simultaneity which does not entail inclusion. These instances are relatively sparse and should be viewed as an optional meaning that accompanies the primary role of signifying the relationship of inclusion.

5.2.2.1 Simultaneity in the Past

One context wherein a participle form expresses a relationship of simultaneity in the past is when the reference time is marked by an adverb that denotes a durative situation. In most of these instances, the participle form also signifies an iterative or durative action in the past. However, instead of encompassing the adverb, the participle overlaps it:[26]

(240) גַּם בַּיָּמִים הָהֵם חֹרֵי יְהוּדָה **מַרְבִּים** אִגְּרֹתֵיהֶם **הוֹלְכוֹת** עַל טוֹבִיָּה וַאֲשֶׁר לְטוֹבִיָּה **בָּאוֹת** אֲלֵיהֶם :

Also in those days, the nobles of Judah **kept up (E=R(<S))** a brisk correspondence, that **was sent (E=R(<S))** to Tobiah, and **returned (E=R(<S))** by Tobiah to them. (Neh 6:17)

(241) וַיָּקוּמוּ עַל עָמְדָם וַיִּקְרְאוּ בְּסֵפֶר תּוֹרַת יְהֹוָה אֱלֹהֵיהֶם רְבִעִית הַיּוֹם וּרְבִעִית **מִתְוַדִּים וּמִשְׁתַּחֲוִים** לַיהֹוָה אֱלֹהֵיהֶם :

Standing in their places, they read from the scroll of the Teaching of the LORD their God for one-fourth of the day, and for another fourth they **confessed**

---

26. Also see Esther 2:11, 13, 14; Nehemiah 13:15, 16.

(E=R(<S)) and **prostrated** (E=R(<S)) themselves before the LORD their God. (Neh 9:3)

(242) וְכָל יִשְׂרָאֵל בִּימֵי זְרֻבָּבֶל וּבִימֵי נְחֶמְיָה מְנָיוֹת הַמְשֹׁרְרִים וְהַשֹּׁעֲרִים **נֹתְנִים** דְּבַר יוֹם בְּיוֹמוֹ **וּמַקְדִּשִׁים** לַלְוִיִּם וְהַלְוִיִּם **מַקְדִּשִׁים** לִבְנֵי אַהֲרֹן :

And in the time of Zerubbabel, and in the time of Nehemiah, all Israel **contributed** (E=R(<S)) the daily portions of the singers and the gatekeepers, and **made sacred contributions** (E=R(<S)) for the Levites, and the Levites **made sacred contributions** (E=R(<S)) for the Aaronites. (Neh 12:47)

These adverbs delimit the signified actions; hence, the participles do not contain the events:

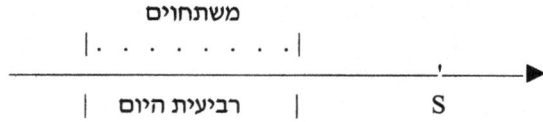

The participle form is capable of expressing an instance of simultaneity even in cases where the R-time is another verb that expresses a durative action. Unlike the previous cases, the participle does not denote an iterative or habitual action in these situations:

(243) וְעוֹד אֲנִי מְדַבֵּר בַּתְּפִלָּה וְהָאִישׁ גַּבְרִיאֵל אֲשֶׁר רָאִיתִי בֶחָזוֹן בַּתְּחִלָּה **מֻעָף** בִּיעָף **נֹגֵעַ** אֵלַי

[W]hile I was uttering my prayer, the man Gabriel, whom I had previously seen in the vision, **was sent forth** (E=R(<S)) in flight and **reached** (E=R(<S)) me. (Dn 9:21)

(244) וַאֲנִי הָיִיתִי מֵבִין וְהִנֵּה צְפִיר הָעִזִּים **בָּא** מִן הַמַּעֲרָב עַל פְּנֵי כָל הָאָרֶץ וְאֵין וֹ(!) **נוֹגֵעַ** בָּאָרֶץ

As I looked on, a he-goat **came** (E=R(<S)) from the west, passing over the entire earth without **touching** (E=R(<S)) the ground. (Dn 8:5)

5.2.2.2   Simultaneity vis-à-vis Speech Time

Occurrences in which the participle runs parallel to speech time are rarer and limited to a very narrow field. The quintessential example of this phenomenon is referred to as the "performative," namely an action that is effected by an utterance. For instance, in the passage below, the treaty declaration and its transfer into writing also signal the consummation of these actions:

(245) הִנֵּה אֲנַחְנוּ הַיּוֹם עֲבָדִים וְהָאָרֶץ אֲשֶׁר נָתַתָּה לַאֲבֹתֵינוּ לֶאֱכֹל אֶת פִּרְיָהּ וְאֶת

טוֹבָה הִנֵּה אֲנַחְנוּ עֲבָדִים עָלֶיהָ. . . . וּבְכָל זֹאת אֲנַחְנוּ **כֹּרְתִים** אֲמָנָה וְכֹתְבִים וְעַל הֶחָתוּם שָׂרֵינוּ לְוִיֵּנוּ כֹּהֲנֵינוּ :

Today we are slaves, and the land that you gave our fathers to enjoy its fruit and bounty—here we are slaves on it! . . . In view of all this, we make **(E=R(=S))** this pledge and put it in writing; and on the sealed copy are subscribed our officials, our Levites, and our priests. (Neh 9:36-10:1)

5.2.3 Denoting the Near Future (S=R<E)

On the face of things, the most prominent exception to the participle form's cardinal role of marking a relationship of inclusion or simultaneity is the expression of the near future—a phenomenon that exists in both classical and Second Temple period Hebrew. The most widely accepted explanation in the literature for these cases is that the speaker perceives the action depicted by the participle as having already begun. For example, Driver (1892:168) averred that:[27] "The ptcp. is used, lastly, of future time (the *fut. instans*), which it represents as already beginning: hence, if the event designated can only in fact occur after some interval." In other words, these cases should be viewed as a quasi-expansion of the participle's role as a signifier of the real present.

This broadening of the real present to include the *futurum instans* has been documented in other languages as well (Joosten 1989:144). Whereas actions falling under the category of the real present "really" transpire, the reader understands actions in the near future as starting out as potentialities anchored in the speech time, even if they come to fruition:[28]

```
    |---------O
 __'_____'_____▶
  S,R      E
```

This particular usage of the participle is found within the framework of both free indirect speech (*oratio obliqua*),[29] which is signified by the particle הנה (examples 246-249), and relative clauses of direct speech (examples 250-252):[30]

(246) וַיֹּאמֶר הִנְנִי **מוֹדִיעֲךָ** אֵת אֲשֶׁר יִהְיֶה בְּאַחֲרִית הַזָּעַם כִּי לְמוֹעֵד קֵץ :

---

27. Joüon and Muraoka (1996:§121e); Gesenius, Kautzsch, and Cowley (1910:§116p); and Joosten (1989:135, 144) offer similar descriptions of this phenomenon.
28. Hatav claims that in these instances the reference time runs parallel to the speech time (1997:112).
29. This distinction is based on Sternberg's insights (1983).
30. See Joosten (1989:135-136) and Gross (1975:24).

[A]nd [he] said, I **am going to inform you** ((S=) R = ? / <?E) of what will happen when wrath is at an end, for *it refers* to the time appointed for the end. (Dn 8:19)

(247) הִנֵּה בֵן נוֹלָד לָךְ הוּא יִהְיֶה אִישׁ מְנוּחָה וַהֲנִחוֹתִי לוֹ מִכָּל אוֹיְבָיו מִסָּבִיב כִּי שְׁלֹמֹה יִהְיֶה שְׁמוֹ וְשָׁלוֹם וָשֶׁקֶט אֶתֵּן עַל יִשְׂרָאֵל בְּיָמָיו :

But you **are about to have** ((S=) R = ? / <?E) a son who will be a man at rest, for I will give him rest from all his enemies on all sides; Solomon will be his name and I shall confer peace and quiet on Israel in his time. (1 Chr 22:9)

(248) הִנֵּה אֲנִי בוֹנֶה בַּיִת לְשֵׁם יְהֹוָה אֱלֹהָי

[S]ee, I **am about to build** ((S=) R = ? / <?E) a house for the name of the LORD my God. (2 Chr 2:3)

(249) הִנֵּה יְהֹוָה נֹגֵף מַגֵּפָה גְדוֹלָה בְּעַמֶּךָ וּבְבָנֶיךָ וּבְנָשֶׁיךָ וּבְכָל רְכוּשֶׁךָ :

[T]herefore, the LORD **is about to inflict** ((S=) R = ? / <?E) a great blow upon your people, your sons, and your wives and all your possessions. (2 Chr 21:14)

(250) וְעַתָּה מַה נֹּאמַר אֱלֹהֵינוּ אַחֲרֵי זֹאת כִּי עָזַבְנוּ מִצְוֹתֶיךָ : אֲשֶׁר צִוִּיתָ בְּיַד עֲבָדֶיךָ הַנְּבִיאִים לֵאמֹר הָאָרֶץ אֲשֶׁר אַתֶּם בָּאִים לְרִשְׁתָּהּ אֶרֶץ נִדָּה הִיא בְּנִדַּת עַמֵּי הָאֲרָצוֹת

Now, what can we say in the face of this, O our God, for we have forsaken your commandments, which you gave us through your servants the prophets when you said, The land that you **are about** ((S=) R = ? / <?E) to possess is a land unclean through the uncleanness of the peoples of the land. . . . (Ezr 9:10-11)

(251) וְהַבַּיִת אֲשֶׁר אֲנִי בוֹנֶה גָּדוֹל כִּי גָדוֹל אֱלֹהֵינוּ מִכָּל הָאֱלֹהִים :

The House that I **am about to build** ((S=) R = ? / <?E) will be great, inasmuch as our God is greater than all gods. (2 Chr 2:4)

(252) וּלְהָכִין לִי עֵצִים לָרֹב כִּי הַבַּיִת אֲשֶׁר אֲנִי בוֹנֶה גָּדוֹל וְהַפְלֵא :

. . .to provide me with a great stock of timber; for the House that I **am about to build** ((S=) R = ? / <?E) will be singularly great. (2 Chr 2:8)

In each of these passages, the speaker implies that these potentialities are already underway at the S-time, despite the fact that they will be realized in the near future (thereby substantiating the assumptions raised by Driver and others).

A somewhat anomalous example of this phenomenon is found in a prophecy from the book of Daniel:

(253) וַאֲנִי בִּשְׁנַת אַחַת לְדָרְיָוֶשׁ הַמָּדִי עָמְדִי לְמַחֲזִיק וּלְמָעוֹז לוֹ : וְעַתָּה אֱמֶת אַגִּיד לָךְ הִנֵּה עוֹד שְׁלֹשָׁה מְלָכִים עֹמְדִים לְפָרַס וְהָרְבִיעִי יַעֲשִׁיר עֹשֶׁר גָּדוֹל מִכֹּל וּכְחֶזְקָתוֹ בְעָשְׁרוֹ יָעִיר הַכֹּל אֵת מַלְכוּת יָוָן :

In the first year of Darius the Mede, I took my stand to strengthen and fortify him. And now I will tell you the truth: Persia **will have (participle)** three more kings, and the fourth will be wealthier than them all; by the power he obtains through his wealth, he will stir everyone up against the kingdom of Greece. (Dn 11:1-2)

As opposed to the examples above, this passage does not refer to the immediate future, but to actions that will take place years later. Nonetheless, the participle form "עמדים" evokes a similar sense to that of examples 246 to 252, namely the speaker is so confident that these events will come to pass that it is as though they have commenced at the very moment of utterance.

Although at first glance the near future appears to be an exception to the general rule whereby participle forms express inclusion, the cited passages indicate that this phenomenon can be viewed as a unique broadening of this relationship.

5.2.4 The Blurring of Reference Time in Generic and Habitual Actions

The habitual usage of participle forms (i.e., a general truth, the habitual present, an iterative action in the past) tends to blur the link between the action and its R-time. When the participle is cast in a generic role, the reader may be unable to point to a concrete reference time, especially when the form appears on its own. For instance:[31]

(254) וּבְכָל מְדִינָה וּמְדִינָה מְקוֹם אֲשֶׁר דְּבַר הַמֶּלֶךְ וְדָתוֹ **מַגִּיעַ** אֵבֶל גָּדוֹל לַיְּהוּדִים
וְצוֹם וּבְכִי וּמִסְפֵּד שַׂק וָאֵפֶר יֻצַּע לָרַבִּים :

Also, in every province that the king's command and decree **reached (iterative)**, there was great mourning among the Jews, with fasting, weeping, and wailing, and everybody used to be offered a sackcloth and ashes. (Est 4:3)

(255) וְהָעֹשֶׁר וְהַכָּבוֹד מִלְּפָנֶיךָ וְאַתָּה **מוֹשֵׁל** בַּכֹּל

Riches and honor are yours to dispense; you **have dominion (general truth)** over all. (1 Chr 29:12)

The difficulty of pinpointing the reference time in these two cases is tied to the fact that participial forms represent habitual actions (an iterative action in the past and a general truth) rather than particular ones. Nevertheless, these verses accord with the basic meaning of a relationship of inclusion or simultaneity.[32] Bybee claims that: "Generic or gnomic situations are often regarded as timeless because they hold for all time, but they still can be regarded as in effect at the moment of speech" (1994:141).

---

31. For further elaboration, see §2.2.4 above.
32. See the disquisition on the particle's role as a signifier of relationships of inclusion or simultaneity within the framework of habitual actions: §5.2.1.4-5; §5.2.4.

For example, the verb "מושל" in the last verse denotes a general truth, but it can still be conceived as an accurate depiction of the present. Or as Comrie put it:

> The situation referred by the verb in the present tense is simply a situation holding literally at the present moment; whether or not this situation is part of a larger situation extending into the past or the future is an implicature, rather than part of the meaning of the present tense. (1985:38)

Comrie's definition also enables him to consider generic or habitual actions that can be construed as taking place at any given moment, including the moment of speech (even if the action has yet to actually occur), as one of the possible meanings of the participial form (Comrie 1985:39). The following verse substantially bolsters Comrie's argument:

(256) וַיֹּאמֶר הָמָן לַמֶּלֶךְ אֲחַשְׁוֵרוֹשׁ יֶשְׁנוֹ עַם אֶחָד **מְפֻזָּר וּמְפֹרָד** [33] בֵּין הָעַמִּים בְּכֹל מְדִינוֹת מַלְכוּתֶךָ וְדָתֵיהֶם שֹׁנוֹת מִכָּל עָם וְאֶת דָּתֵי הַמֶּלֶךְ **אֵינָם עֹשִׂים** וְלַמֶּלֶךְ אֵין **שֹׁוֶה לְהַנִּיחָם**:

> Haman then said to King Ahasuerus, There is a certain people, **scattered (general truth)** and **dispersed (general truth)** among the other peoples in all the provinces of your realm, whose laws are different from those of any other people and who **do not obey (general truth)** the king's laws; and **it is not (general truth)** in your Majesty's interest to tolerate them. (Est 3:8)

All the participles herein express a general truth, which applies, inter alia, to the verse's speech time. Therefore, these forms can be interpreted as including the present.

5.3 The Participle Form's Link to the Modal Axis

Defining the participle's link to the modal axis is more complicated than that of *qatal* and *wayyiqtol* forms. Earlier on, we claimed that *qatal* is inherently an indicative, non-modal form [+actual, -modal, -habitual, -iterative]. Moreover, the fact that *qatal* denotes antecedence in modal contexts was explained as a last resort, for Biblical Hebrew lacks another form capable of signifying this relationship. In these cases, the link to the modal axis is weakened on account of the de-actualization that the *qatal* form has undergone. However, this explanation can be only partially applied to the participle form. In our estimation, participle forms that signify a relationship of inclusion are also inherently indicative. In other words, the action that is expressed in these situations is an actual one that transpires at a concrete point in time.

---

33. The verbs "מפוזר" and "ומפורד" are passive participles and thus do not fall under the purview of the present topic. However, they have been highlighted on account of their resemblance to participle forms in this particular context.

Similar to *qatal*, participle forms can also appear in modal contexts, such as passages where it denotes a relationship of inclusion in the future:[34]

(257) וְיַעַשׂ הַבָּא אֵלָיו כִּרְצוֹנוֹ וְאֵין **עוֹמֵד** לְפָנָיו

His opponent will do as he pleases, for none **will hold out** (|---E---|) against him. (Dn 11:16)   (S<) R

These cases are akin to *qatal*'s role as a signifier of antecedence in the future, especially with respect to the de-actualization that participle forms undergo. This occurs because there are no specific modal forms that express inclusion and attendace; as a result, the indicative forms are used. For example:

(258) עַתָּה בְנִי יְהִי יְהוָה עִמָּךְ וְהִצְלַחְתָּ וּבָנִיתָ בֵּית יְהוָה אֱלֹהֶיךָ כַּאֲשֶׁר **דִּבֶּר** עָלֶיךָ :

Now, my son, may the LORD be with you, and may you succeed in building the House of the LORD your God as **he will have instructed** ((S<) E<R) you. (1 Chr 22:11)

To this point, we have explored the similarities between the *qatal* and participle forms, but there are also considerable differences between them. While the *qatal* form ordinarily does not bear its own modal meaning, the participle denotes habituality on a regular basis. In fact, it is this distinction that renders the link to the modal axis complex.[35]

Given the fact that the habitual meaning breaks off in several different directions, it is worth surveying the rest of the participle's functions for the purpose of shedding light on the form's habitual usage. With this in mind, we will also contrast the participle's role with *yiqtol* and the infinitive construct in the Second Temple period, as well as its own usage in Mishnaic Hebrew. The objective of this comparison is twofold: From a synchronic standpoint, we will point out the areas of overlap and mutual exclusivity between the the participle form and those that we deem to be modal forms. From a diachronic standpoint, we will demonstrate how the fields of usage that pertain to another system—Mishnaic Hebrew—are categorized in a completely different manner.

At the outset of our discussion on the participle, we demonstrated that there is a certain degree of overlap between the participle and the *yiqtol* and infinitive construct forms in all that concerns the expression of habituality in the Second Temple period. For example:

---

34. See the discussion on this relationship in §5.2.1.3 above.
35. Comrie (1985:40) asserts that habituality straddles the fence between the categories of tense, aspect, and mood.

(259) וּבְכָל מְדִינָה וּמְדִינָה מְקוֹם אֲשֶׁר דְּבַר הַמֶּלֶךְ וְדָתוֹ **מַגִּיעַ** אֵבֶל גָּדוֹל לַיְּהוּדִים
וְצוֹם וּבְכִי וּמִסְפֵּד שַׂק וָאֵפֶר **יֻצַּע** לָרַבִּים :

Also, in every province that the king's command and decree **would reach
(iterative, participle),** there would be great mourning among the Jews, with
fasting, weeping, and wailing, and everybody **use to be offered (iterative
yiqtol)** [a] sackcloth and ashes. (Est 4:3)

(260) וַיִּסָּפְרוּ הַלְוִיִּם מִבֶּן שְׁלֹשִׁים שָׁנָה וָמַעְלָה וַיְהִי מִסְפָּרָם לְגֻלְגְּלֹתָם לִגְבָרִים שְׁלֹשִׁים
וּשְׁמוֹנָה אָלֶף : מֵאֵלֶּה **לְנַצֵּחַ** עַל מְלֶאכֶת בֵּית יְהוָה עֶשְׂרִים וְאַרְבָּעָה אָלֶף וְשֹׁטְרִים
וְשֹׁפְטִים שֵׁשֶׁת אֲלָפִים : וְאַרְבַּעַת אֲלָפִים שֹׁעֲרִים וְאַרְבַּעַת אֲלָפִים **מְהַלְלִים** לַיהוָה
בַּכֵּלִים אֲשֶׁר עָשִׂיתִי לְהַלֵּל :[36]

The Levites, from the age of thirty and upward, were counted; the head-count
of their males was 38000: of these there **were (iterative infinitive construct)**
24000 **in charge** of the work of the House of the LORD, 6000 officers and
magistrates, 4000 gatekeepers, and 4000 **would praise (iterative participle)**
the LORD with instruments I devised for singing praises. (1 Chr 23:3-5)

Despite the sense of neutralization that these substitutions are likely to arouse,
the forms are not completely interchangeable. For instance, its habitual capacities
notwithstanding, the participle does not appear in the language of the law. Instead,
deontic (directive) modal expressions are intermingled with habitual expressions
in juridical passages; *yiqtol* and the infinitive construct are the exclusive signifiers
of the language of the law throughout this period:

(261) וַיִּמְצְאוּ כָּתוּב בַּתּוֹרָה אֲשֶׁר צִוָּה יְהוָה בְּיַד מֹשֶׁה אֲשֶׁר **יֵשְׁבוּ** בְנֵי יִשְׂרָאֵל בַּסֻּכּוֹת
בֶּחָג בַּחֹדֶשׁ הַשְּׁבִיעִי : וַאֲשֶׁר **יַשְׁמִיעוּ וְיַעֲבִירוּ** קוֹל בְּכָל עָרֵיהֶם וּבִירוּשָׁלַ͏ִם

They found written in the Teaching that the LORD had commanded Moses that
the Israelites **must dwell** in booths during the festival of the seventh month,
and that they **must announce and proclaim** throughout all their towns and
Jerusalem. . . (Neh 8:14-15)

(262) אֵלֶּה פְקֻדָּתָם לַעֲבֹדָתָם **לָבוֹא** לְבֵית יְהוָה כְּמִשְׁפָּטָם בְּיַד אַהֲרֹן אֲבִיהֶם כַּאֲשֶׁר
צִוָּהוּ יְהוָה אֱלֹהֵי יִשְׂרָאֵל :

According to this allocation of offices by tasks, **they should enter (infinitive
construct)** the House of the LORD as was laid down for them by Aaron their
father, as the LORD God of Israel had commanded him. (1 Chr 24:19)

The same picture emerges from the Dead Sea Scrolls, as in the following passage
from *The Community Rule*:

אלה החוקים למשכיל **להתהלך** בם עם כול חי לתכון עת ועת ולמשקל איש
ואיש לעשות את רצון אל ככול הנגלה לעת בעת

---
36. These are the same examples that were cited at the beginning of this chapter.

These are the statutes for the Instructor. **[He] shall conduct (infinitive construct)** himself by them with every living person, guided by the precepts appropriate to each era and the value of each person. He shall work the will of God according to what has been revealed for each period of history (1QS 9:12-13)

However, in Mishnaic Hebrew, the language of the law is marked by the participle form as well:

הַמְקַבֵּל עָלָיו לִהְיוֹת חָבֵר **אֵינוֹ מוֹכֵר** לְעַם הָאָרֶץ לַח וְיָבֵשׁ **וְאֵינוֹ לוֹקֵחַ** מִמֶּנּוּ לַח **וְאֵינוֹ מִתְאָרֵחַ** אֵצֶל עַם הָאָרֶץ **וְלֹא מְאָרְחוֹ** אֶצְלוֹ בִּכְסוּתוֹ

Whoever undertakes to become a member **may not sell (law)** to an *am ha'aretz* anything moist or dry, **nor may he buy (law)** from him anything moist, and he **may not be the guest (law)** of an *am ha'aretz*, **nor may he receive (law)** him as his guest in his garments.[37] (Demai 2:3)

אֵין **עוֹמְדִין** לְהִתְפַּלֵּל אֶלָּא מִתּוֹךְ כּוֹבֶד רֹאשׁ

One should only **pray (law)** in a reverent mood. (Berakhot 5:1)

הָאוֹכֵל תְּרוּמַת חָמֵץ בְּפֶסַח **מְשַׁלֵּם** קֶרֶן וְחֹמֶשׁ

One who eats *terumah* of ḥametz on Pesaḥ, **must pay (law)** the principal plus a fifth. (Pesahim 2:4)

The other functions of the *yiqtol* and infinitive construct forms in the Second Temple era are also characterized by a strong link to the modal meaning. As already noted,[38] these forms are used to signify both epistemic modality (e.g., the expression of the future or a condition) and deontic modality (e.g., an order, prohibition, request, wish, oath, or desire). That said, during the Mishnaic period, the participle infiltrates much deeper into the modal realm, serving nearly all the above mentioned meanings (Azar 1995:15-16, 20-25; Sharvit 1980:114-117).

To follow, then, is a brief sampling of the assorted meanings that the participle assumes in Mishnaic Hebrew:

Future:[39]

דּוֹר הַמִּדְבָּר אֵין לָהֶם חֵלֶק לָעוֹלָם הַבָּא וְאֵין **עוֹמְדִין** בַּדִּין

---

37. See Azar (1995:20); Mishor (1983:272-274); and Sharvit (1980:117).
38. See the sections on *yiqtol* (§3.3); and the infinitive construct (§5.2).
39. Sharvit (1980:113) notes that over the course of the discussion in the *Mishnah* from which this passage derives, the use of the participle "עומדים" is compared to that of the *yiqtol* form in Psalms 1:5:

ר' נחמיה אומר אלו ואלו אין **עומדים** בדין, שנאמר 'על כן לא **יקומו** רשעים במשפט'"

The generation of the wilderness has no portion in the world-to-come and **will not stand (future)** in judgement (Sanhedrin 10:3)

A conditional sentence:

שֶׁאִם תִּפְּלוּ בְיָדָם **אֵין מְרַחֲמִין** עֲלֵיכֶם

If you should fall into their hands, they **would have no mercy (conditional)** on you (Sotah 8:1)

An oath:

נִשְׁבָּע אֲנִי בְשִׁמְךָ הַגָּדוֹל שֶׁ**אֵינִי זָז** מִכָּאן

I swear by your great name that **I will not move (oath)** from here (Ta'anit 3:8)

Unreal situations:

אָמַר ר׳ אֱלִיעֶזֶר וְכִי הֵיאַךְ הֶעָנִי הַזֶּה **מַחֲלִיף** דָּבָר שֶׁלֹּא בָא בִרְשׁוּתוֹ

Rabbi Eliezer said, And how can this poor person **exchange (irrealis)** something which has not come into his possession? (Pe'ah 5:2)

As we can see, the rules that govern usage in the Mishnaic language vastly differ from those of the Second Temple period in all that concerns the link to the modal axis.

This comparison brings us back to the role of the participial form in our own corpus. As argued above, despite the rise in the participle's habitual usage, it should still be viewed as an integral part of the indicative system. While taking into account the view that associates the habitual meaning with the broadening of the relationship of inclusion, we may conclude that this usage maintains a connection to the participle's classical role as an adjective, which can also be characterized as an attribute or situation.

B. The Modal System
a. The General Modal Forms

6. The Functions of *Yiqtol* in the Hebrew of the Second Temple Period

6.1 Introduction

From a diachronic standpoint, there is an affinity between the usages of *yiqtol* in the First and Second Temple periods with respect to both the reference-time and modal axes, but the form has expanded its range of functions. One of the central features of this expansion is tied to the fact that, alongside the classical task of expressing the chronological relationship R≤E, *yiqtol* often encompasses its own reference time [R,E]. Although this usage indeed exists in classical Hebrew, it is exceedingly rare.[1] Broadly speaking, this phenomenon is tied to the breaking of the classical sequential forms' "monopoly" during this period.[2] Lastly, from a paradigmatic standpoint, it is worth noting that *yiqtol* and infinitive construct (predicative) forms essentially "compete" over the same functions.

The branching out of *yiqtol* forms to the field of successions not only has ramifications on the link to the reference-time axis, but on the modal axis as well. Given the *yiqtol* form's wherewithal to occupy a clause's initial position and establish the reference time, the area of overlap between the latter and the volitive forms (cohortative, imperative, and jussive) has swelled. Since the *yiqtol* forms during the Second Temple period can also signify successions in modal expressions (a task that is denoted in classical Hebrew by *weqatal* and *waw*-prefixed volitive forms), they can be found in volitive sequences, where they are arrayed alongside the marked volitive forms. What is more, this feature may have accelerated the obfuscation between the roles of the *yiqtol* and volitive forms during this period.[3]

6.2 The *Yiqtol* Form's Link to Reference Time

6.2.1 Relations of Subsequence R<E

6.2.1.1 Subsequence to an Action in the Past

6.2.1.1.1 Events Situated in the Past—R<E<S

On account of its relative characteristics, a *yiqtol* form that is situated in the past is capable of maintaining relation of subsequence R<E with another past action. Within this framework, the R-time can be established by means of *wayyiqtol* and *qatal* forms, or by *yiqtol* and participle forms that express an iterative action in the

---

1. We will expand upon this issue in the main body of this chapter.
2. Cf. a similar phenomenon involving the *qatal* (§3.2.3 above), infinitive absolute (§10.1.2 below), and infinitive construct forms (§8.4 below).
3. A glaring exception to this rule is the aberrant alignment in chapter 11 of the book of Daniel; see §9.3.2.2 below.

past.[4] In general, this relationship involves *yiqtol* forms in subordinate clauses, while the main clause provides the reference time:

(263) וַיָּשֶׂם דָּנִיֵּאל עַל לִבּוֹ אֲשֶׁר לֹא **יִתְגָּאַל** בְּפַת בַּג הַמֶּלֶךְ וּבְיֵין מִשְׁתָּיו וַיְבַקֵּשׁ מִשַּׂר
הַסָּרִיסִים אֲשֶׁר לֹא **יִתְגָּאָל** :

Daniel resolved not **to defile** (R<E(<S)) himself with the king's food or the wine he drank, so he sought permission of the chief officer not **to defile** (R<E(<S)) himself. (Dn 1:8)

(264) רַק הַכֹּהֲנִים הָיוּ לִמְעָט וְלֹא יָכְלוּ לְהַפְשִׁיט אֶת כָּל הָעֹלוֹת וַיְחַזְּקוּם אֲחֵיהֶם
הַלְוִיִּם עַד כְּלוֹת הַמְּלָאכָה וְעַד **יִתְקַדְּשׁוּ** הַכֹּהֲנִים כִּי הַלְוִיִּם יִשְׁרֵי לֵבָב לְהִתְקַדֵּשׁ
מֵהַכֹּהֲנִים :

The priests were too few to be able to flay all the burnt offerings, so their kinsmen, the Levites, reinforced them till the end of the work, and till the rest of the priests **sanctified** (R<E(<S)) themselves. (The Levites were more conscientious about sanctifying themselves than the priests.) (2 Chr 29:34)

In examples 263 and 264, the R-times of the *yiqtol* forms are *wayyiqtol* forms in main clauses. A similar usage of *yiqtol* turns up within the context of indirect speech in the past:

(265) וַיְהִי כַּאֲשֶׁר צָלֲלוּ שַׁעֲרֵי יְרוּשָׁלַ͏ִם לִפְנֵי הַשַּׁבָּת וָאֹמְרָה וַיִּסָּגְרוּ הַדְּלָתוֹת וָאֹמְרָה
אֲשֶׁר לֹא **יִפְתָּחוּם** עַד אַחַר הַשַּׁבָּת וּמִנְּעָרַי הֶעֱמַדְתִּי עַל הַשְּׁעָרִים לֹא יָבוֹא[5] מַשָּׂא
בְּיוֹם הַשַּׁבָּת :

When shadows filled the gateways of Jerusalem at the approach of the sabbath, I gave orders that the doors be closed, and ordered them not **to be opened** (R<E(<S)) until after the sabbath. I stationed some of my servants at the gates, so that no goods should enter on the sabbath. (Neh 13:19)

(266) וַיְהִי באמרם (כְּאָמְרָם) אֵלָיו יוֹם וָיוֹם וְלֹא שָׁמַע אֲלֵיהֶם וַיַּגִּידוּ לְהָמָן לִרְאוֹת
הֲיַעַמְדוּ דִּבְרֵי מָרְדֳּכַי כִּי הִגִּיד לָהֶם אֲשֶׁר הוּא יְהוּדִי :

When they spoke to him day after day and he would not listen to them, they told Haman, in order to see whether Mordecai's resolve **would prevail** (R<E(<S)) for he had explained to them that he was a Jew. (Est 3:4)

Hence, the chronological relations in these cases can be outlined thus:[6]

---

4. For more on this matter, see the discussion on relations of subsequence between itera-
    tive actions in the past (§6.2.1.5 below).
5. The verb "יבוא" also denotes a similar chronological relation.
6. An abstruse passage that can perhaps be interpreted in a similar fashion is Nehemiah
    3:14–15; see Joosten (1999:24). The difficulty stems from the fact that the same structure
    surfaces in verse 13, albeit with *qatal* and *wayyiqtol*. The question of whether verse 13 is
    chronologically distinct from the next two appears to be beyond resolve.

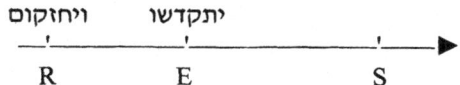

6.2.1.1.2 Events Situated in the Future—R<S<E

By its very nature, relative time ignores speech time in its capacity as a deictic axis. Consequently, there are R<S<E relationships in this category that are identical to those of the previous section, with the exception that the events related to an R-time in the past are in the future realm.

(267) וּבָאתִי֙ לַהֲבִינְךָ֔ אֵ֛ת אֲשֶׁר **יִקְרָ֥ה** לְעַמְּךָ֖ בְּאַחֲרִ֣ית הַיָּמִ֑ים כִּ֖י עוֹד חָז֥וֹן לַיָּמִֽים׃

So I have come to make you understand what **is to befall (R(<S)<E)** your people in the days to come, for there is yet a vision for those days. (Dn 10:14)

(268) וַיְהִ֤י עָלַי֙ דְּבַר־יְהוָ֣ה לֵאמֹ֔ר דָּ֤ם לָרֹב֙ שָׁפַ֔כְתָּ וּמִלְחָמ֥וֹת גְּדֹל֖וֹת עָשִׂ֑יתָ **לֹא־תִבְנֶ֥ה** בַ֙יִת֙ לִשְׁמִ֔י כִּ֚י דָּמִ֣ים רַבִּ֔ים שָׁפַ֖כְתָּ אַ֥רְצָה לְפָנָֽי׃

But the word of the LORD came to me, saying, you have shed much blood and fought great battles; you **shall not build (R(<S)<E)** a House for my name for you have shed much blood on the earth in my sight. (1 Chr 22:8)

(269) וְהִנֵּ֣ה בְעָנְיִ֡י הֲכִינ֪וֹתִי לְבֵית־יְהוָ֡ה זָהָב֩ כִּכָּרִ֨ים מֵאָה־אֶ֜לֶף וְכֶ֣סֶף אֶ֥לֶף אֲלָפִ֣ים כִּכָּרִ֗ים וְלַנְּחֹ֤שֶׁת וְלַבַּרְזֶל֙ אֵ֣ין מִשְׁקָ֔ל כִּ֥י לָרֹ֖ב הָיָ֑ה וְעֵצִ֤ים וַאֲבָנִים֙ הֲכִינ֔וֹתִי וַעֲלֵיהֶ֖ם **תּוֹסִֽיף**׃

See, by denying myself, I have laid aside for the House of the LORD one hundred thousand talents of gold and one million talents of silver, and so much copper and iron it cannot be weighed; I have also laid aside wood and stone, and **you shall add (R(<S)<E)** to them. (1 Chr 22:14)

Since the context of these verses is direct speech, the argument can be made that there is a link to S-time. However, we prefer to view these cases as a special instance that is informed by a chronological relationship stemming from an R<E alignment:

6.2.1.2   Subsequence to Speech Time—S=R<E

Within the framework of direct speech, *yiqtol* often refrains from signifying an explicit reference time. For example:

(270) וַיֹּאמְרוּ **נָקוּם** וּבָנִינוּ

[A]nd they said, **Let us get up ((S=)R<E)** and start building! (Neh 2:18)

Hatav (1997:5-6) and others[7] contend that, in the absence of a palpable reference time, the S-time can be interpreted as filling this role because it is "the first unmarked R-time."

As noted, the chronological relationship S=R<E is among the most prominent characteristics of direct speech, and this feature is responsible for the close affinity between the *yiqtol* and volitive forms (the cohortative, the imperative, and the jussive). In the first chapter, we asserted that the difference between *yiqtol* and the volitive forms does not pertain to modality because both groups belong to the modal field. Instead, it rests on the fact that the volitive forms are marked as signifiers of the volitive mode, while this is but one of several possible meanings that *yiqtol* denotes. Perhaps this distinction can be illuminated by means of an analysis of both groups' link to reference time. The relationship that is signified by the volitive forms is S=R<E. However, in contrast to the *yiqtol* form, where this meaning is a variation on the R≤E relationship, it is obligatory insofar as the volitives are concerned. In other words, the volitive forms are the designated signifiers of the chronological relationship S=R<E.

The link between the *yiqtol* form's chronological meanings and the modal axis in both fields of deontic and epistemic modality is richer and more complex. For example:[8]

(271) אִם עַל הַמֶּלֶךְ טוֹב **יִכָּתֵב לְאַבְּדָם**

If it please your Majesty, **let** an edict **be drawn up ((S=)R<E)** for their destruction. (Est 3:9)

(272) וָאֹמַר לַמֶּלֶךְ הַמֶּלֶךְ לְעוֹלָם **יִחְיֶה**

[B]ut I answered the king, **May the king live ((S=)R<E)** forever! (Neh 2:3)

The expression of the future is inherently linked to the modal axis. However, examples 271 and 272 attest to the fact that, in addition to expressing the chronological relations S=R<E, *yiqtol* forms can also convey a meaning from the field of deontic modality; for example, Esther 3:9 also connotes a [+request] and Nehemiah

---

7.   See Partee (1984) and Prior (1967), who are mentioned by Hatav (1997:5-6).

8.   Given the pervasiveness of these functions (over 90 in the corpus under examination), we will not list all the examples that fall under this heading. For more on these cases, see the discussion on the *weqatal* form's link to the modal axis in §7.3 below.

2:3 connotes a [+wish]. In principle, epistemic modality also encompasses the signification of the future. In this group, *yiqtol* frequently appears in the protasis of conditional and interrogative sentences. For instance:[9]

(273) אִם **תִּדְרְשֶׁנּוּ** יִמָּצֵא לָךְ וְאִם **תַּעַזְבֶנּוּ** יַזְנִיחֲךָ לָעַד ׃

[I]f **you seek him** he will be available to you, but if **you forsake him** he will abandon you forever. (1 Chr 28:9)

(274) וְהֵיךְ **יוּכַל** עֶבֶד אֲדֹנִי זֶה לְדַבֵּר עִם אֲדֹנִי זֶה

How **can** this servant of my Lord speak with my Lord? (Dn 10:17)

Besides those instances where the R-time is vague, there are cases where it explicitly corresponds to the speech time. For example:

(275) וְעַתָּה **אָשׁוּב** לְהִלָּחֵם עִם שַׂר פָּרָס

Now **I must go back** ((S=)R<E) to fight the prince of Persia. (Dn 10:20)

(276) וַאֲנִי מֵעַתָּה לֹא **יַעֲמָד** בִּי כֹחַ וּנְשָׁמָה לֹא נִשְׁאֲרָה בִי ׃

. . .from this point my strength **will fail me** ((S=)R<E) and no spirit will be left in me. (Dn 10:17)

In these cases, simultaneity between the R-time and the S-time is evinced by dint of the semantic essence of the particle עתה. In other words, עתה indicates that the R-time is synonymous with the S-time, whereas the *yiqtol* forms signify that the action takes place later. Example 276 underscores the disparate relations of *yiqtol* and *qatal*—subsequence and antecedence, respectively—to the same reference time:

6.2.1.3 Subsequence to a Future Action

A relation of subsequence can also appear in the context of a future action, as *yiqtol* forms are capable of denoting the future of the future, namely an action that is slated to occur after a future one.

---

9.   We will expand upon these cases in the forthcoming section on the *yiqtol* form's link to the modal axis (§6.3.1.1.3).

(277) וָאוֹמַר לַמֶּלֶךְ אִם עַל הַמֶּלֶךְ טוֹב אִגְּרוֹת יִתְּנוּ לִי עַל פַּחֲווֹת עֵבֶר הַנָּהָר אֲשֶׁר **יַעֲבִירוּנִי** עַד אֲשֶׁר **אָבוֹא** אֶל יְהוּדָה[10].

Then I said to the king, If it please the king, let me have letters to the governors of the province of Beyond the River, saying that **they shall let me pass ((S<) R<E)** until **I reach ((S<)R<E)** Judah. (Neh 2:7)

This verse features a string of *yiqtol* forms in embedded clauses, each of which signifies a future action vis-à-vis its predecessor:

This relationship turns up alongside adverbial clauses that denote future events:

(278) וְאַחֲרֵי הַשָּׁבֻעִים שִׁשִּׁים וּשְׁנַיִם **יִכָּרֵת** מָשִׁיחַ וְאֵין לוֹ

And after those sixty-two weeks, the anointed one **will disappear ((S<)R<E)** and vanish. (Dn 9:26)

(279) וּלְקֵץ שָׁנִים **יִתְחַבָּרוּ** וּבַת מֶלֶךְ הַנֶּגֶב **תָּבוֹא** אֶל מֶלֶךְ הַצָּפוֹן לַעֲשׂוֹת מֵישָׁרִים[11]

After some years, **an alliance will be made ((S<)R<E)**, and the daughter of the king of the south **will come ((S<)R<E)** to the king of the north to effect the agreement. (Dn 11:6)

This chronological relationship tends to crop up within the syntactical context of conditional sentences:[12]

(280) כִּי אִם הַחֲרֵשׁ תַּחֲרִישִׁי בָּעֵת הַזֹּאת רֶוַח וְהַצָּלָה **יַעֲמוֹד** לַיְּהוּדִים מִמָּקוֹם אַחֵר

On the contrary, if you keep silent in this crisis, relief and deliverance **will come ((S<)R<E)** to the Jews from another quarter. (Est 4:14)

(281) אִם תִּדְרְשֶׁנּוּ **יִמָּצֵא** לָךְ וְאִם תַּעַזְבֶנּוּ **יַזְנִיחֲךָ** לָעַד:

[If] you seek him **he will be available ((S<)R<E)** to you, but if you forsake him **he will abandon you ((S<)R<E)** forever. (1 Chr 28:9)

---

10. Also see Esther 1:20; 2:4; 4:16; Ezra 9:14; Nehemiah 2:8; 4:5, 14; 6:13; 1 Chronicles 28:8; 2 Chronicles 2:15; 20:12; 25:8, 16; 31:4.
11. Also see Daniel 11:13.
12. Also see Esther 1:19; Nehemiah 1:8, 9; 2:5; 13:21; 2 Chronicles 15:2; 20:20; 30:9.

6.2.1.4 Subsequence in the Habitual Present

There are cases where *yiqtol* forms denote a relation of subsequence within habitual actions.[13] These cases are akin to relations of antecedence that are signified by *qatal* forms within habitual or iterative actions, for a relation of subsequence evidently materializes every time the habitual action transpires:

(282) וּמִבְּנֵי יִשָּׂשכָר יוֹדְעֵי בִינָה לַעִתִּים לָדַעַת מַה **יַּעֲשֶׂה** יִשְׂרָאֵל רָאשֵׁיהֶם מָאתַיִם וְכָל אֲחֵיהֶם עַל פִּיהֶם:[14]

[O]f the Issacharites, men who know how to interpret the signs of the times, (and) know how Israel **should act (R<E)**; their chiefs were 200, and all their kinsmen followed them. (1 Chr 12:33)

(283) כָּל עַבְדֵי הַמֶּלֶךְ וְעַם מְדִינוֹת הַמֶּלֶךְ יֹדְעִים אֲשֶׁר כָּל אִישׁ וְאִשָּׁה אֲשֶׁר **יָבוֹא** אֶל הַמֶּלֶךְ אֶל הֶחָצֵר הַפְּנִימִית

All the king's courtiers and the people of the king's provinces know that if any person, man or woman, **enters (E<R)** the king's presence in the inner court (Est 4:11)

In 1 Chronicles 12, "יעשה" and "לדעת" maintain a relation of subsequence, and the same might be said for "יבוא" and "יודעים" in Esther 4.[15] The verb "לדעת" signifies the habitual present or a general truth, whereas the habitual verb "יעשה" denotes a subsequent action, namely "יודעים מה עליו לעשות" (they know what he must do):[16]

---

13. See the discussion on the obfuscation of the link to the reference time in generic actions (§6.2.3 below).
14. For a discussion on the use of the infinitive construct form, see §8.2.4-5 below.
15. Alternatively, the argument can be made that the link to the reference time has been blurred here as well. Perhaps the very fact that this verse can be understood in both ways constitutes a harbinger of the emergent obfuscation.
16. In this diagram, the letter "e" stands for the concrete event of knowing about the habitual action in 1 Chronicles 12:33.

6.2.1.5 Subsequence in Iterative Actions in the Past

Despite the tendency of an iterative action in the past to blur the link to R-time in generic actions,[17] there is at least one clear example of a relation of subsequence within this framework:

(284) בְּנֶה הַנַּעֲרָה בָּאָה אֶל הַמֶּלֶךְ אֵת כָּל אֲשֶׁר תֹּאמַר **יִנָּתֵן** לָהּ

> [A]nd it was after that that the girl would go to the king, whatever she asked for **would be given (R<E)** to her. (Est 2:13)

Similar to the verses in the previous section, a relation of subsequence is triggered every time a candidate states her desire. The fact that there are relatively few examples of this sort of relationship within the context of either iterative actions in the past or the habitual present might be tied to the obfuscation of the R-time link that informs these categories.

6.2.1.6 Subsequence within the Language of the Law

Similar to the habitual present and iterative actions in the past, relations of subsequence appear in legal passages that call upon the faithful to perform a habitual action:

(285) וַיִּמְצְאוּ כָּתוּב בַּתּוֹרָה אֲשֶׁר צִוָּה יְהוָה בְּיַד מֹשֶׁה אֲשֶׁר **יֵשְׁבוּ** בְנֵי יִשְׂרָאֵל בַּסֻּכּוֹת בֶּחָג בַּחֹדֶשׁ הַשְּׁבִיעִי : וַאֲשֶׁר **יַשְׁמִיעוּ וְיַעֲבִירוּ** קוֹל בְּכָל עָרֵיהֶם וּבִירוּשָׁלַם

> They found written in the Teaching that the LORD had commanded Moses that the Israelites **must dwell (R<E)** in booths during the festival of the seventh month, and that they **must announce (R<E) and proclaim (R<E)** throughout all their towns and Jerusalem. . . . (Neh 8:14-15)

(286) וְלֹא תִדְרְשׁוּ שְׁלֹמָם וְטוֹבָתָם עַד עוֹלָם לְמַעַן **תֶּחֶזְקוּ**

> [D]o nothing for their well-being or advantage, then **you will be strong (R<E)**. (Ezr 9:12)

(287) וְכֹל אֲשֶׁר לֹא יִדְרֹשׁ לַיהוָה אֱלֹהֵי יִשְׂרָאֵל **יוּמָת** לְמִן קָטֹן וְעַד גָּדוֹל לְמֵאִישׁ וְעַד אִשָּׁה :

> Whoever would not worship the LORD God of Israel **would be put to death (R<E)**, whether small or great, whether man or woman. (2 Chr 15:13)

Examples 286 and 287 are redolent of the relations in the previous two sections. However, the first passage is mildly different because the reference time is manifested in a verb ("צוה") that constitutes a part of the narrative rather than the language of the law. In any event, it also serves as the reference time for each and every future action:

---

17. See §6.2.3 below for a discussion on the blurring of the R-time link in generic actions.

צוה   ישבו   ישבו   ישבו
————'———————'———————'———————'————▶
R   E₁   E₂   E3. . .

6.2.2 Relations of Simultaneity—R=E

In addition to subsequence vis-à-vis R-time, *yiqtol* signifies simultaneity in the First and Second Temple periods. Given that *qatal* also signifies the relation R=E, what is the difference between *qatal* and *yiqtol*? The answer concerns each of the forms' links to the modal axis: *yiqtol* signifies this relationship in modal contexts, whereas *qatal* surfaces in other, non-modal frameworks.[18] Unlike the relation of antecedence, the signification of R=E by *qatal* forms is limited to the realm of the past. Conversely, the *yiqtol* form denotes this relation in both the future and past in iterative/habitual actions in the past, which also belong to the modal field.[19]

6.2.2.1 Simultaneity in the Future—S<R=E

6.2.2.1.1 Simultaneity with an Adverbial Phrase

Relations of simultaneity in the future are common in cases where the reference time is an adverbial clause. For example:[20]

(288) וּכְעָמְדוֹ **תִּשָּׁבֵר** מַלְכוּתוֹ וְתֵחָץ לְאַרְבַּע רוּחוֹת הַשָּׁמָיִם

But when he will appear, his kingdom **will be broken** ((S<)R=E) up and scattered to the four winds of heaven. (Dn 11:4)

(289) וּבָעִתִּים הָהֵם רַבִּים **יַעַמְדוּ** עַל מֶלֶךְ הַנֶּגֶב

In those times, many **will resist** ((S<)R=E) the king of the south. (Dn 11:14)

(290) וּבְהִכָּשְׁלָם **יֵעָזְרוּ** עֵזֶר מְעָט

In defeat, they **will receive** ((S<)R=E) a little help. (Dn 11:34)

The chronological relations in these cases are:

---

18. For more on the marking of simultaneity, see the beginning of the chapter on the *qatal* form (§3.2.2 above).
19. See the chapter on the *yiqtol* form's connection to the modal axis (§6.3 below) for a comprehensive look at its use within the framework of iterative actions in the past.
20. Also see Esther 9:25; Daniel 1:13; 9:27, 27; 11:8, 20, 23, 29, 40; 12:1, 1, 2, 3, 7.

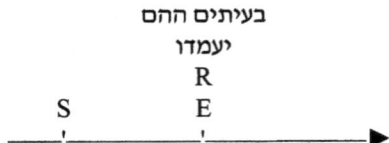

6.2.2.1.2 Simultaneity and the Link between *Yiqtol* and Other Verb Forms

6.2.2.1.2.1 Simultaneity with Verb Forms Denoting the Future

Reference time in the future can be signified not only by an adverbial phrase (as seen in the previous section), but by another verb—*yiqtol* or *weqatal*—that is situated in the future. This is indeed the most prevalent means of signification in our corpus, especially with respect to the following syntactic environments: sentences in which the form comprising the reference time signifies an action that is a generalization or elaboration, wherein the details or summary are conveyed by means of a *yiqtol* form; and causal clauses. For example:

(291) בְּשַׁלְוָה וּבְמִשְׁמַנֵּי מְדִינָה יָבוֹא וְעָשָׂה אֲשֶׁר לֹא עָשׂוּ אֲבֹתָיו וַאֲבוֹת אֲבֹתָיו בָּזֶּה
וְשָׁלָל וּרְכוּשׁ לָהֶם **יִבְזוֹר** וְעַל מִבְצָרִים **יְחַשֵּׁב** מַחְשְׁבֹתָיו וְעַד עֵת :

He will invade the richest of provinces unawares, and will do what his father and forefathers never did; **he will lavish ((S<)R=E)** on them spoil, booty, and wealth; **he will have designs ((S<)R=E)** upon strongholds, but only for a time. (Dn 11:24)

(292) וַיֹּאמְרוּ נָשִׁיב וּמֵהֶם לֹא נְבַקֵּשׁ כֵּן **נַעֲשֶׂה** כַּאֲשֶׁר אַתָּה אוֹמֵר

They replied, We shall give them back, and not demand anything of them; **we shall do ((S<)R=E)** just as you say. (Neh 5:12)

In Daniel 11:24, "יבזור" and "יחשב" constitute elaborations of the subsequent action "ועשה". Accordingly, they do not engender a new reference time, but lean on the verb "ועשה" for this purpose. Conversely, in Nehemiah 5:12, the verb "נעשה" signifies an abstract characterisation of "נשיב" and "נבקש". As in Daniel 11, no new reference time is created; instead, the *yiqtol* form is simultaneous with the preceding verbs. The chronological relations in this section are identical to the previous one:

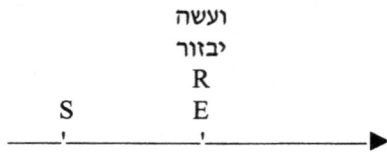

The *yiqtol* forms in the next two verses appear within explanatory clauses. As in examples 291 and 292, the *yiqtol* forms maintain relations of simultaneity:

(293) וְלֹא יַעֲמֹד כִּי **יַחְשְׁבוּ** עָלָיו מַחֲשָׁבוֹת :

. . .but will not stand fast, for **they will devise** ((S<)R=E) plans against him. (Dn 11:25)

(294) וְעַל אֱלֹהֵי אֲבֹתָיו לֹא יָבִין וְעַל חֶמְדַּת נָשִׁים וְעַל כָּל אֱלוֹהַּ לֹא יָבִין כִּי עַל כֹּל **יִתְגַּדָּל** :

He will not have regard for the god of his ancestors or for the one dear to women; he will not have regard for any god, because **he will magnify** ((S<)R=E) himself above all. (Dn 11:37)

The attributive clause "אשר ימצא את עמי" in the example below is essentially what Esther believes she will have trouble countenancing, namely the content of the scenario that she raises. The prospective event and the act of contending with it maintain a relation of simultaneity, which resembles the one outlined in examples 291 and 292 above.

(295) כִּי אֵיכָכָה אוּכַל וְרָאִיתִי בָּרָעָה אֲשֶׁר **יִמְצָא** אֶת עַמִּי וְאֵיכָכָה אוּכַל וְרָאִיתִי בְּאָבְדַן מוֹלַדְתִּי :

For how can I bear to see the disaster which **will befall** ((S<)R=E) my people! And how can I bear to see the destruction of my kindred! (Est 8:6)

6.2.2.1.2.2 Contrast to an Action Represented by *Yiqtol*

Certain relations of simultaneity between *yiqtol* and a corresponding form can be interpreted as signifying a contrast:

(296) וְיָעֵר כֹּחוֹ וּלְבָבוֹ עַל מֶלֶךְ הַנֶּגֶב בְּחַיִל גָּדוֹל וּמֶלֶךְ הַנֶּגֶב **יִתְגָּרֶה** לַמִּלְחָמָה בְּחַיִל גָּדוֹל וְעָצוּם עַד מְאֹד

He will muster his strength and courage against the king of the south with a great army. The king of the south **will wage** ((S<)R=E) war with a very great and powerful army (Dn 11:25)

(297) וְלֹא יָבִינוּ כָּל רְשָׁעִים וְהַמַּשְׂכִּלִים **יָבִינוּ** :

[A]nd none of the wicked will understand; but the knowledgeable **will understand** ((S<)R=E) (Dn 12:10)

This resembles those cases where *qatal* stands in contrast to *wayyiqtol* in the realm of the past. As noted, these instances are analogous to an indicative usage of *qatal*:[21]

---

21. See §3.2.2.3 above for more on these sorts of contrasts involving *qatal* forms.

(298) וַיָּשָׁב מָרְדֳּכַי אֶל שַׁעַר הַמֶּלֶךְ וְהָמָן **נִדְחַף** אֶל בֵּיתוֹ אָבֵל וַחֲפוּי רֹאשׁ :

Then Mordecai returned to the king's gate, while Haman **hurried (E=R(<S))** home, his head covered in mourning. (Est 6:12)

In all three examples, the highlighted verbs do not engender a new R-time. The very fact that their respective clause stands in contradistinction to the prior clause enables them to draw on the latter for their reference time. The chronological relations herein are identical to those in the previous section:

6.2.2.1.2.3 Negation

Another major group in which a relationship of simultaneity is maintained between *yiqtol* and other verb forms in the future tense consists of *yiqtol* forms that follow the negative particle לא. Similar to negative sentences with *qatal* forms, the argument can be made that the preference for *yiqtol* over sequential *weqatal* forms is a direct result of the fact that the negative particle assumes the opening clausal slot. However, the claim that we raised concerning *qatal*[22] is true here as well, for *yiqtol*'s arrayal in a position other than the sentence's opening slot still does not explain why or how the *yiqtol* form was selected. Similar to the use of *qatal* after a negative particle, these negative clauses do not spawn their own reference time, but lean predominantly on the R-time furnished by the affirmative clause that the *yiqtol* forms refer to. Put differently, negative clauses can maintain a relation of simultaneity with the corresponding positive clause. When a future action is negated, *yiqtol* is the natural candidate because the signification of the R=E relationship is part of the form's meaning. In this respect, these cases share an affinity with the contrasts that were cited in the previous section:

(299) וַיֹּאמְרוּ נָשִׁיב וּמֵהֶם **לֹא נְבַקֵּשׁ**[23]

They replied, We shall give them back, and **not demand ((S<)R=E)** anything of them (Neh 5:12)

(300) לַמּוֹעֵד יָשׁוּב וּבָא בַנֶּגֶב **וְלֹא תִהְיֶה** כָרִאשֹׁנָה וְכָאַחֲרוֹנָה :

---

22. See the discussion in §3.2.2.3.2 above on negations that are executed by *qatal* forms.
23. Similar cases include Nehemiah 2:17; Daniel 11:6 (twice), 17 (twice), 19, 25, 27; 12:10; 2 Chronicles 2:5; 7:13; 12:7; 19:10; 20:12.

At the appointed time, he will again invade the south, but the second time **will not be ((S<)R=E)** like the first. (Dn 11:29)

(301) וְנִשָּׂא הֲמוֹן יָרוּם (וְרָם) לְבָבוֹ וְהִפִּיל רִבֹּאוֹת **וְלֹא יָעוֹז**: 24.

But when the multitude is carried off, he will grow arrogant; he will cause myriads to perish, but **will not prevail ((S<)R=E)**. (Dn 11:12)

(302) וַיֹּאמֶר דָּוִיד לִשְׁלֹמֹה בְנוֹ חֲזַק וֶאֱמַץ וַעֲשֵׂה אַל תִּירָא וְאַל תֵּחָת כִּי יְהוָה אֱלֹהִים אֱלֹהַי עִמָּךְ **לֹא יַרְפְּךָ וְלֹא יַעַזְבֶךָ**

David said to his son Solomon, Be strong and of good courage and do it; do not be afraid or dismayed, for the LORD God my God is with you; **he will not fail you or forsake you ((S<)R=E)**. (1 Chr 28:20)

(303) אַל תִּלָּחֲמוּ עִם יְהוָה אֱלֹהֵי אֲבֹתֵיכֶם כִּי **לֹא תַצְלִיחוּ**:

[D]o not fight the LORD God of your fathers, because **you will not succeed ((S<)R=E)**. (2 Chr 13:12)

These verses attest to the fact that the reference time can be manifested by *yiqtol* (example 299), *weqatal* (300 and 301), or the volitive forms (302 and 303). The chronological relation herein is similar to the above noted categories of simultaneity with future forms and contrasts:

```
          ישוב ובא
          לא תהיה
———————'—————————'————————▶
   S         R, E
```

6.2.2.1.3 Simultaneity following the Particles גם, אז, and עד

Yiqtol forms that follow גם and אז constitute yet another group in which relations of simultaneity are expressed in the future:

(304) וּבָא בְּמָעוֹז מֶלֶךְ הַצָּפוֹן וְעָשָׂה בָהֶם וְהֶחֱזִיק: וְגַם אֱלֹהֵיהֶם עִם נְסִכֵיהֶם עִם כְּלֵי חֶמְדָּתָם כֶּסֶף וְזָהָב בַּשְּׁבִי **יָבִא** מִצְרָיִם

[A]nd enter the fortress of the king of the north; he will fight and overpower them. **He will also take ((S<)R=E)** their gods with their molten images and their precious vessels of silver and gold back to Egypt as booty (Dn 11:7-8)

(305) אַף יִתֶּן לְךָ יְהוָה שֵׂכֶל וּבִינָה וִיצַוְּךָ עַל יִשְׂרָאֵל וְלִשְׁמוֹר אֶת תּוֹרַת יְהוָה אֱלֹהֶיךָ: אָז **תַּצְלִיחַ** אִם תִּשְׁמוֹר לַעֲשׂוֹת אֶת הַחֻקִּים וְאֶת הַמִּשְׁפָּטִים

---

24. Similar cases include Daniel 11:15, 37, 37; 2 Chronicles 19:10.

Only let God give you sense and understanding and put you in charge of
Israel and the observance of the Teaching of the LORD your God. Then **you
shall succeed ((S<)R=E)**, if you observantly carry out the laws and the rules.
(1 Chr 22:12-13)

Verb forms that are concatenated by וגם mark a relation of simultaineity vis-à-vis
their predecessors. On the other hand, אז precludes a new reference time by creat-
ing the R-time point on its own. In so doing, these traits obviate the use of subsequent consecutive forms:

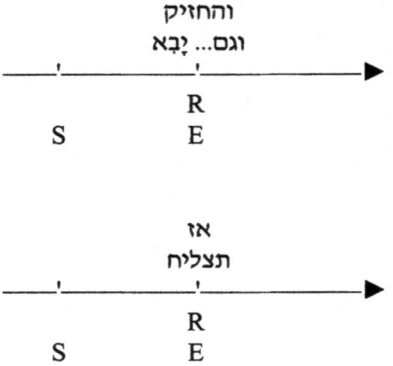

Since the collocation אז + יקטל has provoked so much discussion in biblical schol-
arship, let us delve deeper into the last example, 1 Chronicles 22:12-13. At a relatively early stage in the research,[25] there were grammarians who pointed to the
fact that there are cases where this collocation appears in the past. By virtue of
Bauer's work (1910:27),[26] the comparative Semitic perspective merited a prominent role in the discussion on the Hebrew verbal system. In consequence, attention
was turned to the connection between the following syntactical environments: the
use of the forms that are prefixed by what is termed the *Waw Conversivum* (or
convertive); and those headed by the particles אז, טרם, and עד. Put differently,
the adherents of this descriptive method claim that the ancient Semitic preterite form *yaqtul was preserved in collocations with the *Waw Conversivum* and
the above noted particles.[27] However, the morphological evidence casts serious

---

25. Scholars had pointed to this phenomenon in the nineteenth century, even before the rise
    of the comparative Semitic perspective. Ewald, among others, examined this phenom-
    enon at great length (1870:§136a; 337c).
26. Also see Bergsträsser (1929:§7g).
27. To this very day, there are scholars who believe that *wayyiqtol* and אז + יקטל are
    environments in which the ancient preterite form *yaqtul has remained extant; see
    Greenstein (1988:8), inter alios.

doubt on this approach: In those same places (the derivations ע״י, ע״י, ל״ה and the verbal stem הפעיל) where a distinction can be made, the collocation אז + יקטל corresponds, from a morphological standpoint, to the forms that derive from the ancient **yaqtulu* form.[28] Therefore, in all that concerns the morphological level, the analysis of this collocation is an indivisible part of the analysis of *yiqtol* forms.

These cases are tied to the question of the relative nature of biblical verb forms. From an R-time perspective, a survey of collocations comprised of a particle (אז, טרם(ב), or עד) and a trailing *yiqtol* or *qatal* demonstrates that these cases abide by their meaning. Wherefore, there are no cardinal differences between these instances and the other environments in which verb forms maintain the following sorts of chronological relations with their reference time:

	In the Past	In the Future (and Generic Actions)
אז + קטל:	$R>E$ or $R=E$[29]	$R>E$
אז + יקטל:	$R<E$	$R<E$ or $R=E$

Within this framework, *qatal* and *yiqtol* are ordinarily used to signify relations of

---

28. This rule applies to both the field of prose and the fields of poetry, prophecy, and wisdom literature. See Genesis 24:41; Exodus 15:1; Leviticus 26:34; Numbers 21:17; Deuteronomy 4:41; Joshua 1:8 (twice); 8:30; 20:6; 1 Kings 11:7; 12:18; 15:16; 16:5; 1 Chronicles 22:13; 2 Chronicles 5:2; as well as Ezekiel 32:14; Zephaniah 3:11; Psalms 56:5; 69:5; 119:6; Job 3:13; 33:16; Proverbs 2:5, 9. There is a single exception to this morphological rule—"אָז יַקְהֵל" in 1 Kings 8:1 (the corresponding verse in 2 Chronicles 5:2 reads "אָז יַקְהִיל"). The question of how to interpret this occurrence is a matter of research temperament. Greenstein (1988:8) avers that it is the sole remnant of an archaic usage. On the one hand, the argument can be made that this formulation constitutes an error. However, neither of these claims muddles the lucid synchronic picture of the structure's tight morphological link to the *yiqtol* form, rather than *wayyiqtol*. As a result, it behooves us to examine these cases against the background of the form's various documented roles.

29. There is only one apparent exception to this rule in the Hebrew Bible:
וַיֹּאמֶר קַח הַחִצִּים וַיִּקָּח וַיֹּאמֶר לְמֶלֶךְ יִשְׂרָאֵל הַךְ אַרְצָה וַיַּךְ שָׁלֹשׁ פְּעָמִים וַיַּעֲמֹד׃ וַיִּקְצֹף עָלָיו אִישׁ הָאֱלֹהִים וַיֹּאמֶר לְהַכּוֹת חָמֵשׁ אוֹ שֵׁשׁ פְּעָמִים **אָז הִכִּיתָ** אֶת אֲרָם עַד כַּלֵּה וְעַתָּה שָׁלֹשׁ פְּעָמִים תַּכֶּה אֶת אֲרָם׃ (2 Kgs 13:18-19)
In the Septuagint and the Vulgate, this verse is understood differently than in the Masoretic text; instead of "להכות", it has been rendered into something along the lines of "לו הכית" (if only you struck); see *BHS*. However, this interpretation does not solve the problem, for it still appears as though "הכית" expresses a future action. Be that as it may, this is not an aberration that testifies to the rule. It could very well be that the relationship between the particle "אז" and the verb "הכית" is tied to an error concerning the formulation of "להכות".

antecedence and subsequence, respectively. More specifically, when a *qatal* form trails the particle אז, it is likely to denote that the action precedes the reference time manifested by אז. On account of *qatal*'s relative characteristics, this relation can be maintained in both the past and future. Conversely, the affiliated actions of *yiqtol* forms that are preceded by אז tend to take place after the R-time established by the particle. Here too, the context can be either the past or future due to *yiqtol*'s relative nature. In addition to relations of antecedence and subsequence, these forms also denote simultaneity. Like other syntactical structures, there is a clear division between the roles: *qatal* signifies simultaneity in the realm of the past, while *yiqtol* marks simultaneity in the future (and generic actions). This description is applicable to the prose of both the First and Second Temple periods.[30] Moreover, it bears noting that, in the lone instance of אז + קוטל, the verb form's paradigmatic meaning—the relationship of inclusion in the past—is preserved:

(306) וַיְהִי רִיב בֵּין רֹעֵי מִקְנֵה אַבְרָם וּבֵין רֹעֵי מִקְנֵה לוֹט וְהַכְּנַעֲנִי וְהַפְּרִזִּי **אָז יֹשֵׁב** בָּאָרֶץ:

And there was quarreling between the herdsmen of Abram's cattle and those of Lot's cattle. The Canaanites and Perizzites **were then dwelling** (|---E---| (<S) in the land. (Gn 13:7)   **R**

The Canaanites apparently dwelled in the land both before and after the shepherds' dispute, so that the chronological relation is thus:

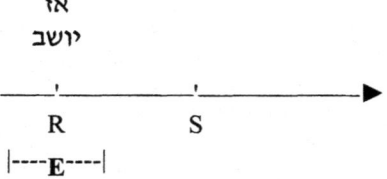

The chart below outlines the differences between the meanings borne by *qatal* and *yiqtol* forms in the collocation under discussion:

---

30. Given the material's limited scope, I will cite all the occurrences from both the First and Second Temple periods.

אז + יקטל	אז + קטל
Subsequence in the Future:	**Antecedence in the Future:**
(308) וַיֹּאמְרוּ אִם מְשַׁלְּחִים אֶת אֲרוֹן אֱלֹהֵי יִשְׂרָאֵל אַל תְּשַׁלְּחוּ אֹתוֹ רֵיקָם כִּי הָשֵׁב תָּשִׁיבוּ לוֹ אָשָׁם אָז תֵּרָפְאוּ[31]	(307) וִיהִי בְשָׁמְעֲךָ (כְּשָׁמְעֲךָ) אֶת קוֹל צְעָדָה בְּרָאשֵׁי הַבְּכָאִים אָז תֶּחֱרָץ כִּי אָז יָצָא יְהוָה לְפָנֶיךָ לְהַכּוֹת בְּמַחֲנֵה פְלִשְׁתִּים:
They answered, If you are going to send the Ark of the God of Israel away, do not send it away without anything; you must also pay an indemnity to him. **Then you will be healed ((S<)R<E).** (1 Sm 6:3)	And when you hear the sound of marching in the tops of the baca trees, then go into action, for the LORD **will have gone ((S<)E<R)** in front of you to attack the Philistine forces. (2 Sm 5:24)
Subsequence in the Past:[32]	**Antecedence in the Past:**[33]
(310) וַיְהִי כִּרְאוֹת זִמְרִי כִּי נִלְכְּדָה הָעִיר וַיָּבֹא אֶל אַרְמוֹן בֵּית הַמֶּלֶךְ וַיִּשְׂרֹף עָלָיו אֶת בֵּית מֶלֶךְ בָּאֵשׁ וַיָּמֹת. . . . אָז יֵחָלֵק הָעָם יִשְׂרָאֵל לַחֵצִי חֲצִי הָעָם הָיָה אַחֲרֵי תִבְנִי בֶן גִּינַת לְהַמְלִיכוֹ וְהַחֲצִי אַחֲרֵי עָמְרִי:	(309) וַיִּתֵּן יְהוָה אֶת לָכִישׁ בְּיַד יִשְׂרָאֵל וַיִּלְכְּדָהּ בַּיּוֹם הַשֵּׁנִי וַיַּכֶּהָ לְפִי חֶרֶב וְאֶת כָּל הַנֶּפֶשׁ אֲשֶׁר בָּהּ כְּכֹל אֲשֶׁר עָשָׂה לְלָבְנָה: אָז עָלָה הֹרָם מֶלֶךְ גֶּזֶר לַעְזֹר אֶת לָכִישׁ וַיַּכֵּהוּ יְהוֹשֻׁעַ וְאֶת עַמּוֹ עַד בִּלְתִּי הִשְׁאִיר לוֹ שָׂרִיד:
When Zimri saw that the town was taken, he went into the citadel of the royal palace and burned down the royal palace over himself. And so he died. . . . Then the people of Israel **split (R<E(<S))** into two factions: a part of the people followed Tibni son of Ginath to make him king, and the other part followed Omri. (1 Kgs 16:18-21)	The LORD delivered Lachish into the hands of Israel. They captured it on the second day and put it and all the people in it to the sword, just as they had done to Libnah. The King Horam of Gezer **had marched (E<R(<S)** to help Lachish; but Joshua defeated him and his army, letting none of them escape. (Josh 10:32-33)

---

31. This verse can perhaps also be interpreted as expressing simultaneity in the future.
32. Also see Exodus 15:1; Numbers 21:17; Deuteronomy 4:41; Joshua 8:30; 10:12; 22:1; 1 Kings 3:16; 8:1; 9:11; 2 Kings 12:18; 15:16; 16:5; 2 Chronicles 5:2. One would be hard pressed to definitively establish the chronological relation. That said, instances that probably belong to this category are 1 Kings 11:7; 2 Kings 8:22 and the corresponding verse in 2 Chronicles 21:10.
33. Also see 1 Kings 9:24.

אז + יקטל	אז + קטל
Simultaneity in the Future:[34]	**Simultaneity in the Past:**[35]
(312) וִיהִי כְּשָׁמְעֲךָ אֶת קוֹל הַצְּעָדָה בְּרָאשֵׁי הַבְּכָאִים אָז **תֶּצֵא** בַמִּלְחָמָה כִּי יָצָא הָאֱלֹהִים לְפָנֶיךָ לְהַכּוֹת אֶת מַחֲנֵה פְלִשְׁתִּים: And when you hear the sound of marching in the tops of the baca trees, then **go out ((S<)R=E)** to battle, for God will be going in front of you to attack the Philistine forces. (1 Chr 14:15)	(311) וַיֹּאמֶר פִּינְחָס בֶּן אֶלְעָזָר הַכֹּהֵן אֶל בְּנֵי רְאוּבֵן וְאֶל בְּנֵי גָד וְאֶל בְּנֵי מְנַשֶּׁה הַיּוֹם יָדַעְנוּ כִּי בְתוֹכֵנוּ יְהוָה אֲשֶׁר לֹא מְעַלְתֶּם בַּיהוָה הַמַּעַל הַזֶּה אָז **הִצַּלְתֶּם** אֶת בְּנֵי יִשְׂרָאֵל מִיַּד יְהוָה: The priest Phinehas son of Eleazar said to the Reubenites, the Gadites, and the Manassites, Now we know that the LORD is in our midst, since you have not committed such treachery against the LORD. **You have** indeed **saved (E=R(<S))** the Israelites from punishment by the LORD. (Josh 22:31)
Subsequence in the Language of the Law:[36] (313) זֹאת חֻקַּת הַפָּסַח כָּל בֶּן נֵכָר לֹא יֹאכַל בּוֹ: וְכָל עֶבֶד אִישׁ מִקְנַת כָּסֶף וּמַלְתָּה אֹתוֹ אָז **יֹאכַל** בּוֹ. . . . וְכִי יָגוּר אִתְּךָ גֵּר וְעָשָׂה פֶסַח לַיהוָה הִמּוֹל לוֹ כָל זָכָר וְאָז **יִקְרַב** לַעֲשֹׂתוֹ This is the law of the passover offering: No foreigner shall eat of it. But any slave a man has bought may only **eat (R<E)** of it after [his master] has circumcised him. . . . If a stranger who dwells with you would offer the passover to the LORD, all his males must be circumcised; only then **he shall be admitted (R<E)** to offer it. (Ex 12:43-48)	

2 Samuel 5:24 constitutes an important example, for two collocations are contrasted within a single verse: "אָז תֶּחֱרָץ כִּי אָז יָצָא". The first denotes simultaneity with "כשמעך" and the second antecedence to this event. In the corresponding verse from 1 Chronicles 14, *qatal* denotes a relation of antecedence even in the absence of the particle אז.

From a pragmatic standpoint, אז + יקטל also fills another, unique function.

---

34. Also see Genesis 24:41; Exodus 20:12; Leviticus 26:34, 41 (twice); Deuteronomy 29:19; Joshua 20:6; 2 Samuel 5:24; 2 Kings 5:3; 1 Chronicles 22:13.

35. Also see Genesis 4:26 (49:4); Exodus 4:26 (15:15); Judges 8:3; 13:21; 2 Samuel 2:27; 21:17, 18; 1 Kings 8:12; 22:50; 2 Kings 14:8; 1 Chronicles 15:2; 16:7; 20:4; 2 Chronicles 6:1; 8:12, 17; 24:17.

36. Also see Joshua 1:8 (twice).

Unlike the other collocations involving the particle אז, this variation also demarcates the boundary between distinct textual units. For instance, in the passage from
1 Kings 16, יקטל + אז partitions Zimri's life story from the inheritance struggle.[37]

6.2.2.2 Simultaneity in Iterative Actions in the Past

Like the corresponding relations of subsequence, there are habitual contexts in
which the relation of simultaneity comes to expression despite the obscurity concerning the form's link to the reference time:[38]

(314) וּבְהַגִּיעַ תֹּר נַעֲרָה וְנַעֲרָה לָבוֹא אֶל הַמֶּלֶךְ אֲחַשְׁוֵרוֹשׁ מִקֵּץ הֱיוֹת לָהּ כְּדָת הַנָּשִׁים
שְׁנֵים עָשָׂר חֹדֶשׁ כִּי כֵּן **יִמְלְאוּ** יְמֵי מְרוּקֵיהֶן

Every time a girl's turn came to go to King Ahasuerus at the end of the twelve
months' treatment prescribed for women for that was the period **allocated
(R=E)** for beautifying them. . . . (Est 2:12)

(315) וּבָזֶה הַנַּעֲרָה בָאָה אֶל הַמֶּלֶךְ אֵת כָּל אֲשֶׁר **תֹּאמַר** יִנָּתֶן לָהּ

[A]nd it was after that that the girl would go to the king, whatever she **would
ask (R=E)** for would be given her. (Est 2:13)

(316) וּבְכָל מְדִינָה וּמְדִינָה מְקוֹם אֲשֶׁר דְּבַר הַמֶּלֶךְ וְדָתוֹ **מַגִּיעַ** אֵבֶל גָּדוֹל לַיְּהוּדִים
וְצוֹם וּבְכִי וּמִסְפֵּד שַׂק וָאֵפֶר **יֻצַּע** לָרַבִּים :

Also, in every province that the king's command and decree **would reach
(participle)**, there was great mourning among the Jews, with fasting, weeping,
and wailing, and everybody **used to be offered** (*yiqtol*) [a] sackcloth and
ashes. (Est 4:3)

(317) כִּי לְעֶת יוֹם בְּיוֹם **יָבֹאוּ** עַל דָּוִיד לְעָזְרוֹ עַד לְמַחֲנֶה גָדוֹל כְּמַחֲנֵה אֱלֹהִים :

Day in day out, people **used to come (R=E)** to David to give him support, until
there was an army as vast as the army of God. (1 Chr 12:23)

The reference time in these verses can be ascertained from the context. Just as
relations of subsequence are denoted within the framework of a habitual action,
in these examples they apply to each and every action in an independent fashion.

---

37. In this context, it would be interesting to determine the connection between אז יקטל
which denotes a relation of subsequence in the past and serves as a border mark between textual units, and the cases in which the border is delineated by phrases such as
"ככלות כל זאת קטל". For an in-depth discussion on this topic, see the section on the
opening of narrative units that serve as a background for narrative chains (§3.2.1.6).
38. The obfuscation of these forms' link to the R-time axis is discussed in the next section.

Relations of simultaneity within the framework of iterative actions in the past can also be found in negative sentences:

(318) וְכָל עַבְדֵי הַמֶּלֶךְ אֲשֶׁר בְּשַׁעַר הַמֶּלֶךְ כֹּרְעִים וּמִשְׁתַּחֲוִים לְהָמָן כִּי כֵן צִוָּה לוֹ הַמֶּלֶךְ וּמָרְדֳּכַי **לֹא יִכְרַע וְלֹא יִשְׁתַּחֲוֶה** :

All the king's courtiers in the palace gate would kneel and bow low to Haman, for such was the king's order concerning him; but Mordecai **would not kneel or bow low (R=E)**. (Est 3:2)

Negative clauses are dependent on the affiliated positive clauses. In Esther 3:2, positive and negative clauses form a relation of simultaneity. Let us compare this structure with a negative sentence that contains a *qatal* form:

(319) וָאֱהִי עֹלֶה בַנַּחַל לַיְלָה וָאֱהִי שֹׁבֵר בַּחוֹמָה וָאָשׁוּב וָאָבוֹא בְּשַׁעַר הַגַּיְא וָאָשׁוּב : וְהַסְּגָנִים **לֹא יָדְעוּ** אָנָה הָלָכְתִּי

So I went up the wadi by night, surveying the wall, and, entering again by the Valley Gate, I returned. The prefects **knew nothing (E=R(<S))** of where I had gone. (Neh 2:15-16)

The difference between examples 318 and 319 is the context rather than the chronological framework, as both cases express relations of simultaneity in the past tense. Whereas *yiqtol* forms turn up in habitual-modal frameworks, *qatal* forms serve in actual-indicative ones.

6.2.3 Obfuscation of *Yiqtol*'s Link to Reference Time in Generic and Habitual Actions

When *yiqtol* fills a habitual role, its link to R-time is frequently blurred. This characteristic stems from these verbs' predisposition for marking a generic action that is not bound to any specific point in time. The obfuscation of the R-time link is a direct result of the indeterminate nature of these actions. Consequently, they tend to be "atemporal," especially in the case of independent *yiqtol* forms. For example:

(320) וָאֹמְרָה הַאִישׁ כָּמוֹנִי **יִבְרָח** וּמִי כָמוֹנִי אֲשֶׁר יָבוֹא אֶל הַהֵיכָל וָחָי

I replied, Would a man like me **take flight (habitual present)**? Besides, who such as I can go into the sanctuary and live? (Neh 6:11)

(321) לְאַרְבַּע רוּחוֹת **יִהְיוּ** הַשֹּׁעֲרִים מִזְרָח יָמָּה צָפוֹנָה וָנֶגְבָּה :

The gatekeepers **were (general truth)** on the four sides, east, west, north, and south. (1 Chr 9:24)

In these two verses, *yiqtol* forms signify the habitual present/general truth and stand alone; as a result, there is no connection between the event and reference time. The ambiguity concerning these forms' R-time link does not contradict their meaning R≤E. For as we have already seen,[39] when these verbs are arrayed in a habitual succession consisting of multiple forms that maintain chronological relations with one another, they adhere to their fundamental meaning. Against this background, it would appear to be more accurate to consider this phenomenon a neutralization of the R-time link than an aberration from these forms' role.

The next passage attests to the fact that, even in successions comprised of habitual actions, it is not always easy to determine the chronological relationships:

(322) וַאֲחֵיהֶם בְּחַצְרֵיהֶם **לָבוֹא** לְשִׁבְעַת הַיָּמִים מֵעֵת אֶל עֵת עִם עַם אֵלֶּה : כִּי בֶאֱמוּנָה הֵמָּה אַרְבַּעַת גִּבֹּרֵי הַשֹּׁעֲרִים הֵם הַלְוִיִּם וְהָיוּ עַל הַלְּשָׁכוֹת וְעַל הָאֹצָרוֹת בֵּית הָאֱלֹהִים : וּסְבִיבוֹת בֵּית הָאֱלֹהִים **יָלִינוּ** כִּי עֲלֵיהֶם מִשְׁמֶרֶת וְהֵם עַל הַמַּפְתֵּחַ וְלַבֹּקֶר לַבֹּקֶר : וּמֵהֶם עַל כְּלֵי הָעֲבוֹדָה כִּי בְמִסְפָּר **יְבִיאוּם** וּבְמִסְפָּר **יוֹצִיאוּם** :

> [A]nd their kinsmen in their villages **would join (iterative)** them every seven days, according to a fixed schedule. The four chief gatekeepers, who were Levites, were entrusted to be over the chambers and the treasuries of the House of God. They **used to spend (iterative)** the night near the House of God; for they had to do guard duty, and they were in charge of opening it every morning. Some of them had charge of the service vessels, for they were counted when they **were brought back (iterative)** and **taken out (iterative)**. (1 Chr 9:25-28)

What is the connection between "לבוא" and "ילינו" and between "יביאום" and "יוציאום"? On the one hand, the argument can be made that the second verb maintains a relation of subsequence with the first, for in each shift, say, the men had to first arrive before going to sleep. On the other hand, there is also a possibility that each form should be viewed as signifying an independent action in which the relation to the reference time is undefined.

6.2.4 Sequential Forms [R,E]

One of the attributes that distinguishes *yiqtol* in the Second Temple period is the profusion of cases in which it denotes the relationship [R,E]. As established in the first chapter of this work, the expression of this relationship is the hallmark of sequential forms in Biblical Hebrew. During the First Temple period, this feature characterized both the *wayyiqtol* form in the indicative field and the *weqatal* form in the modal field. Exceptions to this rule are quite rare. For example, Hatav found only seven cases (0.65%) in classical texts where *yiqtol* serves as a consecutive

---

39. See §6.2.1.4-6 and §6.2.2.2 above for discussions on relations of antecedence and simultaneity within the framework of the habitual present, iterative actions in the past, and the language of the law.

form (1997:57). In contrast, 58 (or 15.84%) of the 366 *yiqtol* forms in our corpus express the relation [R,E].[40]

In light of the above, it appears as though the classical framework in which *yiqtol* is the exclusive signifier of the chronological relationship R≤E is steadily breached in the Biblical Hebrew of the Second Temple period, as during this era the form also denoted the meaning [R,E]. From a systematic standpoint, this development should also be viewed as part of the shifts that consecutive forms underwent[41] as well as the decrease in the use of *weqatal* (Joosten 2005 and 2006). The next passage attests to the extensive overlap with respect to the purview of various sequential forms:[42]

(323) וַיֵּרָא יְהוָה אֶל שְׁלֹמֹה בַּלַּיְלָה וַיֹּאמֶר לוֹ. . . . **וְיִכָּנְעוּ** עַמִּי אֲשֶׁר נִקְרָא שְׁמִי עֲלֵיהֶם **וְיִתְפַּלְלוּ וִיבַקְשׁוּ** פָנַי **וְיָשֻׁבוּ** מִדַּרְכֵיהֶם הָרָעִים וַאֲנִי אֶשְׁמַע מִן הַשָּׁמַיִם **וְאֶסְלַח** לְחַטָּאתָם **וְאֶרְפָּא** אֶת אַרְצָם. . . . **וְהָיוּ** עֵינַי וְלִבִּי שָׁם כָּל הַיָּמִים: וְאַתָּה אִם תֵּלֵךְ לְפָנַי כַּאֲשֶׁר הָלַךְ דָּוִיד אָבִיךָ **וְלַעֲשׂוֹת** כְּכֹל אֲשֶׁר צִוִּיתִיךָ וְחֻקַּי וּמִשְׁפָּטַי תִּשְׁמוֹר: **וַהֲקִימוֹתִי** אֶת כִּסֵּא מַלְכוּתֶךָ:

> The LORD appeared to Solomon at night and said to him. . . . [W]hen my people, who bear my name, **humble [R,E]** themselves, **pray [R,E]**, and **seek [R,E]** my favor and **turn [R,E]** from their evil ways, I will hear in my heavenly abode and **forgive [R,E]** their sins and **heal [R,E]** their land. . . . my eyes and my heart **shall always be [R,E]** there. As for you, if you will walk before me as your father David walked before me, and **will do [R,E]** all that I have commanded you, keeping my laws and rules, **I will establish [R,E]** your royal throne over Israel forever. (2 Chr 7:12-18)

As demonstrated, a succession can be marked by the *yiqtol* (verse 14), *weqatal* (verses 16 and 18), and infinitive construct (17) forms. However, I would be hard pressed to point to any pragmatic motivation behind the decision to use one form over the next, for *weqatal*'s exclusive hold over clausal leadoff slots and *yiqtol*'s placement in any other position—rules that we are familiar with from classical Hebrew—are evidently no longer in force. Therefore, it stands to reason that the

---

40. These figures warrant qualification, as 33 out of the 58 occurrences are from Daniel 11, where the *yiqtol* and jussive forms are indistinguishable. However, even if we were to exclude this chapter from the tally, we would be left with 25 occurrences, namely 7.5% of the form's 333 occurrences. Reduced as it may be, this figure still constitutes a significant change compared to the consecutive *yiqtol* form in First Temple period prose, where they comprise less than 1% of its total occurrences. (Daniel 11 is also anomalous in other respects, including the distribution of *yiqtol* forms vis-à-vis the jussive [see the discussion in §8.2.2 below]).

41. §3.2.3 above and §10.2 below examine the changes that the *qatal* form and the infinitive absolute undergo in this context.

42. Also see Esther 1:19; Nehemiah 6:13; 8:15; Daniel 1:12, 13; 12:4, 10 (twice); 1 Chronicles 13:2; 2 Chronicles 2:15; 7:14 (six times); 12:8; 14:6.

consecutive forms *yiqtol*, *weqatal*, and the infinitive construct have undergone a certain degree of neutralization.[43]

Sequential *yiqtol* forms are capable of following not only *yiqtol* forms, but cohortative and imperative ones as well:

(324) לְכוּ **וְנִבְנֶה** אֶת חוֹמַת יְרוּשָׁלַם וְלֹא נִהְיֶה עוֹד חֶרְפָּה:

Come, **let us rebuild [R,E]** the wall of Jerusalem and suffer no more disgrace. (Neh 2:17)

(325) וְאַתָּה לֵךְ לַקֵּץ **וְתָנוּחַ** וְתַעֲמֹד לְגֹרָלְךָ לְקֵץ הַיָּמִין:

But you, go on to the end; and **rest [R,E]**, and arise to your destiny at the end of the days. (Dn 12:13)

(326) וַיֹּאמֶר דָּנִיֵּאל אֶל הַמֶּלְצַר אֲשֶׁר מִנָּה שַׂר הַסָּרִיסִים עַל דָּנִיֵּאל חֲנַנְיָה מִישָׁאֵל וַעֲזַרְיָה: נַס נָא אֶת עֲבָדֶיךָ יָמִים עֲשָׂרָה **וְיִתְּנוּ** לָנוּ מִן הַזֵּרְעִים וְנֹאכְלָה וּמַיִם **וְנִשְׁתֶּה**: **וְיֵרָאוּ** לְפָנֶיךָ מַרְאֵינוּ וּמַרְאֵה הַיְלָדִים הָאֹכְלִים אֵת פַּתְבַּג הַמֶּלֶךְ

Daniel replied to the guard whom the chief officer had put in charge of Daniel, Hananiah, Mishael and Azariah, Please test your servants for ten days, and legumes **should be provided [R,E]** so we can eat and water so **we can drink [R,E]**. Then **compare [R,E]** our appearance with that of the youths who eat of the king's food (Dn 1:11-13)

(327) אִם תָּבוֹא עָלֵינוּ רָעָה חֶרֶב שְׁפוֹט וְדֶבֶר וְרָעָב **נַעַמְדָה** לִפְנֵי הַבַּיִת הַזֶּה וּלְפָנֶיךָ כִּי שִׁמְךָ בַּבַּיִת הַזֶּה **וְנִזְעַק** אֵלֶיךָ מִצָּרָתֵנוּ **וְתִשְׁמַע וְתוֹשִׁיעַ**:

Should misfortune befall us—the punishing sword, pestilence, or famine—we shall stand before this House and before you, for your name is in this House, **and we shall cry [R,E]** out to you in our distress, **and you will listen [R,E] and deliver [R,E]** us. (2 Chr 20:9)

6.3 The *Yiqtol* Form's Link to the Modal Axis

As illustrated in the first chapter of this book, there is a complicated debate over whether the Hebrew verbal system should be considered from an aspectual or modal framework. In this discussion, we follow in the footsteps of Kuryłowicz (1973a, b) who urges scholars to reserve the terms perfective and imperfective for languages that are endowed with a full-fledged oppositional system comprised of both categories, such as the Slavic languages or Greek; Biblical Hebrew indeed lacks such a dichotomy. Moreover, we will draw on the works of Hatav (1997:117-162, 189-192) and Joosten (2002), who expand upon Kuryłowicz's thesis and en-

---

43. See the discussion on the infinitive construct form's relation to the reference-time axis in §5.4 above.

deavor to organize Biblical Hebrew's system of paradigmatic contrasts along the modal axis.

In the following discussion, the terminology is largely based on Palmer (2001). One of the fundamental distinctions that Palmer (and others) draws is between "propositional" and "event" modality, the second of which encompasses deontic modality.[44] This distinction will accompany us over the next few pages.

6.3.1 Propositional Modality

Propositional modality refers to the veracity or the degree of factuality and actuality that speakers attribute to the content of a proposition. Within this category, Palmer contends that quite a few languages maintain a secondary distinction between "epistemic" and "evidential" modality. In cases of propositional modality, the speaker opines on the extent of a certain action's factuality, whereas in the evidential variety the speaker refers to his knowledge about the way in which the action/situation has come to his or her attention. (In certain languages, there is a clear distinction between, say, actions that speakers report about from a secondary source or are part of their general knowledge and an event that is ascertained in a direct, observed fashion.)[45] In the sections that follow, we will employ Palmer's categorization with the objective of discerning the various types of propositional modality that appear in late Biblical Hebrew.[46]

6.3.1.1 Epistemic Modality

As noted, epistemic modality pertains to the speaker's judgment concerning a particular event's veracity or factuality. Put differently, this category touches upon the range of possibilities between unmitigated certainty and absolute doubt (i.e., between a real and unreal proposition). With respect to the biblical verbal system, *yiqtol* forms that denote the future can be perceived as signifiers of epistemic modality. In many languages, the future, as opposed to the past, is used not only to express chronological relations, but various modal meanings as well. According to Lyons (1977:677): "[T]he future is not like the past from the point of view of our experience and conceptualization of time. Futurity is never a purely temporal concept; it necessarily includes an element of prediction or some related modal notion." In other words, futures can be formed from modal expressions. There is a

---

44. According to Palmer, event modality is a principal category, which includes the distinction between deontic and dynamic modality; but this nuance appears to be superfluous insofar as Biblical Hebrew is concerned. Therefore, the primary foil that we will erect opposite propositional modality is deontic modality.

45. See Palmer (2001:35-52).

46. I expand upon the theoretical aspects of this topic in §2.2.3 above.

connection between future forms and the expression of various gradients of epistemic modality in various languages. Along with the signification of the future, these forms mark the extent of the speaker's confidence that the event will occur (Bybee 1994:247-248).

6.3.1.1.1 The Future

Yiqtol forms that appear within the framework of direct speech or prose prophecies and refer to the future are closely linked to the modal axis.[47] This relation can fall under the purview of both deontic modality (discussed below) and epistemic modality, the last of which covers a wide range of occurrences that run the gamut of the probability scale, beginning with cases in which the speaker is absolutely certain that an action will come to fruition and ending with those in which it is highly doubtful:

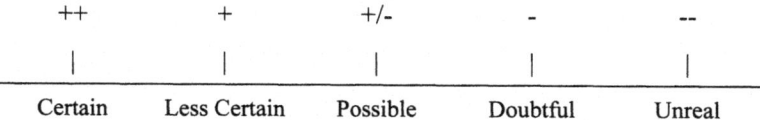

++	+	+/-	-	--
Certain	Less Certain	Possible	Doubtful	Unreal

The following examples represent the different levels of the probability scale:[48]

‏(328) הִנֵּה בֵן נוֹלָד לָךְ הוּא **יִהְיֶה** אִישׁ מְנוּחָה וַהֲנִיחוֹתִי לוֹ מִכָּל אוֹיְבָיו מִסָּבִיב כִּי שְׁלֹמֹה **יִהְיֶה** שְׁמוֹ וְשָׁלוֹם וָשֶׁקֶט **אֶתֵּן** עַל יִשְׂרָאֵל בְּיָמָיו : הוּא **יִבְנֶה** בַיִת לִשְׁמִי וְהוּא **יִהְיֶה** לִּי לְבֵן וַאֲנִי לוֹ לְאָב וַהֲכִינוֹתִי כִּסֵּא מַלְכוּתוֹ עַל יִשְׂרָאֵל עַד עוֹלָם : (++)

But you will have a son who **will be** (++) a man at rest, for I will give him rest from all his enemies on all sides; Solomon **will be** (++) his name and **I shall confer** (++) peace and quiet on Israel in his time. **He will build** (++) a House for my name; **he shall be** (++) a son to me and I to him a father, and I will establish his throne of kingship over Israel forever. (1 Chr 22:9)

‏(329) וַיֹּאמְרוּ **נָשִׁיב** וּמֵהֶם לֹא **נְבַקֵּשׁ** כֵּן **נַעֲשֶׂה** כַּאֲשֶׁר אַתָּה אוֹמֵר (++)

They replied, **We shall give** (++) them back, and not **demand** (++) anything of them; **we shall do** (++) just as you say. (Neh 5:12)

---

47. See the discussion on the link between the modal and reference-time axis in §2.2.4 above.

48. Categorizing occurrences according to the above noted division entails a fair share of personal discretion. Therefore, my interpretations are feasible, but not inalterable.

(330) אִם מָצָאתִי חֵן בְּעֵינֵי הַמֶּלֶךְ . . . יָבוֹא הַמֶּלֶךְ וְהָמָן אֶל הַמִּשְׁתֶּה אֲשֶׁר **אֶעֱשֶׂה** לָהֶם וּמָחָר אֶעֱשֶׂה כִּדְבַר הַמֶּלֶךְ : (+)

If your Majesty will do me the favor . . . let your Majesty and Haman come to the feast which **I will prepare (+)** for them; and tomorrow I will do your Majesty's bidding. (Est 5:8)

(331) וְהַיּוֹם הַזֶּה **תֹּאמַרְנָה** שָׂרוֹת פָּרַס וּמָדַי אֲשֶׁר שָׁמְעוּ אֶת דְּבַר הַמַּלְכָּה לְכֹל שָׂרֵי הַמֶּלֶךְ וּכְדַי בִּזָּיוֹן וָקָצֶף : (+/-)

This very day the ladies of Persia and Media, who have heard of the queen's behavior, **might mention (-/+)** it to all your Majesty's officials, and there will be no end of scorn and provocation! (Est 1:18)

(332) בִּמְקוֹם אֲשֶׁר **תִּשְׁמְעוּ** אֶת קוֹל הַשּׁוֹפָר שָׁמָּה תִּקָּבְצוּ אֵלֵינוּ : (+/-)

When **you hear (-/+)** a trumpet call, gather yourselves to me at that place; (Neh 4:14)

(333) כִּי אֵיכָכָה **אוּכַל** וְרָאִיתִי בָּרָעָה אֲשֶׁר יִמְצָא אֶת עַמִּי וְאֵיכָכָה **אוּכַל** וְרָאִיתִי בְּאָבְדַן מוֹלַדְתִּי : (-)

For how **can I bear (-)** to see the disaster which will befall my people! And how **can I bear (-)** to see the destruction of my kindred! (Est 8:6)

(334) וְכִי מִי אֲנִי וּמִי עַמִּי כִּי **נַעֲצֹר** כֹּחַ לְהִתְנַדֵּב כָּזֹאת כִּי מִמְּךָ הַכֹּל וּמִיָּדְךָ נָתַנּוּ לָךְ : (--)

Who am I and who are my people that **we could find (--)** the means to make such a freewill offering; but all is from you, and it is your gift that we have given to you. (1 Chr 29:14)

(335) וּמִי **יַעֲצָר** כֹּחַ לִבְנוֹת לוֹ בַיִת כִּי הַשָּׁמַיִם וּשְׁמֵי הַשָּׁמַיִם לֹא יְכַלְכְּלֻהוּ וּמִי אֲנִי אֲשֶׁר **אֶבְנֶה** לוֹ בַיִת כִּי אִם לְהַקְטִיר לְפָנָיו : (--)[49]

Who indeed **is capable (--)** of building a House for him! Even the heavens to their uttermost reaches cannot contain him, and who am I that **I could build (--)** him a House, except as a place for making burnt offerings to him? (2 Chr 2:5)

In examples 328 and 329, the speaker is highly confident that the actions marked by a *yiqtol* will come to pass. This meaning is common when the speaker is God (as in example 328) or a seer presuming to speak in God's name.[50] However, a non-divinely inspired speaker can also be reasonably confident that a specific action will take place (as in example 329).[51]

---

49. Also see Nehemiah 3:35; 6:11.
50. Also see Daniel 8:19-26; 9:24-27; 11:2b-12:3; 1 Chronicles 28:6.
51. One can perhaps also include "אצום" in Esther 4:16.

An appreciable level of certitude can also be ascribed to the queen's words in example 330, but the link of "אעשה" to the subsequent conditional clause somewhat diminishes the likelihood that the feast will be held. Therefore, the event's probability level has been ratcheted down to mere certainty (+).[52]

The next two examples are positioned in the middle of the scale (+/-), as the speakers' attitude appears to be that the actions "have a decent chance" of occurring. In example 331, the officials claim that, on account of Vashti's conduct, the rest of the elites' wives are liable to behave in a similar fashion. The verb "תשמענ", in example 332 pertains to the instructions given to the men building the wall. As in the previous verse, the speaker (Nehemiah) apparently believes that the event is likely to take place. If this is indeed the case, then the verse could have also been formulated as a conditional sentence—something along the lines of "אם תשמעו את קול השופר" (if you hear the sound of the shofar).

In example 333, Esther expresses doubts concerning her ability to restrain herself were the sword of annihilation to dangle over her people's heads. Here too, the speaker's mindset seems to fall under the rubric of deontic modality, as the queen articulates something along the lines of "I don't want to see what would happen if. . ." However, as in some of the previous examples, this meaning does not necessarily contradict the verse's epistemic meaning.

As in the previous verse, the final two examples are rhetorical question sentences. However, the speakers do not appear to harbor doubts concerning the probability of the actions that are conveyed by the *yiqtol* forms. Instead, they are certain that they are beyond the realm of the possible, namely these actions are designated unrealistic scenarios.

In sum, the field of epistemic modality in Biblical Hebrew encompasses those same cases where *yiqtol* is used in direct speech or prophetic prose. Within this framework, the form can be situated anywhere along the probability scale, from absolute certainty to an unreal proposition.

6.3.1.1.2 Interrogative Sentences

Another special context in which *yiqtol* expresses epistemic modality is the interrogative sentence. Palmer (2001:11-12) avers that both interrogative and negative sentences are frameworks where verb forms signify "non-assertiveness." According to this approach, verb forms in languages with a modal system are capable of

---

52. The argument can be made that this instance should be classified under the rubric of deontic modality, for the verse can also be interpreted as an expression of Esther's desire for the event to be held. In any case, this reading does not necessarily contradict the verse's epistemic meaning.

expressing irrealis propositions in these contexts.[53] Several Hebrew scholars have already pointed to the syntactic and semantic uniqueness of biblical interrogative sentences.[54] The signification of interrogative sentences is not the exclusive domain of *yiqtol*, as other verb forms fill this role as well. However, the *yiqtol* form stands out for its link to the above noted probability scale. Specifically, *yiqtol* forms denote various degrees of likelihood in the syntactical context of the interrogative sentence.

a.   Probable (+)

(336) וַיָּבוֹא הָמָן וַיֹּאמֶר לוֹ הַמֶּלֶךְ מַה לַעֲשׂוֹת בָּאִישׁ אֲשֶׁר הַמֶּלֶךְ חָפֵץ בִּיקָרוֹ וַיֹּאמֶר הָמָן בְּלִבּוֹ **לְמִי יַחְפֹּץ הַמֶּלֶךְ** לַעֲשׂוֹת יְקָר יוֹתֵר מִמֶּנִּי :

Haman entered, and the king asked him, What should be done for a man whom the king desires to honor? Haman said to himself, **Whom would the king desire (+) to honor** more than me? (Est 6:6)

(337) וַיֹּאמֶר שַׂר הַסָּרִיסִים לְדָנִיֵּאל יָרֵא אֲנִי אֶת אֲדֹנִי הַמֶּלֶךְ אֲשֶׁר מִנָּה אֶת מַאֲכַלְכֶם וְאֶת מִשְׁתֵּיכֶם אֲשֶׁר **לָמָּה יִרְאֶה** אֶת פְּנֵיכֶם זֹעֲפִים מִן הַיְלָדִים אֲשֶׁר כְּגִילְכֶם וְחִיַּבְתֶּם אֶת רֹאשִׁי לַמֶּלֶךְ :

The chief officer said to Daniel, I fear from my lord the king, who allotted food and drink to you, **lest he notice (+)** that you look out of sorts, unlike the other youths of your age, and you will put my life in jeopardy with the king. (Dn 1:10)

b.   Improbable (-)

(338) וַיְהִי כַּאֲשֶׁר שָׁמַע סַנְבַלַּט כִּי אֲנַחְנוּ בוֹנִים אֶת הַחוֹמָה וַיִּחַר לוֹ וַיִּכְעַס הַרְבֵּה וַיַּלְעֵג עַל הַיְּהוּדִים : וַיֹּאמֶר לִפְנֵי אֶחָיו וְחֵיל שֹׁמְרוֹן וַיֹּאמֶר מָה הַיְּהוּדִים הָאֲמֵלָלִים עֹשִׂים **הֲיַעַזְבוּ** לָהֶם **הֲיִזְבָּחוּ הֲיְכַלּוּ** בַיּוֹם **הַיְחַיּוּ** אֶת הָאֲבָנִים מֵעֲרֵמוֹת הֶעָפָר וְהֵמָּה שְׂרוּפוֹת :

[S]aying in the presence of his brothers and the Samarian force, What are the miserable Jews doing? **Will they restore(-), offer sacrifice (-), and finish (-)** one day? **Can they revive (-)** those stones out of the dust heaps, burned as they are? (Neh 3:33-34)

(339) **וְהֵיךְ יוּכַל** עֶבֶד אֲדֹנִי זֶה לְדַבֵּר עִם אֲדֹנִי זֶה וַאֲנִי מֵעַתָּה לֹא יַעֲמָד בִּי כֹחַ וּנְשָׁמָה לֹא נִשְׁאֲרָה בִי :

---

53. Also see Palmer (2001:52-55, 172-174). Moreover, he (172) notes that there are languages in which a form that is designated as a signifier of an unreal action can denote a question without any other marking (e.g., a question particle).

54. See, for example, Driver (1892:39[γ]), Hatav (1997:140-141, 147), and Joosten (2002:54).

How can (-) this servant of my Lord speak with my Lord, seeing that my strength has failed and no spirit is left in me? (Dn 10:17)

(340) הֲנָשׁוּב לְהָפֵר מִצְוֹתֶיךָ וּלְהִתְחַתֵּן בְּעַמֵּי הַתֹּעֵבוֹת הָאֵלֶּה הֲלוֹא תֶאֱנַף בָּנוּ עַד כַּלֵּה לְאֵין שְׁאֵרִית וּפְלֵיטָה: [55]

[S]hall we return (-) to violate your commandments by intermarrying with these peoples who follow such abhorrent practices? Will you not rage against us till we are destroyed without remnant or survivor? (Ezr 9:14)

In the first two verses, the speakers basically ask the following questions regarding the event's probability level: Who is the most likely candidate for the king's honors? Why aren't you eating the king's bread—he's liable to notice that your faces are sullen? Examples 338 to 340 differ in that the questions therein are rhetorical. More specifically, the speaker is not inquiring as to the actions' likelihood, but essentially claims that there is little chance they will come to fruition.

These verses can be compared to question sentences containing the *qatal* form:

(341) וַיֹּאמֶר הַמֶּלֶךְ מַה **נַּעֲשָׂה** יְקָר וּגְדוּלָּה לְמָרְדֳּכַי עַל זֶה וַיֹּאמְרוּ נַעֲרֵי הַמֶּלֶךְ מְשָׁרְתָיו לֹא נַעֲשָׂה עִמּוֹ דָּבָר:

What honor or advancement **has been conferred** on Mordecai for this? the king inquired. Nothing at all has been done for him, replied the king's servants who were in attendance on him. (Est 6:3)

(342) וָאָרִיבָה אֶת הַסְּגָנִים וָאֹמְרָה מַדּוּעַ **נֶעֱזַב** בֵּית הָאֱלֹהִים וָאֶקְבְּצֵם וָאַעֲמִדֵם עַל עָמְדָם:

I censured the prefects, saying, How is it that the House of God **has been neglected**? Then I recalled *the Levites* and installed them again in their posts. (Neh 13:11)

In these verses, *qatal* forms appear within the framework of question sentences, which semantically belong to the modal field.[56] As noted in chapter one,[57] these cases are reminiscent of *qatal* forms in other modal contexts (such as the future and the language of the law). This usage stems from the fact that there is only one form in Biblical Hebrew for marking the relation of antecedence E<R. To some extent, the modal context blurs *qatal*'s paradigmatic function [+actual, -modal] in all that concerns the modal axis. The distinction between the last two verses and examples 336 and 337 is more pronounced in all that concerns the ties to the reference-time axis (antecedence versus subsequence), but they also differ with respect to modality. In 341 and 342, the blurring of the link to the modal axis is

---

55. Also see Esther 8:6; Daniel 10:17; Ezra 9:10; 2 Chronicles 2:5.
56. See §3.3.2 above for more on the role of *qatal* forms in modal contexts.
57. §2.2.4.

negligible, so that that the actions' actuality are not tangibly undermined, at least from the vantage point of the speaker. To wit: in Esther 6:3, the king believes that Mordecai has been rewarded for his actions (even though nothing had been done in practice); and the speaker in Nehemiah 13:11 knows that the action has indeed come to pass.

6.3.1.1.3 Conditional Sentences

Yiqtol forms also denote epistemic modality in conditional sentences. Palmer groups these sentences under the category of propositional modality and argues that, in languages where unreal scenarios are marked syntactically, both real and unreal conditional sentences can be placed under this heading (2001:177-178).[58]

Besides *wayyiqtol*, conditional sentences can be formulated by means of *qatal*, the participle, *weqatal*, and directive forms and even nominal clauses.[59] However, in Hatav's estimation, the necessity of marking the relation of antecedence and the relation of inclusion (the R-time axis) is responsible for the use of non-modal forms (*qatal*, the participle) in this context (1997:146-147). As we have already argued,[60] the presence of these forms in modal contexts stems from the fact that the Hebrew is compelled, due to its relative paucity of verb forms, to utilize them whenever expressing a relation of antecedence or inclusion, as in conditional sentences.

A *yiqtol* form can turn up within the protasis and/or apodosis of a conditional clause. The primary function of *yiqtol* in protases is the signification of epistemic modality:[61]

(343) אִם הַחֲרֵשׁ **תַּחֲרִישִׁי** בָּעֵת הַזֹּאת רֶוַח וְהַצָּלָה **יַעֲמוֹד** לַיְּהוּדִים מִמָּקוֹם אַחֵר

[I]f you **keep silent** (+/-) in this crisis, relief and deliverance **will come** to the Jews from another quarter. (Est 4:14)

(344) זְכָר נָא אֶת הַדָּבָר אֲשֶׁר צִוִּיתָ אֶת מֹשֶׁה עַבְדְּךָ לֵאמֹר **אַתֶּם תִּמְעֲלוּ אֲנִי אָפִיץ** אֶתְכֶם בָּעַמִּים: וְשַׁבְתֶּם אֵלַי וּשְׁמַרְתֶּם מִצְוֹתַי וַעֲשִׂיתֶם אֹתָם אִם יִהְיֶה נִדַּחֲכֶם בִּקְצֵה הַשָּׁמַיִם מִשָּׁם **אֲקַבְּצֵם**[62]

---

58. Also see Lyons (1977:847) who deems a condition to be one of the frameworks for expressing epistemic modality.
59. See Joüon and Muraoka (1996:§167), inter alios.
60. See §2.1.2 and §2.2.4 above.
61. Other verses include Esther 1:17; 1 Chronicles 28:9; 2 Chronicles 7:13-14; 15:2.
62. Conditional sentences that are comprised entirely of two adjoining clauses are relatively rare in Biblical Hebrew, yet commonplace in the language of the Sages; see Joüon and Muraoka (1996:§a167) and Segal (1932:192). On the other hand, Segal shows (1932:192-195) that although this structure, which he indeed describes as "consecutiveness of the protasis and apodosis without a link," is quite popular in the language of the Sages, it is habitated by *qatal* rather than *yiqtol* forms.

Be mindful of the promise you gave to your servant Moses: If **you will be unfaithful** (+/-), **I will scatter** you among the peoples; but if you turn back to me, faithfully keep my commandments, even if **you were to be** dispersed (+/-) at the ends of the earth, **I will gather** them from there. (Neh 1:8-9)

(345) וְטוֹבִיָּה הָעַמֹּנִי אֶצְלוֹ וַיֹּאמֶר גַּם אֲשֶׁר הֵם בּוֹנִים אִם **יַעֲלֶה** שׁוּעָל וּפָרַץ חוֹמַת אַבְנֵיהֶם:

Tobiah the Ammonite, alongside him, said, That stone wall they are building – if a fox **were to climb** (+/-) it he would breach it! (Neh 3:35)

The verbs in the protasis of these sentences (e.g., "תחרשי", "תמעלו", and "יהיה") express probability, namely the speaker asserts that the scenario is likely to occur. Although the forms in the apodosis of these examples connote a similar meaning, there are also cases in which they may be interpreted as deontic modality:

(346) אִם עַל הַמֶּלֶךְ טוֹב **יֵצֵא** דְבַר מַלְכוּת מִלְּפָנָיו[63]

If it pleases your Majesty, let a royal edict **be issued** by you. (Est 1:19)

(347) וַיֵּצֵא דָוִיד לִפְנֵיהֶם וַיַּעַן וַיֹּאמֶר לָהֶם אִם לְשָׁלוֹם בָּאתֶם אֵלַי לְעָזְרֵנִי **יִהְיֶה** לִּי עֲלֵיכֶם לֵבָב לְיָחַד וְאִם לְרַמּוֹתַנִי לְצָרַי בְּלֹא חָמָס בְּכַפַּי יֵרֶא אֱלֹהֵי אֲבוֹתֵינוּ וְיוֹכַח:[64]

[A]nd David went out to meet them, saying to them, If you come on a peaceful errand, to support me, then **I will make** common cause with you, but if to betray me to my foes, for no injustice on my part, then let the God of our fathers take notice and give judgment. (1 Chr 12:18)

In example 346, a *yiqtol* form is used to express a request.[65] Although this verse also conveys probability (high certainty), it is accompanied by the formulation of a guarantee. The link to deontic modality is reinforced by the jussive forms that appear in the same capacity toward the end of this passage. The following example also involves a guarantee:

(348) כִּי חַנּוּן וְרַחוּם יְהוָה אֱלֹהֵיכֶם **וְלֹא יָסִיר** פָּנִים מִכֶּם אִם תָּשׁוּבוּ אֵלָיו:

[F]or the LORD your God is gracious and merciful; **he will not turn** his face from you if you return to him. (2 Chr 30:9)

---

63. Also see Esther 3:9; 5:4; Nehemiah 2:5, 7.
64. Also see Nehemiah 13:21; 2 Chronicles 20:20.
65. See the ensuing discussion (§6.3.2) on the use of *yiqtol* forms for expressing deontic modality.

6.3.1.2 Evidential Modality

As posited in the first part of this book,[66] evidential modality falls under the rubric of propositional modality. In contrast to epistemic modality, which focuses on the speaker's estimation of the veracity of the proposition, evidential modality's primary concern is the source of the evidence from which the speaker learns about the proposition. Given that *yiqtol* expresses both propositional (epistemic) and deontic modality in the Second Temple period corpus, we argued that any attempt to determine the form's habitual meanings should be approached from the link to the rest of its modal meanings. In so doing, we have chosen to place habitual actions within the framework of evidential modality. Put differently, these forms indicate the source of the evidence from which the speaker learns about the event. This decision is based, inter alia, on a typological comparison between languages with morphological categories for designating evidential modality. In these sorts of languages, the meaning of a habitual action/general truth is occasionally classified under "habitual modality."[67] Unlike the category of the future, wherein the speaker judges the probability of a future action, evidential modality concerns the manner in which the speaker learns about an occurrence, namely the specific action that comes to his or her attention from more general information.

6.3.1.2.1 General Truth/Habitual Present

The connection of actions constituting a general truth/habitual present to the time axis tends to be neutralized.[68] In other words, the action can take place before, during, or after the speech time regardless of whether it is an iterative action (a) or a general truth that displays a feature (b):[69]

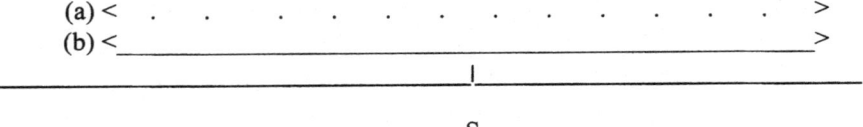

$$\text{S}$$

---

66. See §2.2.3 above.
67. See Palmer (2001:8), who notes that in Central Pomo there are five categories of "evidence," among them general information.
68. As averred in §2.2.4 of this work, when these verbs are arrayed within the framework of a distinct proposition, there are advantages to claiming that the link to the reference-time axis, which we designated as MØ, has been neutralized. Also see the discussion in this chapter (§6.2.3) on the blurring of the link to the R-time axis.
69. At this juncture, we will not attempt to untangle the complex differences between generics and habituals. For an in-depth look at this topic, see Dahl (1975), Comrie (1976:26-32), and Hatav (1997:131-138); the latter also provides a bibliography.

For example:

(349) לְאַרְבַּע רוּחוֹת **יִהְיוּ** הַשֹּׁעֲרִים מִזְרָח יָמָּה צָפוֹנָה וָנֶגְבָּה :

The gatekeepers **were (GT)** on the four sides, east, west, north, and south.
(1 Chr 9:24)

(350) כָּל עַבְדֵי הַמֶּלֶךְ וְעַם מְדִינוֹת הַמֶּלֶךְ יֹדְעִים אֲשֶׁר כָּל אִישׁ וְאִשָּׁה אֲשֶׁר **יָבוֹא** אֶל
הַמֶּלֶךְ אֶל הֶחָצֵר הַפְּנִימִית אֲשֶׁר לֹא יִקָּרֵא אַחַת דָּתוֹ לְהָמִית לְבַד מֵאֲשֶׁר **יוֹשִׁיט** לוֹ
הַמֶּלֶךְ אֶת שַׁרְבִיט הַזָּהָב וְחָיָה וַאֲנִי לֹא נִקְרֵאתִי לָבוֹא אֶל הַמֶּלֶךְ זֶה שְׁלוֹשִׁים יוֹם :

All the king's courtiers and the people of the king's provinces know that if
any person, man or woman, **enters (HP)** the king's presence in the inner
court without having been summoned, there is but one law for him—that
he be put to death. Only if the king **extends (HP)** the golden scepter to him
may he live. Now I have not been summoned to visit the king for the last
thirty days. (Est 4:11)

(351) כִּי אֶל הַלְּשָׁכוֹת **יָבִיאוּ** בְנֵי יִשְׂרָאֵל וּבְנֵי הַלֵּוִי אֶת תְּרוּמַת הַדָּגָן הַתִּירוֹשׁ וְהַיִּצְהָר

For it is to the storerooms that the Israelites and the Levites **bring (HP)** the
gifts of grain, wine, and oil. (Neh 10:40)

These verb forms do not mark the duration of generic actions, so that the time span
must be ascertained from the context. As Dahl (1975) and Hatav (1997:131-138)
show, duration is highly dependent on the nature of the subject. The actions are not
identified with a particular point in time. These actions might circumscribe a fixed
duration, but this has no bearing on the habitual nature of these actions.

6.3.1.2.2 Iterative Actions in the Past

On the face of things, an account of the modal meaning of an iterative action in
the past would appear to be more difficult to comprehend than, say, a habitual
one because modal expressions tend to refer to the future, whereas an action that
occurs in the past lacks an immediate connection to modality (Palmer 2001:179;
Givón 1994:270-271). However, in many languages, full-fledged modal forms include a subsidiary role that expresses iteration in the past. From this perspective,
the difference between the iterative past and habitual present is that the former is
limited to the past:

. . . .   Habitual Present

. . . .   Iterative Action in the Past

S

Here are several examples of iterative actions in the past:

(352) וּבְהַגִּיעַ תֹּר נַעֲרָה וְנַעֲרָה לָבוֹא אֶל הַמֶּלֶךְ אֲחַשְׁוֵרוֹשׁ מִקֵּץ הֱיוֹת לָהּ כְּדָת הַנָּשִׁים שְׁנֵים עָשָׂר חֹדֶשׁ כִּי כֵּן **יִמְלְאוּ** יְמֵי מְרוּקֵיהֶן שִׁשָּׁה חֳדָשִׁים בְּשֶׁמֶן הַמֹּר וְשִׁשָּׁה חֳדָשִׁים בַּבְּשָׂמִים וּבְתַמְרוּקֵי הַנָּשִׁים: וּבָזֶה הַנַּעֲרָה בָּאָה אֶל הַמֶּלֶךְ אֵת כָּל אֲשֶׁר **תֹּאמַר יִנָּתֵן** לָהּ לָבוֹא עִמָּהּ מִבֵּית הַנָּשִׁים עַד בֵּית הַמֶּלֶךְ:

When each girl's turn came to go to King Ahasuerus at the end of the twelve months' treatment prescribed for women (for that was the period **spent on (IP)** beautifying them: six months with oil of myrrh and six months with perfumes and women's cosmetics, and it was after that that the girl would go to the king), whatever **she asked for (IP) would be given (IP)** her to take with her from the harem to the king's palace. (Est 2:12-13)

(353) וְכָל עַבְדֵי הַמֶּלֶךְ אֲשֶׁר בְּשַׁעַר הַמֶּלֶךְ כֹּרְעִים וּמִשְׁתַּחֲוִים לְהָמָן כִּי כֵן צִוָּה לוֹ הַמֶּלֶךְ וּמָרְדֳּכַי **לֹא יִכְרַע וְלֹא יִשְׁתַּחֲוֶה**:

All the king's courtiers in the palace gate knelt and bowed low to Haman, for such was the king's order concerning him; but Mordecai **would not kneel (IP) or bow low (IP)**. (Est 3:2)

(354) וּבְכָל מְדִינָה וּמְדִינָה מְקוֹם אֲשֶׁר דְּבַר הַמֶּלֶךְ וְדָתוֹ מַגִּיעַ אֵבֶל גָּדוֹל לַיְּהוּדִים וְצוֹם וּבְכִי וּמִסְפֵּד שַׂק וָאֵפֶר **יֻצַּע לָרַבִּים**:

Also, in every province that the king's command and decree would reach, there was great mourning among the Jews, with fasting, weeping, and wailing and everybody **used to be offered (IP)** [a] sackcloth and ashes. (Est 4:3)

(355) כִּי לְעֶת יוֹם בְּיוֹם **יָבֹאוּ** עַל דָּוִיד לְעָזְרוֹ עַד לְמַחֲנֶה גָדוֹל כְּמַחֲנֵה אֱלֹהִים:

Day in day out, people **would come (IP)** to David to give him support, until there was an army as vast as the army of God. (1 Chr 12:23)

(356) וַיְהִי אַחֲרֵי בוֹא אֲמַצְיָהוּ מֵהַכּוֹת אֶת אֲדוֹמִים וַיָּבֵא אֶת אֱלֹהֵי בְּנֵי שֵׂעִיר וַיַּעֲמִידֵם לוֹ לֵאלֹהִים וְלִפְנֵיהֶם **יִשְׁתַּחֲוֶה** וְלָהֶם **יְקַטֵּר**:

After Amaziah returned from defeating the Edomites, he had the gods of the men of Seir brought, and installed them as his gods; he prostrated himself before them, and to them **he would bow low (IP)** and **would give a sacrifice (IP)**. (2 Chr 25:14)

The last two verses indicate that iterative meaning can be established by means of either an adverb, such as "לעת יום ביום" in 1 Chronicles 12:23, or exclusively by a *yiqtol* form, as in 2 Chronicles 25:14 where the shift from *wayyiqtol* to *yiqtol* forms denotes a transition from the narrative to habitual actions.

6.3.2 Deontic Modality

As aforementioned, the primary difference between propositional and event modality is that the former is concerned with the speaker's assessment of a proposition's veracity [+probability] and the latter with the expression of the speaker's desire toward a future event [+desire]. In the discussion that follows, we will examine the two principal contexts of deontic modality: the directive and the language of the law.

6.3.2.1 The Directive

The directive consists of various gradients of the speaker's desire with respect to a stated proposition, including orders, prohibitions, oaths, requests, wishes, and desire. In Biblical Hebrew, the marked directive forms are the cohortative (אקטלה), imperative, and jussive,[70] which appear in complementary distributions in the first, second, and third persons, respectively. Whereas the directive meaning is compulsory insofar as the cohortative, imperative, and jussive are concerned, it is optional for *yiqtol*.

We have already demonstrated that there is a close tie between the R-time axis and the attributes that pertain to the modal axis.[71] From a chronological standpoint, we posited that the directive forms are limited to marking the relation S,R<E, while *yiqtol* can also denote several other chronological alignments, all within the framework of its paradigmatic R≤E relationship. As a result, in those same cases where *yiqtol* expresses S,R<E, the similarities to the directive forms become all the more salient. This feature is also true of classical Hebrew. However, given the fact that in the Second Temple period (unlike classical Hebrew) *yiqtol* marks the relation of succession [R,E], it is used within successions of directive forms as well. It stands to reason that this last trait also contributes to the obfuscation of the differences between the various forms during the period in question.

6.3.2.1.1 The Imperative Mood

The imperative is one of the directive moods connoted by *yiqtol* forms:

(357) וְהִנֵּה בְעָנְיִי הֲכִינוֹתִי לְבֵית יְהוָה זָהָב כִּכָּרִים מֵאָה אֶלֶף וְכֶסֶף אֶלֶף אֲלָפִים כִּכָּרִים וְלַנְּחֹשֶׁת וְלַבַּרְזֶל אֵין מִשְׁקָל כִּי לָרֹב הָיָה וְעֵצִים וַאֲבָנִים הֲכִינוֹתִי וַעֲלֵיהֶם תּוֹסִיף:

See, by denying myself, I have laid aside for the House of the LORD one hundred thousand talents of gold and one million talents of silver, and so much

---

70. For more on this matter, see the discussion on the volitive forms in §9 below.

71. See the discussion on the *yiqtol* form's link to the reference-time axis.

copper and iron it cannot be weighed; I have also laid aside wood and stone,
and **you shall add (impv.)** to them. (1 Chr 22:14)

(358) וְאַתָּה לֵךְ לַקֵּץ **וְתָנוּחַ וְתַעֲמֹד** לְגֹרָלְךָ לְקֵץ הַיָּמִין: [72]

But you, go on to the end; **you shall rest (impv.)** and **arise (impv.)** to your
destiny at the end of the days. (Dn 12:13)

In 1 Chronicles 22:14, David not only tells Solomon what the future holds, but
issues him instructions by dint of the verb "תּוֹסִיף". This interpretation is bolstered
by the sentence's context, namely the string of directive forms in the two adjacent
verses (13 and 15-16):

(359) אָז תַּצְלִיחַ אִם תִּשְׁמוֹר לַעֲשׂוֹת אֶת הַחֻקִּים וְאֶת הַמִּשְׁפָּטִים אֲשֶׁר צִוָּה יְהוָה
אֶת מֹשֶׁה עַל יִשְׂרָאֵל **חֲזַק וֶאֱמָץ אַל תִּירָא וְאַל תֵּחָת.** . . . **קוּם וַעֲשֵׂה** וִיהִי יְהוָה עִמָּךְ:

Then you shall succeed, if you observantly carry out the laws and the rules that
the LORD charged Moses to lay upon Israel. **Be strong and of good courage;
do not be afraid or dismayed.** . . . . **Go and do** it, and may the LORD be with
you (1 Chr 22:13-16)

In Daniel 12:13 (example 358), the *yiqtol* forms also convey a directive. More
specifically, they serve as consecutive forms that are preceded by an imperative
("לֵךְ"). The latter is positioned at the outset of a series of instructions and marks
the succession as a directive chain. This alignment testifies to the fact that *yiqtol*
forms are capable of signifying commands.

6.3.2.1.2 The Prohibitive Mood

The prohibitive mood is the negative mirror image of the imperative. As in the latter, the most common method for signifying the prohibitive in Biblical Hebrew is
via the marked prohibitive form—the jussive:

(360) וְאַתֶּם חִזְקוּ **וְאַל יִרְפּוּ** יְדֵיכֶם כִּי יֵשׁ שָׂכָר לִפְעֻלַּתְכֶם:

As for you, be strong; **do not be disheartened (juss.-prohib.)** for there is
reward for your labor. (2 Chr 15:7)

---

72. Perhaps the following passage from Daniel can be added to this category (Dn 1:3-5):
וַיֹּאמֶר הַמֶּלֶךְ לְאַשְׁפְּנַז רַב סָרִיסָיו לְהָבִיא מִבְּנֵי יִשְׂרָאֵל וּמִזֶּרַע הַמְּלוּכָה וּמִן הַפַּרְתְּמִים: יְלָדִים אֲשֶׁר
אֵין בָּהֶם כָּל מאוּם וְטוֹבֵי מַרְאֶה וּמַשְׂכִּלִים בְּכָל חָכְמָה וְיֹדְעֵי דַעַת וּמְבִינֵי מַדָּע וַאֲשֶׁר כֹּחַ בָּהֶם לַעֲמֹד
בְּהֵיכַל הַמֶּלֶךְ וּלְלַמְּדָם סֵפֶר וּלְשׁוֹן כַּשְׂדִּים: וַיְמַן לָהֶם הַמֶּלֶךְ דְּבַר יוֹם בְּיוֹמוֹ מִפַּת בַּג הַמֶּלֶךְ וּמִיֵּין
מִשְׁתָּיו **וּלְגַדְּלָם** שָׁנִים שָׁלוֹשׁ וּמִקְצָתָם **יַעַמְדוּ** לִפְנֵי הַמֶּלֶךְ.
If we interpret the verbs "ולגדלם" and "יעמדו" as continuation of the instructions in the
first two verses, then verse 5 can also be entered under the heading of the imperative
mood. See the discussion on this verse in §8.2.7 below.

Nevertheless, 2 Chronicles 28:13 demonstrates that there are other available options:

(361) וַיֹּאמְרוּ לָהֶם לֹא **תָבִיאוּ** אֶת הַשִּׁבְיָה הֵנָּה כִּי לְאַשְׁמַת יְהוָה עָלֵינוּ אַתֶּם אֹמְרִים לְהֹסִיף עַל חַטֹּאתֵנוּ וְעַל אַשְׁמָתֵנוּ

[A]nd said to them, **Do not bring (*yiqtol*-prohib.)** these captives here, for it would mean our offending the Lord, adding to our sins and our offenses.

The command to refrain from bringing all the captives is a concrete prohibition, which is tantamount to the one in the first example. The chronological relations herein is S,R<E, and the distinction between the marked directive form and *yiqtol* has been obfuscated.

6.3.2.1.3 The Language of the Oath

The *yiqtol* form also appears within oath language. In the following example, Nehemiah administers an oath to the nation, whereby they will refrain from betrothing their children to gentiles:

(362) וָאָרִיב עִמָּם וָאֲקַלְלֵם וָאַכֶּה מֵהֶם אֲנָשִׁים וָאֶמְרְטֵם וָאַשְׁבִּיעֵם בֵּאלֹהִים אִם **תִּתְּנוּ** בְנֹתֵיכֶם לִבְנֵיהֶם וְאִם **תִּשְׂאוּ** מִבְּנֹתֵיהֶם לִבְנֵיכֶם וְלָכֶם :

I censured them, cursed them, flogged them, tore out their hair, and adjured them by God, saying, **You shall not give (oath)** your daughters in marriage to their sons, or **take (oath)** any of their daughters for your sons or yourselves. (Neh 13:25)

The conjunction אם bears a negative meaning.[73] Since this verse constitutes a direct oath, the structure is conjugated in the second person. An indirect oath turns up in Nehemiah 5:12:

(363) וָאַשְׁבִּיעֵם לַעֲשׂוֹת כַּדָּבָר הַזֶּה :

I put them under oath to keep this promise.

Nehemiah 10:29-32 also contains several vows:

(364) וּשְׁאָר הָעָם . . . מַחֲזִיקִים עַל אֲחֵיהֶם אַדִּירֵיהֶם וּבָאִים בְּאָלָה וּבִשְׁבוּעָה לָלֶכֶת בְּתוֹרַת הָאֱלֹהִים. . . . וַאֲשֶׁר **לֹא נִתֵּן** בְּנֹתֵינוּ לְעַמֵּי הָאָרֶץ וְאֶת בְּנֹתֵיהֶם **לֹא נִקַּח** לְבָנֵינוּ : וְעַמֵּי הָאָרֶץ הַמְבִיאִים אֶת הַמַּקָּחוֹת וְכָל שֶׁבֶר בְּיוֹם הַשַּׁבָּת לִמְכּוֹר **לֹא נִקַּח** מֵהֶם בַּשַּׁבָּת וּבְיוֹם קֹדֶשׁ **וְנִטֹּשׁ** אֶת הַשָּׁנָה הַשְּׁבִיעִית וּמַשָּׁא כָל יָד :

---

73. Joüon and Muraoka (1996:§165a).

And the rest of the people . . . [j]oin with their noble brothers, and take an oath with sanctions to follow the Teaching of God. . . . Namely: **We will not give (oath)** our daughters in marriage to the peoples of the land, **or take (oath)** their daughters for our sons. The peoples of the land who bring their wares and all sorts of foodstuff for sale on the sabbath day, **we will not buy (oath)** from them on the sabbath or a holy day. **We will forgo (oath)** the produce of the seventh year, and every outstanding debt.

6.3.2.1.4 Request

Among the *yiqtol* form's directive meanings is the request. The difference between an order and a request often stems from the speaker's status vis-à-vis the addressee. Accordingly, the request meaning is prevalent within the context of solicitations to more dignified addressees, like a king or God:

(365) אִם עַל הַמֶּלֶךְ טוֹב **יֵצֵא** דְבַר מַלְכוּת מִלְּפָנָיו **וְיִכָּתֵב** בְּדָתֵי פָרַס וּמָדַי **וְלֹא יַעֲבוֹר** אֲשֶׁר לֹא תָבוֹא וַשְׁתִּי לִפְנֵי הַמֶּלֶךְ אֲחַשְׁוֵרוֹשׁ וּמַלְכוּתָהּ **יִתֵּן** הַמֶּלֶךְ לִרְעוּתָהּ הַטּוֹבָה מִמֶּנָּה:

If it please your Majesty, **let** a royal edict **be issued (req.)** by you, and **let it be written (req.)** into the laws of Persia and Media, **so that it cannot be abrogated (req.)**, that Vashti shall never enter the presence of King Ahasuerus. And let your Majesty **bestow (req.)** her royal state upon another who is more worthy than she. (Est 1:19)

(366) וַיֹּאמְרוּ נַעֲרֵי הַמֶּלֶךְ מְשָׁרְתָיו **יְבַקְשׁוּ** לַמֶּלֶךְ נְעָרוֹת בְּתוּלוֹת טוֹבוֹת מַרְאֶה: [74]

The king's servants who attended him said, **Let** beautiful young virgins **be sought (req.)** out for your Majesty. (Est 2:2)

(367) נַס נָא אֶת עֲבָדֶיךָ יָמִים עֲשָׂרָה **וְיִתְּנוּ** לָנוּ מִן הַזֵּרֹעִים וְנֹאכְלָה וּמַיִם וְנִשְׁתֶּה: **וְיֵרָאוּ** לְפָנֶיךָ מַרְאֵינוּ וּמַרְאֵה הַיְלָדִים הָאֹכְלִים אֵת פַּתְבַּג הַמֶּלֶךְ וְכַאֲשֶׁר תִּרְאֵה עֲשֵׂה עִם עֲבָדֶיךָ:

Please test your servants for ten days, legumes **should be provided (req.)** so we can eat and water so we can drink. Then **compare (req.)** our appearance with that of the youths who eat of the king's food, and do with your servants as you see fit. (Dn 1:12-13)

(368) אֱלֹהֵינוּ הֲלֹא **תִשְׁפָּט** בָּם כִּי אֵין בָּנוּ כֹּחַ לִפְנֵי הֶהָמוֹן הָרָב הַזֶּה הַבָּא עָלֵינוּ וַאֲנַחְנוּ לֹא נֵדַע מַה נַּעֲשֶׂה כִּי עָלֶיךָ עֵינֵינוּ: [75]

---

74. Also see Esther 5:4; Nehemiah 2:5, 7.
75. The findings warrant some qualification. Out of all the relevant occurrences, there is not a single designated *yiqtol* form. Put differently, none of the *yiqtol* forms can be morphologically distinguished from the jussive. For example, the verb "ויתנו" in Daniel 1:12-13 appears within a succession of marked directive forms: "נס", "ונאכלה",

O our God, surely **you will punish (req.)** them, for we are powerless before this great multitude that has come against us, and do not know what to do, but our eyes are on you. (2 Chr 20:12)

6.3.2.1.5 The Optative Mood

The expression of wishes is yet another function of the *yiqtol* form:

(369) וָאֹמַר לַמֶּלֶךְ הַמֶּלֶךְ לְעוֹלָם יִחְיֶה

[B]ut I answered the king, **May** the king **live (opt.)** forever! (Neh 2:3)

(370) כִּי הִתְפַּלֵּל יְחִזְקִיָּהוּ עֲלֵיהֶם לֵאמֹר יְהוָה הַטּוֹב **יְכַפֵּר** בְּעַד :

Hezekiah prayed for them, saying, The good LORD **will provide (opt.)** atonement for . . . (2 Chr 30:18)

Example 369 is among the verses that Hurvitz (1972:21) cites for the purpose of illustrating the differences between the language in our corpus and that of classical texts, where we find the following structure:

(371) וַתִּקֹּד בַּת שֶׁבַע אַפַּיִם אֶרֶץ וַתִּשְׁתַּחוּ לַמֶּלֶךְ וַתֹּאמֶר **יְחִי אֲדֹנִי הַמֶּלֶךְ דָּוִד לְעֹלָם** :

Bathsheba bowed low in homage to the king with her face to the ground, and she said, **May my lord King David live (jussive opt.) forever!** (1 Kgs 1:31)

In Hurvitz's estimation, the word order in Nehemiah 2:3 was influenced by con- temporaneous Aramaic. As evidence, he compares this verse to Daniel 2:4: "מַלְכָּא לְעָלְמִין חֱיִי". However, it bears noting that the forms in Kings and Daniel are marked directives (jussive and imperative forms), while Nehemiah expresses a wish by means of a *yiqtol* form.

6.3.2.1.6 Expressing Desire

In certain directive contexts, the *yiqtol* form articulates a general desire. Although these cases share an affinity with those in the previous clause (the optative), the expression of desire is more general and does not fall under any of the other cat- egories. For example:

---

and "ונשתה". If this passage were from the First Temple period corpus, then we would probably have deemed "ויתנו" and "ויראו" to be jussives due to their position at the beginning of the clauses. However, as we have already seen, the *yiqtol* form is capable of filling this slot in the Second Temple period and can be aligned within a succession of marked directive forms.

(372) וְעַתָּה **נִכְרָת** בְּרִית לֵאלֹהֵינוּ לְהוֹצִיא כָל נָשִׁים וְהַנּוֹלָד מֵהֶם בַּעֲצַת אֲדֹנָי
וְהַחֲרֵדִים בְּמִצְוַת אֱלֹהֵינוּ וְכַתּוֹרָה **יֵעָשֶׂה** : קוּם כִּי עָלֶיךָ הַדָּבָר וַאֲנַחְנוּ עִמָּךְ חֲזַק
וַעֲשֵׂה :

Now then, **let us make (des.)** a covenant with our God to expel all these
women and those who have been born to them, in accordance with the bidding
of the Lord and of all who are concerned over the commandment of our God,
and **let** the Teaching **be obeyed (des.)**. Take action, for the responsibility is
yours and we are with you. Act with resolve! (Ezr 10:3-4)

(373) וָאוֹמַר אֲלֵהֶם אַתֶּם רֹאִים הָרָעָה אֲשֶׁר אֲנַחְנוּ בָהּ אֲשֶׁר יְרוּשָׁלַם חֲרֵבָה וּשְׁעָרֶיהָ
נִצְּתוּ בָאֵשׁ לְכוּ וְנִבְנֶה אֶת חוֹמַת יְרוּשָׁלַם וְלֹא נִהְיֶה עוֹד חֶרְפָּה : וָאַגִּיד לָהֶם אֶת
יַד אֱלֹהַי אֲשֶׁר הִיא טוֹבָה עָלַי וְאַף דִּבְרֵי הַמֶּלֶךְ אֲשֶׁר אָמַר לִי וַיֹּאמְרוּ **נָקוּם** וּבָנִינוּ
וַיְחַזְּקוּ יְדֵיהֶם לַטּוֹבָה :

Then I said to them, you see the bad state we are in—Jerusalem lying in ruins
and its gates destroyed by fire. Come, let us rebuild the wall of Jerusalem and
suffer no more disgrace. I told them of my God's benevolent care for me, also
of the things that the king had said to me, and they said, **Let us start (des.)**
building! They were encouraged by *his* benevolence. (Neh 2:17-18)

(374) וַיֹּאמְרוּ **נָשִׁיב** וּמֵהֶם לֹא נְבַקֵּשׁ כֵּן נַעֲשֶׂה כַּאֲשֶׁר אַתָּה אוֹמֵר וָאֶקְרָא אֶת
הַכֹּהֲנִים וָאַשְׁבִּיעֵם לַעֲשׂוֹת כַּדָּבָר הַזֶּה :

They replied, **We shall give them back (des.)**, and not demand anything of
them; we shall do just as you say. Summoning the priests, I put them under
oath to keep this promise. (Neh 5:12)

(375) וַאֲנִי בָאתִי בֵּית שְׁמַעְיָה בֶן דְּלָיָה בֶּן מְהֵיטַבְאֵל וְהוּא עָצוּר וַיֹּאמֶר **נִוָּעֵד** אֶל
בֵּית הָאֱלֹהִים אֶל תּוֹךְ הַהֵיכָל וְנִסְגְּרָה דַּלְתוֹת הַהֵיכָל כִּי בָּאִים לְהָרְגֶךָ וְלַיְלָה בָּאִים
לְהָרְגֶךָ : [76]

Then I visited Shemaiah son of Delaiah son of Mehetabel when he was
housebound, and he said, **Let us meet (des.)** in the House of God, inside the
sanctuary. And let us shut the doors of the sanctuary, for they are coming to kill
you, by night they are coming to kill you. (Neh 6:10)

The succession in the fourth passage is comprised of the verbs "נועד" and the cohortative "ונסגרה", both of which essentially convey the expression of a desire. In
example 372, Shecaniah avails himself of *yiqtol* forms when speaking about what
the nation must do and utilizes imperative forms when addressing Ezra. This usage
engenders a sort of parallelism between the two forms, so that here too there is
evidently a link between the designated volitive meanings of both forms.

---

76. Also see Nehemiah 6:11; 1 Chronicles 22:8; 28:3; 2 Chronicles 2:15; 14:6; 20:20;
28:23.

6.3.2.2 The Language of the Law

Unlike classical literature, the amount of passages of the language of the law in late classical Hebrew is relatively scant. However, this clearly does not imply that only a few laws were written during this period, as a short perusal through the Dead Sea Scrolls is enough to demonstrate the opposite.[77] That said, only a handful of juridical passages have survived. As a result, the examples below do not derive from lengthy legal compendia, but from shorter segments dispersed throughout the texts.

The decision to classify the *yiqtol* forms that denote the language of the law under the heading of deontic modality is tied to the fact that these contexts naturally include the meaning of instruction. The main point of divergence between commandments within the language of the law and those belonging to the directive group is that the former are generic/general instructions, whereas the latter are concrete orders which refer to an actual event. For example, when the angel orders Abraham "אל תשלך ידך אל הנער" in Genesis 22:12, he is referring to a specific event. Conversely, the commandment "לא תרצח" Thou shall not kill (Exodus 20:13) is a general directive, namely a generic prohibition that applies to any future situation in which a person is liable to kill another human being. The following are examples of *yiqtol* in juridical passages:

(376) וַיִּמְצְאוּ כָּתוּב בַּתּוֹרָה אֲשֶׁר צִוָּה יְהוָה בְּיַד מֹשֶׁה אֲשֶׁר **יֵשְׁבוּ** בְנֵי יִשְׂרָאֵל בַּסֻּכּוֹת בֶּחָג בַּחֹדֶשׁ הַשְּׁבִיעִי : וַאֲשֶׁר **יַשְׁמִיעוּ וְיַעֲבִירוּ** קוֹל בְּכָל עָרֵיהֶם וּבִירוּשָׁלַם[78]

They found written in the Teaching that the LORD had commanded Moses that the Israelites **must dwell (law)** in booths during the festival of the seventh month, and that **they must announce (law) and proclaim (law)** throughout all their towns and Jerusalem. (Neh 8:14-15)

(377) בַּיּוֹם הַהוּא נִקְרָא בְּסֵפֶר מֹשֶׁה בְּאָזְנֵי הָעָם וְנִמְצָא כָתוּב בּוֹ אֲשֶׁר לֹא **יָבוֹא** עַמֹּנִי וּמֹאָבִי בִּקְהַל הָאֱלֹהִים עַד עוֹלָם :[79]

At that time they read to the people from the book of Moses, and it was found written that no Ammonite or Moabite **might** ever **enter (law)** the congregation of God. (Neh 13:1)

(378) וַיְצַו עֲלֵיהֶם לֵאמֹר כֹּה **תַעֲשׂוּן**[80] בְּיִרְאַת יְהוָה בֶּאֱמוּנָה וּבְלֵבָב שָׁלֵם : וְכָל רִיב אֲשֶׁר **יָבוֹא** עֲלֵיכֶם מֵאֲחֵיכֶם הַיֹּשְׁבִים בְּעָרֵיהֶם בֵּין דָּם לְדָם בֵּין תּוֹרָה לְמִצְוָה לְחֻקִּים

---

77. §8.2.1 examines the infinitive construct's role as a signifier of the language of the law.
78. Cf. Leviticus 23:22 and Deuteronomy 16:13-17.
79. Cf. Deuteronomy 23:4.
80. The use of the יקטלון form during this period essentially constitutes an archaic vestige, which stems from an attempt to hark back to the classical style of the language of the law; see Garr (2006).

וּלְמִשְׁפָּטִים וְהִזְהַרְתֶּם אֹתָם וְלֹא **יֶאְשְׁמוּ** לַיהוה וְהָיָה קֶצֶף עֲלֵיכֶם וְעַל אֲחֵיכֶם כֹּה
תַּעֲשׂוּן וְלֹא תֶאְשָׁמוּ.[81]

He charged them, This is how **you shall act (law)**: in fear of the LORD, with
fidelity, and with whole heart. When a dispute **comes (law)** before you from
your brothers living in their towns, whether about homicide, or about ritual,
or laws or rules, you must instruct them so that they **do not incur guilt (law)**
before the LORD and wrath be upon you and your brothers. **Thus you shall do
(law)** and **you will not incur guilt (law)**. (2 Chr 19:9-10)

There is an interesting connection between the language of the law (the promulga-
tion of general/generic directives), the habitual present, and iterative actions in the
past. The common denominator between these three groups is the nature of the
actions that they mark (i.e., iterative and habitual actions), while the chronological
field sets them apart: the habitual present is atemporal; an iterative action in the
past obviously occurs in the past; and the language of the law takes effect from the
moment the law is given onward:

An iterative action in the past: [.   .   .   .   .   .]
The language of the law: >.   .   .   .   .   .   .>
The habitual present: <.   .   .   .   .>

S

---

81. Also see Ezra 2:63, Nehemiah 7:3, and 2 Chronicles 15:13, which can be understood
    as either the habitual present or the language of the law itself. One can perhaps add
    occurrences in Nehemiah 10:30-40, as this string of oaths that can be interpreted as a
    sort of general language of the law.

7. Usages of *Weqatal* in the Second Temple Period

7.1 Introduction

As in First Temple period Hebrew, *weqatal* serves as a modal consecutive form throughout the Second Temple period. Although the contexts that host *weqatal* in the Second Temple period bear a strong resemblance to those of the First, there are substantial differences between the two eras. These differences are tied to the fall-off in *weqatal*'s use during the Second Temple period, which stems from several concurrent developments that, in the final equation, have engendered an overall picture of retrenchment.

The prime indicator of the *weqatal* form's diminishing use is the number of occurrences. In our corpus, there are 117 instances of *weqatal*, which constitute some 3.7% of the total occurrences of all the verb forms surveyed.[1] On the one hand, this state of affairs may be the product of chance, as it is a distinct possibility that the number of occurrences is linked to the sort of texts that have reached our hands.[2] On the other hand, it is important to note that 63 occurrences (54% of the total) are concentrated in chapter 11 of the book of Daniel. Therefore, if we were to subtract these instances from the final count, the scarcity of this form is even greater than the sum total of its occurrences suggests.[3] Given the limited material, one would be hard-pressed to determine whether the drop in *weqatal*'s usage is the fruit of chance. However, in light of the functional decline, which will be examined herein, it appears as though the statistical data should be viewed as but one element of a larger body of evidence.

The fact that *weqatal* is far from a mainstay in our corpus is apparently connected to several processes that transpire during this period. To begin with, the form's position as the exclusive signifier of succession in the modal field is undermined. Whereas the function of marking successions in the modal field was primarily filled by *weqatal* forms during the First Temple period,[4] by the time of the Second Temple several other forms "compete" over this role. For example, the

---

1. For comparison's sake, Hatav (1997:57) found 573 occurrences of *weqatal* (9.5% of all verbs surveyed) in the Hebrew of the First Temple period.
2. For example, only one instance of this form was found within the framework of the language of the law in the Second Temple period (see §7.3.2.2 in this chapter). However, given the scarcity of legal directives in this era's biblical texts, this isolated occurrence merely offers a partial view of the situation. A comparison with the Dead Sea Scrolls shows that *weqatal*'s usage within the framework of the language of the law is well established and even routine in the era that followed the Second Temple period.
3. If Daniel 11, which constitutes a glaring anomaly vis-à-vis the rest of the corpus, is omitted from the final tally, *weqatal* forms comprise only 1.7% of the total number of occurrences of all verb forms.
4. This does not include successions utilizing volitive forms (the cohortative, the imperative, and the jussive), as these constructions (*waw* + volitive) can also mark succession in these contexts.

waw + *yiqtol* and *waw* + infinitive construct tandems denote modal succession. In addition, the infinitive absolute assumes this same function and is also capable of serving as a modal consecutive form. The fact that other forms fill this role takes away from the unique standing of *weqatal*. For example:

(379) וְעָמַד מִנֵּצֶר שָׁרָשֶׁיהָ כַּנּוֹ וְיָבֹא אֶל הַחַיִל וְיָבֹא בְּמָעוֹז מֶלֶךְ הַצָּפוֹן וְעָשָׂה בָהֶם
וְהֶחֱזִיק׃

A shoot from her stock **will appear** (*weqatal*) in his place, **will come** (*yiqtol*) against the army **and enter** (*yiqtol*) the fortress of the king of the north; **he will fight** (*weqatal*) and **overpower** (*weqatal*) them. (Dn 11:7)

Not only does this period bear witness to an increase in the number of forms vying over the signification of succession, but other tasks that were previously entrusted to *weqatal* are assumed by "rival" forms. For instance, the signification of habitual actions (the habitual present, general truth, and iterative actions in the past), which was the exclusive domain of *weqatal* and *yiqtol* during the First Temple period,[5] is taken up by infinitive construct and participle forms:

(380) עַל כֵּן הַיְּהוּדִים הַפְּרוֹזִים (הַפְּרָזִים) הַיֹּשְׁבִים בְּעָרֵי הַפְּרָזוֹת **עֹשִׂים** אֵת יוֹם
אַרְבָּעָה עָשָׂר לְחֹדֶשׁ אֲדָר שִׂמְחָה וּמִשְׁתֶּה וְיוֹם טוֹב

That is why village Jews, who live in unwalled towns, **observe (habitual present: participle)** the fourteenth day of the month of Adar a day of merrymaking and feasting, and as a holiday. (Est 9:19)

(381) וַאֲנַחְנוּ יְהוָה אֱלֹהֵינוּ וְלֹא עֲזַבְנֻהוּ וְכֹהֲנִים **מְשָׁרְתִים** לַיהוָה בְּנֵי אַהֲרֹן וְהַלְוִיִּם
בַּמְּלָאכֶת׃ **וּמַקְטִרִים** לַיהוָה עֹלוֹת בַּבֹּקֶר בַּבֹּקֶר וּבָעֶרֶב בָּעֶרֶב וּקְטֹרֶת סַמִּים וּמַעֲרֶכֶת
לֶחֶם עַל הַשֻּׁלְחָן הַטָּהוֹר וּמְנוֹרַת הַזָּהָב וְנֵרֹתֶיהָ **לְבָעֵר** בָּעֶרֶב בָּעֶרֶב כִּי שֹׁמְרִים אֲנַחְנוּ
אֶת מִשְׁמֶרֶת יְהוָה אֱלֹהֵינוּ וְאַתֶּם עֲזַבְתֶּם אֹתוֹ׃

As for us, the LORD is our God, and we have not forsaken him. The priests who **minister (habitual present: participle)** to the LORD are the sons of Aaron, and the Levites are at their tasks. **They offer (habitual present: participle)** burnt offerings in smoke each morning and each evening, and the aromatic incense, the rows of bread on the pure table; **they kindle (habitual present: infinitive construct)** the golden lampstand with its lamps burning each evening, for we keep the charge of the LORD our God, while you have forsaken it. (2 Chr 13:10-11)

---

5. Like the rest of the functions of the *weqatal* and *yiqtol* forms in classical prose, there is a clear distinction herein between *weqatal*, which serves as a habitual consecutive form, and *yiqtol*, which expresses subsequence or concurrence within a habitual context.

These changes are responsible for *weqatal*'s near banishment from the habitual present/general truth and, in all likelihood, iterative actions in the past.[6]

In sum, several variables have combined to weaken the standing of *weqatal* in the Second Temple period. The undermining of the classical system of consecutive forms and the changes in the usage of other forms, which do not compete with *weqatal* in classical Hebrew, stand behind the form's waning status. This shift did not impact the entire system in one fell swoop. While *weqatal* has indeed been virtually eliminated from certain areas, in others it has only absorbed minor setbacks at the expense of rival forms. In the pages that follow, we will attempt to shed some light on this complicated situation.

7.2 The *Weqatal* Form's Link to Reference Time

7.2.1 Consecutive Forms—Establishing R-Time [R,E]

As noted in the second chapter of this book,[7] our depiction of consecutive forms is predicated on the studies of Kamp and Rohrer (1983) and Kamp and Reyle (1993), as well as Hatav's incorporation of these works into the field of Biblical Hebrew (1997, 2000a, and 2004). These scholars' definition of consecutive forms leans on Reichenbach's concept of reference time (1947). According to Reichenbach, the distinguishing feature of a consecutive form is that it encompasses its own R-time [E,R]. In other words, the very use of this form in a given phrase situates the reference time within it, and the R-time need not be discerned from the context. What is more, it is the inclusion of the reference time within the form itself that allows the writer to construct the succession. In classical Biblical Hebrew, *wayyiqtol* and *weqatal* are the primary building blocks of sequencing in the indicative and modal fields, respectively.

In the second chapter, we demonstrated that the purpose of a textual continuum is not necessarily the advancement of reference time along the time axis.[8] Although the signification of chronological relationships is indeed one of the most prevalent results of concatenating sequential forms, these verbs can also express other meanings, such as a change in the narrative perspective, a generalization, and the provision of further details. Additionally, consecutive forms can mark a geographical succession, such as border lists.

7.2.1.1 Chronological Successions

Concatenating a sequence of events and advancing them along the time axis is, as above mentioned, one of the principal functions of the *weqatal* consecutive form.

---

6.   See §7.3.1.2.3 below.

7.   §2.1.3 above.

8.   Despite the fact that this is how Hatav defines the role of consecutive forms (2000).

Since the sequential form encompasses its own reference time, in these cases every appearance of this form presents a new R-time that advances the chain of occurrences along the time axis.

(382) וּלְקֵץ שָׁנִים יִתְחַבָּרוּ וּבַת מֶלֶךְ הַנֶּגֶב תָּבוֹא אֶל מֶלֶךְ הַצָּפוֹן לַעֲשׂוֹת מֵישָׁרִים וְלֹא תַעְצֹר כּוֹחַ הַזְּרוֹעַ וְלֹא יַעֲמֹד וּזְרֹעוֹ וְתִנָּתֵן הִיא וּמְבִיאֶיהָ וְהַיֹּלְדָהּ וּמַחֲזִקָהּ בָּעִתִּים: **וְעָמַד** מִנֵּצֶר שָׁרָשֶׁיהָ כַּנּוֹ וְיָבֹא אֶל הַחַיִל וְיָבֹא בְּמָעוֹז מֶלֶךְ הַצָּפוֹן **וְעָשָׂה** בָהֶם **וְהֶחֱזִיק**: וְגַם אֱלֹהֵיהֶם עִם נְסִכֵיהֶם עִם כְּלֵי חֶמְדָּתָם כֶּסֶף וְזָהָב בַּשְּׁבִי יָבָא מִצְרָיִם וְהוּא שָׁנִים יַעֲמֹד מִמֶּלֶךְ הַצָּפוֹן: **וּבָא** בְּמַלְכוּת מֶלֶךְ הַנֶּגֶב **וְשָׁב** אֶל אַדְמָתוֹ:[9]

After some years, an alliance will be made, and the daughter of the king of the south will come to the king of the north to effect the agreement, but she will not maintain her strength, nor will his strength endure. She will be surrendered together with those who escorted her and the one who begot her and helped her during those times. A shoot from her stock **will appear [R,E]** in his place, will come against the army and enter the fortress of the king of the north; he **will fight [R,E]** and **overpower [R,E]** them. He will also take their gods with their molten images and their precious vessels of silver and gold back to Egypt as booty. For some years he will leave the king of the north alone, who will *later* **invade [R,E]** the realm of the king of the south, but **will go back [R,E]** to his land. (Dn 11:6-9)

(383) וְעַתָּה בְּנוֹתֵיכֶם אַל תִּתְּנוּ לִבְנֵיהֶם וּבְנֹתֵיהֶם אַל תִּשְׂאוּ לִבְנֵיכֶם וְלֹא תִדְרְשׁוּ שְׁלֹמָם וְטוֹבָתָם עַד עוֹלָם לְמַעַן תֶּחֶזְקוּ **וַאֲכַלְתֶּם** אֶת טוּב הָאָרֶץ **וְהוֹרַשְׁתֶּם** לִבְנֵיכֶם עַד עוֹלָם:

Now then, do not give your daughters in marriage to their sons or let their daughters marry your sons; do nothing for their well-being or advantage, then you will be strong **and enjoy [R,E]** the bounty of the land **and bequeath [R,E]** it to your children forever. (Ezr 9:12)

7.2.1.2 Non-chronological Successions

As illustrated in the next few examples, *weqatal* does not always push the reference time forward along the time axis:

(384) וּזְרֹעִים מִמֶּנּוּ יַעֲמֹדוּ וְחִלְּלוּ הַמִּקְדָּשׁ הַמָּעוֹז **וְהֵסִירוּ** הַתָּמִיד **וְנָתְנוּ** הַשִּׁקּוּץ מְשֹׁמֵם:

Forces will be levied by him; they will desecrate the temple, the fortress; **they will abolish [R,E]** the regular offering **and set up [R,E]** the appalling abomination. (Dn 11:31)

---

9.   Also see the remainder of this chapter (Daniel 11), to exclude those passages that are cited in the ensuing clause.

(385) וַיִּקְרָא יַעְבֵּץ לֵאלֹהֵי יִשְׂרָאֵל לֵאמֹר אִם בָּרֵךְ תְּבָרְכֵנִי **וְהִרְבִּיתָ** אֶת גְּבוּלִי **וְהָיְתָה** יָדְךָ עִמִּי **וְעָשִׂיתָ** מֵּרָעָה לְבִלְתִּי עָצְבִּי וַיָּבֵא אֱלֹהִים אֵת אֲשֶׁר שָׁאָל:

Jabez invoked the God of Israel, saying, Oh, bless me, **enlarge [R,E]** my territory, **stand [R,E]** by me, and **make [R,E]** me not suffer pain from misfortune! And God granted what he asked. (1 Chr 4:10)

Drawing on examples from the French language in which the interpretation of the chronological relations between different sequential forms is context-dependent, Kamp and Rohrer show that the premise according to which consecutive forms invariably move the reference time forward is problematic (1983:260-261).[10] Another exception to the signification of chronological succession in our corpus is verbs depicting a general action that is followed by a string of actions, which basically expands upon the former. For instance, the elimination of the regular offering and the introduction of the "appalling abomination" in Daniel 11:31 supply details of the Temple's desecration. Likewise, the verbs "והרבית", "והיתה", and "ועשית" in 1 Chronicles 4:10 elaborate on the blessing bestowed by God.

An additional example of a *weqatal* form that does not advance its R-time is found in Daniel 12:1:

(386) וּבָעֵת הַהִיא יַעֲמֹד מִיכָאֵל הַשַּׂר הַגָּדוֹל הָעֹמֵד עַל בְּנֵי עַמֶּךָ **וְהָיְתָה** עֵת צָרָה אֲשֶׁר לֹא נִהְיְתָה מִהְיוֹת גּוֹי עַד הָעֵת הַהִיא

At that time, the great prince, Michael, who stands beside the sons of your people, will appear. **It will be [R,E]** a time of trouble, the like of which has never been since the nation came into being. (Dn 12:1)

This example somewhat differs from the first two. The verse opens with the adverb "ובעת ההיא", which constitutes the sentence's reference time. The verb "יעמד" follows on the heels of "בעת ההיא" and refers to the latter as its R-time. "והיתה" engenders a new reference time, which changes the speaker's perspective from Michael's actions to a general description of the period, rather than referring to a later time.

From a typological standpoint, the next passage from the First Temple period offers us an opportunity to compare the previous example with a different consecutive form (*wayyiqtol*) that marks a change in the speaker's perspective:

(387) וַיָּסֹבּוּ וַיֶּאֶרְבוּ לוֹ כָל הַלַּיְלָה בְּשַׁעַר הָעִיר וַיִּתְחָרְשׁוּ כָל הַלַּיְלָה לֵאמֹר עַד אוֹר הַבֹּקֶר וַהֲרַגְנֻהוּ: **וַיִּשְׁכַּב שִׁמְשׁוֹן** עַד חֲצִי הַלַּיְלָה וַיָּקָם בַּחֲצִי הַלַּיְלָה וַיֶּאֱחֹז בְּדַלְתוֹת שַׁעַר הָעִיר וּבִשְׁתֵּי הַמְּזוּזוֹת

[S]o they gathered and laid in ambush for him in the town gate the whole night; and all night long they kept whispering to each other, When daylight comes, we'll kill him. **But Samson laid [R,E]** in bed only till midnight. At midnight

---

10. See §2.1.3 above.

he got up, and grasped the doors of the town gate together with the two
gateposts. (Jgs 16:2-3)

Here too, the consecutive form ("וישכב") merely shifts the narrative perspective.
The first verbal succession ("ויסבו", "ויארבו", and "ויתחרשו") depicts the Philistines' actions, while the second ("ויאחז", "ויקם", "וישכב") refers to Samson. The
transition from the last verb of the Philistines' succession to the one that opens the
subsequent verse about Samson does not denote chronological advancement. As
in Daniel 12:1, the author shifts the narrative perspective by taking advantage of
the fact that sequential forms establish a new reference time.

There are also cases where it is difficult to determine the precise nature of the
chronological relationship between neighboring sequential forms:

(388) וְעָמַד מֶלֶךְ גִּבּוֹר וּמָשַׁל מִמְשָׁל רַב וְעָשָׂה כִּרְצוֹנוֹ :

Then a warrior king will appear who **will have [R,E]** an extensive dominion
and do [R,E] as he pleases. (Dn 11:3)

(389) וּבָאוּ בוֹ צִיִּים כִּתִּים וְנִכְאָה וְשָׁב וְזָעַם עַל בְּרִית קוֹדֶשׁ וְעָשָׂה וְשָׁב וְיָבֵן עַל עֹזְבֵי
בְּרִית קֹדֶשׁ :

Ships from Kittim will come against him. He will be checked, **and will turn
back [R,E], and will rage [R,E]** against the holy covenant. **Having done
[R,E]** so, he will return and then attend to those who forsake the holy covenant.
(Dn 11:30)

7.3 The *Weqatal* Form's Link to the Modal Axis

Insofar as the modal axis is concerned, both *yiqtol* and *weqatal* express a wide
range of modal meanings.[11] The cardinal difference between *yiqtol* and *weqatal*
centers almost entirely on the link to the reference-time axis,[12] but there is much
in common between the two forms with respect to the modal axis. For instance,
every modal function of the *weqatal* form is also filled by *yiqtol*. In the pages that
follow, we will attempt to show that the decline in *weqatal*'s use during the Second
Temple period stems from the loss of its exclusive role as the modal consecutive
form, rather than a deterioration in its modal uses. Similar to *yiqtol*, the distinction
that we draw between *weqatal*'s sundry roles follows Palmer's basic differentiation between propositional and deontic modality (2001).[13]

---

11. See the chapter on the *yiqtol* form for an in-depth discussion on this topic (§6.3 above).
12. This was also touched on in §2.2.4 above.
13. See §2.2.3 above.

7.3.1 Propositional Modality

Propositional modality is concerned with the feasibility, or the degree of factuality and actuality, a speaker ascribes to his or her proposition. One of the standard distinctions in this field is between *epistemic modality*, namely the speaker's judgment concerning the extent of a certain action's factuality, and *evidential modality*, which pertains to the quality of the evidence via which the speaker is familiar with the action.[14] These categories will underpin the forthcoming discussion.

7.3.1.1 Epistemic Modality

7.3.1.1.1 The Future

As above mentioned, epistemic modality measures the speaker's judgment regarding a communicated action's factuality. Like the epistemic use of *yiqtol*, one can characterize the occurrences of sequential *weqatal* forms that express the future in accordance with the degree of certainty that the speaker ascribes to the action. For the purposes of this discussion, we will avail ourselves of the following levels of certitude: strong (++), possible (+/-), and highly unlikely (--).

The overall impression of the usages of *weqatal* to expperss future events in our corpus is influenced by the fact that most of the relevant occurrences are in the book of Daniel, especially its eleventh chapter. Over the course of this book, *weqatal* forms appear within the framework of a prophetic future. This context is naturally informed by a high level of certainty, for the prophet expresses his own self-confidence that his words will come to fruition, while endeavoring to persuade his audience:

(390) **וְעַתָּה אֱמֶת אַגִּיד לָךְ** הִנֵּה עוֹד שְׁלֹשָׁה מְלָכִים עֹמְדִים לְפָרַס וְהָרְבִיעִי יַעֲשִׁיר
עֹשֶׁר גָּדוֹל מִכֹּל וּכְחֶזְקָתוֹ בְעָשְׁרוֹ יָעִיר הַכֹּל אֵת מַלְכוּת יָוָן ׃ **וְעָמַד** מֶלֶךְ גִּבּוֹר **וּמָשַׁל**
מִמְשָׁל רַב **וְעָשָׂה** כִּרְצוֹנוֹ ׃[15]

And now I will tell (++) you the truth: Persia will have three more kings, and the fourth will be wealthier than them all; by the power he obtains through his wealth, he will stir everyone up against the kingdom of Greece. Then a warrior king **will appear (++) and he will have (++)** an extensive dominion **and he will do (++)** as he pleases. (Dn 11:2-3)

The beginning of this passage, "ועתה אמת אגיד לך", bolsters our hypothesis with respect to the sense of certitude that the speaker undertakes to convey. In addition to the prophecies in the book of Daniel, the following cases also fall under this category:

---

14. For more on these categories and related bibliographic referrals, see §6.3.1.1-2 above.
15. Also see the rest of this chapter, as well as Daniel 8:24, 25; 9:25, 27; 12:1, 10.

(391) הִנֵּה בֵן נוֹלָד לָךְ הוּא יִהְיֶה אִישׁ מְנוּחָה **וַהֲנִיחוֹתִי** לוֹ מִכָּל אוֹיְבָיו מִסָּבִיב כִּי
שְׁלֹמֹה יִהְיֶה שְׁמוֹ וְשָׁלוֹם וָשֶׁקֶט אֶתֵּן עַל יִשְׂרָאֵל בְּיָמָיו : הוּא יִבְנֶה בַיִת לִשְׁמִי וְהוּא
יִהְיֶה לִּי לְבֵן וַאֲנִי לוֹ לְאָב **וַהֲכִינוֹתִי** כִּסֵּא מַלְכוּתוֹ עַל יִשְׂרָאֵל עַד עוֹלָם :

But you will have a son who will be a man at rest, for **I will give** (++) him rest
from all his enemies on all sides; Solomon will be his name and I shall confer
peace and quiet on Israel in his time. He will build a House for my name; he
shall be a son to me and I to him a father, **and I will establish** (++) his throne
of kingship over Israel forever. (1 Chr 22:9–10)

(392) וּבִרְאוֹת יְהוָה כִּי נִכְנָעוּ הָיָה דְבַר יְהוָה אֶל שְׁמַעְיָה לֵאמֹר נִכְנָעוּ לֹא אַשְׁחִיתֵם
וְנָתַתִּי לָהֶם כִּמְעַט לִפְלֵיטָה וְלֹא תִתַּךְ חֲמָתִי בִּירוּשָׁלַם בְּיַד שִׁישָׁק :[16]

When the Lord saw that they had submitted, the word of the Lord came to
Shemaiah, saying, Since they have humbled themselves, I will not destroy
them but **will grant** (++) them some measure of deliverance, and my wrath
will not be poured out on Jerusalem through Shishak. (2 Chr 12:7)

These passages resemble the occurrences in the book of Daniel in that the speakers
(either God or his messenger) are confident that their prophecies will be fulfilled.
Speaker confidence is weaker in the following passages:

(393) וַיֹּאמְרוּ צָרֵינוּ לֹא יֵדְעוּ וְלֹא יִרְאוּ עַד אֲשֶׁר נָבוֹא אֶל תּוֹכָם **וַהֲרַגְנוּם וְהִשְׁבַּתְנוּ**
אֶת הַמְּלָאכָה : (‎-/+)

And our foes were saying, Before they know or see it, we shall be in among
them **and kill them** (+/-) **and put a stop** (+/-) to the work. (Neh 4:5)

(394) וַיֹּאמֶר לִי שְׁלֹמֹה בִנְךָ הוּא יִבְנֶה בֵיתִי וַחֲצֵרוֹתָי כִּי בָחַרְתִּי בוֹ לִי לְבֵן וַאֲנִי אֶהְיֶה
לּוֹ לְאָב : **וַהֲכִינוֹתִי** אֶת מַלְכוּתוֹ עַד לְעוֹלָם אִם יֶחֱזַק לַעֲשׂוֹת מִצְוֹתַי וּמִשְׁפָּטַי כַּיּוֹם
הַזֶּה : וְעַתָּה לְעֵינֵי כָל יִשְׂרָאֵל קְהַל יְהוָה וּבְאָזְנֵי אֱלֹהֵינוּ שִׁמְרוּ וְדִרְשׁוּ כָּל מִצְוֹת יְהוָה
אֱלֹהֵיכֶם לְמַעַן תִּירְשׁוּ אֶת הָאָרֶץ הַטּוֹבָה **וְהִנְחַלְתֶּם** לִבְנֵיכֶם אַחֲרֵיכֶם עַד עוֹלָם :
(‎-/+)

He said to me, It will be your son Solomon who will build my House and my
courts, for I have chosen him to be a son to Me, and I will be a father to him.
I will establish (+/-) his kingdom forever, if he keeps firmly to the observance
of my commandments and rules as he does now. And now, in the sight of all
Israel, the congregation of the Lord, and in the hearing of our God, *I say:*
Observe and apply yourselves to all the commandments of the Lord your God
in order that you may possess this good land **and bequeath** (+/-) it to your
children after you forever. (1 Chr 28:6–8)

In example 393, the speakers—the enemies of Judah—are deliberating over what
would happen should they attempt to infiltrate Jerusalem and attack the Jews who
are rebuilding the city. Although the commentators have mixed opinions as to the

---

16. Also see 2 Chronicles 20:16.

assailants' confidence in their plan, it is evidently less than that of the first three passages. In example 394, the two actions represented by *weqatal* forms are conditioned on the fulfillment of other actions ("שמרו ודרשו", "אם יחזק", and "למען") and thus express possibility (+/-) rather than certainty (++).

Like the *yiqtol* form, the level of certainty of *weqatal* forms that express the future in our corpus cover the entire range of the possibility axis. However, on account of our corpus's diminutive dimensions, the high concentration of *weqatal* forms in prophetic verses, and the general decrease in the form's usage, *weqatal* lacks the relative abundance and diversity that informs *yiqtol* in this particular context.

7.3.1.1.2 Question Sentences

Question sentences constitute a special group in which *weqatal* forms convey epistemic modality.[17] Similar to *yiqtol*, the attribute that singles out *weqatal*'s use in question sentences is its link to the same probability scale that was outlined in the previous section. In other words, *weqatal* forms express various levels of plausibility within the semantic context of the question sentence. As opposed to the regular future, where it is possible to express a high degree of certainty concerning the future, question sentences are limited to denoting either possibility (+/-) or a lack thereof (--):

(395) וַיִּקָּבְצוּ עַם רָב וַיִּסְתְּמוּ אֶת כָּל הַמַּעְיָנוֹת וְאֶת הַנַּחַל הַשּׁוֹטֵף בְּתוֹךְ הָאָרֶץ לֵאמֹר לָמָּה יָבוֹאוּ מַלְכֵי אַשּׁוּר **וּמָצְאוּ** מַיִם רַבִּים : (-/+)

A large force was assembled to stop up all the springs and the wadi that flowed through the land, saying: Why should the kings of Assyria come **and find** (+/-) water in abundance. (2 Chr 32:4)

(396) וָאֹמְרָה הַאִישׁ כָּמוֹנִי יִבְרָח וּמִי כָמוֹנִי אֲשֶׁר יָבֹא אֶל הַהֵיכָל **וָחָי** לֹא אָבוֹא : (--)

I replied, Will a man like me take flight? Besides, who such as I can go into the sanctuary **and live?** (--) I will not go in. (Neh 6:11)

In the first example, the assumption is that the Assyrian forces will probably make their way to Jerusalem and besiege the city. Therefore, the speaker suggests that the wells be sealed lest the enemy find them. In example 396, Nehemiah broods over whether to seek haven inside the sanctuary in order to protect himself from his enemies, but the speaker does not believe that this is a realistic option.

---

17. See the discussion on the usage of the *yiqtol* form in question sentences: §6.3.1.1.1 above.

7.3.1.1.3 Conditional Sentences

Conditional sentences are another category of modal sentences that have *weqatal* forms. In the chapter on *yiqtol*, we elaborated on the position of conditional sentences within the framework of epistemic modality.[18] Moreover, we opined that the modal expression pertains to the plausibility level of the actions conveyed therein. Similar to the other usages that are connected to the modal axis, there is no essential difference between the functions of the *yiqtol* and *weqatal* forms in their modal meaning.

Here are all the occurrences in our corpus of *weqatal* forms within the framework of conditional sentences:

(397) וַהֲכִינוֹתִי אֶת מַלְכוּתוֹ עַד לְעוֹלָם אִם יֶחֱזַק לַעֲשׂוֹת מִצְוֹתַי וּמִשְׁפָּטַי כַּיּוֹם הַזֶּה:[19]

I will establish (conditional) his kingdom forever, if he keeps firmly to the observance of my commandments and rules as he does now. (1 Chr 28:7)

(398) וְטוֹבִיָּה הָעַמֹּנִי אֶצְלוֹ וַיֹּאמֶר גַּם אֲשֶׁר הֵם בּוֹנִים אִם יַעֲלֶה שׁוּעָל וּפָרַץ חוֹמַת אַבְנֵיהֶם:

Tobiah the Ammonite, alongside him, said, That stone wall they are building— if a fox **climbed** it, **he would breach (conditional)** it! (Neh 3:35)

(399) זְכָר נָא אֶת הַדָּבָר אֲשֶׁר צִוִּיתָ אֶת מֹשֶׁה עַבְדְּךָ לֵאמֹר אַתֶּם תִּמְעָלוּ אֲנִי אָפִיץ אֶתְכֶם בָּעַמִּים: **וְשַׁבְתֶּם**[20] אֵלַי **וּשְׁמַרְתֶּם** מִצְוֹתַי **וַעֲשִׂיתֶם** אֹתָם אִם יִהְיֶה נִדַּחֲכֶם בִּקְצֵה הַשָּׁמַיִם מִשָּׁם אֲקַבְּצֵם והבואתים (**וַהֲבִיאוֹתִים**) אֶל הַמָּקוֹם אֲשֶׁר בָּחַרְתִּי לְשַׁכֵּן אֶת שְׁמִי שָׁם:

Be mindful of the promise you gave to your servant Moses: If you are unfaithful, I will scatter you among the peoples; but **if you turn back (conditional)** to me, faithfully **keep (conditional) and fulfill (conditional)** my commandments, even if your dispersed are at the ends of the earth, I will gather them from there **and bring (conditional)** them to the place where I have chosen to establish my name. (Neh 1:8-9)

Since the *weqatal* form is restricted to the opening slot of a conditional sentence, it cannot be preceded by the particle אם (Joüon and Muraoka 1996:§167h). Therefore, when the form is used in the protasis (as in example 399), it appears without a conditional particle.

---

18. See §6.3.1.1 above.
19. We also took advantage of this example in the earlier discussion on the future realm.
20. The function of this particular *weqatal* form can be discerned from the passage's context. The conditional sentence that opens with "ושבתם" basically stands in succession with the conditional clause "אתם תמעלו אני אפיץ". A similar usage turns up in classical Hebrew: (Gn 44:22) וַנֹּאמֶר אֶל אֲדֹנִי לֹא יוּכַל הַנַּעַר לַעֲזֹב אֶת אָבִיו וְעָזַב אֶת אָבִיו וָמֵת.

7.3.1.1.4 Purpose Clauses

The expression of purpose also falls within the purview of the epistemic mood. In the following example, *weqatal* forms appear within the framework of a purpose clause that begins with a *yiqtol* form:

(400) וְעַתָּה בְּנוֹתֵיכֶם אַל תִּתְּנוּ לִבְנֵיהֶם וּבְנֹתֵיהֶם אַל תִּשְׂאוּ לִבְנֵיכֶם וְלֹא תִדְרְשׁוּ
שְׁלֹמָם וְטוֹבָתָם עַד עוֹלָם לְמַעַן תֶּחֶזְקוּ **וַאֲכַלְתֶּם** אֶת טוּב הָאָרֶץ **וְהוֹרַשְׁתֶּם** לִבְנֵיכֶם
עַד עוֹלָם:

Now then, do not give your daughters in marriage to their sons or let their daughters marry your sons; do nothing for their well-being or advantage, then you will be strong **and enjoy** (+/-) the bounty of the land **and bequeath** (+/-) it to your children forever. (Ezr 9:12)

7.3.1.2 Evidential Modality

Whereas epistemic modality focuses on a proposition's level of truthfulness, evidential modality is concerned with the quality of the evidence from which the speaker learns about the proposition. Given the fact that *weqatal* and *yiqtol* forms also express propositional (epistemic) and deontic modality, it is incumbent upon us to assay their habitual meanings on the basis of their connection to their other functions, including the modal ones. Within the current framework, this sort of modality signifies, inter alia, that the information concerning the proposition reaches the speaker as part of his or her general knowledge and is not obtained on a first-hand basis.

7.3.1.2.1 The Decline in *Weqatal*'s Habitual Usage

One of the most important developments concerning *weqatal* in the Biblical Hebrew of the Second Temple period is the steep decline in its habitual usage. In his grammatical study comparing the book of Chronicles to Samuel and Kings, Kropat concludes that the *weqatal* form never denotes iterative meanings. This claim is perhaps valid with respect to the Hebrew of the Second Temple period, but the iterative usage is well documented throughout the First Temple period.[21] In our corpus, there are only three documented occurrences of a *weqatal* form filling the role of the habitual present. Moreover, there is only one, dubious instance of an iterative action in the past.

In light of these findings, how are we to view the *weqatal* form's habitual usage? Joosten (2006:145) suggests a number of complementary explanations: the

---

21. Joosten has already criticized Kropat on this matter (2006:144).

disappearance of *weqatal*'s role as an iterative action in the past is reflected by
the growing presence of the construction *waw* + *yiqtol* as a signifier of succession
in the past. This phenomenon is also linked to the increased use of both *waw* +
yiqtol for denoting modal succession and the participle as a signifier of habituality.
Moreover, we can bolster Joosten's argument by pointing to the fact that the infinitive construct form also competes over this role.

This development is part of a broader contraction of *weqatal*'s use, which involves the phasing out of the signification of various modal directives. Our findings buttress Joosten's analysis. However, these claims warrant some qualification, for in habitual contexts the evidence upon which we seek to establish the
weqatal form's meaning is silence. More specifically, our premise is based on the
fact that this usage does not occur at all in Second Temple period texts. However,
this usage is circumscribed and relatively limited, so that instances of "evidence
from silence" are liable to entail a fair share of arbitrariness. For example, our
corpus has only one *weqatal* form within the context of the language of the law.
Can we thus infer that this form is no longer used to signify the language of the
law in this period? The absence of *weqatal* forms from this category can be tied
to the relative paucity of these contexts in the Second Temple period texts. This
hypothesis is reinforced by comparing our corpus to the sectarian language that
emerges from the Dead Sea Scrolls, as these texts feature numerous legal passages
that avail themselves of *weqatal* (as well as *yiqtol* and infinitive construct) forms.

7.3.1.2.2 The General Truth or Habitual Present

As noted above, there are only three instances of a *weqatal* form marking a general
truth or the habitual present in biblical prose of the Second Temple period:

(401) כָּל עַבְדֵי הַמֶּלֶךְ וְעַם מְדִינוֹת הַמֶּלֶךְ יֹדְעִים אֲשֶׁר כָּל אִישׁ וְאִשָּׁה אֲשֶׁר יָבוֹא
אֶל הַמֶּלֶךְ אֶל הֶחָצֵר הַפְּנִימִית אֲשֶׁר לֹא יִקָּרֵא אַחַת דָּתוֹ לְהָמִית לְבַד מֵאֲשֶׁר יוֹשִׁיט
לוֹ הַמֶּלֶךְ אֶת שַׁרְבִיט הַזָּהָב **וְחָיָה** וַאֲנִי לֹא נִקְרֵאתִי לָבוֹא אֶל הַמֶּלֶךְ זֶה שְׁלוֹשִׁים
יוֹם:

All the king's courtiers and the people of the king's provinces know that
if any person, man or woman, enters the king's presence in the inner court
without having been summoned, there is but one law for him—that he be
put to death. Only if the king extends the golden scepter to him may **he live
(habitual)**. Now I have not been summoned to visit the king for the last thirty
days. (Est 4:11)

(402) וָאֹמְרָה הַאִישׁ כָּמוֹנִי יִבְרָח וּמִי כָמוֹנִי אֲשֶׁר יָבֹא אֶל הַהֵיכָל **וָחָי** לֹא אָבוֹא:

I replied, Will a man like me take flight? Besides, who such as I can go into the
sanctuary and **live (habitual)**? I will not go in. (Neh 6:11)

(403) כִּי בְדִבְרֵי דָוִיד הָאַחֲרֹנִים הֵמָּה מִסְפַּר בְּנֵי לֵוִי מִבֶּן עֶשְׂרִים שָׁנָה וּלְמָעְלָה. . . .
וְלַעֲמֹד בַּבֹּקֶר בַּבֹּקֶר לְהֹדוֹת וּלְהַלֵּל לַיהוָה וְכֵן לָעָרֶב. . . . **וְשָׁמְרוּ** אֶת מִשְׁמֶרֶת אֹהֶל
מוֹעֵד וְאֵת מִשְׁמֶרֶת הַקֹּדֶשׁ וּמִשְׁמֶרֶת בְּנֵי אַהֲרֹן אֲחֵיהֶם לַעֲבֹדַת בֵּית יְהוָה:

Among the last acts of David was the counting of the Levites from the age of
twenty and upward. . . . [A]nd [they] attend every morning to praise and extol
the LORD, and in the evening too. . . . [A]nd [they] **keep (habitual)** watch
over the Tent of Meeting, over the holy things, and over the Aaronites their
kinsmen, for the service of the House of the LORD. (1 Chr 23:27-32)

In the first two examples, *weqatal* forms express resultativity more than habituality—should the king extend his scepter or should Nehemiah enter the sanctuary,
a person's life will be spared—and the habitual meaning can be discerned from
the context. In Esther 4:11, the chain of *yiqtol* forms articulates habituality, thus
enabling the reader to interpret the *weqatal* form in a similar fashion. Likewise,
the *yiqtol* forms in Nehemiah 6:11 denote a general truth. The fact that this passage's succession of verbs appears within the framework of a rhetorical question
sentence also adds a tint of epistemic modality [-feasibility] to the meaning of the
general truth. Therefore, it appears as if the *weqatal* form does not entirely serve
as a signifier of habituality in the First two examples, but expresses resultativity
as well. In the third example, however, the *weqatal* form's signification of the
habitual present is more pronounced than the first two.[22]

Against this background, it is reasonable to assume that Joosten's arguments
concerning the disappearance of *weqatal* in its capacity as a signifier of an iterative
action in the past also applies to the habitual present. On the one hand, the evidence regarding the gradual decline of the *weqatal* form's habitual use is indeed
predicated on silence, namely the scarcity of this usage throughout the Second
Temple period. Consequently, we must also take into account the possibility that
this state of affairs is happenstance. On the other hand, the convergence of several
prominent developments during this era increases the likelihood that more than
chance is at work here. It is not difficult to see how the use of the *yiqtol* form as a
signifier of modal succession, along with the proliferation in the use of participial
and infinitive construct forms to denote habituality, is liable to whittle away at
weqatal's standing, which is informed by a decline in the syntactical contexts that
host this form.[23]

---

22. There are three more examples of this usage during the Second Temple period:
   1. אֵין טוֹב בָּאָדָם שֶׁיֹּאכַל וְשָׁתָה וְהֶרְאָה אֶת נַפְשׁוֹ טוֹב בַּעֲמָלוֹ (Eccl 2:24)
   2. וְגַם כָּל הָאָדָם שֶׁיֹּאכַל וְשָׁתָה וְרָאָה טוֹב בְּכָל עֲמָלוֹ מַתַּת אֱלֹהִים הִיא: (Eccl 3:13)
   3. וְגַם בַּדֶּרֶךְ כשהסכל (כְּשֶׁסָּכָל) הֹלֵךְ לִבּוֹ חָסֵר וְאָמַר לַכֹּל סָכָל הוּא: (Eccl 10:3)
   Unlike the prose examples cited in the main text, these verses are from wisdom literature. Therefore, it is preferable that they be examined in a different venue.
23. There is also a plausible explanation as to why *weqatal* forms serve as consecutive
   forms in the Dead Sea Scrolls within the framework of the language of the law. This

7.3.1.2.3 Iterative Actions in the Past?

Has the *weqatal* form's role as a signifier of iterative actions in the past vanished completely from the biblical prose of the Second Temple period? Joosten (2006) avers that this has indeed transpired and considers this phenomenon a part of the reorganization of the late Biblical Hebrew verbal system. As we have seen, this process is connected to the following developments: the rise in the number of verb forms marking successions within the framework of habitual actions; and the general lapse in the *weqatal* form's habitual uses.

Nevertheless, we have located one instance of *weqatal* in our corpus that can perhaps be interpreted as expressing an iterative/habitual action in the past. However, even if we were convinced that this is indeed the case, the passage fails to dispel the overall impression that the *weqatal* form's habitual usages are heading toward extinction.

(404) בִּמְקוֹם אֲשֶׁר תִּשְׁמְעוּ אֶת קוֹל הַשּׁוֹפָר שָׁמָּה תִּקָּבְצוּ אֵלֵינוּ אֱלֹהֵינוּ יִלָּחֶם לָנוּ :
וַאֲנַחְנוּ עֹשִׂים בַּמְּלָאכָה וְחֶצְיָם מַחֲזִיקִים בָּרְמָחִים מֵעֲלוֹת הַשַּׁחַר עַד צֵאת הַכּוֹכָבִים :
גַּם בָּעֵת הַהִיא אָמַרְתִּי לָעָם אִישׁ וְנַעֲרוֹ יָלִינוּ בְּתוֹךְ יְרוּשָׁלִַם וְהָיוּ לָנוּ הַלַּיְלָה מִשְׁמָר
וְהַיּוֹם מְלָאכָה : וְאֵין אֲנִי וְאַחַי וּנְעָרַי וְאַנְשֵׁי הַמִּשְׁמָר אֲשֶׁר אַחֲרָי אֵין אֲנַחְנוּ פֹשְׁטִים
בְּגָדֵינוּ אִישׁ שִׁלְחוֹ הַמָּיִם :

> When you hear a trumpet call, gather yourselves to me at that place; our God will fight for us! And so we worked on, while half were holding lances, from the break of day until the stars appeared. I further said to the people at that time, Let every man with his servant lodge in Jerusalem and the night **will be (iterative?)** for standing guard and the day for working. Nor did I, my brothers, my servants, or the guards following me ever take off our clothes, *or each his weapon, even at the water.* (Neh 4:14-17)

How, then, are we to understand the verb "והיו" in verse 16? Most of the commentaries interpret it as part of the imperative language that begins with the verb "ילינו", but there is another possible reading. A comparison between this verse and the first two reveals an abrupt transition from the imperative tone in verse 14 to the descriptive language of the habitual action in verse 15. Likewise, "והיו" may be interpreted as signifying an iterative action in the past, namely Nehemiah describes the conduct of Jerusalem's defenders over the course of the night and day shifts. According to this reading, the imperative does not give way to habituality

---

context differs from habitual actions in that it straddles the fence between deontic modality (articulating an order) and habituality. *Weqatal*'s presence in these contexts may be tied to the fact that it signifies various shades of deontic modality. During this period, the difference between the language of the law, the habitual present, and an iterative action in the past comes to expression not only in the context of the *weqatal* form's usages, but in those of the participle as well (see §5.2.1.4-5 below). Unlike *weqatal*, the participle marks the habitual present and an iterative action in the past, but not the language of the law.

during the transition from verse 16 to 17. Instead, the entire process takes place within the confines of the former and the habitual mood is maintained throughout the next verse.

7.3.2 Deontic Modality
7.3.2.1 The Directive Mood
7.3.2.1.1 The Imperative Mood

Within the framework of the deontic mood, *weqatal* is likely to express a direct command:

(405) וַיֹּאמֶר לָהֶם אַתֶּם רָאשֵׁי הָאָבוֹת לַלְוִיִּם הִתְקַדְּשׁוּ אַתֶּם וַאֲחֵיכֶם **וְהַעֲלִיתֶם**
אֵת אֲרוֹן יְהֹוָה אֱלֹהֵי יִשְׂרָאֵל אֶל הֲכִינוֹתִי לוֹ :

He said to them, You are the heads of the clans of the Levites; sanctify yourselves, you and your kinsmen, **and bring up (command)** the Ark of the LORD God of Israel to *the place* I have prepared for it. (1 Chr 15:12)

Since the form that opens this chain of instructions is the imperative "התקדשו", the succession can be said to convey an order. Even though this sort of chain is usually expressed by a concatenation of imperative forms, the transition to *weqatal* constitutes a natural choice because it serves as a modal consecutive form. This usage is also widespread throughout classical Biblical Hebrew. For example:

(406) עֲשֵׂה לְךָ תֵּבַת עֲצֵי גֹפֶר קִנִּים תַּעֲשֶׂה אֶת הַתֵּבָה **וְכָפַרְתָּ** אֹתָהּ מִבַּיִת וּמִחוּץ
בַּכֹּפֶר :

Make yourself an ark of gopher wood; make it an ark with compartments, and **cover (command)** it inside and out with pitch. (Gn 6:14)

7.3.2.1.2 The Hortative Mood

Using *weqatal* to formulate a request is among the meanings of the optative mood. This usage is generally found in situations where the speaker's stature is inferior to that of his addressee:

(407) וַיִּקְרָא יַעְבֵּץ לֵאלֹהֵי יִשְׂרָאֵל לֵאמֹר אִם[24] בָּרֵךְ תְּבָרְכֵנִי **וְהִרְבִּיתָ** אֶת גְּבוּלִי
וְהָיְתָה יָדְךָ עִמִּי **וְעָשִׂיתָ** מֵרָעָה לְבִלְתִּי עָצְבִּי וַיָּבֵא אֱלֹהִים אֵת אֲשֶׁר שָׁאָל :

Jabez invoked the God of Israel, saying, Oh, bless me, **enlarge (hor.)**

---

24. The task of the particle "אם" herein is not to express a condition. As in Biblical Hebrew of the First Temple period, this particle can signify a request or wish (the optative mood). See Joüon and Muraoka (1996:§163d).

my territory, **stand (hor.)** by me, and **make (hor.)** me not suffer pain from misfortune! And God granted what he asked. (1 Chr 4:10)

(408) וַיֹּאמֶר הָמָן אֶל הַמֶּלֶךְ אִישׁ אֲשֶׁר הַמֶּלֶךְ חָפֵץ בִּיקָרוֹ : יָבִיאוּ לְבוּשׁ מַלְכוּת אֲשֶׁר לָבַשׁ בּוֹ הַמֶּלֶךְ וְסוּס אֲשֶׁר רָכַב עָלָיו הַמֶּלֶךְ וַאֲשֶׁר נִתַּן כֶּתֶר מַלְכוּת בְּרֹאשׁוֹ : **וְנָתוֹן** הַלְּבוּשׁ וְהַסּוּס עַל יַד אִישׁ מִשָּׂרֵי הַמֶּלֶךְ הַפַּרְתְּמִים **וְהִלְבִּישׁוּ** אֶת הָאִישׁ אֲשֶׁר הַמֶּלֶךְ חָפֵץ בִּיקָרוֹ **וְהִרְכִּיבֻהוּ** עַל הַסּוּס בִּרְחוֹב הָעִיר **וְקָרְאוּ** לְפָנָיו כָּכָה יֵעָשֶׂה לָאִישׁ אֲשֶׁר הַמֶּלֶךְ חָפֵץ בִּיקָרוֹ :

So Haman said to the king, For the man whom the king desires to honor, let royal garb which the king has worn be brought, and a horse on which the king has ridden and on whose head a royal diadem has been set; and let the attire and the horse be put in the charge of one of the king's noble courtiers. And **let the man whom the king desires to honor be attired (hor.) and paraded (hor.)** on the horse through the city square, while **they proclaim (hor.)** before him: This is what is done for the man whom the king desires to honor! (Est 6:7–9)

In the first example, a *yiqtol* form ("תברכני") opens the chain of requests, while *weqatal* forms serve in a sequential capacity. Although the passage from Esther 6 also commences with a *yiqtol* form, the first consecutive form is the infinitive absolute "נתון"[25] and the *weqatal* forms follow in its footsteps.

7.3.2.1.3 The Optative Mood

Another possibility in the realm of the directive is a wish or blessing:

(409) עַתָּה בְנִי *יְהִי* יְהֹוָה עִמָּךְ **וְהִצְלַחְתָּ וּבָנִיתָ** בֵּית יְהֹוָה אֱלֹהֶיךָ

Now, my son, may the LORD be with you, **and may you succeed (opt.) and build (opt.)** the House of the LORD your God. (1 Chr 22:11)

In this verse, *weqatal* forms stand in succession with a jussive form ("יהי"). The semantic connotation of the wish is evinced by means of the form that opens the chain, and the *weqatal* form subsequently concatenates the modal sequence.

7.3.2.1.4 Expressions of Will

Like the *yiqtol* form, in certain scenarios the speaker can express a more general desire via *weqatal*. These instances closely resemble the directive mood's other meanings in that they pertain to the speaker's will. However, the wishes tend to be less personal, as in the following verse:

---

25. During this period, the infinitive absolute is used as a consecutive form that is un-marked from a modal standpoint; see the discussion on the infinitive absolute in §10.2 below.

(410) וָאָשִׁיב אוֹתָם דָּבָר וָאוֹמַר לָהֶם אֱלֹהֵי הַשָּׁמַיִם הוּא יַצְלִיחַ לָנוּ וַאֲנַחְנוּ עֲבָדָיו נָקוּם **וּבָנִינוּ** וְלָכֶם אֵין חֵלֶק וּצְדָקָה וְזִכָּרוֹן בִּירוּשָׁלָם :

I said to them in reply, The God of Heaven will grant us success, and **we**, his servants, will stand and **build** [will]. But you have no share or claim or stake in Jerusalem! (Neh 2:20)

In this example, Nehemiah informs his interlocutors of the Jews' desire to build Jerusalem without their assistance.

7.3.2.2 The Language of the Law[26]

In Second Temple period texts, passages transmitting legal materials are relatively scarce and brief, and the few passages that exist are randomly scattered throughout the corpus. Furthermore, there is only one instance of a *weqatal* form in the language of the law:

(411) וַיְצַו עֲלֵיהֶם לֵאמֹר כֹּה תַעֲשׂוּן בְּיִרְאַת יְהוָה בֶּאֱמוּנָה וּבְלֵבָב שָׁלֵם : וְכָל רִיב אֲשֶׁר יָבוֹא עֲלֵיכֶם מֵאֲחֵיכֶם הַיֹּשְׁבִים בְּעָרֵיהֶם בֵּין דָּם לְדָם בֵּין תּוֹרָה לְמִצְוָה לְחֻקִּים וּלְמִשְׁפָּטִים **וְהִזְהַרְתֶּם** אֹתָם וְלֹא יֶאְשְׁמוּ לַיהוָה וְהָיָה קֶצֶף עֲלֵיכֶם וְעַל אֲחֵיכֶם כֹּה תַעֲשׂוּן וְלֹא תֶאְשָׁמוּ :

He charged them, This is how you shall act: in fear of the LORD, with fidelity, and with whole heart. When a dispute comes before you from your brothers living in their towns, whether about homicide, or about ritual, or laws or rules, **you must instruct (law)** them so that they do not incur guilt before the LORD and wrath be upon you and your brothers. Act so and you will not incur guilt. (2 Chr 19:9-10)

The fact that this is the only occurrence of *weqatal* in the language of the law throughout our corpus testifies more to the nature of the biblical texts that were preserved than the *weqatal* form's usages during this era. A quick perusal through the Dead Sea Scrolls reveals that *weqatal* appears quite frequently within juridical passages, as in the following example from *The Community Rule* (or *the Manual of Discipline*):

והוסיפו הכוהנים והלויים **ואמרו** ארור בגלולי לבו לעבור הבא בברית הזות ומכשול עוונו ישים לפניו להסוג בו **והיה** בשומעו את דברי הברית הזות יתברך בלבבו לאמור שלום יהי לי כיא בשרירות לבי אלך **ונספתה** רוחו הצמאה עם הרווה לאין סליחה אף אל וקנאת משפטיו יבערו בו לכלת עולמים **ודבקו** בו כול אלות הברית הזות ויבדילהו אל לרעה **ונכרת** מתוך כול בני אור בהסוגו מאחרי אל בגלוליו ומכשול עוונו יתן גורלו בתוך ארורי עולמים וכול באי הברית יענו **ואמרו** אחריהם אמן אמן

---

26. For more on the uniqueness of the language of the law vis-à-vis the rest of the deontic modal contexts, see the discussion on the *yiqtol* form in §6.3.2.2 below.

Then the priests and Levites shall go on **to declare**, Damned be anyone initiated with unrepentant heart, who enters this covenant, then sets up the stumbling block of his sin, so turning apostate. **It shall come to pass**, when he hears the words of this covenant, that he shall bless himself in his heart, saying Peace be with me, though I walk in the stubbornness of my heart. Surrounded by abundant water, his spirit shall nevertheless **expire** thirsty, without forgiveness. God's anger and zeal for his commandments shall burn against him for eternal destruction. All the curses of this covenant **shall cleave to** him, and God shall separate him out for a fate befitting his wickedness. **He shall be cut off** from all the Sons of Light because of his apostasy from God, brought about by unrepentance and the stumbling block of sin. He shall cast his lot with those damned for all time. The initiates are all to respond **and say** in turn, Amen, amen. (1QS 2:11-18)

8. Usages of the Infinitive Construct Form in the Hebrew of the Second Temple Period

8.1 Introduction

The predicative usages of the infinitive construct during the Second Temple period constitutes one of the most significant diachronic developments in our corpus. The shift from the subordinated adverbial form to the independent modal infinitive did not transpire in one fell swoop. Instead, it was a gradual transition that was tied to the level of explicitness of the relationship between the framework sentence's main verb and infinitive form. Since this relationship is often less than transparent, the infinitive's syntactical role also tends to be vague, as evidenced by the following examples:

(412) וַתִּשְׁלַח בְּגָדִים **לְהַלְבִּישׁ** אֶת מָרְדֳּכַי

She sent clothing **in order to dress [adv. complement-purpose]** Mordecai. (Est 4:4)

(413) וְעַתָּה שְׁלַח לִי אִישׁ חָכָם לַעֲשׂוֹת בַּזָּהָב וּבַכֶּסֶף וּבַנְּחֹשֶׁת וּבַבַּרְזֶל וּבָאַרְגְּוָן וְכַרְמִיל וּתְכֵלֶת וְיֹדֵעַ לְפַתֵּחַ פִּתּוּחִים עִם הַחֲכָמִים אֲשֶׁר עִמִּי בִּיהוּדָה וּבִירוּשָׁלַ͏ִם אֲשֶׁר הֵכִין דָּוִיד אָבִי : וּשְׁלַח לִי עֲצֵי אֲרָזִים בְּרוֹשִׁים וְאַלְגּוּמִּים מֵהַלְּבָנוֹן כִּי אֲנִי יָדַעְתִּי אֲשֶׁר עֲבָדֶיךָ יוֹדְעִים לִכְרוֹת עֲצֵי לְבָנוֹן וְהִנֵּה עֲבָדַי עִם עֲבָדֶיךָ : **וּלְהָכִין** לִי עֵצִים לָרֹב

Now send me a craftsman to work in gold, silver, bronze, and iron, and in purple, crimson, and blue yarn, and who knows how to engrave, alongside the craftsmen I have here in Judah and in Jerusalem, whom my father David provided. Send me cedars, cypress, and algum wood from the Lebanon, for I know that your servants are skilled at cutting the trees of Lebanon and behold my servants will work with yours. **And prepare [predicative-request]** me a great stock of timber. (2 Chr 2:6-8)

(414) וַיִּכְתֹּב בְּשֵׁם הַמֶּלֶךְ אֲחַשְׁוֵרֹשׁ וַיַּחְתֹּם בְּטַבַּעַת הַמֶּלֶךְ וַיִּשְׁלַח סְפָרִים בְּיַד הָרָצִים בַּסּוּסִים רֹכְבֵי הָרֶכֶשׁ הָאֲחַשְׁתְּרָנִים בְּנֵי הָרַמָּכִים : אֲשֶׁר נָתַן הַמֶּלֶךְ לַיְּהוּדִים אֲשֶׁר בְּכָל עִיר וָעִיר **לְהִקָּהֵל וְלַעֲמֹד** עַל נַפְשָׁם **לְהַשְׁמִיד וְלַהֲרֹג וּלְאַבֵּד** אֶת כָּל חֵיל עַם וּמְדִינָה הַצָּרִים אֹתָם טַף וְנָשִׁים וּשְׁלָלָם **לָבוֹז** : בְּיוֹם אֶחָד בְּכָל מְדִינוֹת הַמֶּלֶךְ אֲחַשְׁוֵרוֹשׁ בִּשְׁלוֹשָׁה עָשָׂר לְחֹדֶשׁ שְׁנֵים עָשָׂר הוּא חֹדֶשׁ אֲדָר : פַּתְשֶׁגֶן הַכְּתָב **לְהִנָּתֵן** דָּת בְּכָל מְדִינָה וּמְדִינָה גָּלוּי לְכָל הָעַמִּים **וְלִהְיוֹת** (הַיְּהוּדִיים) עתודים (הַיְּהוּדִים) (**עֲתִידִים**) לַיּוֹם הַזֶּה לְהִנָּקֵם מֵאֹיְבֵיהֶם :

He had them written in the name of King Ahasuerus and sealed with the king's signet. Letters were dispatched by mounted couriers, riding steeds used in the king's service, bred of the royal stud, [letters] that the king has given to the Jews of every city [saying:] **[They] shall assemble (predicative-command?)** **and fight (predicative-command?)** for their lives; if any people or province attacks them, **[they] shall destroy, massacre, and exterminate (predicative-command?)** its armed force together with women and children, and **plunder (predicative-command?)** their possessions. On a single day in all the provinces of King Ahasuerus, namely, on the thirteenth day of the twelfth month, that is, the month of Adar. The copy of the document **shall be given (predicative-command?)** as a law in every single province: it is to be publicly displayed to all the peoples, so that the Jews **shall be ready (predicative-command?)** for that day to avenge themselves on their enemies. (Est 8:10-13)

In the first passage, the syntactic link between the inflected verb "ותשלח" and the infinitive form "להלביש" is immediate and clear. Therefore, we readily interpret the form as an adverbial complement (purpose) of the verb. Conversely, the link in the second passage between the infinitive form "ולהכין" and the anterior imperative "שלח" is rather flimsy, so that the infinitive can be deemed an independent modal form. The situation is more complicated in Esther 8, for the relation between the chain of infinitive forms and the framework verb is abstruse. On the one hand, the argument can be made that these forms are subordinated to the verb "נתן" (permitted); on the other hand, they may be seen as independent modal forms that divulge the content of the king's missives.[1] Given the ambiguities involved, any attempt at discerning the infinitive's function in these sorts of cases must inevitably draw on our knowledge of the form's usages during this period.

The connection between the adverbial form's usages and their independent modal counterparts is not a coincidence. In essence, there are occasions where it would be more accurate to refer to these two meanings as disparate expressions of the extent to which the infinitive has distanced itself from the explicit verb form.[2] These two usages—the adverbial complement and independent modal form—are essentially the opposite poles of a succession that pertains to the degree of explicitness of the infinitive's link to the verb in the framework sentence, on the one hand, and their transformation into independent forms, on the other.

In addition to Second Temple period Hebrew, this phenomenon is also well-documented in many Semitic languages, among others. However, the Second Temple period language is unique in that the predicative uses of the infinitve—out of the 486 occurrences of the infinitive construct form that were found in the corpus, 104 (21.39%) serve in assorted predicative roles—prompted a major shift, as the embedded adverbial usage increasingly gave way to an independent modal form.

8.2 The Infinitive Construct Form's Link to the Modal Axis

An examination of all the occurrences of the infinitive construct form during this period reveals that its most prevalent uses are in the modal realm.[3] From a dia-

---

1. See Cohen (2005) for an in-depth discussion on on the predicative roles of the infinitive construct in the Hebrew of the Second Temple.
2. As Palmer demonstrates, there is a connection between subjunctive forms and modality in many languages (1986:131-136); also see Lyons (1968:311-313).
3. According to Kesterson, "The *liqtol*, which is very flexible in meaning and in function,

chronic standpoint, there is almost a complete overlap between the predicative uses of the infinitive construct and the historical roles of *yiqtol* and *weqatal*. On the basis of a comparison with the language of the Dead Sea Scrolls, the argument can be made (Cohen 2005) that these forms' initial and primary usage was in the language of the law, whereupon their purview subsequently expanded to the rest of the historical roles of *yiqtol* and *weqatal*. A similar picture arises from the corpus in question, as most of the uses are of the modal variety—the language of the law, the language of instruction, the future, the habitual present, iterative actions in the past, wishes, and the volitive—and there are very few exceptions to this rule.

8.2.1 Using the Infinitive Form to Express Commandments or the Law[4]

One of the methodological stumbling blocks that hinder comparisons between the First and Second Temple periods in all that concerns the use of the infinitive construct within the framework of directives and the language of the law is the fact that the latter era is largely comprised of narrative material with few juridical contexts. As in many other areas, the discovery of the Dead Sea Scrolls has contributed immensely to the research of the Second Temple period language. Since the secterians' literature is brimming with legal compendia, which shed light on the sect's lifestyles and beliefs, these texts fill the void that informs our own corpus. For instance, a comparison with the Scrolls enhances our understanding of the infinitive forms' role in Esther 8:10-13:[5]

(415) וַיִּכְתֹּב בְּשֵׁם הַמֶּלֶךְ אֲחַשְׁוֵרֹשׁ וַיַּחְתֹּם בְּטַבַּעַת הַמֶּלֶךְ וַיִּשְׁלַח סְפָרִים בְּיַד הָרָצִים בַּסּוּסִים רֹכְבֵי הָרֶכֶשׁ הָאֲחַשְׁתְּרָנִים בְּנֵי הָרַמָּכִים : אֲשֶׁר נָתַן הַמֶּלֶךְ לַיְּהוּדִים אֲשֶׁר בְּכָל עִיר וָעִיר **לְהִקָּהֵל וְלַעֲמֹד** עַל נַפְשָׁם **לְהַשְׁמִיד וְלַהֲרֹג וּלְאַבֵּד** אֶת כָּל חֵיל עַם וּמְדִינָה הַצָּרִים אֹתָם טַף וְנָשִׁים וּשְׁלָלָם **לָבוֹז** : בְּיוֹם אֶחָד בְּכָל מְדִינוֹת הַמֶּלֶךְ אֲחַשְׁוֵרוֹשׁ בִּשְׁלוֹשָׁה עָשָׂר לְחֹדֶשׁ שְׁנֵים עָשָׂר הוּא חֹדֶשׁ אֲדָר : פַּתְשֶׁגֶן הַכְּתָב **לְהִנָּתֵן** דָּת בְּכָל מְדִינָה וּמְדִינָה גָּלוּי לְכָל הָעַמִּים **וְלִהְיוֹת** היהודיים (הַיְּהוּדִים) עתודים **(עֲתִידִים)** לַיּוֹם הַזֶּה לְהִנָּקֵם מֵאֹיְבֵיהֶם :

He had them written in the name of King Ahasuerus and sealed with the king's signet. Letters were dispatched by mounted couriers, riding steeds used in the

---

is common in Serakim and CD. The flexibility is related to the fact that it has the ability to borrow heavily from its context. Person, number, gender, tense, mood, voice, aspect— none of these does it express on its own" (1984:228). Kesterson's observation is accurate with respect to person, gender, and number, but must be qualified in all that concerns mood.

4. Esther 1:22; 3:13 (four times), 14 (twice); 4:11?; 8:11 (six times), 13 (twice); 9:21, 22, 31; Ezra 10:7?; 1 Chronicles 22:19; 24:19; 2 Chronicles 30:1?.
5. Very similar occurrences can be found in Esther 1:22; 3:13-14; 9:21-22, 31 and perhaps 2 Chronicles 30:1 (twice).

king's service, bred of the royal stud, [letters] that the king has given to the Jews of every city [saying:] [They] **shall assemble (predicative-command?)** **and fight (predicative-command?)** for their lives; if any people or province attacks them, [they] **shall destroy, massacre,** and **exterminate (predicative-command?)** its armed force together with women and children, and **plunder (predicative-command?)** their possessions. On a single day in all the provinces of King Ahasuerus, namely, on the thirteenth day of the twelfth month, that is, the month of Adar. The copy of the document **shall be given (predicative-command?)** as a law in every single province: it is to be publicly displayed to all the peoples, so that the Jews **shall be ready (predicative-command?)** for that day to avenge themselves on their enemies. (Est 8:10-13)

As already discussed, there are serious doubts as to the role of this passage's inflected infinitive forms: Do they serve as complements of the verb "נתן" (permit), or are they independent modal forms? A comparison with the language of the law in the Dead Sea Scrolls strengthens the claim that these forms should be classified under this same heading. In other words, they serve as independent modal forms. For example:

אלה החוקים למשכיל **להתהלך** בם עם כול חי לתכון עת ועת ולמשקל איש ואיש **לעשות** את רצון אל ככול הנגלה לעת בעת **ולמוד** את כול השכל הנמצא לפי העתים ואת חוק העת

These are the statutes for the instructor. [He] **shall conduct (law)** himself by them with every living person, guided by the precepts appropriate to each era and the value of each person: [He] **shall carry out (law)** the will of God according to what has been revealed for each period of history **and shall study (law)** all the wise legal findings of earlier times, as well as every statute applying to his own time (1QS 9:12-14)

This string of commandments does not open with a main verb, but by declaring that this sequence consists of a list of laws intended for the "instructor." Accordingly, the lack of a main verb renders the infinitives independent forms. This usage closely resembles that of 1 Chronicles 24:19 and perhaps Esther 4:11:

(416) אֵלֶּה פְקֻדָּתָם לַעֲבֹדָתָם **לָבוֹא** לְבֵית יְהוָה כְּמִשְׁפָּטָם בְּיַד אַהֲרֹן אֲבִיהֶם כַּאֲשֶׁר צִוָּהוּ יְהוָה אֱלֹהֵי יִשְׂרָאֵל:

These are the orders regarding their work: [They] **shall enter (law)** the House of the LORD as was laid down for them by Aaron their father, as the LORD God of Israel commanded him. (1 Chr 24:19)

(417) כָּל עַבְדֵי הַמֶּלֶךְ וְעַם מְדִינוֹת הַמֶּלֶךְ יֹדְעִים אֲשֶׁר כָּל אִישׁ וְאִשָּׁה אֲשֶׁר יָבוֹא אֶל הַמֶּלֶךְ אֶל הֶחָצֵר הַפְּנִימִית אֲשֶׁר לֹא יִקָּרֵא אַחַת דָּתוֹ **לְהָמִית** לְבַד מֵאֲשֶׁר יוֹשִׁיט לוֹ הַמֶּלֶךְ אֶת שַׁרְבִיט הַזָּהָב וְחָיָה

All the king's courtiers and the people of the king's provinces know that if any person, man or woman, enters the king's presence in the inner court without having been summoned, there is but one law for him: **[He] shall be put to death (law?)**. Only if the king extends the golden scepter to him may he live. (Est 4:11)

The argument whereby these infinitives should be understood as independent modal forms is bolstered by the fact that the Bible's format for promulgating laws is echoed in several verses of *The Community Rule* (whose readership was certainly familiar with Hebrew scripture). In some of the contexts where biblical law employs *yiqtol*, the authors of the *Rule* availed themselves of the infinitive form. For example:

(418) **לֹא תָסוּר** מִן הַדָּבָר אֲשֶׁר יַגִּידוּ לְךָ יָמִין וּשְׂמֹאל

You must not deviate (*yiqtol* law) from the verdict that they announce to you neither to the right nor to the left. (Dt 17:11)

ולא **לסור** מחוקי אמתו ללכת ימין ושמאול[6]

[They] must not deviate (infinitive construct law) from his unerring laws neither to the right nor the left. (1QS 1:15)

Or:

(419) וְלֹא **תָתוּרוּ** אַחֲרֵי לְבַבְכֶם וְאַחֲרֵי עֵינֵיכֶם אֲשֶׁר אַתֶּם זֹנִים אַחֲרֵיהֶם :

[A]nd **you shall not follow (*yiqtol* law)** your heart and eyes in your lustful urge. (Nm 15:39)

ולוא **ללכת** עוד בשרירות לב ואשמה ועיני זנות[7]

[A]nd [you] shall no longer **walk (infinitive construct law)** with a wanton, guilty heart and lustful desires. (1QS 1:6)

In light of the findings from the Dead Sea Scrolls, it appears as though the infinitives in Esther 8 should be interpreted as independent modal forms that provide the content of the king's decree.

There are two more pertinent cases in which the role of the infinitive form is ambiguous:

(420) וַיַּעֲבִירוּ קוֹל בִּיהוּדָה וִירוּשָׁלַם לְכֹל בְּנֵי הַגּוֹלָה **לְהִקָּבֵץ** יְרוּשָׁלָם : וְכֹל אֲשֶׁר לֹא יָבוֹא לִשְׁלֹשֶׁת הַיָּמִים כַּעֲצַת הַשָּׂרִים וְהַזְּקֵנִים יָחֳרַם כָּל רְכוּשׁוֹ וְהוּא יִבָּדֵל מִקְּהַל הַגּוֹלָה :

Then a proclamation was issued in Judah and Jerusalem: All who had returned from the exile **shall assemble (law?)** in Jerusalem, and that anyone who did

---

6.　See Licht 1965:62.

7.　Ibid.:60.

not come in three days would, by decision of the officers and elders, have his property confiscated and himself excluded from the congregation of the returning exiles. (Ezr 10:7-8)

(421) עַתָּה תְּנוּ לְבַבְכֶם וְנַפְשְׁכֶם לִדְרוֹשׁ לַיהוָה אֱלֹהֵיכֶם וְקוּמוּ וּבְנוּ אֶת מִקְדַּשׁ יְהוָה הָאֱלֹהִים **לְהָבִיא** אֶת אֲרוֹן בְּרִית יְהוָה וּכְלֵי קֹדֶשׁ הָאֱלֹהִים לַבַּיִת הַנִּבְנֶה לְשֵׁם יְהוָה:

Now, set your minds and hearts on worshiping the LORD your God, and go build the Sanctuary of the LORD your God **so that you may bring (adv?/law?)** the Ark of the Covenant of the LORD and the holy vessels of God to the house that is built for the name of the LORD. (1 Chr 22:19)

Determining whether the infinitives are independent predicates or adverbial forms is far from simple. Nevertheless, given the prevalence of this usage throughout the period at hand, it is possible to view them as independent modal forms that denote a general instruction.

It is worth comparing the openings of sectarian compendia of law to chains of inflected infinitive forms in the book of Esther, as the literary context of most of these constructions is the same:

ל<משכיל. . .>שים לחיןו? <**ספר סר**>**כ** היחד לדרוש

. . .to live according to **[the book of]** the *Yahad's* **[Ru]le.** (He is to teach them) to seek (1QS 1:1)

וזה **הסרך** לאנשי היחד

This is **the rule** for the men of the *Yahad* (1QS 5:1)

This structure turns up in the book of Esther, namely a succession appears immediately after the reader is informed that X wrote the instructions and sent them to Y:[8]

(422) וַיִּקָּרְאוּ סֹפְרֵי הַמֶּלֶךְ בַּחֹדֶשׁ הָרִאשׁוֹן בִּשְׁלוֹשָׁה עָשָׂר יוֹם בּוֹ **וַיִּכָּתֵב** כְּכָל אֲשֶׁר צִוָּה הָמָן אֶל אֲחַשְׁדַּרְפְּנֵי הַמֶּלֶךְ וְאֶל הַפַּחוֹת אֲשֶׁר עַל מְדִינָה וּמְדִינָה וְאֶל שָׂרֵי עַם וָעָם מְדִינָה וּמְדִינָה כִּכְתָבָהּ וְעַם וָעָם כִּלְשׁוֹנוֹ בְּשֵׁם הַמֶּלֶךְ אֲחַשְׁוֵרֹשׁ נִכְתָּב וְנֶחְתָּם בְּטַבַּעַת הַמֶּלֶךְ: **וְנִשְׁלוֹחַ** סְפָרִים בְּיַד הָרָצִים אֶל כָּל מְדִינוֹת הַמֶּלֶךְ **לְהַשְׁמִיד לַהֲרֹג וּלְאַבֵּד** אֶת כָּל הַיְּהוּדִים מִנַּעַר וְעַד זָקֵן טַף וְנָשִׁים בְּיוֹם אֶחָד בִּשְׁלוֹשָׁה עָשָׂר לְחֹדֶשׁ שְׁנֵים עָשָׂר הוּא חֹדֶשׁ אֲדָר וּשְׁלָלָם **לָבוֹז**: פַּתְשֶׁגֶן הַכְּתָב **לְהִנָּתֵן** דָּת בְּכָל מְדִינָה וּמְדִינָה גָּלוּי לְכָל הָעַמִּים לִהְיוֹת עֲתִדִים לַיּוֹם הַזֶּה:[9]

On the thirteenth day of the first month, the king's scribes were summoned and a decree **was issued**, as Haman directed, to the king's satraps, to the governors of every province, and to the officials of every people, to every province in its own script and to every people in its own language. The orders were issued in

---

8. The phrase "כי נמכרנו אני ועמי להשמיד להרוג ולאבד" (Esther 7:7) is essentially a direct quote from the decrees that the king has dispatched throughout the empire.
9. Also see Esther 1:22; 8:9-13; 9:20-22, 29-31.

the name of King Ahasuerus and sealed with the king's signet. Accordingly, written instructions **were dispatched** by couriers to all the king's provinces: **[They] shall destroy, massacre, and exterminate (law)** all the Jews, young and old, children and women, on a single day, on the thirteenth day of the twelfth month—that is, the month of Adar—and **[they] shall plunder (law)** their possessions. The copy of the document **shall be given (law)** as a law in every single province; it was to be publicly displayed to all the peoples, so that they might be ready for that day. (Est 3:12-14)

The similarity between the above noted passages in the *Rule* and the book of Esther should come as no surprise, for both contain a series of instructions. In light of the usage in the Scrolls, the occurrences in Esther should also be understood as independent modal forms, rather than adverbial complements. Just as the chain of infinitive forms comprises the juridical content of the *Rule*, the chain in Esther should be viewed as signifying the content of the king's directive. Moreover, the infinitive forms in the next verse can also be interpreted as the content of missives:

(423) וַיִּשְׁלַ֨ח יְחִזְקִיָּ֜הוּ עַל כָּל יִשְׂרָאֵל וִיהוּדָה וְגַם אִגְּרוֹת **כָּתַב** עַל אֶפְרַיִם וּמְנַשֶּׁה **לָבוֹא** לְבֵית יְהוָה בִּירוּשָׁלַ֫ם **לַעֲשׂוֹת** פֶּסַח לַיהוָה אֱלֹהֵי יִשְׂרָאֵל׃

Hezekiah **sent word** to all Israel and Judah; he also **wrote** letters to Ephraim and Manasseh: **[You] shall come [command]** to the House of the LORD in Jerusalem, **[you] shall keep [command]** the Passover for the LORD God of Israel. (2 Chr 30:1)

The chain of instructions that begins in column 5 of the *Rule* opens with the words "וזה הסרך לאנשי היחד" (1QS 5:1). This pattern is already familiar from biblical law of the First Temple period, but the instructions in classical Hebrew are transmitted via *yiqtol* and *weqatal*. For example:

(424) וַיְדַבֵּר יְהוָה אֶל מֹשֶׁה לֵּאמֹר׃ צַו אֶת אַהֲרֹן וְאֶת בָּנָיו לֵאמֹר זֹאת תּוֹרַת הָעֹלָה הִוא הָעֹלָה עַל מוֹקְדָה עַל הַמִּזְבֵּחַ כָּל הַלַּיְלָה עַד הַבֹּקֶר וְאֵשׁ הַמִּזְבֵּחַ **תּוּקַד** בּוֹ׃ **וְלָבַשׁ** הַכֹּהֵן מִדּוֹ בַד וּמִכְנְסֵי בַד **יִלְבַּשׁ** עַל בְּשָׂרוֹ **וְהֵרִים** אֶת הַדֶּשֶׁן אֲשֶׁר תֹּאכַל הָאֵשׁ אֶת הָעֹלָה עַל הַמִּזְבֵּחַ **וְשָׂמוֹ** אֵצֶל הַמִּזְבֵּחַ׃ **וּפָשַׁט** אֶת בְּגָדָיו **וְלָבַשׁ** בְּגָדִים אֲחֵרִים **וְהוֹצִיא** אֶת הַדֶּשֶׁן אֶל מִחוּץ לַמַּחֲנֶה אֶל מָקוֹם טָהוֹר׃[10]

The LORD spoke to Moses, saying: Command Aaron and his sons thus: This is the ritual of the burnt offering: The burnt offering itself shall remain where it is burned upon the altar all night until morning, while the fire on the altar **is kept going (*yiqtol*)** on it. The priest **shall dress (*weqatal*)** in linen raiment, **he shall wear (*yiqtol*)** linen breeches next to his body; and **he shall take up (*weqatal*)** the ashes to which the fire has reduced the burnt offering on the altar and **place (*weqatal*)** them beside the altar. **He shall then take off (*weqatal*)** his vestments and **put on (*weqatal*)** other vestments, and **carry (*weqatal*)** the ashes outside the camp to a clean place. (Lv 6:1-4)

---

10. Also see the string of instructions in Leviticus 6:7-11, inter alia.

A comparison of the aforementioned cases from our corpus with the compendium of instructions in the "books" from the First Temple period clearly attests that the verb forms' usage in the texts from the First Temple period accords with the extant language-of-the-law segments from that same period. For example:

(425) וַיִּכְתֹּב יֵהוּא סְפָרִים וַיִּשְׁלַח שֹׁמְרוֹן אֶל שָׂרֵי יִזְרְעֶאל הַזְּקֵנִים וְאֶל הָאֹמְנִים אַחְאָב לֵאמֹר: וְעַתָּה כְּבֹא הַסֵּפֶר הַזֶּה אֲלֵיכֶם וְאִתְּכֶם בְּנֵי אֲדֹנֵיכֶם וְאִתְּכֶם הָרֶכֶב וְהַסּוּסִים וְעִיר מִבְצָר וְהַנָּשֶׁק: וּרְאִיתֶם הַטּוֹב וְהַיָּשָׁר מִבְּנֵי אֲדֹנֵיכֶם וְשַׂמְתֶּם עַל כִּסֵּא אָבִיו וְהִלָּחֲמוּ עַל בֵּית אֲדֹנֵיכֶם:

Jehu **wrote** letters and **sent** them to Samaria, to the elders and officials of Jezreel and to the guardians of the children of Ahab, as follows: Now, when this letter reaches you—since your master's sons are with you and you also have chariots and horses, and a fortified city, and weapons—**select** (*weqatal*) the best and the most suitable of your master's sons and **set** (*weqatal*) him on his father's throne, and **fight** (imperative) for your master's house. (2 Kgs 10:1-3)

8.2.2 Using the Infinitive Form to Express a Wish or Grant Permission[11]

In the following example from 2 Chronicles, the infinitive form turns up in a letter that King Solomon sends to King Huram of Tyre requesting a master craftsman and materials for the construction of the Temple:

(426) וַיִּשְׁלַח שְׁלֹמֹה אֶל חוּרָם מֶלֶךְ צֹר לֵאמֹר. . . [6]וְעַתָּה שְׁלַח לִי אִישׁ חָכָם לַעֲשׂוֹת בַּזָּהָב וּבַכֶּסֶף וּבַנְּחֹשֶׁת וּבַבַּרְזֶל וּבָאַרְגְּוָן וְכַרְמִיל וּתְכֵלֶת וְיֹדֵעַ לְפַתֵּחַ פִּתּוּחִים עִם הַחֲכָמִים אֲשֶׁר עִמִּי בִּיהוּדָה וּבִירוּשָׁלַ͏ִם אֲשֶׁר הֵכִין דָּוִיד אָבִי: וּשְׁלַח לִי עֲצֵי אֲרָזִים בְּרוֹשִׁים וְאַלְגּוּמִּים מֵהַלְּבָנוֹן כִּי אֲנִי יָדַעְתִּי אֲשֶׁר עֲבָדֶיךָ יוֹדְעִים לִכְרוֹת עֲצֵי לְבָנוֹן וְהִנֵּה עֲבָדַי עִם עֲבָדֶיךָ: וּלְהָכִין לִי עֵצִים לָרֹב כִּי הַבַּיִת אֲשֶׁר אֲנִי בוֹנֶה גָּדוֹל וְהַפְלֵא:

Solomon sent this message to King Huram of Tyre, saying . . . [N]ow **send** (imperative) me a craftsman to work in gold, silver, bronze, and iron, and in purple, crimson, and blue yarn, and who knows how to engrave, alongside the craftsmen I have here in Judah and in Jerusalem, whom my father David provided. **Send** (imperative) me cedars, cypress, and algum wood from the Lebanon, for I know that your servants are skilled at cutting the trees of Lebanon, and behold my servants will work with yours. And **provide** (infinitive construct) me with a great stock of timber; for the House that I intend to build will be singularly great. (2 Chr 2:2-8)

The succession commences with imperative forms (שלח); however, these are subsequently replaced with an infinitive (להכין), which should also be viewed as bearing the volitive meaning that is expressed by "שלח" and "ושלח".

---

11. 1 Chronicles 13:4; 22:5 (twice); 2 Chronicles 2:8.

The next passage also features a request:

(427) וַיֹּאמֶר דָּוִיד לְכֹל קְהַל יִשְׂרָאֵל אִם עֲלֵיכֶם טוֹב וּמִן יְהוָה אֱלֹהֵינוּ נִפְרְצָה
נִשְׁלְחָה עַל אַחֵינוּ הַנִּשְׁאָרִים בְּכֹל אַרְצוֹת יִשְׂרָאֵל וְעִמָּהֶם הַכֹּהֲנִים וְהַלְוִיִּם בְּעָרֵי
מִגְרְשֵׁיהֶם וְיִקָּבְצוּ אֵלֵינוּ: וְנָסֵבָּה אֶת אֲרוֹן אֱלֹהֵינוּ אֵלֵינוּ כִּי לֹא דְרַשְׁנֻהוּ בִּימֵי
שָׁאוּל: וַיֹּאמְרוּ כָל הַקָּהָל **לַעֲשׂוֹת** כֵּן [12]

David said to the entire assembly of Israel, If you approve, and if the Lord our God concurs, let us send far and wide to our remaining kinsmen throughout the territories of Israel, including the priests and Levites in the towns where they have pasturelands, that they should gather together to us in order to transfer the Ark of our God to us, for throughout the days of Saul we paid no regard to it. The entire assembly said: **[We] will do** so **(infinitive construct)**. (1 Chr 13:2-4)

Contrasting the use of the infinitive form "לעשות" with the rest of its occurrences indicates that it is possible to interpret it as a signifier of direct speech in which the infinitive serves as a volitive form, rather than an instance of indirect speech or an adverbial complement. This usage is reminiscent of the following verse from the First Temple period:

(428) וַיֹּאמֶר אֲלֵהֶם **יְהִי כֵן** יְהוָה עִמָּכֶם

But he said to them, The Lord **be (jussive)** with you. (Ex 10:10)

By its very nature, the volitive is not limited to requests or wishes, but encompasses a broad spectrum of connotations. For example:

(429) וַיֹּאמֶר דָּוִיד שְׁלֹמֹה בְנִי נַעַר וָרָךְ וְהַבַּיִת **לִבְנוֹת** לַיהוָה **לְהַגְדִּיל** לְמַעְלָה לְשֵׁם
וּלְתִפְאֶרֶת לְכָל הָאֲרָצוֹת אָכִינָה נָּא לוֹ וַיָּכֶן דָּוִיד לָרֹב לִפְנֵי מוֹתוֹ:

For David thought, My son Solomon is an untried youth, and the House **should be built (infinitive construct)** for the Lord, **[and it] should be enlarged (infinitive construct)** to be exceedingly great to win fame and glory throughout all the lands; let me then lay aside material for him. So David laid aside much material before he died. (1 Chr 22:5)

The infinitive forms in this sentence do not express a request, for David is not addressing anyone in particular. Instead, he expresses what, in his estimation, needs to be done, namely a sort of wish.

---

12. For a discussion on the cardinal difference between this case and those in which the infinitive form appears after the declarative verb root אמ"ר. An example of this usage turns up in the following verse (Esther 6:1-2): "בַּלַּיְלָה הַהוּא נָדְדָה שְׁנַת הַמֶּלֶךְ **וַיֹּאמֶר לְהָבִיא**
אֶת סֵפֶר הַזִּכְרֹנוֹת דִּבְרֵי הַיָּמִים"; see §6.2.7 below.

8.2.3 Expressing the Future with the Infinitive

Besides the infinitive form's deontic roles, Qimron points to a less pervasive usage in the Dead Sea Scrolls that he dubs the "indicative future" (Qimron 1986:§400.02).[13] For example:

כי ביד אביונים **תסגיר** [או]יבי כול הארצות וביד כורעי עפר **להשפיל** גיבורי עמים
להשיב גמול רשעים בראש אש[מתם] **ולהצדיק** משפט אמתכה בכול בני איש
ולעשות לכה שם עולם בעם המלחמות **ולהתגדל ולהתקדש** לעיני שאר הגוים

For into the hand of the oppressed **you will deliver** (*yiqtol*) the [ene]mies of all the lands; into the hands of those who are prostrate in the dust, [you] will **bring down (infinitive construct)** all mighty men of the peoples, [you] will **retaliate (infinitive construct)** against the wicked at the height of their guilt; [you]**will pronounce (infinitive construct)** the just judgement of your truth on all sons of man, and [you] **will make (infinitive construct)** for yourself an everlasting name among the people of the wars, and [you] **will show yourself great (infinitive construct) and holy (infinitive construct)** before the rest of the nations. (1QM 11:13-15)

As in the previous discussion, there are doubts as to the function that these infinitives fill. Given the context, however, they appear to be independent forms, rather than complements of the verb "תסגיר". Accordingly, Qimron posits that these infinitives do not express a directive or order, but inform the reader of what will transpire in the future.[14]

With respect to our own corpus, one example was found that can be interpreted in this fashion:

(430) עַתָּה אַל תַּקְשׁוּ עָרְפְּכֶם כַּאֲבוֹתֵיכֶם תְּנוּ יָד לַיהוָה וּבֹאוּ לְמִקְדָּשׁוֹ אֲשֶׁר הִקְדִּישׁ
לְעוֹלָם וְעִבְדוּ אֶת יְהוָה אֱלֹהֵיכֶם וְיָשֹׁב מִכֶּם חֲרוֹן אַפּוֹ : כִּי בְשׁוּבְכֶם עַל יְהוָה אֲחֵיכֶם
וּבְנֵיכֶם לְרַחֲמִים לִפְנֵי שׁוֹבֵיהֶם **וְלָשׁוּב** לָאָרֶץ הַזֹּאת כִּי חַנּוּן וְרַחוּם יְהוָה אֱלֹהֵיכֶם
וְלֹא יָסִיר פָּנִים מִכֶּם אִם תָּשׁוּבוּ אֵלָיו :

Now do not be stiffnecked like your fathers; submit yourselves to the LORD and come to his sanctuary, which he consecrated forever, and serve the LORD

---

13. Also see Cohen's view of this term (2005:84).
14. This usage also appears, inter alia, in the following passage from the Dead Sea Scrolls:
ואתם התחזקו ואל תיראום <. .> המה לתהו ולבהו תשוקתם ומשענתם בלוא ה<. . .
וי?ל?וא <. .> ישראל כול הו?י?זה ונהיה ו<. . .>ה <. . .>ל בכול נהיי עולמים היום מועדו
להכניע ולהשפיל שר ממשלת רשעה **וישלח** עזר ?עו?ל?מים לגורל <פ?>זד?ותו בגבורת מלאך
האדיר למשרת ?<. . .>? מיכאל באור עולמים **להאיר** בשמחה ברית ישראל שלו?ם? וברכה
(1QM 17:4-8) לגורל אל **להרים** באלים משרת מיכאל וממשלת ישראל בכול בשר.
Also see 1QH 7:30-31; 1QM 2:2-4; 1QSa 1:4-5; 1QS 3:24; CD-A 7:9-10; CD-B 19:5-6. Lastly, if we interpret the infinitive forms in 1QM 3:4-6 and 3:8-9 as the text that will be written on the trumpets of the Sons of Light, then perhaps these passages should be understood in a similar vein.

your God so that his anger may turn back from you.[9] If you return to the LORD, your brothers and children will be regarded with compassion by their captors, **and will return (infinitive construct)** to this land; for the LORD your God is gracious and merciful; he will not turn his face from you if you return to him. (2 Chr 30:8-9)

The missive that Hezekiah dispatches opens with several orders to the people of Israel. However, verse 9 shifts to a description of what will happen should the people of Israel heed the king's words and return to God. In consequence, "ולשוב" should be interpreted as signifying the future. Although this constitutes the lone occurrence of this usage in our corpus, the language of the Scrolls indicates that its distribution was perhaps wider than the existing biblical texts suggest.

8.2.4 The Habitual Present or General Truth[15]

Like classical *yiqtol* and *weqatal*, the infinitive forms in the Second Temple period also express the habitual present:

(431) וְהֵם וּבְנֵיהֶם עַל הַשְּׁעָרִים לְבֵית יְהוָה לְבֵית הָאֹהֶל לְמִשְׁמָרוֹת: לְאַרְבַּע רוּחוֹת יִהְיוּ הַשֹּׁעֲרִים מִזְרָח יָמָּה צָפוֹנָה וָנֶגְבָּה: וַאֲחֵיהֶם בְּחַצְרֵיהֶם **לָבוֹא** לְשִׁבְעַת הַיָּמִים מֵעֵת אֶל עֵת עִם אֵלֶּה:

They and their descendants were in charge of the gates of the House of the LORD, that is, the House of the Tent, as guards. The gatekeepers were on the four sides, east, west, north, and south; and their kinsmen in their villages **join (infinitive construct)** them every seven days, according to a fixed schedule. (1 Chr 9:23-25)

The adverbial phrase "מעת אל עת" underscores that "their brethren" arrive on a regular (habitual) basis.

In the next three examples, the infinitive is associated with forms that express the habitual present or a general truth:

(432) וַיֵּצֵא אֶל פָּנָיו יֵהוּא בֶן חֲנָנִי הַחֹזֶה וַיֹּאמֶר אֶל הַמֶּלֶךְ יְהוֹשָׁפָט הֲלָרָשָׁע **לַעְזֹר** וּלְשֹׂנְאֵי יְהוָה **תֶּאֱהָב**

Jehu son of Hanani the seer went out to meet King Jehoshaphat and said to him, Should **[you] give (infinitive construct)** aid to the wicked and **befriend (*yiqtol*)** those who hate the LORD? (2 Chr 19:2)

---

15. Nehemiah 10:35?, 36?, 37?; 12:24 (twice); 13:18?; Daniel 12:11; 1 Chronicles 5:1; 9:25, 32; 12:9; 23:4, 13? (thrice), 30 (thrice); 25:5; 26:12; 29:17; 2 Chronicles 2:17?; 13:11, 12; 19:2; 31:18; 33:14; 34:12.

(433) וּלְלֶחֶם הַמַּעֲרֶכֶת וּלְסֹלֶת לְמִנְחָה וְלִרְקִיקֵי הַמַּצּוֹת וְלַמַּחֲבַת וְלַמֻּרְבָּכֶת וּלְכָל־
מְשׂוּרָה וּמִדָּה : **וְלַעֲמֹד** בַּבֹּקֶר בַּבֹּקֶר **לְהֹדוֹת וּלְהַלֵּל**[16] לַיהוָה וְכֵן לָעָרֶב : וּלְכֹל הַעֲלוֹת
עֹלוֹת לַיהוָה לַשַּׁבָּתוֹת לֶחֳדָשִׁים וְלַמֹּעֲדִים בְּמִסְפָּר כְּמִשְׁפָּט עֲלֵיהֶם תָּמִיד לִפְנֵי יְהוָה :
וְשָׁמְרוּ אֶת־מִשְׁמֶרֶת אֹהֶל מוֹעֵד וְאֵת מִשְׁמֶרֶת הַקֹּדֶשׁ וּמִשְׁמֶרֶת בְּנֵי אַהֲרֹן אֲחֵיהֶם
לַעֲבֹדַת בֵּית יְהוָה :

[A]nd the rows of bread, and the fine flour for the meal offering, and the
unleavened wafers, and the cakes made on the griddle and soaked, and every
measure of capacity and length; and **[they] are present (infinitive construct)**
every morning **to praise (infinitive construct)** and **to extol (infinitive
construct)** the LORD, and at evening too, and whenever offerings were made
to the LORD, according to the quantities prescribed for them, on sabbaths, new
moons and holidays, regularly, before the LORD; and so **they keep (*weqatal*)**
watch over the Tent of Meeting, over the holy things, and over the Aaronites
their kinsmen, for the service of the House of the LORD. (1 Chr 23:29-32)

(434) וַאֲנַחְנוּ יְהוָה אֱלֹהֵינוּ וְלֹא עֲזַבְנֻהוּ וְכֹהֲנִים מְשָׁרְתִים לַיהוָה בְּנֵי אַהֲרֹן וְהַלְוִיִּם
בַּמְּלָאכֶת : **וּמַקְטִרִים** לַיהוָה עֹלוֹת בַּבֹּקֶר בַּבֹּקֶר וּבָעֶרֶב בָּעֶרֶב וּקְטֹרֶת סַמִּים וּמַעֲרֶכֶת
לֶחֶם עַל הַשֻּׁלְחָן הַטָּהוֹר וּמְנוֹרַת הַזָּהָב וְנֵרֹתֶיהָ **לְבָעֵר** בָּעֶרֶב בָּעֶרֶב כִּי שֹׁמְרִים אֲנַחְנוּ
אֶת־מִשְׁמֶרֶת יְהוָה אֱלֹהֵינוּ וְאַתֶּם עֲזַבְתֶּם אֹתוֹ [17]:

As for us, the LORD is our God, and we have not forsaken him. The priests
who minister to the LORD are the sons of Aaron, and the Levites are at their
tasks. **They offer (participle)** burnt offerings in smoke each morning and each
evening, and the aromatic incense, the rows of bread on the pure table; they
kindle (infinitive construct) the golden lampstand with its lamps burning
each evening, for we keep the charge of the LORD our God, while you have
forsaken it. (2 Chr 13:10-11)

In 2 Chronicles 19:2, the infinitive form appears within a question. The author
utilizes an infinitive in the verse's first clause, while a *yiqtol* form carries out a
similar function in the parallel clause. The infinitive forms in 1 Chronicles 23 are
arrayed within a list, whereupon a *weqatal* form ("ושמרו") is deployed in a similar
capacity. We can thus see how a new form, the infinitive, assumes a role that was
customarily filled by *yiqtol* and *weqatal* in the First Temple period. Alternatively,
example 434 demonstrates that the infinitive maintains a link to the participial
form, which also denotes the habitual present during the Second Temple period. The structure that is utilized for marking the habitual present in example 433
(1 Chr 23:29-32) is commonplace in the lists from this period.[18] However, it also
turns up in direct speech, as in examples 432 and 434.

---

16. These forms can be interpreted as adverbial complements of "ולעמד" (i.e., in order to
"להודות ולהלל").
17. An infinitive form also replaces a participle in 2 Chronicles 34:12.
18. Also see Nehemiah 10:35?, 36?, 37?; 12:24 (twice); 1 Chronicles 9:25, 32; 12:9;
23:13? (thrice), 30 (thrice); 25:5; 26:12; 2 Chronicles 2:17?; 31:18; 34:12.

The following three verses enable us to compare the ways in which the habitual present is expressed in negative sentences over the different periods:

(435) וַיֹּאמֶר לָבָן **לֹא יֵעָשֶׂה** כֵן בִּמְקוֹמֵנוּ לָתֵת הַצְּעִירָה לִפְנֵי הַבְּכִירָה׃

Laban said, **It is not (*yiqtol*)** the practice in our place to marry off the younger before the older. (Gn 29:26)

(436) וּבְנֵי רְאוּבֵן בְּכוֹר יִשְׂרָאֵל כִּי הוּא הַבְּכוֹר וּבְחַלְּלוֹ יְצוּעֵי אָבִיו נִתְּנָה בְּכֹרָתוֹ לִבְנֵי יוֹסֵף בֶּן יִשְׂרָאֵל **וְלֹא לְהִתְיַחֵשׂ** לַבְּכֹרָה׃

The sons of Reuben the first-born of Israel. (He was the first-born; but when he defiled his father's bed, his birthright was given to the sons of Joseph son of Israel, so **he is not reckoned (infinitive construct)** as first-born in the genealogy; (1 Chr 5:1)

(437) וַאֲנִי שְׂנֵאתִיהוּ כִּי **אֵינֶנּוּ מִתְנַבֵּא** עָלַי לְטוֹבָה כִּי כָל יָמָיו לְרָעָה

[B]ut I hate him, because **he never prophesies (participle)** anything good for me but always misfortune. (2 Chr 18:7)

The first verse represents the standard pattern of the First Temple period wherein the habitual present (custom) is denoted by the *yiqtol* form. The next example's structure is a revised edition of the classical pattern in which *yiqtol* has been exchanged for the infinitive construct. Likewise, the participle's usage in 2 Chronicles 18:7 is among the attributes of the later language.[19]

Another role that the infinitive form plays within the framework of the habitual present/general truth is the depiction of a delineated space's geographical boundaries:

(438) וַיִּתְפַּלֵּל אֵלָיו וַיֵּעָתֶר לוֹ וַיִּשְׁמַע תְּחִנָּתוֹ וַיְשִׁיבֵהוּ יְרוּשָׁלַ͏ִם לְמַלְכוּתוֹ וַיֵּדַע מְנַשֶּׁה כִּי יְהוָה הוּא הָאֱלֹהִים׃ וְאַחֲרֵי כֵן בָּנָה חוֹמָה חִיצוֹנָה לְעִיר דָּוִיד מַעְרָבָה לְגִיחוֹן בַּנַּחַל **וְלָבוֹא** בְשַׁעַר הַדָּגִים **וְסָבַב** לָעֹפֶל וַיַּגְבִּיהֶהָ מְאֹד וַיָּשֶׂם שָׂרֵי חַיִל בְּכָל הֶעָרִים הַבְּצֻרוֹת בִּיהוּדָה׃

He prayed to him, and he granted his prayer, heard his plea, and returned him to Jerusalem to his kingdom. Then Manasseh knew that the LORD alone was God. Afterward he built the outer wall of the City of David west of Gihon in the wadi and **[it] touches (infinitive construct)** the Fish Gate, and **it encircles (*weqatal*)** the Ophel; he raised it very high. He also placed army officers in all the fortified towns of Judah. (2 Chr 33:13-14)

---

19. Although the structure "אין + pronoun + participle" appears four times in the First Temple period corpus (Leviticus 11:4, 26; Deuteronomy 21:18, 20), it is relegated to the language of the law. However, the structure's distribution is wider in the Second Temple period corpus (2 Chronicles 18:7; Nehemiah 13:24; Esther 3:8; 5:13) and is commonplace in Ecclesiastes (1:7; 4:17; 5:11; 6:2; 8:7, 13; 9:5, 16).

This usage is also familiar to us from classical Hebrew, where *yiqtol* and *weqatal* assume this same task:

(439) וַיֵּצֵא הַגּוֹרָל לִבְנֵי יוֹסֵף מִיַּרְדֵּן יְרִיחוֹ לְמֵי יְרִיחוֹ מִזְרָחָה הַמִּדְבָּר עֹלֶה עָלָה מִירִיחוֹ בָּהָר בֵּית אֵל: **וְיָצָא** מִבֵּית אֵל לוּזָה **וְעָבַר** אֶל גְּבוּל הָאַרְכִּי עֲטָרוֹת: **וְיָרַד** יָמָּה אֶל גְּבוּל הַיַּפְלֵטִי עַד גְּבוּל בֵּית חוֹרֹן תַּחְתּוֹן וְעַד גֶּזֶר **וְהָיוּ** תֹצְאֹתָו יָמָּה:

The portion that fell by lot to the Josephites ran from the Jordan at Jericho—from the waters of Jericho east of the wilderness. From Jericho it ascended through the hill country to Bethel. From Bethel **it runs** (*weqatal*) to Luz **and passes** (*weqatal*) on to the territory of the Archites at Ataroth, **descends** (*weqatal*) westward to the territory of the Japhletites as far as the border of Lower Beth-horon and Gezer, **and runs** (*weqatal*) on to the Sea. (Josh 16:1-3)

Just as the shift from the narrative to the description of the border in Joshua is marked by the transition from *wayyiqtol* to *weqatal*, the shift in our own corpus from Manasseh's concrete actions to the description of the wall's layout is marked by a transition from *wayyiqtol* to infinitive construct and *weqatal* forms.

The infinitive construct also signifies the habitual present or general truth in the texts from Qumran (Cohen 2005:85-86), including the following passage:

ועל השלט השני יכתובו זיקי דם **להפיל** חללים באף אל ועל הזרק השלישי יכתובו שלהובת חרב **אוכלת** חללי און במשפט אל

On the second weapon they shall write Missiles of blood **kill (infinitive construct)** by the wrath of God. On the third dart they shall write The blade of a sword **devours (participle)** the slain of wickedness by the judgement of God. (1QM 6:2-3)

As Qimron has suggested (1986:§400.02), the infinitive form "להפיל" expresses the same meaning as the participial "אוכלת". Therefore, it should be perceived as a signifier of the habitual present/general truth.

8.2.5 An Iterative Action in the Past[20]

An additional usage of the infinitive is the signification of iterative actions in the past. This constitutes yet another example of a function that was filled by the modal *yiqtol* and *weqatal* forms in classical Hebrew.

(440) **וַיַּעֲמִידוּ** הַלְוִיִּם אֶת הֵימָן בֶּן יוֹאֵל וּמִן אֶחָיו אָסָף בֶּן בֶּרֶכְיָהוּ וּמִן בְּנֵי מְרָרִי אֲחֵיהֶם אֵיתָן בֶּן קוּשָׁיָהוּ: וְעִמָּהֶם אֲחֵיהֶם הַמִּשְׁנִים זְכַרְיָהוּ בֶּן וְעֲזִיאֵל וּשְׁמִירָמוֹת וִיחִיאֵל וְעֻנִּי אֱלִיאָב וּבְנָיָהוּ וּמַעֲשֵׂיָהוּ וּמַתִּתְיָהוּ וֶאֱלִיפְלֵהוּ וּמִקְנֵיָהוּ וְעֹבֵד אֱדֹם וִיעִיאֵל הַשֹּׁעֲרִים: וְהַמְשֹׁרְרִים הֵימָן אָסָף וְאֵיתָן בִּמְצִלְתַּיִם נְחֹשֶׁת **לְהַשְׁמִיעַ**:

---

20. Ezra 3:12; 6:24; Nehemiah 8:13?; 10:30? (thrice); 1 Chronicles 6:34; 10:10?; 15:19, 21; 16:4 (thrice); 23:4; 2 Chronicles 12:12.

וּזְכַרְיָה וַעֲזִיאֵל וּשְׁמִירָמוֹת וִיחִיאֵל וְעֻנִּי וֶאֱלִיאָב וּמַעֲשֵׂיָהוּ וּבְנָיָהוּ בִּנְבָלִים עַל
עֲלָמוֹת׃ וּמַתִּתְיָהוּ וֶאֱלִיפְלֵהוּ וּמִקְנֵיָהוּ וְעֹבֵד אֱדֹם וִיעִיאֵל וַעֲזַזְיָהוּ בְּכִנֹּרוֹת עַל
הַשְּׁמִינִית **לְנַצֵּחַ**׃

So the Levites **installed (wayyiqtol)** Heman son of Joel and, of his kinsmen,
Asaph son of Berechiah; and, of the sons of Merari their kinsmen, Ethan son of
Kushaiah. Together with them were their kinsmen of second rank, Zechariah,
Ben, Jaaziel, Shemiramoth, Jehiel, Unni, Eliab, Benaiah, Maaseiah, Mattithiah,
Eliphalehu, Mikneiah, Obed-edom and Jeiel the gatekeepers. Also the singers
Heman, Asaph, and Ethan **used to sound (infinitive construct)** the bronze
cymbals, and Zechariah, Aziel, Shemiramoth, Jehiel, Unni, Eliab, Maaseiah,
and Benaiah with harps on alamoth; also Mattithiah, Eliphalehu, Mikneiah,
Obed-edom, Jeiel, and Azaziah **used to lead (infinitive construct)** on the
sheminith with lyres; (1 Chr 15:17-21)

(441) וְאֵלֶּה אֲשֶׁר **הֶעֱמִיד** דָּוִיד עַל יְדֵי שִׁיר בֵּית יְהוָה מִמְּנוֹחַ הָאָרוֹן׃ **וַיִּהְיוּ** מְשָׁרְתִים
לִפְנֵי מִשְׁכַּן אֹהֶל מוֹעֵד בַּשִּׁיר עַד בְּנוֹת שְׁלֹמֹה אֶת בֵּית יְהוָה בִּירוּשָׁלָם **וַיַּעַמְדוּ**
כְמִשְׁפָּטָם עַל עֲבוֹדָתָם׃ וְאֵלֶּה הָעֹמְדִים וּבְנֵיהֶם מִבְּנֵי הַקְּהָתִי הֵימָן הַמְשׁוֹרֵר בֶּן יוֹאֵל
בֶּן שְׁמוּאֵל׃ . . . . וְאַהֲרֹן וּבָנָיו **מַקְטִירִים** עַל מִזְבַּח הָעוֹלָה וְעַל מִזְבַּח הַקְּטֹרֶת לְכֹל
מְלֶאכֶת קֹדֶשׁ הַקֳּדָשִׁים **וּלְכַפֵּר** עַל יִשְׂרָאֵל כְּכֹל אֲשֶׁר צִוָּה מֹשֶׁה עֶבֶד הָאֱלֹהִים׃

These were appointed by David to be in charge of song in the House of the
Lord, from the time the Ark came to rest. **They served** at the Tabernacle of
the Tent of Meeting with song until Solomon built the House of the Lord in
Jerusalem; and **they carried** out their duties as prescribed for them. Those
were the appointed men; and their sons were: the Kohathites: Heman the
singer, son of Joel son of Samuel. . . . But Aaron and his sons **used to give
offerings (participle)** upon the altar of burnt offering and upon the altar of
incense, performing all the tasks of the most holy place, **and used to make
atonement (infinitive construct)** for Israel, according to all that Moses the
servant of God had commanded. (1 Chr 6:16-34)

In both these examples, the wayyiqtol and qatal forms set the temporal framework
and thus situate the action in the past. Consequently, the infinitive forms should be
interpreted as expressing iterative actions in the past. The next passage is similar
in this respect:

(442) **וַיָּבִיאוּ** אֶת אֲרוֹן הָאֱלֹהִים **וַיַּצִּיגוּ** אֹתוֹ בְּתוֹךְ הָאֹהֶל אֲשֶׁר נָטָה לוֹ דָּוִיד **וַיַּקְרִיבוּ**
עֹלוֹת וּשְׁלָמִים לִפְנֵי הָאֱלֹהִים׃ **וַיְכַל** דָּוִיד מֵהַעֲלוֹת הָעֹלָה וְהַשְּׁלָמִים **וַיְבָרֶךְ** אֶת הָעָם
בְּשֵׁם יְהוָה׃ **וַיְחַלֵּק** לְכָל אִישׁ יִשְׂרָאֵל מֵאִישׁ וְעַד אִשָּׁה לְאִישׁ כִּכַּר לֶחֶם וְאֶשְׁפָּר
וַאֲשִׁישָׁה׃ **וַיִּתֵּן** לִפְנֵי אֲרוֹן יְהוָה מִן הַלְוִיִּם מְשָׁרְתִים **וּלְהַזְכִּיר וּלְהוֹדוֹת וּלְהַלֵּל** לַיהוָה
אֱלֹהֵי יִשְׂרָאֵל׃

They brought (wayyiqtol) in the Ark of God **and set (wayyiqtol)** it up inside
the tent that David had pitched for it, **and they sacrificed (wayyiqtol)** burnt
offerings and offerings of well being before God. When David **finished
(wayyiqtol)** sacrificing the burnt offerings and the offerings of well being, **he**

blessed (*wayyiqtol*) the people in the name of the LORD. **And he distributed** (*wayyiqtol*) to every person in Israel—man and woman alike—to each a loaf of bread, a cake made in a pan, and a raisin cake. **He appointed** (*wayyiqtol*) Levites to minister before the Ark of the LORD, **and [they] used to invoke (infinitive construct) [the name of], praise (infinitive construct), and extol (infinitive construct)** the LORD God of Israel. (1 Chr 16:1-4)

This passage exemplifies the Second Temple era's transition from narrative successions that are denoted by *wayyiqtol* forms to habitual actions marked by infinitive construct forms. In classical Hebrew, this task is effected by substituting *wayyiqtol* for *yiqtol* and *weqatal* forms:

(443) **וַיֹּאמֶר** יְהֹוָה אֶל מֹשֶׁה אֱמֹר אֶל בְּנֵי יִשְׂרָאֵל אַתֶּם עַם קְשֵׁה עֹרֶף רֶגַע אֶחָד אֶעֱלֶה בְקִרְבְּךָ וְכִלִּיתִיךָ וְעַתָּה הוֹרֵד עֶדְיְךָ מֵעָלֶיךָ וְאֵדְעָה מָה אֶעֱשֶׂה לָּךְ : **וַיִּתְנַצְּלוּ** בְנֵי יִשְׂרָאֵל אֶת עֶדְיָם מֵהַר חוֹרֵב : וּמֹשֶׁה **יִקַּח** אֶת הָאֹהֶל **וְנָטָה** לוֹ מִחוּץ לַמַּחֲנֶה הַרְחֵק מִן הַמַּחֲנֶה **וְקָרָא** לוֹ אֹהֶל מוֹעֵד **וְהָיָה** כָּל מְבַקֵּשׁ יְהֹוָה **יֵצֵא** אֶל אֹהֶל מוֹעֵד אֲשֶׁר מִחוּץ לַמַּחֲנֶה : **וְהָיָה** כְּצֵאת מֹשֶׁה אֶל הָאֹהֶל **יָקוּמוּ** כָּל הָעָם **וְנִצְּבוּ** אִישׁ פֶּתַח אָהֳלוֹ **וְהִבִּיטוּ** אַחֲרֵי מֹשֶׁה עַד בֹּאוֹ הָאֹהֱלָה : **וְהָיָה** כְּבֹא מֹשֶׁה הָאֹהֱלָה **יֵרֵד** עַמּוּד הֶעָנָן **וְעָמַד** פֶּתַח הָאֹהֶל **וְדִבֶּר** עִם מֹשֶׁה :

The LORD **said** (*wayyiqtol*) to Moses, Say to the Israelite people, you are a stiffnecked people. If I were to go in your midst for one moment, I would destroy you. Now, then, leave off your finery, and I will consider what to do to you. So the Israelites **remained** (*wayyiqtol*) stripped of the finery from Mount Horeb on. Now Moses **would take** (*yiqtol*) the Tent **and pitch** (*weqatal*) it outside the camp, at some distance from the camp. And he **called** (*weqatal*) it the Tent of Meeting, and **whoever sought** (*weqatal*) the LORD **would go out** (*yiqtol*) to the Tent of Meeting that was outside the camp. Whenever Moses **would go out** (*weqatal*) to the Tent, all the people **would rise** (*yiqtol*) **and stand** (*weqatal*), each at the entrance of his tent, and **would gaze** (*weqatal*) after Moses until he had entered the Tent. And when Moses **would enter** (*weqatal*) the Tent, the pillar of cloud **would descend** (*yiqtol*) and **stand** (*weqatal*) at the entrance of the Tent, while **he would speak** (*weqatal*) with Moses (Ex 33:5-9)

Similarly, iterative successions feature infinitive and participle forms that convey the same meaning:

(444) וְדָוִיד זָקֵן וְשָׂבַע יָמִים וַיַּמְלֵךְ אֶת שְׁלֹמֹה בְנוֹ עַל יִשְׂרָאֵל : וַיֶּאֱסֹף אֶת כָּל שָׂרֵי יִשְׂרָאֵל וְהַכֹּהֲנִים וְהַלְוִיִּם : וַיִּסָּפְרוּ הַלְוִיִּם מִבֶּן שְׁלֹשִׁים שָׁנָה וָמַעְלָה נַיְהִי מִסְפָּרָם לְגֻלְגְּלֹתָם לִגְבָרִים שְׁלֹשִׁים וּשְׁמוֹנָה אָלֶף : מֵאֵלֶּה **לְנַצֵּחַ** עַל מְלֶאכֶת בֵּית יְהֹוָה עֶשְׂרִים וְאַרְבָּעָה אָלֶף וְשֹׁטְרִים וְשֹׁפְטִים שֵׁשֶׁת אֲלָפִים : וְאַרְבַּעַת אֲלָפִים שֹׁעֲרִים וְאַרְבַּעַת אֲלָפִים **מְהַלְלִים** לַיהֹוָה בַּכֵּלִים אֲשֶׁר עָשִׂיתִי לְהַלֵּל :

When David reached a ripe old age, he made his son Solomon king over Israel. Then David assembled all the officers of Israel and the priests and the Levites. The Levites, from the age of thirty and upward, were counted; the head-count of their males was 38000: of these **there were (infinitive construct)** 24000 **in charge** of the work of the House of the LORD, 6000 officers and

magistrates, 4000 gatekeepers, and 4000 **would praise (participle)** the Lord
with instruments I devised for singing praises. (1 Chr 23:1-5)

(445) וַיַּעֲנוּ בְּהַלֵּל וּבְהוֹדֹת לַיהוָה כִּי טוֹב כִּי לְעוֹלָם חַסְדּוֹ עַל יִשְׂרָאֵל וְכָל הָעָם
הֵרִיעוּ תְרוּעָה גְדוֹלָה בְהַלֵּל לַיהוָה עַל הוּסַד בֵּית יְהוָה: וְרַבִּים מֵהַכֹּהֲנִים וְהַלְוִיִּם
וְרָאשֵׁי הָאָבוֹת הַזְּקֵנִים אֲשֶׁר רָאוּ אֶת הַבַּיִת הָרִאשׁוֹן בְּיָסְדוֹ זֶה הַבַּיִת בְּעֵינֵיהֶם
בֹּכִים בְּקוֹל גָּדוֹל וְרַבִּים בִּתְרוּעָה בְשִׂמְחָה **לְהָרִים** קוֹל:

They sang songs extolling and praising the Lord, For he is good, his steadfast
love for Israel is eternal. All the people raised a great shout extolling the Lord
because the foundation of the House of the Lord had been laid. Many of the
priests and Levites and the chiefs of the clans, the old men who had seen the
first house, **would cry (participle)** loudly at the sight of the founding of this
house. Many others **would shout (infinitive construct)** joyously at the top of
their voices. (Ezr 3:11-12)

The iterative usage also surfaces in the Dead Sea Scrolls (Cohen 2005:86-88):

וברכו שם כולם את אל ישראל ורוממו שמו ביחד שמחה וענו ואמרו ברוך
אל ישראל השומר חסד לבריתו ותעודות ישועה לעם פדותו **ויקרא** כושלים
ל<.>. . . פ<ב>לא וקהל גויים **אסף** לכלה אין שארית **ולהרים** במשפט לב נמס
ולפתוח פה לנאלמים לרן בגבו<רות . . . > רפות **ללמד** מלחמה

There they shall all bless the God of Israel and joyously exalt his name together.
They shall say in response: Blessed is the God of Israel, who guards loving
kindness for his covenant and the appointed times of salvation for the people
he redeems. **He has called** (*wayyiqtol*) those who stumble unto wondrous
[accomplishment]s, and **he has gathered** (*qatal*) a congregation of nations for
annihilation without remnant and **he would raise up (infinitive construct)** in
judgement he whose heart has melted, and **would open (infinitive construct)**
a mouth for the dumb to sing migh[ty deeds . . .], and **would teach (infinitive
construct)** feeble warfare. (1QM 14:3-6)

In this paragraph, the people recall some of God's wondrous feats. The use of
the *wayyiqtol* and *qatal* forms situates the narrative in the past. Therefore, the
subsequent infinitives should be interpreted as forms that refer to the past. However, unlike "ויקרא" and "אסף", which denote a specific action, the infinitive
forms appear to signify iterative actions (God assembled the congregation in
order to bring justice to "those whose hearts have melted" and open "the mouth
of mutes") instead of one-time acts of grace.

   Like their habitual-present contexts, infinitives that signify an iterative action
in the past are situated within lists.[21] That said, in contrast to the habitual present,
the iterative forms are most likely to be found in historical narratives.[22]

---

21. 1 Chronicles 6:34; 15:19, 21; 23:4.
22. Ezra 3:12; 6:24; Nehemiah 8:13; 1 Chronicles 10:13; 16:4 (thrice); 2 Chronicles 12:12.

8.2.6 Other Usages

Two of the 72 instances wherein the infinitive construct serves as an independent predicate do not fall under any of the above-mentioned modal categories:

(446) וַיֹּאמֶר לֵךְ דָּנִיֵּאל כִּי סְתֻמִים וַחֲתֻמִים הַדְּבָרִים עַד עֵת קֵץ : יִתְבָּרֲרוּ וְיִתְלַבְּנוּ
וְיִצָּרְפוּ רַבִּים וְהִרְשִׁיעוּ רְשָׁעִים וְלֹא יָבִינוּ כָּל רְשָׁעִים וְהַמַּשְׂכִּלִים יָבִינוּ : וּמֵעֵת הוּסַר
הַתָּמִיד **וְלָתֵת** שִׁקּוּץ שֹׁמֵם יָמִים אֶלֶף מָאתַיִם וְתִשְׁעִים :

He said, Go, Daniel, for these words are secret and sealed to the time of the end. Many will be purified and purged and refined; the wicked will act wickedly and none of the wicked will understand; but the knowledgeable will understand. (From the time the regular offering is abolished, and an appalling abomination **is set up (infinitive construct)**, it will be a thousand two hundred and ninety days.) (Dn 12:9-11)

(447) וַיִּשְׂרְפוּ אֶת בֵּית הָאֱלֹהִים וַיְנַתְּצוּ אֵת חוֹמַת יְרוּשָׁלָם וְכָל אַרְמְנוֹתֶיהָ שָׂרְפוּ
בָאֵשׁ וְכָל כְּלֵי מַחֲמַדֶּיהָ **לְהַשְׁחִית** :

They burned the House of God and tore down the wall of Jerusalem, burned down all its mansions, and all its precious objects were **consigned to destruction (infinitive construct)**. (2 Chr 36:19)

In the first passage, the verb "ולתת" apparently denotes a protracted action, not a habitual present one. Moreover, it stands in contradistinction to the verb "הוסר"; whereas the removal is a summary act, the "appalling abomination" is to be displayed over the course of 1,290 days. However, the fact that the action is delimited to a set period of time edges it closer to the category of a tangible act. The infinitive in 2 Chronicles 36:19 stands in succession with the *qatal* form "שרפו". In consequence, it appears to expresses a similar quality, namely a concrete, one-time action in the past, and thus should be considered an exception that attests to the rule.[23]

8.2.7 אמר לקטל[24]

In his introduction to the literature of the Bible, Driver (1913:506) avers that there are quite a few occurrences of indirect speech in the later books, especially in contexts that hosted direct speech in earlier Hebrew. For example:

---

23. The situation in the Dead Sea Scrolls appears to be redolent of the biblical texts of the Second Temple period, as the vast majority of the infinitive's occurrences fill the same functions that have historically been filled by *yiqtol* and *weqatal*. See Cohen (2005).
24. Esther 1:11 (twice), 17; 4:15; 6:1; 9:14; Daniel 1:3, 4, 5?; 2:2 (twice); Nehemiah 9:23 (twice); 1 Chronicles 13:4; 15:16, 16?; 22:2; 2 Chronicles 14:3 (twice); 29:21, 27, 30; 31:11; 33:16.

(448) בַּלַּיְלָה הַהוּא נָדְדָה שְׁנַת הַמֶּלֶךְ **וַיֹּאמֶר לְהָבִיא** אֶת סֵפֶר הַזִּכְרֹנוֹת דִּבְרֵי הַיָּמִים
וַיִּהְיוּ נִקְרָאִים לִפְנֵי הַמֶּלֶךְ :

That night, sleep deserted the king, **and he ordered** the book of records, the
annals, **to be brought (predicative?)** and it was read to the king. (Est 6:1)

This verse can, in principle, be interpreted in two different ways: the verb root
אמ״ר is followed by a clause of indirect speech; or "להביא" serves as an independent predicative form, which marks a direct quote of an imperative or instruction.

Let us begin by evaluating the first interpretation. In classical prose, direct
speech is consistently marked by the verb root אמ״ר:[25]

(449) וַתֵּרֶא רָחֵל כִּי לֹא יָלְדָה לְיַעֲקֹב וַתְּקַנֵּא רָחֵל בַּאֲחֹתָהּ **וַתֹּאמֶר** אֶל יַעֲקֹב הָבָה לִּי
בָנִים וְאִם אַיִן מֵתָה אָנֹכִי :

When Rachel saw that she had borne Jacob no children, she became envious
of her sister; and Rachel **said (אמ״ר)** to Jacob, Give me children, or I shall die.
(Gn 30:1)

Conversely, the use of a speech verb other than the אמ״ר root invariably denotes
a shift to indirect speech:

(450) **וַיַּגֵּד** יַעֲקֹב לְרָחֵל כִּי אֲחִי אָבִיהָ הוּא וְכִי בֶן רִבְקָה הוּא

Jacob **told (נג״ד)** Rachel that he was her father's kinsman, that he was
Rebekah's son. (Gn 29:12)

As such, directives are framed in the classical texts in one of three ways:

(451) **וַיֹּאמֶר** הַנִּיחוּ לוֹ אִישׁ אַל יָנַע עַצְמוֹתָיו

Let him be, he **said (אמ״ר)**, let no one disturb his bones. So they left his bones
undisturbed (2 Kgs 23:18)

(452) **וַיְצַו** הַמֶּלֶךְ אֶת כָּל הָעָם **לֵאמֹר** עֲשׂוּ פֶסַח לַיהוָה אֱלֹהֵיכֶם כַּכָּתוּב עַל סֵפֶר
הַבְּרִית הַזֶּה :

The king **commanded (צו״ה)** all the people, **saying (inf. אמ״ר)** Offer the
passover sacrifice to the LORD your God as prescribed in this scroll of the
covenant. (2 Kgs 23:21)

---

25. According to Goldenberg "'*āmar* 'say' will normally define clauses as representing
direct speech, and . . . [a] direct speech clause will, of all *verba dicendi*, require ordinarily '*āmar* 'say' for their presentation in a matrix sentence" (1991:85).

(453) וַעֲלִיתֶם אַחֲרָיו וּבָא וְיָשַׁב עַל כִּסְאִי וְהוּא יִמְלֹךְ תַּחְתָּי וְאֹתוֹ **צִוִּיתִי לִהְיוֹת** נָגִיד
עַל יִשְׂרָאֵל וְעַל יְהוּדָה:

> Then march up after him, and let him come in and sit on my throne. For he
> shall succeed me as king; him **I designate (צו"ה)** to be (**infinitive construct**)
> ruler of Israel and Judah. (1 Kgs 1:35)

In example 451, the author uses an imperative after the root אמ"ר and it heads
direct speech. The imperative form also appears within the framework of direct
speech in the verse from 2 Kings, but the main verb is "ויצו". Therefore, the infinitive form "לאמר" is added to this structure for the purpose of facilitating the
signification of direct speech. Alternatively, the צו"ה verb root in the last example
was not ballasted with "לאמר", and this is evidently the reason why the infinitive
"להיות" is positioned after "צויתי".

Unlike classical Hebrew texts, we have found quite a few cases in the
Second Temple period, such as the above cited Esther 6:1, where the infinitive form supervenes the verb root אמ"ר. Driver claims that the semantic
connotation of אמ"ר is not "to say," but "to command" (Driver 1913:506).
A survey of these constructions indeed shows that the speaker is nearly always
an authoritative figure (usually a king).

Alongside the standard function of the verb root אמ"ר (i.e., "to say"), the Second Temple period also includes another meaning, "to order."[26] This meaning is
one of the prevalent meanings of the אמ"ר root in Biblical Aramaic,[27] so that
there is a strong possibility that the Aramaic influenced the semantic change in
the Hebrew.

Following Goldenberg, the speech verb itself is not the only factor that determines the syntactical construction, as the semantic luggage that it bears must be
taken into account.[28] In other words, the semantic broadening of the purview of
the verb root אמ"ר during the Second Temple period also engendered a change in
the attendant syntactical structure.

---

26. See *BDB*'s fourth entry for אָמַר (pp. 55-56).
27. See *BDB*'s entry for אֲמַר in the Aramaic section (p. 1081). In Arabic, this root's exclu-
    sive meaning is "to order," whereas the root *qwl* is designated entirely for utterance.
    The following structure in Biblical Aramaic is reminiscent of אמר לקטל:
    בֵּאדַיִן נְבוּכַדְנֶצַּר בִּרְגַז וַחֲמָא **אֲמַר לְהַיְתָיָה** לְשַׁדְרַךְ מֵישַׁךְ וַעֲבֵד נְגוֹ (Daniel 3:13).
    Similar to the Hebrew, a king is invariably the speaker in the Aramaic construction.
28. According to Goldenberg, "The differentiation between direct and indirect speech lies
    not in the conjunction, but in the *verbum dicendi* that is selected. . . . If *'āmar* occurs
    in one verse or two with a *'kī'*-clause of indirect speech, it will be found that in those
    cases *'āmar* does not mean 'say,' but 'command' or 'think'" (1991:85-86).

This development does not necessarily refute our contention as to the tension between the infinitive form's adverbial and independent uses. An examination of the infinitive's roles in the אמר לקטל structure reveals disparate usages across the adverbial-independent scale.[29] More specifically, there are cases where it is obvious from the context that the construction signifies indirect speech (example 454 below), namely infinitive forms are subordinated to a speech verb. Alternatively, there are other instances in which infinitive construct should be considered independent forms (example 455). In most cases, however, it is impossible to firmly establish which category the infinitive falls under (example 456 and 457):

(454) **וַיֹּאמֶר** דָּוִיד לְשָׂרֵי הַלְוִיִּם **לְהַעֲמִיד** אֶת אֲחֵיהֶם הַמְשֹׁרְרִים[30]

David **ordered** the officers of the Levites **to install** their kinsmen, the singers. (1 Chr 15:16)

(455) וַיֹּאמֶר דָּוִיד לְכֹל קְהַל יִשְׂרָאֵל אִם עֲלֵיכֶם טוֹב וּמִן יְהוָה אֱלֹהֵינוּ נִפְרְצָה נִשְׁלְחָה עַל אַחֵינוּ הַנִּשְׁאָרִים בְּכֹל אַרְצוֹת יִשְׂרָאֵל. . . . **וַיֹּאמְרוּ** כָל הַקָּהָל **לַעֲשׂוֹת כֵּן** כִּי יָשַׁר הַדָּבָר בְּעֵינֵי כָל הָעָם:[31]

David said to the entire assembly of Israel, If you approve, and if the LORD our God concurs, let us send far and wide to our remaining kinsmen throughout the territories of Israel. . . . The entire assembly **said: We will do** so, for the proposal pleased all the people. (1 Chr 13:2-4)

(456) וַיֹּאמֶר חִזְקִיָּהוּ **לְהַעֲלוֹת** הָעֹלָה לְהַמִּזְבֵּחַ[32]

Hezekiah gave the order (or said:) **To offer** (or **Offer!**) the burnt offering on the altar. (2 Chr 29:27)

(457) וַתֹּאמֶר אֶסְתֵּר **לְהָשִׁיב** אֶל מָרְדֳּכָי:

And Esther gave the order (or said:) **To respond (or Respond!)** to Mordecai. (Est 4:15)

---

29. See the discussion at the outset of this chapter.
30. The use of "אחיהם" rather than אחיכם clearly indicates that this is a case of indirect speech. Also see Esther 1:11 (twice), 17.
31. One would be hard-pressed to interpret "ויאמרו" as "ויצוו" in this particular passage. Therefore, "לעשות" should in all likelihood be considered an independent form, namely a variation of ויאמר: "יעש כן".
32. In this verse, there are doubts as to whether the passage reads ויצו חזקיהו להעלות or ויאמר חזקיהו: העלו את העולה or את העולה. Also see Esther 6:1; 9:14; Daniel 2:2 (twice); Nehemiah 9:23 (twice); 1 Chronicles 22:2; 2 Chronicles 14:3 (twice); 29:21, 30; 31:11; 33:16.

8.3 The Infinitive Construct's Link to the Participle

Besides its aforementioned connection to the modal axis, the infinitive maintains an inherently syntactic relationship with the participial[33] form throughout the Second Temple period.[34]

8.3.1 היה לקטל

The infinitive form's link to the participle is accentuated by the fact that during this period, the former serves as a component of periphrastic verb structures, such as היה + לקטל:

(458) וַיְהִי לִדְרֹשׁ אֱלֹהִים בִּימֵי זְכַרְיָהוּ הַמֵּבִין בִּרְאֹת הָאֱלֹהִים

He **applied himself to the worship** (**לקטל** + **ויהי**) of God during the time of Zechariah, instructor in the visions of God (2 Chr 26:5)

Cases with some sort of separation between the הי"ה verb root and the inflected infinitive form should perhaps also be classified under this rubric:[35]

---

33. In his book on the infinitive form in Semitic languages, Solá-Solé wrote:
     Une attention spéciale doit être accordée au rapport existant entre les noms d'action et infinitifs sémitiques et le participe. On peut remarquer qu'il y a une relation évidente entre ces deux catégories grammaticales. Les parlers qui ont une forme sans préformante à l'infinitif présentent des formes participiales avec préformante; en revanche, ceux qui ont une forme avec préformante à l'infinitif nous donnent des formes nues au participe. En outre, on peut constater le rapport fonctionnel qui parfois existe entre ces deux catégories grammaticales. Dans certains cas, il est possible d'employer le participe à la place du nom d'action ou de l'infinitif. (1961:193)
34. Another aspect of this link surfaces in four passages from the Dead Sea Scrolls containing personal pronouns that supervene inflected infinitives:
     1. ואיש ברבים ילך רכיל **לשלח הואה** מאתם ולוא ישוב עוד (1QS 7:16-17)
     2. כל אדם אשר יחרים אדם מאדם בחוקי הגוים **להמית הוא** (CD-A 9:1)
     3. אל יניא איש שבועה אשר ל?א? <י<דענה <. . .>ם **להקים היא** ואם להניא אם **לעבור ברית הוא** יניאה ואל יקימנה (CD-A 16:10-12)
     One possible reading of these cases is to interpret them as analytic verb structures in which an infinitive form serves as both the predicative nucleus of the verb and the subject of the independent personal pronoun. In three of the passages, the inflected counterpart of the verbal phrase should be passive forms: לשלוח הוא = יְשֻׁלַּח; להמית הוא = יוּמַת; and להקים היא = תּוּקַם. Perhaps these constructions were formulated for the purpose of emphasizing the logical subject of verbs with passive connotations. For a disquisition on these cases, see Cohen (2005:89-92)
35. There is nothing to prevent us from classifying these forms as periphrastic היה + לקטל structures, as there is a precedent from the corresponding participial construction: "וַיִּהְיוּ יָמִים שְׁלוֹשָׁה בֹּזְזִים אֶת הַשָּׁלָל כִּי רַב הוּא" (2 Chr 20:25). Also see 2 Chr 5:8.

(459) נَיֹּאמֶר כִּי אֱלֹהֵי מַלְכֵי אֲרָם הֵם מַעְזְרִים אֹתָם לָהֶם אֲזַבֵּחַ וְיַעְזְרוּנִי וְהֵם הָיוּ
לוֹ **לְהַכְשִׁילוֹ** וּלְכָל יִשְׂרָאֵל:

[F]or he thought, The gods of the kings of Aram help them; I shall sacrifice to
them and they will help me; **but they were his ruin** (היה + לקטל) and that of
all Israel. (2 Chr 28:23)

(460) וַיְהִי אַחֲרֵי כֵן הָיָה עִם לֵב יוֹאָשׁ **לְחַדֵּשׁ** אֶת בֵּית יְהוָה:

Afterward, Joash **decided to renovate** (היה + לקטל) the House of the LORD.
(2 Chr 24:4)

(461) גַּם בִּיהוּדָה **הָיְתָה** יַד הָאֱלֹהִים **לָתֵת** לָהֶם לֵב אֶחָד לַעֲשׂוֹת מִצְוַת הַמֶּלֶךְ
הַשָּׂרִים בִּדְבַר יְהוָה:

The hand of God **was** on Judah as well, **to make** (היה + לקטל) them of a
single mind to carry out the command of the king and officers concerning the
ordinance of the LORD. (2 Chr 30:12)

(462) **וַיְהִי** כְאֶחָד למחצרים (לַמְחַצְּרִים) וְלַמְשֹׁרְרִים **לְהַשְׁמִיעַ** קוֹל אֶחָד **לְהַלֵּל**
וּלְהֹדוֹת לַיהוָה וּכְהָרִים קוֹל בַּחֲצֹצְרוֹת וּבִמְצִלְתַּיִם וּבִכְלֵי הַשִּׁיר וּבְהַלֵּל לַיהוָה כִּי
טוֹב כִּי לְעוֹלָם חַסְדּוֹ

The trumpeters and the singers **sang** (ויהי + לקטל) in unison in order **to praise**
(ויהי + לקטל) and **extol** (ויהי + לקטל) the LORD; and when the song was raised,
with trumpets, cymbals, and other musical instruments, in praise to the LORD,
For he is good, for his steadfast love is eternal. (2 Chr 5:13)

This phenomenon also turns up in the Dead Sea Scrolls (Qimron 1986:§400.02):

> ודג>לי הבנים **יהיו להמס** לבב וגבורת אל מאמ>צת> ל>בב . . .<.

[and the] banners of the infantry **cause** their hearts **to melt** (יהיו + לקטל) (1QM
1:14)

והיו להפריח נצר למטעת עולם **להשריש** טרם יפריחו

so that a shoot **might grow up** (והיו + לקטל) into an eternal planting. **Taking
root** (והיו + לקטל) before they shoot up (1QH 16:6-7)

In these passages, there is a clear link between the infinitive and the participial
form. The periphrastic היה + infinitive construction replaces the classical היה +
participle. Akin to the היה קוטל structure, the deictic elements, which are tied to
both the person and the time/mood/aspect, are expressed by inflected verbs rather
than the participle. Adopting Goldenberg's view whereby the verb is a predicative
complex (1985:332-336) enables us to analyze the infinitive forms as a nominalization of the predicate's lexical content. This is exactly what transpires in the
corresponding participial structure—the content is nominalized by the participle,
while the person and the nexus are signified by the verb root היי/ה.

8.3.2 Using the Infinitive Form as a Nominalized Adjective

Yet another usage that maintains a link to the participle is manifest in 1 Chronicles 12:24-41. These verses list the members of the army's vanguard who came to David in Hebron to transfer the monarchy to him. The list abounds with participial forms that are joined with other nouns in construct chains. For example:

(463) בְּנֵי יְהוּדָה **נֹשְׂאֵי** צִנָּה וָרֹמַח . . . **חֲלוּצֵי** צָבָא:

Judahites, **equipped with (participle)** shield and spear . . . **armed (participle)** men. (25)

מִן בְּנֵי שִׁמְעוֹן **גִּבּוֹרֵי** חַיִל לַצָּבָא

Simeonites, **valiant (participle)** men, fighting troops (26)

וּמִן בְּנֵי אֶפְרַיִם . . . **גִּבּוֹרֵי** חַיִל

[O]f the Ephraimites . . . **valiant (participle)** men (31)

The phrase "מִזְּבֻלוּן **יוֹצְאֵי** צָבָא **עֹרְכֵי** מִלְחָמָה" in verse 34 contrasts with verse 37 where the participle is replaced with an infinitive: "וּמֵאָשֵׁר יוֹצְאֵי צָבָא **לַעֲרֹךְ** מִלְחָמָה". From a syntactical standpoint, "לערך" is a nominalized form that serves as a *nomen regens*. Further examples of this usage can be found in verses 33 and 34:

וּמִבְּנֵי יִשָּׂשכָר **יוֹדְעֵי** בִינָה לַעִתִּים **לָדַעַת** מַה יַּעֲשֶׂה יִשְׂרָאֵל. . . . מִזְּבֻלוּן יוֹצְאֵי צָבָא
עֹרְכֵי מִלְחָמָה בְּכָל כְּלֵי מִלְחָמָה חֲמִשִּׁים אָלֶף **וְלַעֲדֹר** בְּלֹא לֵב וָלֵב:

[O]f the Issacharites, men who **knew how (participle)** to interpret the signs of the times, **who understand (infinitive construct)** how Israel. . . . [O]f Zebulun, those ready for service, able to man a battle line with all kinds of weapons, 50000, **who give (infinitive construct)** support wholeheartedly.

Here too, the infinitives correspond to the sentence's earlier participial forms. Likewise, the infinitive in verse 34—"**ולעדר** בלא לב ולב"—may be compared to the participial form in verse 39:

כָּל אֵלֶּה אַנְשֵׁי מִלְחָמָה **עֹדְרֵי** מַעֲרָכָה בְּלֵבָב שָׁלֵם:

All these, fighting men **manning (participle)** the battle with whole heart.

The following verse also appears to contain an instance of this phenomenon:

(464) וְעַל יָדָם חֵיל צָבָא שְׁלֹשׁ מֵאוֹת אֶלֶף וְשִׁבְעַת אֲלָפִים וַחֲמֵשׁ מֵאוֹת **עוֹשֵׂי** מִלְחָמָה
בְּכֹחַ חָיִל **לַעְזֹר** לַמֶּלֶךְ עַל הָאוֹיֵב:

[U]nder them was the trained army of 307500, **who made war (participle)** with might and power **who aid (infinitive construct)** the king against the enemy. (2 Chr 26:13)

8.4 The Infinitive Construct's Link to Reference Time

Like *yiqtol*, it is quite evident that the distinction between sequential and non-sequential infinitive construct forms has been obfuscated, as the latter is also capable of signifying both the R≤E and [R,E] relationships:

(465) וּשְׁלַח לִי עֲצֵי אֲרָזִים בְּרוֹשִׁים וְאַלְגּוּמִּים מֵהַלְּבָנוֹן כִּי אֲנִי יָדַעְתִּי אֲשֶׁר עֲבָדֶיךָ
יוֹדְעִים לִכְרוֹת עֲצֵי לְבָנוֹן וְהִנֵּה עֲבָדַי עִם עֲבָדֶיךָ: וּלְהָכִין לִי עֵצִים לָרֹב כִּי הַבַּיִת
אֲשֶׁר אֲנִי בוֹנֶה גָּדוֹל וְהַפְלֵא:

Send (imperative) me cedars, cypress, and algum wood from the Lebanon, for I know that your servants are skilled at cutting the trees of Lebanon, and behold my servants will work with yours. **And provide ((S=)R≤E)** me with a great stock of timber; for the House that I intend to build will be singularly great. (2 Chr 2:7-8)

(466) כִּי בְשׁוּבְכֶם עַל יְהֹוָה אֲחֵיכֶם וּבְנֵיכֶם לְרַחֲמִים לִפְנֵי שׁוֹבֵיהֶם וְלָשׁוּב לָאָרֶץ
הַזֹּאת כִּי חַנּוּן וְרַחוּם יְהֹוָה אֱלֹהֵיכֶם וְלֹא יָסִיר פָּנִים מִכֶּם אִם תָּשׁוּבוּ אֵלָיו:

If you return to the LORD, your brothers and children will be regarded with compassion by their captors, **and will return (R≤E)** to this land; for the LORD your God is gracious and merciful; he will not turn his face from you if you return to him. (2 Chr 30: 9)

(467) וַיִּכְתֹּב בְּשֵׁם הַמֶּלֶךְ אֲחַשְׁוֵרֹשׁ וַיַּחְתֹּם בְּטַבַּעַת הַמֶּלֶךְ וַיִּשְׁלַח סְפָרִים בְּיַד
הָרָצִים בַּסּוּסִים רֹכְבֵי הָרֶכֶשׁ הָאֲחַשְׁתְּרָנִים בְּנֵי הָרַמָּכִים: אֲשֶׁר נָתַן הַמֶּלֶךְ לַיְּהוּדִים
אֲשֶׁר בְּכָל עִיר וָעִיר לְהִקָּהֵל וְלַעֲמֹד עַל נַפְשָׁם לְהַשְׁמִיד וְלַהֲרֹג וּלְאַבֵּד אֶת כָּל חֵיל
עַם וּמְדִינָה הַצָּרִים אֹתָם טַף וְנָשִׁים וּשְׁלָלָם לָבוֹז: בְּיוֹם אֶחָד בְּכָל מְדִינוֹת הַמֶּלֶךְ
אֲחַשְׁוֵרֹשׁ בִּשְׁלוֹשָׁה עָשָׂר לְחֹדֶשׁ שְׁנֵים עָשָׂר הוּא חֹדֶשׁ אֲדָר: פַּתְשֶׁגֶן הַכְּתָב לְהִנָּתֵן
דָּת בְּכָל מְדִינָה וּמְדִינָה גָּלוּי לְכָל הָעַמִּים וְלִהְיוֹת הַיְּהוּדִיִּים (הַיְּהוּדִים) עֲתוּדִים
(עֲתִידִים) לַיּוֹם הַזֶּה לְהִנָּקֵם מֵאֹיְבֵיהֶם:

He had them written in the name of King Ahasuerus and sealed with the king's signet. Letters were dispatched by mounted couriers, riding steeds used in the king's service, bred of the royal stud, [letters] that the king has given to the Jews of every city [saying: They] shall assemble and **fight [R,E]** for their lives; if any people or province attacks them, **[they] shall destroy, massacre [R,E]**, **and exterminate [R,E]** its armed force together with women and children, and **plunder [R,E]** their possessions. On a single day in all the provinces of King Ahasuerus, namely on the thirteenth day of the twelfth month, that is the month of Adar. The copy of the document shall be given as a law in every single province: it is to be publicly displayed to all the peoples, so that the Jews **shall be [R,E]** ready for that day to avenge themselves on their enemies. (Est 8:10-13)

In 2 Chronicles 30, the infinitive "ולהכין" serves as a volitive form that corresponds to the imperative form; hence the relationship is (S=)R≤E:

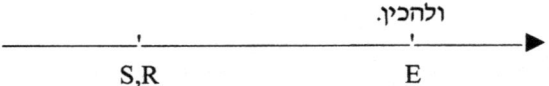

In the second example, the infinitive form also signifies an event in the future, and the form's relationship to its reference time—the preceding clause "כי בשובכם על יהוה"—is R≤E:

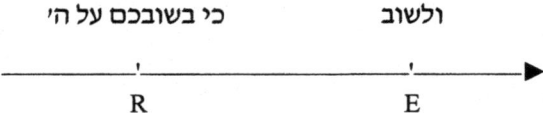

Within the continuum of infinitives in Esther 8, *waw*-less forms open the string of instructions and stand in succession with *waw*-prefixed forms, which bear their own reference time [R,E].

b. The Volitive Forms

9. The Functions of the Volitive Forms in Second Temple Period Hebrew

9.1 Introduction

The morphological uniqueness of Biblical Hebrew's volitive forms—the cohortative, the imperative, and the jussive—is predicated on the fact that, notwithstanding their disparate morphological origins,[1] the three forms essentially comprise one system from a functional standpoint. In consequence, for the purposes of this discussion, the cohortative, the imperative, and the jussive will be viewed as elements that form a single paradigm. Nevertheless, when the need arises, we will spell out the pragmatic differences between the forms, which stem from the distinct person (first, second, or third) that each takes on.

In general, there is no evidence that the volitive group underwent any dramatic changes between the First and Second Temple periods. However, a significant exception to this rule is chapter 11 of the book of Daniel, where the jussive forms are arrayed in a completely different manner than the *yiqtol* forms.[2]

Save for Daniel 11, these forms are distinct from *yiqtol* in all that concerns their link to the modal axis, by virtue of their designation as signifiers of deontic modality. Therefore, the chronological relationships that the jussive forms are capable of expressing are limited compared to *yiqtol*.

9.2 The Volitive Forms' Link to Reference Time

Unlike *yiqtol* which, on account of its relative attributes, can express the relationship of posteriority R<E in past, present, or future contexts, the volitive forms are restricted to conveying the relationship of posteriority to speech time: S=R<E. Just as the volitive meaning is but one component of a wider modal expanse, which is also denoted by *yiqtol* forms, articulating a relationship of posteriority to speech time is but one of many chronological relationships that the *yiqtol* form is capable of marking.

In our corpus, volitive forms also express the sequential relationship [R,E] on account of their deployment in modal chains. As in the First Temple period, both the [R,E] and S<R=E relations appear within the framework of complementary distributions. The latter turns up in situations where the volitives lack a prefix

---

1. There is a consensus among scholars over this distinction. Waltke and O'Connor offer a succinct discussion on the morphological incarnations of the different forms, along with relevant bibliographical references (1990:564-568). Also see Rainey (1986), inter alios.

2. See the discussion in §9.3.2.2 below.

waw, while the relationship [R,E] is conveyed by forms that are preceded by *waw*s in a clause's opening slot.[3]

9.2.1 Subsequence to Speech Time—S=R<E

A relationship of subsequence to speech time (S=R<E) stems directly from the volitive meaning of the the cohortative, imperative, and jussive forms. In other words, there is a connection between the semantic baggage borne by the deontic mood and the fact that nearly all of these forms appear in main clauses within the framework of direct speech:[4]

(468) וְגַם אֲנִי אַחַי וּנְעָרַי נֹשִׁים בָּהֶם כֶּסֶף וְדָגָן **נַעַזְבָה** נָּא אֶת הַמַּשָּׁא הַזֶּה :

I, my brothers, and my servants also have claims of money and grain against them; **let us abandon (S=R<E)** those claims! (Neh 5:10)

(469) וַיֹּאמֶר הַמֶּלֶךְ **מַהֲרוּ** אֶת הָמָן לַעֲשׂוֹת אֶת דְּבַר אֶסְתֵּר

The king commanded, Tell Haman **to hurry (S=R<E)** and do Esther's bidding. (Est 5:5)

(470) אֲדֹנָי כְּכָל צִדְקֹתֶךָ **יָשָׁב** נָא אַפְּךָ וַחֲמָתְךָ מֵעִירְךָ יְרוּשָׁלַם הַר קָדְשֶׁךָ

O Lord, as befits your abundant benevolence, **let** your wrathful fury **turn back (S=R<E)** from your city Jerusalem, your holy mountain. (Dn 9:16)

The chronological relationship in these cases is thus:

ויאמר	מהרו
S,R	E

Examples 468 to 470 represent the vast majority of the volitive forms' usages in our corpus. In those rare instances where the forms are in clauses other than a main one, the chronological relationship appears to be more complex, but still conforms to the rule of subsequence vis-à-vis speech time:

(471) וַיֵּצֵא דָוִד לִפְנֵיהֶם וַיַּעַן וַיֹּאמֶר לָהֶם אִם לְשָׁלוֹם בָּאתֶם אֵלַי לְעָזְרֵנִי יִהְיֶה לִּי
עֲלֵיכֶם לֵבָב לְיָחַד וְאִם לְרַמּוֹתַנִי לְצָרַי בְּלֹא חָמָס בְּכַפַּי **יֵרֶא** אֱלֹהֵי אֲבוֹתֵינוּ וְיוֹכַח :

[A]nd David went out to meet them, saying to them, If you come on a peaceful

---

3. For more on *waw*'s role as a particle that engenders reference time, see Hatav (2004:512-523).
4. All the volitive forms in our corpus appear within the framework of direct speech or prayer. In addition, 191 out of the 202 occurrences (95%) are situated in a main clause.

errand, to support me, then I will make common cause with you, but if to
betray me to my foes, for no injustice on my part, then **let** the God of our
fathers **take notice (S=R<E)** and give judgment. (1 Chr 12:18)

9.2.2 Expressing Succession [R,E]

As noted above, when volitive forms preceded by the conjunction *waw* appear in a
string of actions, they express the relationship of succession [R,E]:[5]

(472) וַיֹּאמֶר לַלְוִיִּם המבונים (הַמְּבִינִים) לְכָל יִשְׂרָאֵל הַקְּדוֹשִׁים לַיהוָה תְּנוּ אֶת
אֲרוֹן הַקֹּדֶשׁ בַּבַּיִת אֲשֶׁר בָּנָה שְׁלֹמֹה בֶן דָּוִיד מֶלֶךְ יִשְׂרָאֵל אֵין לָכֶם מַשָּׂא בַּכָּתֵף
עַתָּה עִבְדוּ אֶת יְהוָה אֱלֹהֵיכֶם וְאֵת עַמּוֹ יִשְׂרָאֵל: והכונו **(וְהָכִינוּ)** לְבֵית אֲבוֹתֵיכֶם
כְּמַחְלְקוֹתֵיכֶם בִּכְתָב דָּוִיד מֶלֶךְ יִשְׂרָאֵל וּבְמִכְתַּב שְׁלֹמֹה בְנוֹ: **וְעִמְדוּ** בַקֹּדֶשׁ לִפְלֻגּוֹת
בֵּית הָאָבוֹת לַאֲחֵיכֶם בְּנֵי הָעָם וַחֲלֻקַּת בֵּית אָב לַלְוִיִּם: **וְשַׁחֲטוּ** הַפָּסַח **וְהִתְקַדְּשׁוּ**
וְהָכִינוּ לַאֲחֵיכֶם לַעֲשׂוֹת כִּדְבַר יְהוָה בְּיַד מֹשֶׁה:

He said to the Levites, consecrated to the LORD, who taught all Israel, Put the
Holy Ark in the House that Solomon son of David, king of Israel, built; as you
no longer carry it on your shoulders, see now to the service of the LORD your
God and his people Israel, **and dispose [R,E]** yourselves by clans according
to your divisions, as prescribed in the writing of King David of Israel and in
the document of his son Solomon, **and attend [R,E]** in the Sanctuary, by clan
divisions, on your kinsmen, the people—by clan divisions of the Levites. **And
slaughter [R,E]** the passover sacrifice **and sanctify [R,E] yourselves and
prepare [R,E]** it for your kinsmen, according to the word of God given by
Moses. (2 Chr 35:3-6)

(473) וְאַל תִּהְיוּ כַּאֲבוֹתֵיכֶם וְכַאֲחֵיכֶם אֲשֶׁר מָעֲלוּ בַּיהוָה אֱלֹהֵי אֲבוֹתֵיהֶם וַיִּתְּנֵם
לְשַׁמָּה כַּאֲשֶׁר אַתֶּם רֹאִים: עַתָּה אַל תַּקְשׁוּ עָרְפְּכֶם כַּאֲבוֹתֵיכֶם תְּנוּ יָד לַיהוָה **וּבֹאוּ**
לְמִקְדָּשׁוֹ אֲשֶׁר הִקְדִּישׁ לְעוֹלָם **וְעִבְדוּ** אֶת יְהוָה אֱלֹהֵיכֶם **וְיָשֹׁב** מִכֶּם חֲרוֹן אַפּוֹ:

Do not be like your fathers and brothers who trespassed against the LORD God
of their fathers and he turned them into a horror, as you see. Now do not be
stiffnecked like your fathers; submit yourselves to the LORD **and come [R,E]**

---

5. A succession is expressed in 70 of the volitive forms' 202 occurrences (35%) in our
corpus. One of the prominent differences between the volitives and *yiqtol* in First
Temple period Biblical Hebrew is that only the former signify successions. However,
this distinction begins to fray in the Second Temple period, as *yiqtol* assumes this
role as well (see §6.2.4 above). Nevertheless, from a quantitative standpoint, the use
of volitive forms for marking a succession within the framework of deontic modality
is much more commonplace. In Hatav's estimation, the particle *waw* is used to construct reference time in Biblical Hebrew, and the forms that it prefixes mark succession
(2004:512-523). There is reason to believe that the volitive forms signify a more complex relationship, namely the structures engender a succession while simultaneously
maintaining a link with the S-time point (on account of their deontic meaning).

to his sanctuary, which he consecrated forever, **and serve [R,E]** the LORD your God so that his anger **may turn back [R,E]** from you. (2 Chr 30:7-8)

(474) מִי בָכֶם מִכָּל עַמּוֹ יְהִי אֱלֹהָיו עִמּוֹ **וְיַעַל** לִירוּשָׁלַם אֲשֶׁר בִּיהוּדָה **וְיִבֶן** אֶת בֵּית יְהֹוָה אֱלֹהֵי יִשְׂרָאֵל הוּא הָאֱלֹהִים אֲשֶׁר בִּירוּשָׁלָם :

Anyone of you of all his people, may his God be with him, **and let him go up [R,E]** to Jerusalem that is in Judah **and build [R,E]** the House of the LORD God of Israel, the God that is in Jerusalem; (Ezr 1:3)

As we can see, one of the most prevalent traits of successions is that the concatenation of the forms advances the reference time along the time axis:

ובאו	ועבדו	וישב
—'—————	—'—————	—'——▶
[R,E₁]	[R,E₂]	[R,E₃]

Although this chronological function is rather common, it is not the sole objective of consecutive forms. There are also quite a few instances of volitive sequential forms that do not advance the reference time along the time axis:

(475) אָז תַּצְלִיחַ אִם תִּשְׁמוֹר לַעֲשׂוֹת אֶת הַחֻקִּים וְאֶת הַמִּשְׁפָּטִים אֲשֶׁר צִוָּה יְהֹוָה אֶת מֹשֶׁה עַל יִשְׂרָאֵל חֲזַק **וֶאֱמָץ** אַל תִּירָא **וְאַל תֵּחָת** :

Then you shall succeed, if you observantly carry out the laws and the rules that the LORD charged Moses to lay upon Israel. Be strong **and be courageous [R,E]**; do not be afraid **and do not be dismayed [R,E]**. (1 Chr 22:13)

(476) רְאֵה עַתָּה כִּי יְהֹוָה בָּחַר בְּךָ לִבְנוֹת בַּיִת לַמִּקְדָּשׁ חֲזַק **וַעֲשֵׂה** :

See then, the LORD chose you to build a house as the sanctuary; be strong **and do it [R,E]**. (1 Chr 28:10)

(477) וְעַתָּה יְהִי פַחַד יְהֹוָה עֲלֵיכֶם שִׁמְרוּ **וַעֲשׂוּ** כִּי אֵין עִם יְהֹוָה אֱלֹהֵינוּ עַוְלָה וּמַשּׂא פָנִים וּמִקַּח שֹׁחַד:[6]

Now let the dread of the LORD be upon you; beware **and act [R,E]** with care, for there is no injustice or favoritism or bribe-taking with the LORD our God. (2 Chr 19:7)

The common denominator between examples 475 through 477 is that they host pairs of actions which can essentially be viewed as a single unit (hendiadys).[7]

---

6. Also see Ezra 8:29; 10:4; 1 Chronicles 22:16, 19; 28:8, 20; 2 Chronicles 19:7, 11; 32:7.

7. According to Hatav, the hendiadys is one of the categories of sequential forms that do not mark chronological succession (1997:62-70); also see Revell (1989:§18). See §4.2.3.1.1.4 above.

9.3 The Volitive Forms' Link to the Modal Axis

With respect to the link to the modal axis, the primary difference between the volitive forms (the cohortative, the imperative, and the jussive) and the forms *yiqtol*, *weqatal*, and the infinitive construct is that the volitive group's purview is more circumscribed and defined than the latter. In other words, within the framework of the Hebrew verbal system, volitive forms serve exclusively as designated signifiers of deontic modality, whereas this function is but one of several that are filled by the second group within a broader expanse, which includes epistemic modality. In this respect, the usage is highly reminiscent of classical Hebrew texts.[8] Similar to the *yiqtol* form's link to the modal axis, there is often no formal linguistic distinction between the various gradients of deontic modality, so that in most cases the exact modal category can only be discerned by means of the extra-textual context. As we will soon see, this context is often driven by the nature of the relations between the speaker and the addressee(s).

9.3.1 Deontic Modality

9.3.1.1 The Imperative Mood

In the following examples, imperative forms are used to convey directives:[9]

(478) וַיֹּאמֶר לַלְוִיִּם המבונים (הַמְּבִינִים) לְכָל יִשְׂרָאֵל הַקְּדוֹשִׁים לַיהוה **תְּנוּ** אֶת אֲרוֹן הַקֹּדֶשׁ בַּבַּיִת אֲשֶׁר בָּנָה שְׁלֹמֹה בֶן דָּוִיד מֶלֶךְ יִשְׂרָאֵל אֵין לָכֶם מַשָּׂא בַּכָּתֵף עַתָּה **עִבְדוּ** אֶת יְהוָה אֱלֹהֵיכֶם וְאֵת עַמּוֹ יִשְׂרָאֵל : והכונו (**וְהָכִינוּ**) לְבֵית אֲבוֹתֵיכֶם כְּמַחְלְקוֹתֵיכֶם בִּכְתָב דָּוִיד מֶלֶךְ יִשְׂרָאֵל וּבְמִכְתַּב שְׁלֹמֹה בְנוֹ : **וְעִמְדוּ** בַקֹּדֶשׁ לִפְלֻגּוֹת בֵּית הָאָבוֹת לַאֲחֵיכֶם בְּנֵי הָעָם וַחֲלֻקַּת בֵּית אָב לַלְוִיִּם : **וְשַׁחֲטוּ** הַפָּסַח **וְהִתְקַדְּשׁוּ וְהָכִינוּ** לַאֲחֵיכֶם לַעֲשׂוֹת כִּדְבַר יְהוָה בְּיַד מֹשֶׁה :

He said to the Levites, consecrated to the Lord, who taught all Israel, **Put (imperative)** the Holy Ark in the House that Solomon son of David, king of Israel, built; as you no longer carry it on your shoulders, now **serve (imperative)** the Lord your God and his people Israel, **and dispose (imperative)** yourselves

---

8. A notable exception to this similitude can be found in Daniel 11, the aberrance of which has already been noted. See the detailed discussion in clause §9.3.2.2 below.

9. Although the three volitives constitute a single paradigm, the articulation of orders is the exclusive domain of imperative forms. However, this division of labor does not pose any difficulties for the following reasons: With respect to the first person, it is unnatural for people to give themselves an order. On account of the distance between the speaker and the third person, the signification of a directive is less immediate and more general; hence, instructions of this sort are formulated as general commandments (i.e., the language of the law) or a request/wish, rather than a full-fledged order. The signification of an order is the most pervasive function of the imperative, as this usage constitutes 109 out of the 129 occurrences (84.5%) of this form in our corpus. See Esther 4:16; 5:5; 6:10; 7:9; 8:8; Ezra 8:29; 10:11; Nehemiah 4:8; 5:11, inter alia.

by clans according to your divisions, as prescribed in the writing of King
David of Israel and in the document of his son Solomon, **and attend
(imperative)** in the Sanctuary, by clan divisions, on your kinsmen, the people—
by clan divisions of the Levites. Having sanctified yourselves, **slaughter
(imperative)** the passover sacrifice, **sanctify yourselves (imperative) and
prepare (imperative)** it for your kinsmen, according to the word of God given
by Moses. (2 Chr 35:3-6)

(479) וַיֹּאמֶר לָהֶם אַתֶּם רָאשֵׁי הָאָבוֹת לַלְוִיִּם **הִתְקַדְּשׁוּ** אַתֶּם וַאֲחֵיכֶם וְהַעֲלִיתֶם
אֵת אֲרוֹן יְהוָה אֱלֹהֵי יִשְׂרָאֵל אֶל הֲכִינוֹתִי לוֹ:

He said to them, you are the heads of the clans of the Levites; **sanctify
yourselves (imperative)**, you and your kinsmen, and bring up the Ark of the
LORD God of Israel to the place I have prepared for it. (1 Chr 15:12)

These examples reflect the fact that the only syntactical environment in which
imperatives denote an order is main clauses within the framework of direct speech,
where practically all the occurrences of this meaning involve an authority figure
speaking to subordinates. Conversely, when subordinates address their superiors,
the instruction harbors a touch of solicitation or encouragement. For example:

(480) וַיַּעַן שְׁכַנְיָה בֶן יְחִיאֵל מִבְּנֵי עוֹלָם (עֵילָם) וַיֹּאמֶר לְעֶזְרָא . . . . **קוּם** כִּי עָלֶיךָ
הַדָּבָר וַאֲנַחְנוּ עִמָּךְ **חֲזַק וַעֲשֵׂה**:

Then Shecaniah son of Jehiel of the family of Elam spoke up and said to
Ezra . . . , **Take action (encouragment)**, for the responsibility is yours and we
are with you. **Be strong and act (encouragment)** with resolve! (Ezr 10:2-4)

As noted above,[10] chains of instructions are designated a volitive succession by
the sentence's first imperative form. Thereafter, the author is likely to continue
marking the succession with other imperative forms (as in example 478) or *weqatal* (example 479). Revell attempts to draw a semantic and pragmatic distinction
between a series that is comprised entirely of volitive forms, such as imperatives
with or without *waws*, and chains of volitives followed by *weqatal* (1989:22-25).
In his estimation, a pair of consecutive imperative forms tends to express a single
action (the action itself is conveyed by the second form, while the first imperative
serves as a quasi-auxiliary verb), whereas a *weqatal* form that is preceded by an
imperative evinces a strong sense of succession or resultativity. That said, a review
of these constructions in our corpus reveals weaknesses in Revell's argument. Although the passage from Ezra adheres to his rule, the first example (2 Chronicles
35) contradicts it, as the imperatives therein fill the same role as *weqatal* in example 479. In other words, the roles of the volitive and *weqatal* forms have been
neutralized.

---

10. See the discussion on marking succession (§9.2.2 below).

9.3.1.2 The Prohibitive Mood[11]

A prohibition can be considered a negative directive. In the Biblical Hebrew of both the First and Second Temple periods, there is a suppletion between the imperative, which connotes a positive instruction, and the prohibition. The ensuing passage offers a salient example of how these forms replace one another within the framework of a complementary distribution:

(481) וַיֹּאמֶר נְחֶמְיָה הוּא הַתִּרְשָׁתָא וְעֶזְרָא הַכֹּהֵן הַסֹּפֵר וְהַלְוִיִּם הַמְּבִינִים אֶת הָעָם לְכָל הָעָם הַיּוֹם קָדֹשׁ הוּא לַיהוָה אֱלֹהֵיכֶם **אַל תִּתְאַבְּלוּ וְאַל תִּבְכּוּ** כִּי בוֹכִים כָּל הָעָם כְּשָׁמְעָם אֶת דִּבְרֵי הַתּוֹרָה : וַיֹּאמֶר לָהֶם **לְכוּ אִכְלוּ** מַשְׁמַנִּים **וּשְׁתוּ** מַמְתַקִּים **וְשִׁלְחוּ** מָנוֹת לְאֵין נָכוֹן לוֹ כִּי קָדוֹשׁ הַיּוֹם לַאֲדֹנֵינוּ **וְאַל תֵּעָצֵבוּ** כִּי חֶדְוַת יְהוָה הִיא מָעֻזְּכֶם : וְהַלְוִיִּם מַחְשִׁים לְכָל הָעָם לֵאמֹר **הַסּוּ** כִּי הַיּוֹם קָדֹשׁ **וְאַל תֵּעָצֵבוּ** :

Nehemiah the Tirshatha, Ezra the priest and scribe, and the Levites who were explaining to the people said to all the people, This day is holy to the LORD your God: **you must not mourn (jussive) nor weep (jussive)**, for all the people were weeping as they listened to the words of the Teaching. He further said to them, **Go (impv.)**, **eat (impv.)** choice foods **and drink (impv.)** sweet drinks **and send (impv.)** portions to whoever has nothing prepared, for the day is holy to our Lord. **Do not be sad (jussive)**, for your rejoicing in the LORD is the source of your strength. The Levites were quieting the people, saying, **Silence (impv.)**, for the day is holy; **do not be sad (jussive)**. (Neh 8:9-11)

Like classical Hebrew, prohibitions that are comprised of jussives are accompanied by the negative particle אַל, whereas negations involving *yiqtol* are headed by לֹא:

(482) **אַל תִּלָּחֲמוּ** עִם יְהוָה אֱלֹהֵי אֲבֹתֵיכֶם כִּי **לֹא תַצְלִיחוּ** :

[D]o not fight (jussive) the LORD God of your fathers, because **you will not succeed (yiqtol)**. (2 Chr 13:12)

The distinction between the two forms in this verse involves both the modal and reference time axes. With respect to the former, "אל תלחמו" expresses deontic modality (a prohibition), while "לא תצליחו" conveys epistemic modality (an irrealis proposition). Insofar as the reference-time axis is concerned, the jussive expresses subsequence to the speech time and *yiqtol* conveys subsequence to a future action.

Similar to the imperative form, the jussive expresses a prohibition when the speaker outranks his or her addressee; and if the speaker occupies an inferior position, then the structure אל + jussive connotes a request.[12]

---

11. 24 out of the jussive form's 61 occurrences (39%) denote the prohibitive mood; for example, Esther 6:10; Daniel 10:12, 19; 1 Chronicles 22:13; 28:20; 2 Chronicles 20:15, 17; 25:7; 29:11.
12. See §9.3.1.4 below.

9.3.1.3   The Incentive Mood[13]

The volitive forms are also used to express encouragement. Most of this usage's occurrences are conjugated in the first person. In the examples that follow, the speaker urges himself and/or his audience to carry out a desired action:

(483) וַיֹּאמֶר דָּוִיד שְׁלֹמֹה בְנִי נַעַר וָרָךְ וְהַבַּיִת לִבְנוֹת לַיהוָה לְהַגְדִּיל לְמַעְלָה לְשֵׁם וּלְתִפְאֶרֶת לְכָל הָאֲרָצוֹת **אָכִינָה נָּא** לוֹ וַיָּכֶן דָּוִיד לָרֹב לִפְנֵי מוֹתוֹ :

For David thought, My son Solomon is an untried youth, and the House to be built for the LORD is to be made exceedingly great to win fame and glory throughout all the lands; **let me** then **lay aside (incentive)** material for him. So David laid aside much material before he died. (1 Chr 22:5)

(484) ויאמר (וָאֹמַר) לֹא טוֹב הַדָּבָר אֲשֶׁר אַתֶּם עֹשִׂים הֲלוֹא בְּיִרְאַת אֱלֹהֵינוּ תֵּלֵכוּ מֵחֶרְפַּת הַגּוֹיִם אוֹיְבֵינוּ : וְגַם אֲנִי אַחַי וּנְעָרַי נֹשִׁים בָּהֶם כֶּסֶף וְדָגָן **נַעַזְבָה נָּא**[14] אֶת הַמַּשָּׁא הַזֶּה :

So I continued, What you are doing is not right. You ought to act in a God-fearing way so as not to give our enemies, the nations, room to reproach us. I, my brothers, and my servants also have claims of money and grain against them; **let us** now **abandon (incentive)** those claims! (Neh 5:9-10)

The next example also connotes encouragement. The imperative form of the verb root הל"ך serves as an exhortation, which is reminiscent of the role that is filled by the imperative הבה:[15]

(485) וָאֹמַר אֲלֵהֶם אַתֶּם רֹאִים הָרָעָה אֲשֶׁר אֲנַחְנוּ בָהּ אֲשֶׁר יְרוּשָׁלַ͏ִם חֲרֵבָה וּשְׁעָרֶיהָ נִצְּתוּ בָאֵשׁ **לְכוּ** וְנִבְנֶה אֶת חוֹמַת יְרוּשָׁלַ͏ִם וְלֹא נִהְיֶה עוֹד חֶרְפָּה :

Then I said to them, You see the bad state we are in—Jerusalem lying in ruins and its gates destroyed by fire. **Come (incentive)**, let us rebuild the wall of Jerusalem and suffer no more disgrace. (Neh 2:17)

Despite the fact that the imperative form marks the second person, here too the solicitation addresses the speakers inclusive group as articulated through the verbs "נבנה" and "נהיה". The chain is marked as a volitive structure by means of its lead imperative form.

---

13. This meaning is uncommon in the Second Temple period.
14. As in classical Hebrew, the particle נא collaborates with the cohortative forms. See Joüon and Muraoka (1996:§114b).
15. See Joüon and Muraoka (1996:§105e; §177e-f); also see Orlinsky (1941-1942).

9.3.1.4 The Hortative Mood

Another function of volitive forms is to express requests. The difference between
a request and a directive is usually connected to the speaker's status vis-à-vis his
or her audience. Accordingly, the hortative mood is most prevalent in cases where
the speaker's status is lower than that of the addressee:

(486) וְעַתָּה אֲדֹנָי אֱלֹהֵינוּ אֲשֶׁר הוֹצֵאתָ אֶת עַמְּךָ מֵאֶרֶץ מִצְרַיִם בְּיָד חֲזָקָה וַתַּעַשׂ
לְךָ שֵׁם כַּיּוֹם הַזֶּה חָטָאנוּ רָשָׁעְנוּ : אֲדֹנָי כְּכָל צִדְקֹתֶךָ **יָשָׁב נָא** אַפְּךָ וַחֲמָתְךָ מֵעִירְךָ
יְרוּשָׁלַם הַר קָדְשֶׁךָ כִּי בַחֲטָאֵינוּ וּבַעֲוֹנוֹת אֲבֹתֵינוּ יְרוּשָׁלַם וְעַמְּךָ לְחֶרְפָּה לְכָל
סְבִיבֹתֵינוּ : וְעַתָּה **שְׁמַע** אֱלֹהֵינוּ אֶל תְּפִלַּת עַבְדְּךָ וְאֶל תַּחֲנוּנָיו **וְהָאֵר** פָּנֶיךָ עַל מִקְדָּשְׁךָ
הַשָּׁמֵם לְמַעַן אֲדֹנָי : **הַטֵּה** אֱלֹהַי אָזְנְךָ **וּשְׁמָע** פקחה (**פְּקַח**) עֵינֶיךָ **וּרְאֵה** שֹׁמְמֹתֵינוּ
וְהָעִיר אֲשֶׁר נִקְרָא שִׁמְךָ עָלֶיהָ כִּי לֹא עַל צִדְקֹתֵינוּ אֲנַחְנוּ מַפִּילִים תַּחֲנוּנֵינוּ לְפָנֶיךָ
כִּי עַל רַחֲמֶיךָ הָרַבִּים : אֲדֹנָי **שְׁמָעָה** אֲדֹנָי **סְלָחָה** אֲדֹנָי **הַקְשִׁיבָה וַעֲשֵׂה אַל תְּאַחַר**
לְמַעַנְךָ אֱלֹהַי כִּי שִׁמְךָ נִקְרָא עַל עִירְךָ וְעַל עַמֶּךָ :

Now, O Lord our God—you who brought your people out of the land of Egypt
with a mighty hand, winning fame for yourself to this very day—we have
sinned, we have acted wickedly. O Lord, as befits your abundant benevolence,
let your wrathful fury **turn back (hortative)** from your city Jerusalem, your
holy mountain; for because of our sins and the iniquities of our fathers,
Jerusalem and your people have become a mockery among all who are around
us. O our God, **hear (hortative)** now the prayer of your servant and his plea,
and show (hortative) your favor to your desolate sanctuary, for the Lord's
sake. **Incline (hortative)** your ear, O my God, and **hear (hortative)**; **open
(hortative)** your eyes **and see (hortative)** our desolation and the city to which
your name is attached. Not because of any merit of ours do we lay our plea
before you but because of your abundant mercies. O Lord, **hear! (hortative)**
O Lord, **forgive! (hortative)** O Lord, **listen (hortative)**, **act (hortative)** and
do not be late (hortative) for your own sake, O my God; for your name is
attached to your city and your people! (Dn 9:15-19)

(487) וַיִּקְרָא אָסָא אֶל יְהוָה אֱלֹהָיו וַיֹּאמַר יְהוָה אֵין עִמְּךָ לַעְזֹר בֵּין רַב לְאֵין כֹּחַ
עָזְרֵנוּ יְהוָה אֱלֹהֵינוּ כִּי עָלֶיךָ נִשְׁעַנּוּ וּבְשִׁמְךָ בָאנוּ עַל הֶהָמוֹן הַזֶּה יְהוָה אֱלֹהֵינוּ אַתָּה
אַל יַעְצֹר עִמְּךָ אֱנוֹשׁ :

Asa called to the LORD his God, and said, O LORD, it is all the same to you
to help the numerous and the powerless. **Help (hortative)** us, O LORD our
God, for we rely on you, and in your name we have come against this great
multitude. You are the LORD our God. **Let** no mortal **hinder (hortative)** you.
(2 Chr 14:10)

(488) וְאִישׁ הָאֱלֹהִים בָּא אֵלָיו לֵאמֹר הַמֶּלֶךְ **אַל יָבֹא** עִמְּךָ צְבָא יִשְׂרָאֵל כִּי אֵין יְהוָה
עִם יִשְׂרָאֵל כֹּל בְּנֵי אֶפְרָיִם : כִּי אִם בֹּא אַתָּה **עֲשֵׂה חֲזַק** לַמִּלְחָמָה יַכְשִׁילְךָ הָאֱלֹהִים
לִפְנֵי אוֹיֵב כִּי יֶשׁ כֹּחַ בֵּאלֹהִים לַעְזוֹר וּלְהַכְשִׁיל :

Then a man of God came to him and said, O king! **Do not let (hortative)** the army of Israel go with you, for the LORD is not with Israel—all these Ephraimites. But **go (hortative)** by yourself and **do (hortative)** it; **take courage (hortative)** for battle, else God will make you fall before the enemy. For in God there is power to help one or make one fall! (2 Chr 25:7-9)

These passages demonstrate that a request can be formulated in both a positive (imperative or jussive) and negative (jussive) manner.

This approach is much less likely to be used by a speaker addressing subordinates. If a superior indeed adopts a hortative tone, it is probably due to a special need or circumstance. For example:

(489) וַיַּקְהֵל דָּוִיד אֶת כָּל שָׂרֵי יִשְׂרָאֵל שָׂרֵי הַשְּׁבָטִים וְשָׂרֵי הַמַּחְלְקוֹת הַמְשָׁרְתִים אֶת הַמֶּלֶךְ וְשָׂרֵי הָאֲלָפִים וְשָׂרֵי הַמֵּאוֹת וְשָׂרֵי כָל רְכוּשׁ וּמִקְנֶה לַמֶּלֶךְ וּלְבָנָיו עִם הַסָּרִיסִים וְהַגִּבּוֹרִים וּלְכָל גִּבּוֹר חָיִל אֶל יְרוּשָׁלָ͏ם: וַיָּקָם דָּוִיד הַמֶּלֶךְ עַל רַגְלָיו וַיֹּאמֶר **שְׁמָעוּנִי** אַחַי וְעַמִּי אֲנִי עִם לְבָבִי לִבְנוֹת בֵּית מְנוּחָה לַאֲרוֹן בְּרִית יְהוָה וְלַהֲדֹם רַגְלֵי אֱלֹהֵינוּ וַהֲכִינוֹתִי לִבְנוֹת:

David assembled all the officers of Israel—the tribal officers, the divisional officers who served the king, the captains of thousands and the captains of hundreds, and the stewards of all the property and cattle of the king and his sons, with the eunuchs and the warriors, all the men of substance—to Jerusalem.[2] King David rose to his feet and said, **Hear me (hortative)**, my brothers, my people! I wanted to build a resting place for the Ark of the Covenant of the LORD, for the footstool of our God, and I laid aside material for building. (1 Chr 28:1-2)

In this passage, the imperative "שמעוני" is part of a rhetorical device that David uses to capture his audience's attention.

When the relation between a speaker and addressee is vague, it may be difficult to establish whether the former is soliciting a request or issuing an order:

(490) וְשָׁם הָיָה נָבִיא לַיהוָה עֹדֵד שְׁמוֹ וַיֵּצֵא לִפְנֵי הַצָּבָא הַבָּא לְשֹׁמְרוֹן וַיֹּאמֶר לָהֶם הִנֵּה בַּחֲמַת יְהוָה אֱלֹהֵי אֲבוֹתֵיכֶם עַל יְהוּדָה נְתָנָם בְּיֶדְכֶם וַתַּהַרְגוּ בָם בְּזַעַף עַד לַשָּׁמַיִם הִגִּיעַ: וְעַתָּה בְּנֵי יְהוּדָה וִירוּשָׁלַ͏ם אַתֶּם אֹמְרִים לִכְבֹּשׁ לַעֲבָדִים וְלִשְׁפָחוֹת לָכֶם הֲלֹא רַק אַתֶּם עִמָּכֶם אֲשָׁמוֹת לַיהוָה אֱלֹהֵיכֶם: וְעַתָּה **שְׁמָעוּנִי וְהָשִׁיבוּ** הַשִּׁבְיָה אֲשֶׁר שְׁבִיתֶם מֵאֲחֵיכֶם כִּי חֲרוֹן אַף יְהוָה עֲלֵיכֶם:

A prophet of the LORD by the name of Oded was there, who went out to meet the army on its return to Samaria. He said to them, Because of the fury of the LORD God of your fathers against Judah, he delivered them over to you, and you killed them in a rage that reached heaven. Do you now intend to subjugate the men and women of Judah and Jerusalem to be your slaves? As it is, you have nothing but offenses against the LORD your God. Now then, **listen to me (hortative?), and send back (hortative?)** the captives you have taken from your kinsmen, for the wrath of the LORD is upon you! (2 Chr 28:9-11)

(491) וַיָּקָם אֲבִיָּה מֵעַל לְהַר צְמָרִים אֲשֶׁר בְּהַר אֶפְרָיִם וַיֹּאמֶר **שְׁמָעוּנִי** יָרָבְעָם וְכָל יִשְׂרָאֵל:

Abijah stood on top of Mount Zemaraim in the hill country of Ephraim and said, **Listen (hortative?)** to me, Jeroboam and all Israel. (2 Chr 13:4)

(492) כֹּה אָמַר סַנְחֵרִיב מֶלֶךְ אַשּׁוּר. . . . וְעַתָּה **אַל יַשִּׁיא** אֶתְכֶם חִזְקִיָּהוּ **וְאַל יַסִּית** אֶתְכֶם כָּזֹאת **וְאַל תַּאֲמִינוּ** לוֹ כִּי לֹא יוּכַל כָּל אֱלוֹהַּ כָּל גּוֹי וּמַמְלָכָה לְהַצִּיל עַמּוֹ מִיָּדִי וּמִיַּד אֲבוֹתָי

Thus said King Sennacherib of Assyria: . . . Now then, **do not let** Hezekiah **delude (hortative?)** you; **do not let** him **seduce (hortative?)** you in this way; **do not believe (hortative?)** him. For no god of any nation or kingdom has been able to save his people from me or from my fathers (2 Chr 32:10-15)

9.3.1.5 The Optative Mood

Volitive forms can also express a wish. The optative mood closely resembles the hortative, but is less immediate. This very distance may account for the fact that the jussive is the most commonly used form in this group:

(493) עַתָּה בְנִי **יְהִי** יְהוָה עִמָּךְ וְהִצְלַחְתָּ וּבָנִיתָ בֵּית יְהוָה אֱלֹהֶיךָ כַּאֲשֶׁר דִּבֶּר עָלֶיךָ:

Now, my son, **may** the LORD **be (optative)** with you, and may you succeed in building the House of the LORD your God as he promised you would. (1 Chr 22:11)

(494) וְלֹא זָכַר יוֹאָשׁ הַמֶּלֶךְ הַחֶסֶד אֲשֶׁר עָשָׂה יְהוֹיָדָע אָבִיו עִמּוֹ וַיַּהֲרֹג אֶת בְּנוֹ וּכְמוֹתוֹ אָמַר **יֵרֶא** יְהוָה **וְיִדְרֹשׁ**:

King Joash disregarded the loyalty that his father Jehoiada had shown to him, and killed his son. As he was dying, he said, **May** the LORD **see (optative) and require (optative)** it. (2 Chr 24:22)

(495) וַיֵּצֵא דָוִיד לִפְנֵיהֶם וַיַּעַן וַיֹּאמֶר לָהֶם אִם לְשָׁלוֹם בָּאתֶם אֵלַי לְעָזְרֵנִי יִהְיֶה לִּי עֲלֵיכֶם לֵבָב לְיָחַד וְאִם לְרַמּוֹתַנִי לְצָרַי בְּלֹא חָמָס בְּכַפַּי **יֵרֶא** אֱלֹהֵי אֲבוֹתֵינוּ **וְיוֹכַח**: [16]

[A]nd David went out to meet them, saying to them, If you come on a peaceful errand, to support me, then I will make common cause with you, but if to betray me to my foes, for no injustice on my part, then **let** the God of our fathers **take notice (optative) and give (optative) judgment**. (1 Chr 12:18)

---

16. Also see 1 Chronicles 22:16; 2 Chronicles 19:11; 30:6.

9.3.1.6 Will

In certain cases, the modal meanings of the volitive forms can be defined as a general desire that cannot be classified under any of the aforementioned groups:

(496) וַיֹּאמֶר הַמֶּלֶךְ לְאֶסְתֵּר בְּמִשְׁתֵּה הַיַּיִן מַה שְּׁאֵלָתֵךְ וְיִנָּתֵן לָךְ וּמַה בַּקָּשָׁתֵךְ עַד חֲצִי הַמַּלְכוּת **וְתֵעָשׂ** :

At the wine feast, the king asked Esther, What is your wish? It shall be granted you. And what is your request? Even to half the kingdom, **it shall be fulfilled (will)**. (Est 5:6)

(497) וַיֹּאמֶר הַמֶּלֶךְ לְאֶסְתֵּר גַּם בַּיּוֹם הַשֵּׁנִי בְּמִשְׁתֵּה הַיַּיִן מַה שְּׁאֵלָתֵךְ אֶסְתֵּר הַמַּלְכָּה וְתִנָּתֵן לָךְ וּמַה בַּקָּשָׁתֵךְ עַד חֲצִי הַמַּלְכוּת **וְתֵעָשׂ** :

On the second day, the king again asked Esther at the wine feast, What is your wish, Queen Esther? It shall be granted you. And what is your request? Even to half the kingdom, **it shall be fulfilled (will)**. (Est 7:2)

(498) מִי בָכֶם מִכָּל עַמּוֹ יְהִי אֱלֹהָיו עִמּוֹ **וְיַעַל** לִירוּשָׁלַם אֲשֶׁר בִּיהוּדָה **וְיִבֶן** אֶת בֵּית יְהוָה אֱלֹהֵי יִשְׂרָאֵל הוּא הָאֱלֹהִים אֲשֶׁר בִּירוּשָׁלָם :

Anyone of you of all his people, may his God be with him, **and let him go up (will)** to Jerusalem that is in Judah **and build (will)** the House of the Lord God of Israel, the God that is in Jerusalem. (Ezr 1:3)

(499) וְעַתָּה **יְהִי** פַחַד יְהוָה עֲלֵיכֶם שִׁמְרוּ וַעֲשׂוּ כִּי אֵין עִם יְהוָה אֱלֹהֵינוּ עַוְלָה וּמַשֹּׂא פָנִים וּמִקַּח שֹׁחַד :

Now **let** the dread of the Lord **be (will)** upon you; act with care, for there is no injustice or favoritism or bribe-taking with the Lord our God. (2 Chr 19:7)

(500) וְיֵשׁ אֲשֶׁר אֹמְרִים בָּנֵינוּ וּבְנֹתֵינוּ אֲנַחְנוּ רַבִּים **וְנִקְחָה** דָגָן **וְנֹאכְלָה וְנִחְיֶה** :

Some said, Our sons and daughters are numerous; **we must get (will)** grain **and eat (will)** in order that **we may live (will)**! (Neh 5:2)

This meaning appears throughout our corpus in both the jussive (examples 496 to 499)[17] and cohortative forms (example 500). In fact, there is reason to believe that the imperative can also serve in this capacity and that the lack of such instances in our corpus is merely a coincidence, for it expresses the speaker's desire in, say, the following verse in classical Hebrew:

(501) עֲלֵה אֶל הַר הָעֲבָרִים הַזֶּה הַר נְבוֹ אֲשֶׁר בְּאֶרֶץ מוֹאָב אֲשֶׁר עַל פְּנֵי יְרֵחוֹ וּרְאֵה אֶת אֶרֶץ כְּנַעַן אֲשֶׁר אֲנִי נֹתֵן לִבְנֵי יִשְׂרָאֵל לַאֲחֻזָּה : **וּמֻת** בָּהָר אֲשֶׁר אַתָּה עֹלֶה שָׁמָּה **וְהֵאָסֵף** אֶל עַמֶּיךָ כַּאֲשֶׁר מֵת אַהֲרֹן אָחִיךָ בְּהֹר הָהָר וַיֵּאָסֶף אֶל עַמָּיו :

---

17. Also see Esther 9:12; Daniel 9:25; 2 Chronicles 36:23.

Ascend these heights of Abarim to Mount Nebo, which is in the land of Moab facing Jericho, and view the land of Canaan, which I am giving the Israelites as their holding. **You shall die (will)** on the mountain that you are about to ascend, **and shall be gathered (will)** to your kin, as your brother Aaron died on Mount Hor and was gathered to his kin. (Dt 32:49-50)

Unlike the verbs "עלה" and "ראה" at the outset of this chain, the imperative forms "מת" and "האסף" cannot be interpreted as connoting an order, request, or wish. Instead, God states his desire that Moses' life end on Mount Nebo.

9.3.2 Exceptions to the Framework of Deontic Modality

9.3.2.1 Conditional Sentences—Articulating Deontic Modality within an Epistemic Modal Context

The volitive forms can serve within the framework of conditional sentences. While they tend to be used in the apodosis, one volitive was also found in a protasis (example 505 below). On the face of things, this would appear to be an exception to the paradigmatic meaning of volitive forms, namely the signification of deontic modality. However, the next four examples show that conditional volitive forms do not deviate from the deontic mood. In essence, these verses express deontic modality within the broader context of epistemic mood:

(502) וַיֵּצֵא דָוִיד לִפְנֵיהֶם וַיַּעַן וַיֹּאמֶר לָהֶם אִם לְשָׁלוֹם בָּאתֶם אֵלַי לְעָזְרֵנִי יִהְיֶה לִּי עֲלֵיכֶם לֵבָב לְיָחַד וְאִם לְרַמּוֹתַנִי לְצָרַי בְּלֹא חָמָס בְּכַפַּי **יֵרֶא** אֱלֹהֵי אֲבוֹתֵינוּ **וְיוֹכַח**׃

And David went out to meet them, saying to them, If you come on a peaceful errand, to support me, then I will make common cause with you, but if to betray me to my foes, for no injustice on my part, then **let** the God of our fathers **take notice (jussive) and give judgment (jussive).** (1 Chr 12:18)

(503) וַיֹּאמֶר דָּוִיד לְכֹל קְהַל יִשְׂרָאֵל אִם עֲלֵיכֶם טוֹב וּמִן יְהוָה אֱלֹהֵינוּ **נִפְרְצָה נִשְׁלְחָה** עַל אַחֵינוּ הַנִּשְׁאָרִים בְּכֹל אַרְצוֹת יִשְׂרָאֵל וְעִמָּהֶם הַכֹּהֲנִים וְהַלְוִיִּם בְּעָרֵי מִגְרְשֵׁיהֶם וְיִקָּבְצוּ אֵלֵינוּ׃ **וְנָסֵבָּה** אֶת אֲרוֹן אֱלֹהֵינוּ אֵלֵינוּ כִּי לֹא דְרַשְׁנֻהוּ בִּימֵי שָׁאוּל׃

David said to the entire assembly of Israel, If you approve, and if the LORD our God concurs, **let us send far (cohortative) and wide (cohortative)** to our remaining kinsmen throughout the territories of Israel, including the priests and Levites in the towns where they have pasturelands, that they should gather together to us **and we will transfer (cohortative)** the Ark of our God to us, for throughout the days of Saul we paid no regard to it. (1 Chr 13:2-3)

(504) אִם תָּבוֹא עָלֵינוּ רָעָה חֶרֶב שְׁפוֹט וְדֶבֶר וְרָעָב **נַעַמְדָה** לִפְנֵי הַבַּיִת הַזֶּה וּלְפָנֶיךָ

Should misfortune befall us—the punishing sword, pestilence, or famine—**we shall stand (cohortative)** before this House and before you (2 Chr 20:9)

(505) וַיַּשְׁכִּימוּ בַבֹּקֶר וַיֵּצְאוּ לְמִדְבַּר תְּקוֹעַ וּבְצֵאתָם עָמַד יְהוֹשָׁפָט וַיֹּאמֶר שְׁמָעוּנִי
יְהוּדָה וְיֹשְׁבֵי יְרוּשָׁלַם **הַאֲמִינוּ** בַּיהוָה אֱלֹהֵיכֶם **וְתֵאָמֵנוּ הַאֲמִינוּ** בִנְבִיאָיו **וְהַצְלִיחוּ** :

Early the next morning they arose and went forth to the wilderness of Tekoa.
As they went forth, Jehoshaphat stood and said, Listen to me, O Judah and
inhabitants of Jerusalem: **Trust firmly** in the Lord your God and **you will
stand firm**; trust firmly in his prophets and **you will succeed**. (2 Chr 20:20)

In these examples volitive forms are situated in the apodosis of a conditional sentence, through which the author expresses his hope that these actions will indeed
come to pass (deontic modality). On the other hand, the verses also convey the
doubt that is manifest in conditional sentences (epistemic modality).

9.3.2.2 The Future—Functional Leveling of the Jussive and *Yiqtol*

In our corpus, volitive forms rarely deviate from the role of expressing deontic
modality. A glaring exception to this rule is the eleventh chapter of the book of
Daniel.[18] As already seen in other contexts,[19] the linguistic picture that emerges
from Daniel 11 differs from the rest of the Second Temple period texts. Consequently, it stands to reason that this chapter should be treated as an independent
entity.

In Daniel 11, both the jussive and *yiqtol* express the prophetic future. With respect to the former, this usage constitutes an aberration from its other roles in our
corpus, for expressing the future falls under the purview of the epistemic mood.
The distinction between the functions of the jussive and *yiqtol* in Daniel 11 is in
the process of being blurred. However, in my estimation, this conclusion may be
insufficient. It appears as though we can also point to the emergence of a novel re-
alignment of these forms. Qimron (1998:38) avers that the difference between the
plene (*yiqtol*) and truncated (jussive) forms in Biblical Hebrew is tied to the verb
forms' clausal position: the truncated forms come in the opening slot after a *waw*,
whereas the plene forms can occupy any position other than the first. According to
Qimron, this new alignment arose following the analogy to the "inverted future"
forms (*wayyiqtol*). Florentin (2000-2001) excoriates this view and endeavors to
prove that Qimron's rule does not fully apply to either the classical or later language of the Hebrew Scriptures. On the basis of my own research, it would appear
that the truth lies with Florentin.

---

18. Much has been written on the anomalies in chapters 10 to 12 in the book of Daniel; see,
    for example, Goldingay (1989:269-319), who also provides a comprehensive listing of
    related bibliographic material (269-271). These chapters are anomalous to the Hebrew
    Scriptures from both a thematic standpoint (apocalyptic literature) and in all that con-
    cerns their historical background, which probably reflects the period of the Antiochian
    decrees (167-164 BCE).
19. For instance, the discussion on *weqatal* forms in §7.1 above.

That said, the situation is different in Daniel 11, for not only is the volitive forms' primary function—signifying deontic modality—undermined, but a new alignment takes root, which complies with Qimron's rule. To wit: the jussive only turns up in the sentence's opening slot after a *waw*; an *yiqtol* forms are excluded from this position, but can be arrayed in any other location.[20] The next two passages exemplify this sort of substitution:

(506) וְיָשֵׂם פָּנָיו לָבוֹא בְּתֹקֶף כָּל מַלְכוּתוֹ וִישָׁרִים עִמּוֹ וְעָשָׂה וּבַת הַנָּשִׁים יִתֶּן לוֹ לְהַשְׁחִיתָהּ וְלֹא תַעֲמֹד וְלֹא לוֹ תִהְיֶה : וְיָשֵׁב (וְיָשֵׂם) פָּנָיו לְאִיִּים וְלָכַד רַבִּים וְהִשְׁבִּית קָצִין חֶרְפָּתוֹ לוֹ בִּלְתִּי חֶרְפָּתוֹ יָשִׁיב לוֹ :

He will set (*waw* + jussive) his mind upon invading the strongholds throughout his foe's kingdom, but in order to destroy it he will effect an agreement with him and give him a daughter in marriage; he will not succeed at it and **it will not come** (*yiqtol*) about. **He will turn** (*waw* + jussive) to the coastlands and capture many; but a consul will put an end to his insults, nay **pay him back** (*yiqtol*) for his insults. (Dn 11:17-18)

(507) וְיָשֵׁב אַרְצוֹ בִּרְכוּשׁ גָּדוֹל וּלְבָבוֹ עַל בְּרִית קֹדֶשׁ וְעָשָׂה וְשָׁב לְאַרְצוֹ : לַמּוֹעֵד יָשׁוּב וּבָא בַנֶּגֶב וְלֹא תִהְיֶה כָרִאשֹׁנָה וְכָאַחֲרוֹנָה :

He will return (*waw* + jussive) to his land with great wealth, his mind set against the holy covenant. Having done his pleasure, he will return to his land. At the appointed time, **he will again invade** (*yiqtol*) the south, but the second time **will not be** (*yiqtol*) like the first. (Dn 11:28-29)

As above mentioned, this sort of complementary distribution is quite rare in biblical prose. This, then, leads us to the question of how to interpret this phenomenon: From a systematic standpoint, this particular complementary distribution differs from the alignments that we find in the rest of the corpus. Linguistically speaking, the jussive and *yiqtol* have edged significantly closer and are thus on the brink of modal neutralization. Conversely, this pattern also gives rise to a new distinction between the forms in all that concerns their clausal placement.

---

20. If we omit those verbs that cannot be readily classified as either jussive or *yiqtol* forms, then our distribution is as follows: eight occurrences of "*waw* + jussive" and 16 occurrences of *yiqtol*. The lone exception to this rule is entirely dependent on the sentences' *q're* (what is read) version. Verse 10 contains two variations of the root גרי: the *ketiv* (what is written) "ויתגרו" and the *q're* "ויתגרה". Given the distribution of these forms throughout this chapter, I prefer the *ketiv* version, which neutralizes the distinction between the jussive and *yiqtol* forms. The "*waw* + jussive" structure turns up in verse 4, 16, 17, 18, 19, 25, 28, 30; and *yiqtol* in verse 2 (twice), 12 (*ketiv*), 17, 18, 23, 25, 29 (twice), 32, 33, 37 (twice), 39, 42. In contrast to Daniel 11, the plene forms in Daniel 12 are prefixed by a *waw*, such as "ותרבח" in verse 4 and "ותנוח" in 13.

Has the author of Daniel 11 devised a new construction, or is it, as Qimron suggests, a new alignment that took form in the mid-second century BCE, under the inspiration of the Hebrew familiar to us from the Dead Sea Scrolls?[21] Alternatively, perhaps this phenomenon should be attributed to the unique literary genre of Daniel 11?

---

21. Qimron (1998:41) contends that "in the language of the Scrolls, the new alignment is remarkably coherent." In addition, "the majority of optative forms serve in a pre-formative capacity" and "are preceded by a *waw*." A computerized search paints the following picture: 41 occurrences of "*waw* + jussive"; 9 occurrences of the jussive in the middle of a sentence (in negative sentences, there are 34 occurrences of the jussive after the particle אל and 3 after לא). This complex state of affairs merits further scholarly research.

C. The Infinitive Absolute—The Unmarked Consecutive Form

10.1 The Usages of the Infinitive Absolute in Second Temple Period Prose

10.1.1 Introduction

From the very inception of modern Biblical Hebrew research, scholars have noticed that besides the conventional non-predicative functions of the infinitive absolute, such as tautological, and other nominal uses, the form can also assume a predicative function.[1] The infinitive can appear at the beginning of a passage as a signifier of a general command, or at the middle of a sentence in a predicative role. In the latter usage, it may serve as a sort of substitute (usually following a *waw*) for the previous verb. For example:

(508) וּבְשׁוּשַׁן הַבִּירָה הָרְגוּ הַיְּהוּדִים **וְאַבֵּד** חֲמֵשׁ מֵאוֹת אִישׁ:

> In the fortress Shushan, the Jews killed **and destroyed [R,E]** a total of five hundred men. (Est 9:6)

This usage has constituted a challenging linguistic conundrum, as the number of solutions that have been proffered over the years appears to be tantamount to the number of researchers. To follow, then, is a brief sampling of some of the major interpretations of the infinitive absolute, beginning with a passage from Gesenius's grammar (Gesenius, Kautzsch, and Cowley 1910:§113y):

> Finally the infinitive absolute sometimes appears as *a substitute for the finite verb*, either when it is sufficient simply to mention the verbal idea . . . or when the hurried or otherwise excited style intentionally contents itself with this infinitive, in order to bring out the verbal idea in a clearer and more expressive manner.

Joüon and Muraoka provide the following observation of the infinitive absolute (1996:§123x):

> The reasons which have motivated the choice of the inf. abs. are not clearly understood: sometimes there is probably a desire for variety or a stylistic affection; sometimes the author wished to use a form with a vague subject like *one* or *they.*

Tur-Sinai (1954:223-224) averred that this pattern is essentially an elliptical structure, which was originally comprised of a conjugated verb and a tautological infinitive. For instance:

---

1. For example, see Gesenius, Kautzsch, and Cowley (1910:§111y-z); Ewald (1870: §351c); Joüon and Muraoka (1996:§123x); and Waltke and O'Connor (1990:594-597).

(509) וְכִי תִמְכְּרוּ מִמְכָּר לַעֲמִיתֶךָ אוֹ (תקנה) קָנֹה מִיַּד עֲמִיתֶךָ

When you sell property to your neighbor, or buy any from your neighbor
(Lv 25:14)

According to this approach, the phenomenon developed from the ellipsis of the
conjugated verb. However, Tur-Sinai's argument is problematic because, as we
will soon see, it fails to explain more nuanced occurrences of this model. Rubinstein (1952:365) offered a no less problematic one in its place:

> The presence of such a popular usage in the OT, however can only be due,
> we suggest, to scribes or copyists, who resorted to it when they could not be
> certain of the form of a finite verb.

Even if this is a stylistic phenomenon, as suggested by Gesenius, Kautzsch, and
Cowley and by Joüon and Muraoka, researchers are not exempt from endeavoring
to discern the linguistic mechanism that generated this phenomenon.

One of the central methodological obstacles to understanding the infinitive
absolute is the fact that the diachronic and genre-related aspects of the text have
been virtually ignored. As such, we will start out with a survey of its diachronic
perspective. This will be followed by an examination of its syntactical contexts
in Second Temple period prose as well as analogous contexts in other corpuses.

Insofar as the infinitive absolute's distribution in First and Second Temple period prose is concerned, there is a consensus among researchers that there was
a steep decline in the form's usage during the later period. For instance, Polzin
(1976:44) claims:

> The Chronicler's usage of [the] infinitive absolute shows . . . a marked
> decrease as opposed to earlier Hebrew. . . . This evidence seems to point to the
> conclusion that, at the time of the Chronicler, the infinitive absolute is well on
> the way to extinction.

A thorough analysis of the data casts serious doubts on Polzin's assertion. In First
Temple period prose (from Genesis to the end of the book of Kings), the infinitive
absolute appears no less than 415 times.[2] In contrast, it makes only 53 appearanc-
es throughout the Second Temple period prose. However, these numbers warrant
qualification, for the scale of the two corpora is markedly different: the First Temple period corpus entails 334 chapters, whereas Second Temple period prose totals
a mere 81. Therefore, the drop in the infinitive absolute's use is not as significant
as suspected. But the fact that infinitive forms are to be found in both corpora does
not necessarily imply that they were used the same way throughout the two periods.

---

2.   The statistics were gleaned from a computerized scan of the Bible using the program
      Accordance.

In fact, the language of the Second Temple period is informed by substantial alterations in the usage of the infinitive absolute.

In sum, out of 53 occurrences in Second Temple period Biblical Hebrew, 32 (61.5%)[3] serve in a predicative role; 11 (21.1%)[4] fill various adverbial functions; and only 9 (17.4%)[5] can be interpreted as tautological infinitives. All the adverbial usages, save one,[6] involve the infinitive הרבה (many)—a form that has remained "fossilized" since the First Temple period. In fact, if the adverbial occurrences are omitted from the tally, nearly 80% of the infinitive absolute forms in the Second Temple period are predicative, compared to about 10% in the First Temple period corpus. Furthermore, the two periods apparently diverge in all that concerns the exact nature of the predicative usage: While the primary predicative function in the First Temple period texts is to denote a general command or the language of the law, the Second Temple period infinitive forms tend to signify unmarked consecutive forms. In the pages below, we will elaborate on the infinitive's functions during both these periods.

10.1.2 Unmarked Consecutive Forms

The main function of infinitive forms in the Second Temple period is to signify that the reference time and event are in the same unit [R,E],[7] namely the standard classical use of consecutive forms (*wayyiqtol* and *weqatal*). Whereas the latter are marked in accordance to their modal significance, the infinitive forms are unmarked because they are likely to appear in succession with both indicative and modal forms. The modal meaning of these infinitive forms is predicated on the context and is not an inherent part of their meaning. Therefore, a third category of consecutive forms, which are unmarked with respect to their relation to the modal axis, emerged during this period.

Understanding the modal significance of these forms and defining the putative subject of successive actions is not straightforward. For example, the infinitive forms do not always refer to the most proximate verb in a succession. Moreover, they do not necessarily share the subject with the verb that they are referring to, as they can also correspond to other components in the sentence, such as the object.

---

3. Esther 2:3; 3:13; 6:9; 8:8; 9:1, 4, 6, 12, 16 (thrice), 17 (twice), 18 (twice), (as well as 23, 27, as per the כתיב, orthographical spelling); Daniel 1:17; 9:5, 11, 23 (twice); Nehemiah 7:3; 8:8?; 9:8, 13; 1 Chronicles 5:20; 15:22; 2 Chronicles 2:8?; 31:10 (thrice).
4. Ezra 10:1; Nehemiah 2:2; 3:33; 4:13; 5:18; 2 Chronicles 11:12; 14:12; 25:9; 32:27; 36:15 (twice).
5. Esther 4:14; 6:13; Daniel 10:3; 11:10, 13; 1 Chronicles 4:10; 21:17, 24; 2 Chronicles 28:19.
6. 2 Chronicles 36:15.
7. See the discussion on the consecutive forms in §2.1.3 above.

10.1.2.1 Consecutive Forms Aligned with *Qatal*

(510) וּשְׁאָר הַיְּהוּדִים אֲשֶׁר בִּמְדִינוֹת הַמֶּלֶךְ **נִקְהֲלוּ וְעָמֹד** עַל נַפְשָׁם **וְנוֹחַ** מֵאֹיְבֵיהֶם
וְהָרוֹג בְּשֹׂנְאֵיהֶם חֲמִשָּׁה וְשִׁבְעִים אָלֶף וּבַבִּזָּה לֹא שָׁלְחוּ אֶת יָדָם : בְּיוֹם שְׁלוֹשָׁה
עָשָׂר לְחֹדֶשׁ אֲדָר **וְנוֹחַ** בְּאַרְבָּעָה עָשָׂר בּוֹ **וְעָשֹׂה** אֹתוֹ יוֹם מִשְׁתֶּה וְשִׂמְחָה : וְהַיְּהוּדִיִּים
(וְהַיְּהוּדִים) אֲשֶׁר בְּשׁוּשָׁן **נִקְהֲלוּ** בִּשְׁלוֹשָׁה עָשָׂר בּוֹ וּבְאַרְבָּעָה עָשָׂר בּוֹ **וְנוֹחַ** בַּחֲמִשָּׁה
עָשָׂר בּוֹ **וְעָשֹׂה** אֹתוֹ יוֹם מִשְׁתֶּה וְשִׂמְחָה :

The rest of the Jews, those in the king's provinces, likewise **mustered (*qatal*)
and fought [R,E]** for their lives **and disposed [R,E]** of their enemies, **and
killed [R,E]** seventy-five thousand of their foes; but they did not lay hands
on the spoil. That was on the thirteenth day of the month of Adar; **and they
rested [R,E]** on the fourteenth day **and made [R,E]** it a day of feasting and
merrymaking. (But the Jews in Shushan **mustered (*qatal*)** on both the thirteenth
and fourteenth days, and so **rested [R,E]** on the fifteenth, **and made[R,E]** it a
day of feasting and merrymaking.) (Est 9:16-18)

The chain of infinitive forms in the first two verses refers to the Jews in the king's
provinces. At the head of the chain stands a *qatal* form (נקהלו) that signifies the
beginning of the succession, which is followed by infinitive forms.

(511) וּבְשׁוּשַׁן הַבִּירָה הָרְגוּ הַיְּהוּדִים **וְאַבֵּד**[8] חֲמֵשׁ מֵאוֹת אִישׁ :[9]

In the fortress Shushan the Jews killed **and destroyed [R,E]** a total of five
hundred men (Est 9:6 = 9:12)

In examples 510 and 511, the infinitive forms appear within a narrative, but they
can also be found in direct speech or oratory:

(512) וָאֶתְפַּלְלָה לַיהוָה אֱלֹהַי וָאֶתְוַדֶּה וָאֹמְרָה אָנָּא אֲדֹנָי הָאֵל הַגָּדוֹל וְהַנּוֹרָא שֹׁמֵר
הַבְּרִית וְהַחֶסֶד לְאֹהֲבָיו וּלְשֹׁמְרֵי מִצְוֹתָיו : חָטָאנוּ וְעָוִינוּ והרשענו (הִרְשַׁעְנוּ) וּמָרָדְנוּ
וְסוֹר מִמִּצְוֹתֶךָ וּמִמִּשְׁפָּטֶיךָ :

I prayed to the LORD my God, making confession thus: O Lord, great and
awesome God, who stays faithful to his covenant with those who love him
and keep his commandments![5] We have sinned; we have gone astray; we have
acted wickedly; we have been rebellious **and have deviated [R,E]** from your
commandments and your rules. (Dn 9:4-5)

(513) וְכָל יִשְׂרָאֵל עָבְרוּ אֶת תּוֹרָתֶךָ **וְסוֹר** לְבִלְתִּי שְׁמוֹעַ בְּקֹלֶךָ

---

8.   Due to the redundancy of הרגו and ואבד, *JPS* makes do with but one verb ("killed").
9.   Another verse that appears to fall under this category is, "the Jews undertook and ir-
    revocably obligated [קימו וקבל] themselves." (Esther 9:27). In Qimron's estimation,
    (1988:359, note 39), the predicative use of infinitive forms is, in all likelihood, more
    prevalent in the book of Esther, but this fact has been obfuscated; and this blurring is
    entirely on account of the Massorah's mediation.

All Israel has violated your teaching **and gone [R,E]** astray, disobeying you. (Dn 9:11)

(514) אַתָּה הוּא יְהוָה הָאֱלֹהִים אֲשֶׁר בָּחַרְתָּ בְּאַבְרָם וְהוֹצֵאתוֹ מֵאוּר כַּשְׂדִּים וְשַׂמְתָּ שְׁמוֹ אַבְרָהָם: וּמָצָאתָ אֶת לְבָבוֹ נֶאֱמָן לְפָנֶיךָ **וְכָרוֹת** עִמּוֹ הַבְּרִית לָתֵת אֶת אֶרֶץ הַכְּנַעֲנִי הַחִתִּי הָאֱמֹרִי וְהַפְּרִזִּי וְהַיְבוּסִי וְהַגִּרְגָּשִׁי

You are the LORD God, who chose Abram, who brought him out of Ur of the Chaldeans and changed his name to Abraham. Finding his heart true to you, **you made [R,E]** a covenant with him to give the land of the Canaanite, the Hittite, the Amorite, the Perizzite, the Jebusite, and the Girgashite. (Neh 9:7-8)

(515) וּבְעַמּוּד עָנָן הִנְחִיתָם יוֹמָם וּבְעַמּוּד אֵשׁ לַיְלָה לְהָאִיר לָהֶם אֶת הַדֶּרֶךְ אֲשֶׁר יֵלְכוּ בָהּ: וְעַל הַר סִינַי יָרַדְתָּ **וְדַבֵּר** עִמָּהֶם מִשָּׁמָיִם

You led them by day with a pillar of cloud, and by night with a pillar of fire, to give them light in the way they were to go. You came down on Mount Sinai **and spoke [R,E]** to them from heaven. (Neh 9:12-13)

The next example indicates that, in these sorts of successions, there need not be a correlation between the subject of the verb and the assumed subject of the infinitive form:

(516) וַיַּעֲשׂוּ מִלְחָמָה עִם הַהַגְרִיאִים וְיְטוּר וְנָפִישׁ וְנוֹדָב: וַיֵּעָזְרוּ עֲלֵיהֶם וַיִּנָּתְנוּ בְיָדָם הַהַגְרִיאִים וְכֹל שֶׁעִמָּהֶם כִּי לֵאלֹהִים **זָעֲקוּ** בַּמִּלְחָמָה **וְנַעְתּוֹר** לָהֶם כִּי בָטְחוּ בוֹ:

They made war on the Hagrites—Jetur, Naphish, and Nodab. They prevailed against them; the Hagrites and all who were with them were delivered into their hands, for **they cried** to God in the battle, **and he responded [R,E]** to their entreaty because they trusted in him. (1 Chr 5:19-20)

In this passage, the logical subject of the infinitive form "נעתור" is God, the indirect object of the previous clause. The opening verse of the ninth chapter of the book of Esther also merits attention:

(517) וּבִשְׁנֵים עָשָׂר חֹדֶשׁ הוּא חֹדֶשׁ אֲדָר בִּשְׁלוֹשָׁה עָשָׂר יוֹם בּוֹ אֲשֶׁר הִגִּיעַ דְּבַר הַמֶּלֶךְ וְדָתוֹ לְהֵעָשׂוֹת בַּיּוֹם אֲשֶׁר שִׂבְּרוּ אֹיְבֵי הַיְּהוּדִים לִשְׁלוֹט בָּהֶם **וְנַהֲפוֹךְ הוּא** אֲשֶׁר יִשְׁלְטוּ הַיְּהוּדִים הֵמָּה בְּשֹׂנְאֵיהֶם:

And so, on the thirteenth day of the twelfth month—that is, the month of Adar— when the king's command and decree were to be executed, the very day on which the enemies of the Jews had expected to get them in their power, **the opposite happened [R,E]**, and the Jews got their enemies in their power. (Est 9:1)

Since the subject of the action is not marked by the form itself, an independent personal pronoun ("הוא") has been added to the infinitive form ("ונהפוך"). This structure mirrors the juxtaposition of a personal pronoun and a participle, wherein the subject of the action is also located outside the structure itself.[10]

The last two examples are critical to understanding the usage of infinitive forms during the Second Temple period. One of general linguistics' widespread contentions concerning the use of infinitive forms in predicative successions is that they are "inflectionally frugal." In other words, if the deictic elements can be deduced from the succession, then it is superfluous to repeat them in each and every occurrence of the verbs standing in succession. Ewald (1870:§351c), who compares this phenomenon to the forms of Ethiopian and Coptic gerunds, formulated this idea in the following manner:

> Noch hat sich eine eigene art von kürze der darstellung dádurch gebildet daß ein zweites verbum welches sich dem vorigen vermittelst irgend eines -ן verbindet, ihm bloß im *inf. abs.* . . . als wäre es genug nachdem einmal die rede eingeleitet ist eine folgende handlung mit dem *und* so kurz als möglich anzuschließen.

According to Ewald, the infinitive and other forms in a succession should be fully correlated with both tense and person. He also noted that "inflectional frugality" is a recognized phenomenon in many languages, such as Turkish.[11]

The picture that arises from the Hebrew of the Second Temple period differs from Ewald's hypothesis. As seen in example 516, agreement in persons between an infinitive and verb form standing in succession is merely optional.[12] Furthermore the exact relation to reference time (R-time), which is marked by the verb and the infinitive form, appears to be optional as well. To wit: in example 516, the *qatal* form's position vis-à-vis the reference time is R>E, while the infinitive assumes an [E,R] alignment. Moreover, example 517, in which an independent personal pronoun has been attached to the infinitive form, raises doubts with regard to the claim that the above mentioned desire for thriftiness constitutes the incentive behind this structure.[13]

---

10. Another example of this can be found in Ecclesiastes 4:1-2:
וְשַׁבְתִּי אֲנִי וָאֶרְאֶה אֶת כָּל הָעֲשֻׁקִים אֲשֶׁר נַעֲשִׂים תַּחַת הַשָּׁמֶשׁ וְהִנֵּה דִּמְעַת הָעֲשֻׁקִים וְאֵין לָהֶם מְנַחֵם
וּמִיַּד עֹשְׁקֵיהֶם כֹּחַ וְאֵין לָהֶם מְנַחֵם: **וְשַׁבֵּחַ אֲנִי** אֶת הַמֵּתִים שֶׁכְּבָר מֵתוּ מִן הַחַיִּים אֲשֶׁר הֵמָּה חַיִּים עֲדֶנָה.

11. For example, see Deny (1971:445): "Si dans une phrase, plusieurs formes personnelles, semblables se succèdent, on peut se contenter d'énoncer seulement les thèmes en n'exprimant les autres éléments. . . qu'une fois, avec le thème du dernier verbe."

12. Another instance that lacks personal agreement between the infinitive and conjugated forms can be found in Esther 3:12-13: וַיִּקָּרְאוּ סֹפְרֵי הַמֶּלֶךְ בַּחֹדֶשׁ הָרִאשׁוֹן בִּשְׁלוֹשָׁה עָשָׂר יוֹם
בּוֹ וַיִּכָּתֵב כְּכָל אֲשֶׁר צִוָּה הָמָן אֶל אֲחַשְׁדַּרְפְּנֵי הַמֶּלֶךְ וְאֶל הַפַּחוֹת אֲשֶׁר עַל מְדִינָה וּמְדִינָה וְאֶל שָׂרֵי
עַם וָעָם מְדִינָה וּמְדִינָה כִּכְתָבָהּ וְעַם וָעָם כִּלְשׁוֹנוֹ בְּשֵׁם הַמֶּלֶךְ אֲחַשְׁוֵרֹשׁ **נִכְתָּב וְנֶחְתָּם** בְּטַבַּעַת הַמֶּלֶךְ:
וְנִשְׁלוֹחַ סְפָרִים בְּיַד הָרָצִים. Although located outside the corpus in question, Genesis
41:43 also constitutes an example of this phenomenon: וַיַּרְכֵּב אֹתוֹ בְּמִרְכֶּבֶת הַמִּשְׁנֶה אֲשֶׁר
לוֹ **וַיִּקְרְאוּ** לְפָנָיו אַבְרֵךְ **וְנָתוֹן** אֹתוֹ עַל כָּל אֶרֶץ מִצְרָיִם. In this case, the anterior verb is grouped
with a different subject than that of the infinitive form.

13. Perhaps we can shed some light on the flaws of this argument by drawing a typological

10.1.2.2 Consecutive Forms Aligned with *Wayyiqtol*

As argued above, the infinitive absolute forms can stand in succession with forms other than *qatal*. For example, in the next passages, the infinitive forms are arrayed with *wayyiqtol*:

(518) וַיִּקָּרְאוּ סֹפְרֵי הַמֶּלֶךְ בַּחֹדֶשׁ הָרִאשׁוֹן בִּשְׁלוֹשָׁה עָשָׂר יוֹם בּוֹ וַיִּכָּתֵב כְּכָל אֲשֶׁר
צִוָּה הָמָן אֶל אֲחַשְׁדַּרְפְּנֵי הַמֶּלֶךְ וְאֶל הַפַּחוֹת אֲשֶׁר עַל מְדִינָה וּמְדִינָה וְאֶל שָׂרֵי עַם
וָעָם מְדִינָה וּמְדִינָה כִּכְתָבָהּ וְעַם וָעָם כִּלְשׁוֹנוֹ בְּשֵׁם הַמֶּלֶךְ אֲחַשְׁוֵרֹשׁ נִכְתָּב וְנֶחְתָּם
בְּטַבַּעַת הַמֶּלֶךְ : וְנִשְׁלוֹחַ סְפָרִים בְּיַד הָרָצִים אֶל כָּל מְדִינוֹת הַמֶּלֶךְ

On the thirteenth day of the first month, the king's scribes **were summoned** (*wayyiqtol*) and a decree **was issued** (*wayyiqtol*), as Haman directed, to the king's satraps, to the governors of every province, and to the officials of every people, to every province in its own script and to every people in its own language. The orders were issued in the name of King Ahasuerus and sealed with the king's signet. Accordingly, written instructions **were dispatched** [R,E] by couriers to all the king's provinces. (Est 3:12-13)

---

comparison to the Phoenician language and the Amarna correspondence, which is to be conducted exclusively from the typological perspective of a structure. Researchers tend to search for a direct relationship between Phoenician, the Amarna letters, Ugarit, and the Bible; e.g., Huesman (1956), Dahood (1952), and others. However, the inclination to lean on a typological connection, while ignoring the fact that the usages of these forms are different in each of the languages, often leads to hasty conclusions.

In the Amarna letters, the pattern *qatāli-ma* + independent pronoun-subject is commonplace; see Moran (1950) and Rainey (1996:383-388). For example, *ù ma-ti-ma šu-ut a-nu / i-di-šu* (EA 89.38-39)—"And when he died, truly I learned of it." (translation is taken from Moran [1950:170]). *Pa-ṭá-ri-ma šu-ut* [*ù*] / *ia-nu ša-a yu-ba-lu* [*tuppi*[pi-ia]] / *a-na mu-ḫi-ka* (EA 113.40-42)—"If he leaves, then there will be no one to carry my letter(s) to thee" (translation and addendums are from Moran as well [ibid.]).

As Moran points out, the phrases *ma-ti-ma šu-ut* and *pa-ṭá-ri-ma šu-ut* are periphrastic constructions that are comprised of the following components: a verbal lexeme (infinitive forms); the genitive *i*- case (for a possible explanation of its meaning in this particular case, see Moran [1950:171-172]); the particle *ma*, which signifies the predication; and an independent personal pronoun in the role of subject. In other words, this constitutes an analytical representation of all the verbal complex's components, as illustrated by Goldenberg (1985). Compared to the verbal complex of conjugated verb forms, this complex is not informed by thriftiness.

A similar phenomenon can be found in the following Phoenician passage from the Azitawada Inscription: *W'NK 'AZTWD 'NTNM YRDM 'NK YŠBM 'NK BQṢT GBLY* (pillar 1, lines 19-21); see Gordon (1949:110). Here too, an infinitive form precedes an independent personal pronoun, which serves as the subject. Moreover, as per the suggestion of Moran (1950:172), who followed in the footsteps of Gordon (1949:114), the particale *ma-* appears in the combinations *YRDM* and *YŠBM* and might resembles the corresponding structure in the Amarna letters.

The infinitive form "וּנשׁלוֹח" is arranged in a continuum with the verbs "ויקראו"
and "ויכתב".

> (519) וַיִּכְתֹּב מָרְדֳּכַי אֶת הַדְּבָרִים הָאֵלֶּה וַיִּשְׁלַח סְפָרִים אֶל כָּל הַיְּהוּדִים אֲשֶׁר בְּכָל
> מְדִינוֹת הַמֶּלֶךְ אֲחַשְׁוֵרוֹשׁ הַקְּרוֹבִים וְהָרְחוֹקִים: לְקַיֵּם עֲלֵיהֶם לִהְיוֹת עֹשִׂים אֵת
> יוֹם אַרְבָּעָה עָשָׂר לְחֹדֶשׁ אֲדָר וְאֵת יוֹם חֲמִשָּׁה עָשָׂר בּוֹ בְּכָל שָׁנָה וְשָׁנָה: כַּיָּמִים אֲשֶׁר
> נָחוּ בָהֶם הַיְּהוּדִים מֵאֹיְבֵיהֶם וְהַחֹדֶשׁ אֲשֶׁר נֶהְפַּךְ לָהֶם מִיָּגוֹן לְשִׂמְחָה וּמֵאֵבֶל לְיוֹם
> טוֹב לַעֲשׂוֹת אוֹתָם יְמֵי מִשְׁתֶּה וְשִׂמְחָה וּמִשְׁלֹחַ מָנוֹת אִישׁ לְרֵעֵהוּ וּמַתָּנוֹת לָאֶבְיֹנִים:
> **וְקִבֵּל**[14] הַיְּהוּדִים אֵת אֲשֶׁר הֵחֵלּוּ לַעֲשׂוֹת וְאֵת אֲשֶׁר כָּתַב מָרְדֳּכַי אֲלֵיהֶם:

Mordecai **recorded** (*wayyiqtol*) these events. And **he sent** (*wayyiqtol*)
dispatches to all the Jews throughout the provinces of King Ahasuerus, near
and far, charging them to observe the fourteenth and fifteenth days of Adar,
every year—the same days on which the Jews enjoyed relief from their foes
and the same month which had been transformed for them from one of grief
and mourning to one of festive joy. They were to observe them as days of
feasting and merrymaking, and as an occasion for sending gifts to one another
and presents to the poor. The Jews accordingly **assumed [R,E]** as an obligation
that which they had begun to practice and which Mordecai prescribed for
them. (Est 9:20-23)

As in the first example, despite being separated, the infinitive stands in succession
with *wayyiqtol* forms ("ויכתב" and "וישלח"). In this particular case, the interim clause
encompasses a string of predicative infinitive construct forms which convey the
content of Mordecai's letters.[15] Both passages show that the components of a succession do not necessarily have to be in close proximity, as they may be divided
by several lines of text.

10.1.2.3 Consecutive Forms Aligned with *Yiqtol* and/or a Jussive

In all the previous examples, the infinitive forms derived their indicative meaning
from the *qatal* and *wayyiqtol* forms. However, in the next examples, the infinitive
forms stand in succession with modal *yiqtol* and/or jussive forms.

> (520) וַיֹּאמְרוּ נַעֲרֵי הַמֶּלֶךְ מְשָׁרְתָיו **יְבַקְשׁוּ** לַמֶּלֶךְ נְעָרוֹת בְּתוּלוֹת טוֹבוֹת מַרְאֶה:
> **וְיַפְקֵד** הַמֶּלֶךְ פְּקִידִים בְּכָל מְדִינוֹת מַלְכוּתוֹ **וְיִקְבְּצוּ** אֶת כָּל נַעֲרָה בְתוּלָה טוֹבַת
> מַרְאֶה אֶל שׁוּשַׁן הַבִּירָה אֶל בֵּית הַנָּשִׁים אֶל יַד הֵגֶא סְרִיס הַמֶּלֶךְ שֹׁמֵר הַנָּשִׁים **וְנָתוֹן**
> תַּמְרֻקֵיהֶן:

The king's servants who attended him said, **Let** beautiful young virgins **be
sought out (jussive)** for your Majesty. **Let** your Majesty **appoint (jussive)**

---

14. As per the orthographical spelling (כתיב). I follow Qimron's estimation (1988:359,
    note 39), that this is a predicative use of an infinitive form.
15. For more on the predicative usage of these types of inflected infinitive forms, see Co-
    hen (2005:93-94).

officers in every province of your realm **to assemble (jussive)** all the beautiful young virgins at the fortress Shushan, in the harem under the supervision of Hege, the king's eunuch, guardian of the women. **Let them be provided [R,E]** with their cosmetics. (Est 2:2-3)

(521) וַיֹּאמֶר הָמָן אֶל הַמֶּלֶךְ אִישׁ אֲשֶׁר הַמֶּלֶךְ חָפֵץ בִּיקָרוֹ: **יָבִיאוּ** לְבוּשׁ מַלְכוּת אֲשֶׁר לָבַשׁ בּוֹ הַמֶּלֶךְ וְסוּס אֲשֶׁר רָכַב עָלָיו הַמֶּלֶךְ וַאֲשֶׁר נִתַּן כֶּתֶר מַלְכוּת בְּרֹאשׁוֹ: **וְנָתוֹן** הַלְּבוּשׁ וְהַסּוּס עַל יַד אִישׁ מִשָּׂרֵי הַמֶּלֶךְ הַפַּרְתְּמִים וְהִלְבִּישׁוּ אֶת הָאִישׁ אֲשֶׁר הַמֶּלֶךְ חָפֵץ בִּיקָרוֹ וְהִרְכִּיבֻהוּ עַל הַסּוּס בִּרְחוֹב הָעִיר וְקָרְאוּ לְפָנָיו כָּכָה יֵעָשֶׂה לָאִישׁ אֲשֶׁר הַמֶּלֶךְ חָפֵץ בִּיקָרוֹ:

So Haman said to the king, For the man whom the king desires to honor, **let** royal garb which the king has worn **be brought** *(yiqtol)*, and a horse on which the king has ridden and on whose head a royal diadem has been set; **and let** the attire and the horse **be put [R,E]** in the charge of one of the king's noble courtiers. And let the man whom the king desires to honor be attired and paraded on the horse through the city square, while they proclaim before him: This is what is done for the man whom the king desires to honor! (Est 6:7-9)

On the face of things, the inflected verbs in the first passage could have been perceived as *yiqtol* forms rather than jussives, for the only verb form that is marked as the latter is "וְיִפָּקֵד". Yet by virtue of the fact that it is marked as a jussive, we can reasonably assume that the rest of the forms in this continuum are jussives as well. In example 520, the infinitive form closes a string of requests on the part of the king's servants.[16] The second example consists of a modal succession that opens with a *yiqtol* form (יביאו) and continues with *weqatal* forms ("והלבישו" etc.). In both cases, the infinitive form can be said to delineate a border between the forms *yiqtol* and *weqatal* (see §10.3 below).

(522) וָאֹמַר (וָאֹמְרָה) לָהֶם לֹא יִפָּתְחוּ שַׁעֲרֵי יְרוּשָׁלַ͏ִם עַד חֹם הַשֶּׁמֶשׁ וְעַד הֵם עֹמְדִים יָגִיפוּ הַדְּלָתוֹת (וַיֹּאחֵזוּ) וֶאֱחֹזוּ[17] **וְהַעֲמֵיד** מִשְׁמְרוֹת יֹשְׁבֵי יְרוּשָׁלַ͏ִם אִישׁ בְּמִשְׁמָרוֹ וְאִישׁ נֶגֶד בֵּיתוֹ:

I said to them, The gates of Jerusalem are not to be opened until the heat of the day, and before you leave your posts let the doors be closed and barred. **And assign [R,E]** the inhabitants of Jerusalem to watches, each man to his watch, and each in front of his own house. (Neh 7:3)

If we adopt the "וְיֹאחֵזוּ" reading, then this passage can be equated with the previous two, for here too an infinitive form seals a chain of commands.

---

16. At first glance, the verse that follows the passages cited in example 1 ("וְהַנַּעֲרָה אֲשֶׁר "תִּיטַב בְּעֵינֵי הַמֶּלֶךְ תִּמְלֹךְ תַּחַת וַשְׁתִּי) also appears to belong to the string of requests noted in the previous two verses. However, from a syntactical standpoint, it is merely a secondary clause, not a main one.

17. On account of the solid evidence in the Septuagint and the Syriac translation, BHS advocates the "וַיֹּאחֵזוּ" rendering.

10.1.2.4 Consecutive Forms Aligned with the Participle

(523) וְאַתֶּם כִּתְבוּ עַל הַיְּהוּדִים כַּטּוֹב בְּעֵינֵיכֶם בְּשֵׁם הַמֶּלֶךְ וְחִתְמוּ בְּטַבַּעַת הַמֶּלֶךְ
כִּי כְתָב אֲשֶׁר **נִכְתָּב** בְּשֵׁם הַמֶּלֶךְ **וְנַחְתּוֹם** בְּטַבַּעַת הַמֶּלֶךְ אֵין לְהָשִׁיב[18].

And you may further write with regard to the Jews as you see fit. Write it
in the king's name and seal it with the king's signet, for an edict that **has
been written (participle)** in the king's name **and sealed [R,E]** with the king's
signet may not be revoked. (Est 8:8)

In this particular case, the infinitive form "וּנחתום" stands in succession with a
participle in the habitual present that imbues the same meaning upon the former.
With respect to R-time, it expresses the relation [R,E], and the same applies to the
rest of the instances in this category. This pattern is reminiscent of the relationship
between the *yiqtol* and *weqatal* forms in texts from the First Temple period. For
instance:

(524) עַל כֵּן **יַעֲזָב** אִישׁ אֶת אָבִיו וְאֶת אִמּוֹ **וְדָבַק** בְּאִשְׁתּוֹ **וְהָיוּ** לְבָשָׂר אֶחָד :

Hence a man **leaves** [*yiqtol*] his father and mother **and clings** [*weqatal*] to his
wife, so that they **become** [*weqatal*] one flesh. (Gn 2:24)

10.1.2.5 Ambiguous Cases

(525) וְהַיְלָדִים הָאֵלֶּה אַרְבַּעְתָּם נָתַן לָהֶם הָאֱלֹהִים מַדָּע **וְהַשְׂכֵּל** בְּכָל סֵפֶר וְחָכְמָה
וְדָנִיֵּאל הֵבִין בְּכָל חָזוֹן וַחֲלֹמוֹת :

God made all four of these young men intelligent and **proficient (infinitive
absolute?)** in all writings and wisdom, and Daniel had understanding of
visions and dreams of all kinds. (Dn 1:17)

(526) וַיִּקְרְאוּ בַסֵּפֶר בְּתוֹרַת הָאֱלֹהִים מְפֹרָשׁ **וְשׂוֹם** שֶׂכֶל וַיָּבִינוּ בַּמִּקְרָא :

They read from the scroll of the Teaching of God, translating it **and giving
(infinitive absolute?)** the sense; so they understood the reading. (Neh 8:8)

In both these examples, the reader would be hard pressed to decide whether "מדע"
"והשכל" or the infinitive forms stand on their own or whether they comprise part
of a phrase—"מפורש ושום שכל". If the infinitive form ("והשכל") in the first verse
is perceived as standing alone,[19] then this clause constitutes another example of a

---

18. This clause closely resembles the one in Esther 3:12 ("נִכְתָּב וְנֶחְתָּם בְּטַבַּעַת הַמֶּלֶךְ")
wherein the consecutive form is a participle, not an infinitive.
19. Lacocque interprets the verse in this fashion, while Goldingay (1989:6) renders the infinitive as a noun. In this case, the biblical accentuation strengthens the assumption that
"מדע והשכל" ("intelligent and proficient" as per *JPS*, or "intelligence and proficiency"
as per the present author) both serve as the object of the verb "נתן" (gave).

succession of an infinitive and *qatal* form (i.e. "God gave (*qatal*) all four of these young men intelligence **and they became knowldgeable [R,E]** in all writings") According to the second reading, the succession constitutes another example of an inflected verb and infinitive form that do not share the same subject, for the indirect object of the previous verse is cast in the role of subject. Insofar as Nehemiah 8 is concerned, the accentuation (the pause under "מפרש") bolsters the assumption that "מפרש" should be separated from "שום שכל". If this interpretation is accepted, then the infinitive form "שום" can also be viewed as standing in succession with *wayyiqtol* forms (Williamson 1985:278-279).[20]

(527) וַיֹּאמֶר אֵלָיו עֲזַרְיָהוּ הַכֹּהֵן הָרֹאשׁ לְבֵית צָדוֹק וַיֹּאמֶר מֵהָחֵל הַתְּרוּמָה לָבִיא בֵית יְהוָה **אָכוֹל וְשָׂבוֹעַ וְהוֹתֵר** עַד לָרוֹב כִּי יְהוָה בֵּרַךְ אֶת עַמּוֹ וְהַנּוֹתָר אֶת הֶהָמוֹן הַזֶּה:

The chief priest Azariah, of the house of Zadok, replied to him, saying, Ever since the gifts began to be brought to the House of the LORD, people have been **eating (infinitive absolute?) to satiety (infinitive absolute?) and leaving (infinitive absolute?)** over in great amounts, for the LORD has blessed his people; this huge amount is left over! (2 Chr 31:10)

Here too, the reader would be hard pressed to determine the role of the infinitive forms, as they can be understood as either nominal forms[21]—something along the lines of: "מהחל התרומה לבוא בית ה' (היתה) אכילה ושביעה והותרה עד לרוב" (When the tithes began to arrive in the House of the LORD [there was] eating and satiety and great excess)—or as predicative forms.[22] The last two infinitives, "ושבוע והותר", evidently function as consecutive forms; in other words, they maintain an [E,R] relationship. However, the form "אכול" differs, for its R-time is the sub-clause "מהחל התרומה לביא בית ה'". In consequence, it appears as though the feasting took place from that point on and is thus informed by an E>R relation.

10.2 Infinitive Forms as Border Markers that Close a Succession

One of the pragmatic uses of the infinitive absolute in the Second Temple period prose is its placement at the end of a succession:

(528) אַתָּה הוּא יְהוָה הָאֱלֹהִים אֲשֶׁר **בָּחַרְתָּ** בְּאַבְרָם **וְהוֹצֵאתוֹ** מֵאוּר כַּשְׂדִּים **וְשַׂמְתָּ** שְׁמוֹ אַבְרָהָם: **וּמָצָאתָ** אֶת לְבָבוֹ נֶאֱמָן לְפָנֶיךָ **וְכָרוֹת** עִמּוֹ הַבְּרִית לָתֵת אֶת אֶרֶץ הַכְּנַעֲנִי הַחִתִּי הָאֱמֹרִי וְהַפְּרִזִּי וְהַיְבוּסִי וְהַגִּרְגָּשִׁי לָתֵת לְזַרְעוֹ **וַתָּקֶם** אֶת דְּבָרֶיךָ כִּי צַדִּיק אָתָּה:

---

20. See Williamson (1985:278-279).
21. Myers (1965:181) and Dillard (1987:247), inter alios, read the clause in this fashion.
22. For example, König (1897:III §217b).

You are the LORD God, who **chose** (*qatal*) Abram, who **brought** (*qatal*) him out of Ur of the Chaldeans and **changed** (*qatal*) his name to Abraham. And **found** (*qatal*) his heart to be true to you, **you made (infinitive absolute)** a covenant with him to give the land of the Canaanite, the Hittite, the Amorite, the Perizzite, the Jebusite, and the Girgashite—to give it to his descendants. And **you kept** (*wayyiqtol*) your word, for you are righteous. (Neh 9:7-8)

(529) וָאֶתְפַּלְלָה לַיהוָה אֱלֹהַי וָאֶתְוַדֶּה וָאֹמְרָה אָנָּא אֲדֹנָי הָאֵל הַגָּדוֹל וְהַנּוֹרָא שֹׁמֵר הַבְּרִית וְהַחֶסֶד לְאֹהֲבָיו וּלְשֹׁמְרֵי מִצְוֹתָיו : **חָטָאנוּ וְעָוִינוּ והרשענו (הִרְשַׁעְנוּ) וּמָרָדְנוּ וְסוֹר** מִמִּצְוֹתֶךָ וּמִמִּשְׁפָּטֶיךָ : **וְלֹא שָׁמַעְנוּ** אֶל עֲבָדֶיךָ הַנְּבִיאִים אֲשֶׁר דִּבְּרוּ בְּשִׁמְךָ אֶל מְלָכֵינוּ שָׂרֵינוּ וַאֲבֹתֵינוּ וְאֶל כָּל עַם הָאָרֶץ :

I prayed to the LORD my God, making confession thus: O Lord, great and awesome God, who stays faithful to his covenant with those who love him and keep his commandments! **We have sinned** (*qatal*), **we have gone astray** (*qatal*), **we have acted wickedly** (*qatal*), **we have been rebellious** (*qatal*), **and have deviated (infinitive absolute)** from your commandments and your rules, **and have not obeyed** (לא + *qatal*) your servants the prophets who spoke in your name to our kings, our officers, our fathers, and all the people of the land. (Dn 9:4-6)

(530) וַיֹּאמֶר הָמָן אֶל הַמֶּלֶךְ אִישׁ אֲשֶׁר הַמֶּלֶךְ חָפֵץ בִּיקָרוֹ : **יָבִיאוּ** לְבוּשׁ מַלְכוּת אֲשֶׁר לָבַשׁ בּוֹ הַמֶּלֶךְ וְסוּס אֲשֶׁר רָכַב עָלָיו הַמֶּלֶךְ וַאֲשֶׁר נִתַּן כֶּתֶר מַלְכוּת בְּרֹאשׁוֹ : **וְנָתוֹן** הַלְּבוּשׁ וְהַסּוּס עַל יַד אִישׁ מִשָּׂרֵי הַמֶּלֶךְ הַפַּרְתְּמִים **וְהִלְבִּישׁוּ** אֶת הָאִישׁ אֲשֶׁר הַמֶּלֶךְ חָפֵץ בִּיקָרוֹ **וְהִרְכִּיבֻהוּ** עַל הַסּוּס בִּרְחוֹב הָעִיר **וְקָרְאוּ** לְפָנָיו כָּכָה יֵעָשֶׂה לָאִישׁ אֲשֶׁר הַמֶּלֶךְ חָפֵץ בִּיקָרוֹ :

So Haman said to the king, For the man whom the king desires to honor, **let royal garb which the king has worn be brought** (*yiqtol*), and a horse on which the king has ridden and on whose head a royal diadem has been set; **and let the attire and the horse be put (infinitive absolute)** in the charge of one of the king's noble courtiers. And let the man whom the king desires to honor **be attired (weqatal) and paraded** (*weqatal*) on the horse through the city square, while **they proclaim** (*weqatal*) before him: This is what is done for the man whom the king desires to honor! (Est 6:7-9)

(531) וַיֹּאמְרוּ נַעֲרֵי הַמֶּלֶךְ מְשָׁרְתָיו **יְבַקְשׁוּ** לַמֶּלֶךְ נְעָרוֹת בְּתוּלוֹת טוֹבוֹת מַרְאֶה : **וְיַפְקֵד** הַמֶּלֶךְ פְּקִידִים בְּכָל מְדִינוֹת מַלְכוּתוֹ **וְיִקְבְּצוּ** אֶת כָּל נַעֲרָה בְתוּלָה טוֹבַת מַרְאֶה אֶל שׁוּשַׁן הַבִּירָה אֶל בֵּית הַנָּשִׁים אֶל יַד הֵגֶא סְרִיס הַמֶּלֶךְ שֹׁמֵר הַנָּשִׁים **וְנָתוֹן** תַּמְרֻקֵיהֶן : וְהַנַּעֲרָה אֲשֶׁר **תִּיטַב** בְּעֵינֵי הַמֶּלֶךְ תִּמְלֹךְ תַּחַת וַשְׁתִּי וַיִּיטַב הַדָּבָר בְּעֵינֵי הַמֶּלֶךְ וַיַּעַשׂ כֵּן :

The king's servants who attended him said, **Let** beautiful young virgins **be sought out (volitive *yiqtol*)** for your Majesty. **Let your Majesty appoint (volitive *yiqtol*)** officers in every province of your realm let all the beautiful young virgins **be assembled (volitive *yiqtol*)** at the fortress Shushan, in the harem under the supervision of Hege, the king's eunuch, guardian of the women. **Let them be provided (volitive infinitive absolute)** with their cosmetics. And the maiden who **will suit (future *yiqtol*)** your Majesty will be queen instead of Vashti. The proposal pleased the king, and he acted upon it. (Est 2:2-4)

(532) וְכָל יִשְׂרָאֵל **עָבְרוּ** אֶת תּוֹרָתֶךָ **וְסוֹר** לְבִלְתִּי שְׁמוֹעַ בְּקֹלֶךָ **וַתִּתַּךְ** עָלֵינוּ הָאָלָה וְהַשְּׁבֻעָה אֲשֶׁר כְּתוּבָה בְּתוֹרַת מֹשֶׁה עֶבֶד הָאֱלֹהִים כִּי חָטָאנוּ לוֹ׃

All Israel **has violated (*qatal*)** your teaching and **gone astray (infinitive absolute)** disobeying you; so the curse and the oath written in the Teaching of Moses, the servant of God, **have been poured (*wayyiqtol*)** down upon us, for we have sinned against him. (Dn 9:11)

In the first passage, the infinitive form is situated at the tail end of a string of *qatal* forms and is followed by a *wayyiqtol* form. Likewise, the infinitive in example 529 closes actions that are expressed by the *qatal* form. As opposed to the first example, however, the infinitive delineates the border between a chain of positive forms and a *qatal* form that is prefaced by a negation ("ולא שמענו"). Example 530 entails a modal succession of *yiqtol* and *weqatal* forms. Notwithstanding the fact that only one form ("יביאו") precedes the infinitive, the latter can be said to denote a transition from *yiqtol* to *weqatal*. In the next example the infinitive form delineates the border between a chain of *yiqtol* forms that expresses volitive (request) and *yiqtol* form that expresses simple future.[23] Although the fifth example lacks a chain and only hosts a single *qatal* verb before the infinitive "וסור", it can nevertheless be classified as signifying the end of one form's usage and the beginning of another.[24]

Whereas the infinitive form in all the previous examples in this section fills a discursive role (that of the border marker), there are two prominent exceptions to this rule, both of which involve a chain of infinitive forms:

(533) וּשְׁאָר הַיְּהוּדִים אֲשֶׁר בִּמְדִינוֹת הַמֶּלֶךְ נִקְהֲלוּ **וְעָמֹד** עַל נַפְשָׁם **וְנוֹחַ** מֵאֹיְבֵיהֶם **וְהָרוֹג** בְּשֹׂנְאֵיהֶם חֲמִשָּׁה וְשִׁבְעִים אָלֶף וּבַבִּזָּה לֹא שָׁלְחוּ אֶת יָדָם׃ בְּיוֹם שְׁלוֹשָׁה עָשָׂר לְחֹדֶשׁ אֲדָר **וְנוֹחַ** בְּאַרְבָּעָה עָשָׂר בּוֹ **וְעָשֹׂה** אֹתוֹ יוֹם מִשְׁתֶּה וְשִׂמְחָה׃ וְהַיְּהוּדִים אֲשֶׁר בְּשׁוּשָׁן נִקְהֲלוּ בִּשְׁלוֹשָׁה עָשָׂר בּוֹ וּבְאַרְבָּעָה עָשָׂר בּוֹ **וְנוֹחַ** בַּחֲמִשָּׁה עָשָׂר בּוֹ **וְעָשֹׂה** אֹתוֹ יוֹם מִשְׁתֶּה וְשִׂמְחָה׃

The rest of the Jews, those in the king's provinces, likewise mustered **and fought (infinitive absolute)** for their lives. **They disposed (infinitive absolute)** of their enemies, **and killed (infinitive absolute)** seventy-five thousand of their foes; but they did not lay hands on the spoil. That was on the thirteenth day of the month of Adar; **and they rested (infinitive absolute)** on the fourteenth day **and made (infinitive absolute)** it a day of feasting and merrymaking. But the Jews in Shushan mustered on both the thirteenth and

---

23. Also see Esther 3:13.
24. This alignment is rather commonplace and includes, inter alia, Esther 9:1, 4, 12, 18, 23, 27; Nehemiah 7:3; 9:13; 1 Chronicles 5:20.

fourteenth days, **and rested (infinitive absolute)** on the fifteenth, **and made (infinitive absolute)** it a day of feasting and merrymaking. (Est 9:16-18)

(534) וַיֹּאמֶר אֵלָיו עֲזַרְיָהוּ הַכֹּהֵן הָרֹאשׁ לְבֵית צָדוֹק וַיֹּאמֶר מֵהָחֵל הַתְּרוּמָה לָבִיא בֵית יְהוָה **אָכוֹל וְשָׂבוֹעַ וְהוֹתֵר** עַד לָרוֹב כִּי יְהוָה בֵּרַךְ אֶת עַמּוֹ וְהַנּוֹתָר אֶת הֶהָמוֹן הַזֶּה:

The chief priest Azariah, of the house of Zadok, replied to him, saying, Ever since the gifts began to be brought to the House of the LORD, people **have been eating (infinitive absolute) to satiety (infinitive absolute) and leaving (infinitive absolute)** over in great amounts, for the LORD has blessed his people; this huge amount is left over! (2 Chr 31:10)

In sum, we can cautiously conclude that the authors of the Second Temple period were inclined toward using the infinitive as a discourse border marker for closing chains of non-infinitive forms. In addition, there are cases in which the chains themselves are comprised of infinitive forms.

10.3. The Predicative Functions of the Infinitive Absolute in the Prose of the First Temple Period

In this section, I will survey the predicative functions of the infinitive absolute in First Temple period prose with the objective of providing a contrast to the Second Temple corpus. This topic has yet to be fully explored by scholars of Biblical Hebrew.

10.3.1 The Language of the Law, the Word of God, and General Commands

Twenty-six instances of the infinitive absolute,[25] accounting for approximately 6% of its occurrences in the First Temple period prose, clearly signify a general instruction or command. Be it a direct dialogue or in the language of the law, the common denominator between the vast majority of these cases is that the speaker is God.[26]

---

25. Genesis 17:10; 30:32; Exodus 12:48; 13:3; 20:8; Leviticus 2:6; 6:7; Num. 4:2, 22; 6:23; 15:35; 25:17; Deuteronomy 1:16; 5:12; 15:2; 17:1; 24:8, 9; 25:17; 27:1; Joshua 1:13; 4:3; 6:3; 2 Samuel 24:12; 2Kings 3:16; 4:43 (twice); 5:10; 19:29.
26. The exceptions are Exodus 13:3 (וַיֹּאמֶר מֹשֶׁה אֶל הָעָם **זָכוֹר** אֶת הַיּוֹם הַזֶּה אֲשֶׁר יְצָאתֶם"
    וַיִּשְׁלַח אֵלָיו") and 2 Kings 5:10 (מִמִּצְרַיִם מִבֵּית עֲבָדִים כִּי בְּחֹזֶק יָד הוֹצִיא יְהוָה אֶתְכֶם מִזֶּה"
    "אֱלִישָׁע מַלְאָךְ לֵאמֹר: הָלוֹךְ וְרָחַצְתָּ שֶׁבַע פְּעָמִים בַּיַּרְדֵּן וְיָשֹׁב בְּשָׂרְךָ לְךָ וּטְהָר:") where the speakers are Moses and Elisha, respectively. That said, these two cases are not substantially different from the majority, as they also involve authority figures who serve as God's representatives. The infinitive forms appear within the context of instructions that the speakers issue.

(535) וַיְדַבֵּר יְהוָה אֶל מֹשֶׁה וְאֶל אַהֲרֹן לֵאמֹר: **נָשֹׂא** אֶת רֹאשׁ בְּנֵי קְהָת מִתּוֹךְ בְּנֵי
לֵוִי לְמִשְׁפְּחֹתָם לְבֵית אֲבֹתָם:

The LORD spoke to Moses and Aaron, saying: **Take (infinitive absolute command)** a separate census of the Kohathites among the Levites, by the clans of their ancestral house. (Nm 4:1-2)

(536) **הִשָּׁמֶר** בְּנֶגַע הַצָּרַעַת לִשְׁמֹר מְאֹד וְלַעֲשׂוֹת כְּכֹל אֲשֶׁר יוֹרוּ אֶתְכֶם הַכֹּהֲנִים
הַלְוִיִּם כַּאֲשֶׁר צִוִּיתִם תִּשְׁמְרוּ לַעֲשׂוֹת: **זָכוֹר** אֵת אֲשֶׁר עָשָׂה יְהוָה אֱלֹהֶיךָ לְמִרְיָם
בַּדֶּרֶךְ בְּצֵאתְכֶם מִמִּצְרָיִם:

In cases of a skin affection **be (infinitive absolute command) most careful** to do exactly as the levitical priests instruct you. Take care to do as I have commanded them. **Remember (infinitive absolute command)** what the LORD your God did to Miriam on the journey after you left Egypt. (Dt 24:8-9)

In these cases, the infinitive forms are always positioned at the head of the sentence. Moreover, there are several instances in which infinitives serve as general instructions that stand on their own, including the following example:

(537) וַיֹּאמֶר מְשָׁרְתוֹ מָה אֶתֵּן זֶה לִפְנֵי מֵאָה אִישׁ וַיֹּאמֶר תֵּן לָעָם וְיֹאכֵלוּ כִּי כֹה אָמַר
יְהוָה **אָכֹל וְהוֹתֵר**:

His attendant replied, How can I set this before a hundred men? But he said, Give it to the people and let them eat. For thus said the LORD: **They shall eat (infinitive absolute command) and have some left over (infinitive absolute command)** (2 Kgs 4:43)

On other occasions, the infinitive serves as a border marker between two textual units, which also introduces a set of laws on a given topic:

(538) מִקֵּץ שֶׁבַע שָׁנִים תַּעֲשֶׂה שְׁמִטָּה: וְזֶה דְּבַר הַשְּׁמִטָּה **שָׁמוֹט** כָּל בַּעַל מַשֵּׁה יָדוֹ
אֲשֶׁר יַשֶּׁה בְּרֵעֵהוּ לֹא יִגֹּשׂ אֶת רֵעֵהוּ וְאֶת אָחִיו כִּי קָרָא שְׁמִטָּה לַיהוָה: אֶת הַנָּכְרִי
תִּגֹּשׂ וַאֲשֶׁר יִהְיֶה לְךָ אֶת אָחִיךָ תַּשְׁמֵט יָדֶךָ: אֶפֶס כִּי לֹא יִהְיֶה בְּךָ אֶבְיוֹן כִּי בָרֵךְ
יְבָרֶכְךָ יְהוָה בָּאָרֶץ אֲשֶׁר יְהוָה אֱלֹהֶיךָ נֹתֵן לְךָ נַחֲלָה לְרִשְׁתָּהּ רַק אִם שָׁמוֹעַ תִּשְׁמַע
בְּקוֹל יְהוָה אֱלֹהֶיךָ לִשְׁמֹר לַעֲשׂוֹת אֶת כָּל הַמִּצְוָה הַזֹּאת אֲשֶׁר אָנֹכִי מְצַוְּךָ הַיּוֹם: כִּי
יְהוָה אֱלֹהֶיךָ בֵּרַכְךָ כַּאֲשֶׁר דִּבֶּר לָךְ וְהַעֲבַטְתָּ גּוֹיִם רַבִּים וְאַתָּה לֹא תַעֲבֹט וּמָשַׁלְתָּ
בְּגוֹיִם רַבִּים וּבְךָ לֹא יִמְשֹׁלוּ:

Every seventh year you shall practice remission of debts. This shall be the nature of the remission: every creditor **shall remit (infinitive absolute general command)** the due that he claims from his fellow; he shall not dun his fellow or kinsman, for the remission proclaimed is of the LORD. You may dun the foreigner; but you must remit whatever is due you from your kinsmen. There shall be no needy among you since the LORD your God will bless you in the land that the LORD your God is giving you as a hereditary portion, if only you heed the LORD your God and take care to keep all this Instruction that I enjoin upon you this day. For the LORD your God will bless you as he has promised you: you will extend loans to many nations, but require none yourself; you will dominate many nations, but they will not dominate you. (Dt 15:1-6)

(539) **שָׁמוֹר** אֶת חֹדֶשׁ הָאָבִיב וְעָשִׂיתָ פֶּסַח לַיהוָה אֱלֹהֶיךָ כִּי בְּחֹדֶשׁ הָאָבִיב הוֹצִיאֲךָ
יְהוָה אֱלֹהֶיךָ מִמִּצְרַיִם לָיְלָה : וְזָבַחְתָּ פֶּסַח לַיהוָה אֱלֹהֶיךָ צֹאן וּבָקָר בַּמָּקוֹם אֲשֶׁר
יִבְחַר יְהוָה לְשַׁכֵּן שְׁמוֹ שָׁם : לֹא תֹאכַל עָלָיו חָמֵץ שִׁבְעַת יָמִים תֹּאכַל עָלָיו מַצּוֹת
לֶחֶם עֹנִי כִּי בְחִפָּזוֹן יָצָאתָ מֵאֶרֶץ מִצְרַיִם לְמַעַן תִּזְכֹּר אֶת יוֹם צֵאתְךָ מֵאֶרֶץ מִצְרַיִם
כֹּל יְמֵי חַיֶּיךָ :

Observe (infinitive absolute general command) the month of Abib and offer a passover sacrifice to the LORD your God, for it was in the month of Abib, at night, that the LORD your God freed you from Egypt. You shall slaughter the passover sacrifice for the LORD your God, from the flock and the herd, in the place where the LORD will choose to establish his name. You shall not eat anything leavened with it; for seven days thereafter you shall eat unleavened bread, bread of distress, for you departed from the land of Egypt hurriedly so that you may remember the day of your departure from the land of Egypt as long as you live. (Dt 16:1-3)

(540) **שָׁמוֹר** אֶת יוֹם הַשַּׁבָּת לְקַדְּשׁוֹ כַּאֲשֶׁר צִוְּךָ יְהוָה אֱלֹהֶיךָ : שֵׁשֶׁת יָמִים תַּעֲבֹד
וְעָשִׂיתָ כָּל מְלַאכְתֶּךָ : וְיוֹם הַשְּׁבִיעִי שַׁבָּת לַיהוָה אֱלֹהֶיךָ לֹא תַעֲשֶׂה כָל מְלָאכָה אַתָּה
וּבִנְךָ וּבִתֶּךָ וְעַבְדְּךָ וַאֲמָתֶךָ וְשׁוֹרְךָ וַחֲמֹרְךָ וְכָל בְּהֶמְתֶּךָ וְגֵרְךָ אֲשֶׁר בִּשְׁעָרֶיךָ לְמַעַן יָנוּחַ
עַבְדְּךָ וַאֲמָתְךָ כָּמוֹךָ :

Observe (infinitive absolute general command) the sabbath day and keep it holy, as the LORD your God has commanded you. Six days you shall labor and do all your work, but the seventh day is a sabbath of the LORD your God; you shall not do any work—you, your son or your daughter, your male or female slave, your ox or your ass, or any of your cattle, or the stranger in your settlements, so that your male and female slave may rest as you do. (Dt 5:12-14)

In the examples above, the infinitive forms are employed in a modal sense. The laws or commandments are general, namely the ordinances are in force from the moment of their transmission and are to be performed on a regular basis. For instance, in the last three passages, the nation of Israel is commanded, inter alia, to remit all debts to their kin once every seven years, keep the commandments of Passover on an annual basis, and observe the sabbath each and every week.

The next two passages consist of a cognate structure that performs a volitive function. Once again, the infinitive forms appear at the head of the clause:

(541) **הָלוֹךְ** וְדִבַּרְתָּ אֶל דָּוִד

Go (infinitive absolute direct command) and tell David (2 Sm 24:12)

(542) וַיִּשְׁלַח אֵלָיו אֱלִישָׁע מַלְאָךְ לֵאמֹר **הָלוֹךְ** וְרָחַצְתָּ שֶׁבַע פְּעָמִים בַּיַּרְדֵּן וְיָשֹׁב
בְּשָׂרְךָ לְךָ וּטְהָר׃

Elisha sent a messenger to say to him, **Go (infinitive absolute direct command)**
and bathe seven times in the Jordan, and your flesh shall be restored and you
shall be clean. (2 Kgs 5:10)

This set of usages constitutes an alternative to the erstwhile "לך + וקטלת" pattern
of First Temple period prose,[27] which also signifies God's word and the beginning
of a prophecy.[28]

10.3.2 Unmarked Consecutive Forms

Whereas predicative infinitive absolute forms arrayed in unmarked sequential
constructions constitute the dominant form of usage in the Second Temple period
prose, there are only twelve examples of this collocation (less than 3%) in the First
Temple period prose.[29] Moreover, if potential textual errors and later editorial re-
visions are taken into account, then the true number of instances is possibly even
less. Similar to Second Temple period prose, these forms signify the chronological
relationship [R, E], which also characterizes the standard consecutive forms (i.e.,
wayyiqtol and *weqatal*). In contrast to the latter, the infinitives are unmarked with
respect to the modal axis, for they can appear in succession with both modal and
indicative forms alike:

a. Consecutive infinitive form aligned with *Wayyiqtol*:

(543) וַיָּבֹא גִדְעוֹן וּמֵאָה אִישׁ אֲשֶׁר אִתּוֹ בִּקְצֵה הַמַּחֲנֶה רֹאשׁ הָאַשְׁמֹרֶת הַתִּיכוֹנָה אַךְ
הָקֵם הֵקִימוּ אֶת הַשֹּׁמְרִים **וַיִּתְקְעוּ וְנָפוֹץ** בַּשּׁוֹפָרוֹת הַכַּדִּים אֲשֶׁר בְּיָדָם׃ [30]

Gideon and the hundred men with him arrived at the outposts of the camp, at
the beginning of the middle watch, just after the sentries were posted. **They
sounded (*wayyiqtol*) the horns and smashed (infinitive absolute)** the jars that
they had with them. (Jgs 7:19)

---

27. This model appears several times in the prose of the First Temple, where it also signifies the word of God; see Exodus 3:16; Judges 4:6; 1 Samuel 15:3, 18; 22:5 (the actual
speaker in this particular passage is Gad the Prophet); 23:2; 2 Samuel 7:5. Also see
Isaiah 6:9; 20:2; 1 Chronicles 17:4; 21:10; in all these cases, the speaker is also God.
This stands in contradistinction to the structure לך + an imperative, examples of which
include: "וַיֹּאמֶר עֵלִי לִשְׁמוּאֵל לֵךְ שְׁכָב וְהָיָה אִם יִקְרָא אֵלֶיךָ וְאָמַרְתָּ דַּבֵּר יְהוָה כִּי שֹׁמֵעַ עַבְדֶּךָ" (1
Sm 3:9); or "וְהִנֵּה אֶשְׁלַח אֶת הַנַּעַר לֵךְ **מְצָא** אֶת הַחִצִּים" (1 Sm 20:21).
28. The "הלוך וקטלת" pattern opens the following prophecies: Isaiah 38:5; Jeremiah 2:2;
3:12; 13:1; 17:19; 19:1; 28:13; 34:2; 35:2, 13; 39:16.
29. Genesis 41:43; Exodus 8:11; 32:6; Leviticus 6:7; Deuteronomy 3:6; Joshua 9:20;
11:11; Judges 7:19; 1 Samuel 2:28; 22:13; 25:26; 1 Kings 9:25.
30. Also see Genesis 41:43; Exodus 8:11; Deuteronomy 3:6.

b. Consecutive infinitive form aligned with *weqatal*:

(544) וְהֶעֱלָה שְׁלֹמֹה שָׁלֹשׁ פְּעָמִים בַּשָּׁנָה עֹלוֹת וּשְׁלָמִים עַל הַמִּזְבֵּחַ אֲשֶׁר בָּנָה לַיהוה וְהַקְטֵיר אִתּוֹ אֲשֶׁר לִפְנֵי יְהוה[31]

Solomon **used to offer (*weqatal*)** burnt offerings and sacrifices of well-being three times a year on the altar that he had built for the LORD, and **he used to offer (infinitive absolute)** incense on the one that was before the LORD. (1 Kgs 9:25)

c. Consecutive infinitive form aligned with *yiqtol*:

(545) זֹאת נַעֲשֶׂה לָהֶם וְהַחֲיֵה אוֹתָם וְלֹא יִהְיֶה עָלֵינוּ קֶצֶף עַל הַשְּׁבוּעָה אֲשֶׁר נִשְׁבַּעְנוּ לָהֶם:

This is what **we will do (*yiqtol*)** to them: **We will spare (infinitive absolute)** their lives, so that there may be no wrath against us because of the oath that we swore to them. (Josh 9:20)

d. Consecutive infinitive form aligned with an infinitive:

(546) וַיַּשְׁכִּימוּ מִמָּחֳרָת וַיַּעֲלוּ עֹלֹת וַיַּגִּשׁוּ שְׁלָמִים וַיֵּשֶׁב הָעָם לֶאֱכֹל וְשָׁתוֹ וַיָּקֻמוּ לְצַחֵק:

Early next day, the people offered up burnt offerings and brought sacrifices of well being; they sat down **to eat (infinitive construct) and drink (infinitive absolute)** and then rose to dance. (Ex 32:6)

(547) וַיֹּאמֶר אֵלָיו שָׁאוּל לָמָּה קְשַׁרְתֶּם עָלַי אַתָּה וּבֶן יִשַׁי בְּתִתְּךָ לוֹ לֶחֶם וְחֶרֶב וְשָׁאוֹל לוֹ בֵּאלֹהִים לָקוּם אֵלַי לְאֹרֵב כַּיּוֹם הַזֶּה:

And Saul said to him, Why have you and the son of Jesse conspired against me? **You gave (infinitive construct)** him food and a sword, **and inquired (infinitive absolute)** of God for him that he may rise in ambush against me, as is now the case. (1 Sm 22:13)

The function of these forms on the modal axis is context-dependent, as is their person; in other words, the infinitives derive their modal meaning from the head of the series. That said, it is also worth noting that the nearest form is not always the one which signifies the person. For instance, in Genesis 41:43 the infinitive links back to the verb "וירכב":

---

31. Also see 1 Samuel 2:28; 25:33. To this may be added, albeit with reservations, Exodus 36:7, as the Samaritan text, the Septuagint, and the Peshitta contain a verb form instead of an infinitive.

(548) **וַיַּרְכֵּב** אֹתוֹ (פרעה) בְּמִרְכֶּבֶת הַמִּשְׁנֶה אֲשֶׁר לוֹ **וַיִּקְרְאוּ** לְפָנָיו אַבְרֵךְ **וְנָתוֹן**
(פרעה) אֹתוֹ עַל כָּל אֶרֶץ מִצְרָיִם :

He had him **ride** (*wayyiqtol* **3m.s.**) in the chariot of his second-in-command,
and they cried (*wayyiqtol* **3m.p.**) before him, "Abrek!" Thus **he placed** him
(**infinitive absolut 3m.s.**) over all the land of Egypt.

10.4 Forms Appearing in Facultative Successions

Yet another small group (totaling three occurrences) consists of infinitives in a fac-
ultative succession. As in consecutive forms, the significance of these infinitives
stem from the constructs that they are affiliated with. All three instances appear
within the language of the law:

a. Refers to *yiqtol*:

(549) אִישׁ כִּי **יִדֹּר** נֶדֶר לַיהוָה **אוֹ הִשָּׁבַע** שְׁבֻעָה לֶאְסֹר אִסָּר עַל נַפְשׁוֹ לֹא יַחֵל דְּבָרוֹ

If a man **makes** (*yiqtol*) a vow to the LORD **or takes** (**infinitive absolute**)
an oath imposing an obligation on himself, he shall not break his pledge.
(Nm 30:3)

(550) וְכִי **תִמְכְּרוּ** מִמְכָּר לַעֲמִיתֶךָ **אוֹ קָנֹה** מִיַּד עֲמִיתֶךָ אַל תּוֹנוּ אִישׁ אֶת אָחִיו :

When **you sell** (*yiqtol*) property to your neighbor, **or buy** (**infinitive absolute**)
any from your neighbor, you shall not wrong one another. (Lv 25:14)

b. Refers to *weqatal*:

(551) לֹא תֹאכְלוּ כָל נְבֵלָה לַגֵּר אֲשֶׁר בִּשְׁעָרֶיךָ תִּתְּנֶנָּה **וַאֲכָלָהּ אוֹ מָכֹר** לְנָכְרִי כִּי עַם
קָדוֹשׁ אַתָּה לַיהוָה אֱלֹהֶיךָ לֹא תְבַשֵּׁל גְּדִי בַּחֲלֵב אִמּוֹ :

You shall not eat anything that has died a natural death; give it to the stranger
in your community **and he will eat it** (*weqatal*) **or you may sell [it]** (**infinitive
absolute**) to a foreigner. For you are a people consecrated to the LORD your
God. You shall not boil a kid in its mother's milk. (Dt 14:21)

10.5 The Infinitive Absolute—Conclusion

Compared to First Temple period prose, the language of the Second Temple period reflects a dramatic break in the use of the infinitive absolute. However, the decline in the construct's use is not as precipitous as commonly thought.[32] With this in mind, the primary difference between the language of the First and Second Temple periods does not pertain to the decline of the infinitive absolute, but to the manner in which it is used. In the First Temple period language, the tautological function is very common (about 73%). When a predicative infinitive does appear, it is usually within the framework of a general command. When positioned at the beginning of a preceptive chain of laws, the infinitive is likely to serve as a border marker that introduces a string of directives touching upon the same particular topic. Alternatively, the construct may stand on its own and convey the word of God. There are also a smattering of cases (some 3%) in which the infinitive absolute appears in unmarked successions.

In contrast to the First Temple period, the predominant usage of infinitive forms in Second Temple period prose is the predicative (some 80%).[33] The majority of these infinitives serve as consecutive forms that are unmarked for mood. When the infinitive absolute is arrayed alongside a chain of other forms, it tends to serve as a marker that signifies the **end of a chain**, while in the First Temple period prose it usually demarcates the **beginning of a succession**. The use of the tautological infinitive falls off dramatically in the Second Temple period, and may constitute an archaic vestige from the First Temple period.

---

32. Smith (2000), who has researched the use of the infinitive absolute in Sirach and the Dead Sea Scrolls, reaches a similar conclusion. According to Smith, an in-depth analysis of all the material from Qumran indicates that the predicative capacity of the infinitive absolute was clearly present in these texts; in particular, see Smith (2000:266-267).
33. This figure excludes the adverb הרבה.

Conclusion

Throughout this book, we have endeavored to shed light on Biblical Hebrew syntax by fashioning a synchronic structural account of the verbal tense system that underpins the prose of the Second Temple period. The importance of singling out the distinct syntax of the biblical texts from this era is tied to the multiple layers of the Biblical Hebrew scriptures. In contrast to syntax, the research on the Bible's phonetic (and morphological) strata is heavily reliant on the testimony of the vocalization tradition, which was compiled more than a thousand years after the texts were first written. Since this tradition's effect on the syntax is less immediate than that of other levels, the syntax serves as a window through which we can observe the dramatic historical vicissitudes that the Hebrew linguistic system underwent during the biblical epoch.

The present work was divided into two main parts. The first explicated the methodological and theoretical fundaments of this book. In this section, we focused on defining the corpus and elucidating key linguistic terms. Moreover, we surveyed various interpretations of the verbal system that researchers have suggested over the years and outlined the research tools that were employed herein. The second part of the work showcased the detailed account of the verbal system present in Second Temple period texts.

Our delineation and classification of the corpus were shaped by a diachronic outlook as well as our decision to concentrate on the era's prose texts. The diachronic comparison prompted us to select only those texts for which there is a broad consensus over Second Temple period origin. In consequence, we have left out those texts whose date of origin remains the subject of debate, such as Jonah and Ruth. As above mentioned, the second parameter is the text's prosaic nature, which is comprised of narratives, direct speech, the language of the law, and lists. Consequently, the book of Ecclesiastes, which belongs to the wisdom literature genre, was removed from our corpus.[1]

Our account is predicated on the methodological decision to adopt the structural approach as the overarching framework for this study. This method had a profound impact on our work and thus the nature of the discussion. Here too, we were guided by two points of reference: the distinction between "langue" and "parole"; and the distinction between the syntagmatic and paradigmatic planes. In accordance with the "langue-parole" parameter, the first step of this work was to aggregate, analyze, and catalog all 4,270 occurrences of the verb in our corpus. The discoveries that were made within the "parole" framework set the stage for generalizations on the "langue" level. The final step of this process was to

---

1. Ecclesiastes stands in complete contradistinction to contemporaneous prose texts in all that concerns the verbal system, see Isaksson (1987).

ascertain the network of links between the "langue" and "parole" spheres as well
as the instances where no such ties exist.

The syntagmatic-paradigmatic distinction also played a crucial role. Exam-
ining the way verb forms interact in a continuum, on the one hand, and how they
replace each other in similar contexts, on the other, led us to the conclusion that
the meaning of any form can only be determined by contrasting it with the other
forms in the system. By proposing a more sophisticated viewpoint, which takes
into account a wide range of mutual relations among all the forms comprising
the system, our description casts doubt on those approaches that seek to place
the verbal system into one inclusive category, such as tense, aspect, or mode.
On account of the linguistic findings from the Second Temple period corpus,
we have predicated our analysis of the Biblical Hebrew tense system on the
reference-time and modal axes.

Grasping the concept of reference time is essential to describing languages
that possess a relative tense system, such as Biblical Hebrew. Therefore, we
opened with a definition of "relative tense systems" and compared them to "absolute tense systems." In this context, one of the prevalent definitions of tense is
"a grammatical category that maintains a chronological link to a defined deictic
axis."

Among the primary distinctions between an absolute and relative tense system is the deictic axis to which the different forms refer. The central axis of
absolute tense systems is the speech (S) point: everything that precedes this
juncture is past; and everything that comes after is in future. As a result, absolute systems contain two deictic centers—speech time and reference (R) time.
Conversely, verb forms in relative tense systems, like Biblical Hebrew, only
maintain a link with the reference-time axis. Therefore, the biblical forms can
denote relations of antecedence, subsequence, and simultaneity, among others,
in all tenses: the past, the present, and the future. The determining factor with
respect to the chronological significance of a verb form in a relative system is its
reference time. In consequence, the notion of R-time is critical to any account of
the biblical tense system.

Over the years, Biblical Hebrew scholars have been hard pressed to categorize
the classical sequential forms (*wayyiqtol* and *weqatal*) accurately. Since the eighteenth century, the prevalent assumption has been that the principal function of
these forms is to signify chronological or logical succession vis-à-vis their ante-
cendent forms.[2] Our desire to formulate a general account of all Second Temple
period forms drove us to search for a definition of the consecutive form that is, inter alia, grounded on a connection to "reference time." With this objective in mind,

2.   For details, see §2.1.3 and §2.2.4 above.

and on the basis of our findings, we have reached the conclusion that sequential forms always encompass their own reference time [R,E]. To bolster this claim, we cited cases in which sequential forms do not express a chronological succession and demonstrated how the inclusion of their R-time enables them to construct a chain of events that the audience perceives to be a chronological succession. Put differently, classifying a verb as a "consecutive form" does not necessarily mean that it marks a chronological succession. Instead, these forms are endowed with a quality that enables Hebrew writers to concatenate chronological successions, among other meanings.[3]

As noted, the second lynchpin of our theory is the modal axis. We have chosen to follow in the footsteps of those scholars who contend that the verb forms of the Hebrew Bible are arrayed according to mood, rather than aspect. Defining the purviews of "mode" and "aspect" is no easy task. The principal obstacle to a facile and consistent outline of the border between these two concepts is the fact that typological comparisons indicate that the semantic categories of different languages are likely to contain disparate items. For instance, the expression of habituality in one language falls under the modal category, while the same meaning serves as part of the aspectual system in another language. In light of the above, the question that begs asking is thus: What is the status of, say, the habitual past within other meanings that are conveyed in the Biblical Hebrew verbal system?

Our decision to cite the example of habitual meanings is no coincidence. This meaning has posed one of the more complicated theoretical problems in all that concerns the role of the *yiqtol* and *weqatal* forms. In many studies, the term modality is restricted to the volitive. However, in the broader sense of the word, the volitive, or deontic modality, is but one component of the modal field, and this is the definition that was adopted for the purpose of this study. For instance, an appraisal of *yiqtol* and *weqatal*'s habitual meanings within the biblical verb system must take into account the fact that these forms express different categories of epistemic modality (e.g., the future, conditions, and questions), deontic modality (the imperative, the prohibitive, oaths, the hortative, optative, and will), and even the language of the law.

The verbs of the Hebrew Bible constitute a system in flux. As a comparison between the First and Second Temple periods indeed reveals, the roles and systematic standing of certain forms (the infinitive construct, the infinitive absolute, and the participle) underwent dramatic transformations, while other forms (*qatal*, *yiqtol*, and *weqatal*) displayed less sweeping changes that moderately expanded upon or detracted from their classical functions. In addition, there were conservative forms (*wayyiqtol* and the volitive forms) whose functions remained stable, but the

---

3.   Other functions include changing a narrative's perspective and emphasizing other aspects of an event.

aforementioned vicissitudes affected their position within the system. Saussure's schematic chart, which was already presented in the introduction, outlines both the continuity and permutations that characterize biblical prose's transition from the First to the Second Temple period (1972:246):

Period A

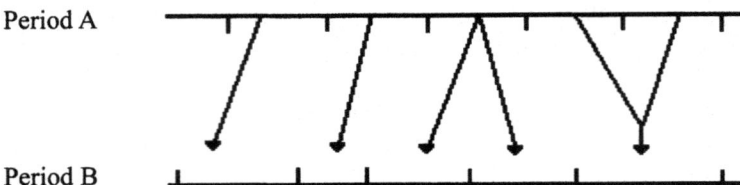

Period B

From a diachronic standpoint, the transition between these two eras attests to the fact that a string of dynamic syntactic and functional changes can transpire even within a conservative morphological framework.

Two central phenomena drew our attention to Second Temple period prose: the steep rise in the predicative use of uninflected forms; and the deterioration of the system of consecutive forms. The first manifestation of the former is the central role that the participle assumes, thereby outshining its functions in First Temple period Hebrew and the language of the Sages. This change engendered occasional overlaps between the participle's usages and that of the *yiqtol* and infinitive construct forms. Another expression of this phenomenon is that the infinitive forms (the infinitive construct and the infinitive absolute) entered the verbal paradigm. Notwithstanding the infinitive construct's established adverbial roles, its predicative use expands appreciably during this period. In its predicative usages, the infinitive construct is a modal form that signifies its meanings in a clear and consistent fashion. Moreover, it apparently covers the same "turf" as *yiqtol* in our corpus. The predicative function of the infinitive absolute (קטול) is practically its only usage during the Second Temple period. Although there are more entrenched uses of this form (such as the tautological function), we contend that these are mere vestiges of an earlier era. The infinitive absolute's debut in the verbal system is tied to the general convulsion that sequential forms underwent during this period. In essence, we are witnesses to the advent of a new consecutive form alongside the two classical ones—*wayyiqtol* and *weqatal*. However, unlike the latter two, the infinitive absolute is neutralized from the standpoint of the modal axis. In other words, it denotes succession in both modal and indicative contexts and a continuation of the respective forms.

The second major phenomenon that transpires during the Second Temple period is the aforementioned undermining of the existing system of consecutive forms. In classical Hebrew, succession is designated almost exclusively by *wayyiqtol* in the indicative field and *weqatal* in the modal field (as well as "*waw* + a volitive form" in volitive frameworks). Several concomitant processes were responsible for the system's collapse in the Second Temple period: the emergence of a new sequential form (the infinitive absolute), which is unmarked from the standpoint of its link to the modal axis; and the growing use of the collocations "*waw* + *qatal*," "*waw* + *yiqtol*," and "*waw* + the infinitive construct" as signifiers of succession. Both these developments are tied to yet another process—the decline in the use of *weqatal* for denoting succession in the modal field.

The charts below summarize the processes that we have discussed throughout this work. The first two outline the Hebrew verbal paradigm of biblical prose texts from the First and Second Temple periods, while the last two tables outline the changes that transpired during these eras with respect to mood and reference time.

a. The Verbal Paradigm in First Temple Period Prose

		Mood					
		Indicative		Modal			
		(+realis, -habitual, -iterative)		General (+irrealis, +future, +habitual, +iterative, +directive)		Volitive (+directive)	
R- time		[R,E]	*Wayyiqtol*	[R,E]	*Weqatal*	[R,E]	*Vol. Forms +* ו
		R≥E	*Qatal*	R≤E	*Yiqtol*	S,R<E	*Volitive Forms*
		|---E---| R	*Participle*				

b. The Verbal Paradigm in Second Temple Period Prose

		Mood					
		Indicative		Modal			
		(realis, -habitual, -iterative)		General (irrealis,+ future, +habitual, +iterative, +directive)		Volitive (+ directive)	
R- time		[R,E]	*Wayyiqtol, Qatal*	[R,E]	*Weqatal, Yiqtol Infinitive Construct*	[R,E]	*Vol.Forms +* ו
						S,R<E	*Volitive Forms*
		R≥E	*Qatal*	R≤E	*Yiqtol Infinitive Construct*		
		|--- E ---| R	*Participle --->* (+habitual, +iterative)				
		[R,E]	*Infinitive Absolute*	[R,E]	*Infinitive Absolute*	[R,E]	*Infinitive Absolute*

c. The Modal Axis
A Summary of the Modal Differences between the Language of the First (I) and Second (II) Temple Periods

Mood / Form	Indicative	Modal				
		Deontic Modality		Propositional Modality		
		Law	Directive	Evidential Modality		Epistemic Modality
				Iterative in Past	Habitual Present	
Yiqtol I	-	+	+	+	+	+
Yiqtol II	-	+	+	+	+	+
Weqatal I	-	+	+	+	+	+
Weqatal II	-	+	+	-	-	+
Participle I	+	-	-	+	-	-
Participle II	+	-	-	+	+	-
Qatal I	+	-	-	-	-	-
Qatal II	+	-	-	-	-	-
Wayyiqtol I	+	-	-	-	-	-
Wayyiqtol II	+	-	-	-	-	-
Volitives I	-	-	+	-	-	-
Volitives II	-	-	+	-	-	-
Infinitive Construct I	-	-	-	-	-	-
Infinitive Construct II	-	+	+	+	+	+
Infinitive Absolute I	-	+	-	-	-	-
Infinitive Absolute II	+	+	+	?	+	+

d. Reference-Time Axis
A Summary of the Differences between the Language of the First (I) and Second (II) Temple Periods in All that Concerns the Link to the Reference-Time Axis

R-Time \\ Form	S,R<E	|—E—| R	R<E	R=E	R>E	[R,E]
Wayyiqtol I	-	-	-	-	-	+
Wayyiqtol II	-	-	-	-	-	+
Weqatal I	-	-	-	-	-	+
Weqatal II	-	-	-	-	-	+
Infinitive Absolute I	-	-	-	-	-	-
Infinitive Absolute II	-	-	-	-	-	+
Yiqtol I	+	-	+	+	-	-
Yiqtol II	+	-	+	+	-	+
Infinitive Construct I	-	-	-	-	-	-
Infinitive Construct II	+	-	+	+	-	+
Qatal I	-	-	-	+	+	-
Qatal II	-	-	-	+	+	+
Participle I	-	+	-	(+)	-	-
Participle II	-	+	-	(+)	-	-
Volitives I	+	-	-	-	-	+
Volitives II	+	-	-	-	-	+

Bibliography

Andersen, Francis I. 1974. *The Sentence in Biblical Hebrew*. The Hague: Mouton.

Azar, Moshe. 1992. "A Step Forward towards Understanding the Structure of a Focused Sentence in Contemporary Hebrew." In *Hebrew: A Living Language*, vol. 1, ed. U. Ornan, R. Ben Shahar, and G. Turi (Haifa: University of Haifa Press), 87-99 [Hebrew].

Baker, David W. 1980. "Further Examples of the Waw Explicativum." *Vetus Testamentum* 30:129-136.

Baltzer, Klaus. 1999. *Deutero-Isaiah*. Minneapolis: Fortress.

Barnes, Oswald. L. 1965. *A New Approach to the Problem of the Hebrew Tenses and Its Solution without Recourse to Waw-Consecutive*. Oxford: Thornton and Son.

Basal, Nasser. 1992. *The Grammatical Theory of Rabbi Judah Ḥayyūj*. PhD diss., Ramat-Gan: Bar-Ilan University [Hebrew].

Bauer, Hans. 1910. "Die Tempora im Semitischen, ihre Entstehung und ihre Ausgestaltung in den Einzelsprachen." *Beiträge zur Assyriologie und Semitischen Sprachwissenschaft* 8:1-53.

———, and Pontus Leander. 1922. *Historische Grammatik der hebräischen Sprache des Alten Testamentes*. Halle: M. Niemeyer.

Ben-Hayyim, Ze'ev. 1977. "The Verbal Tenses in the Biblical Language and the Samaritan Traditions Therein." In *A Book for Dov Sadan*, ed. S. Werses, N. Rotenstreich, and C. Shmeruk (Tel Aviv: Hakibbutz Hameuchad), 66-86 [Hebrew].

———. 1985. "The Historical Unity of the Hebrew Language and its Division into Periods." In *Language Studies*, vol. 1, ed. M. Bar-Asher (Jerusalem: The Hebrew University), 3-25 [Hebrew].

Bergsträsser, Gotthelf. 1918-1929. *Hebräische Grammatik*, vol. 1-2. Leipzig: Vogel.

Berlin, Adele. 1985. *The Dynamics of Biblical Parallelism*. Bloomington: University of Indiana Press.

Blake, Frank R. 1951. *A Resurvey of Hebrew Tenses*. Rome: Pontificium Institutum Biblicum.

Blau, Yehoshua. 1971. "On the Repetition of the Predicate in the Bible." In *Bible and Jewish History—Studies in Bible and Jewish History Dedicated to the Memory of Jacob Liver*, ed. B. Uffenheimer (Tel Aviv: University of Tel Aviv), 234-240 [Hebrew].

———. 1983. "On Polyphony in Biblical Hebrew." In *Proceedings of the Israel Academy of Sciences and Humanities* 6:105-183.

Böttcher, Friedrich. 1866. *Ausführliches Lehrbuch der hebräischen Sprache I*. Leipzig: F. Mühlau.

Brockelmann, Carl. 1956. *Hebräische Syntax*. Neukirchen: Moers.

Bybee, Joan, Revere Perkins, and William Pagliuca. 1994. *The Evolution of Grammar*. Chicago–London: University of Chicago Press.

Chao, Yuen R. 1954-1955. "Review of G. Fant and M. Halle, *Preliminaries to Speech Analysis*." *Romance Philology* 8:40-46.

Charlap, Luba. 1999. *Rabbi Abraham Ibn-Ezra's Linguistic System: Tradition and Innovation*. Beer Sheva: Ben Gurion University Press [Hebrew].

Chomsky, William. 1952. *David Kimhi's Hebrew Grammar (Mikhlol)*. New York: Bloch Publishing Co.

Clifford, John E. 1969. *Tense and Tense Logic*. The Hague: Mouton.

Cohen, David. 1984. *La Phrase nominale et l'évolution du système verbal en sémitique*. Leuven: Peeters.

Cohen, Ohad. 2005. "Predicative Uses of the Infinitive Construct לקטל in the Hebrew of the Second Temple Period: The Language of Esther and the Dead Sea Scrolls." In *Language Studies* 10:75-99. [Hebrew].

——. 2011. "ויאכל וישת ויקם וילך ויבז עשו את הבכורה"—On the Meaning of the Sequential Forms in Biblical Hebrew." In *Language Studies* 13:13-37 [Hebrew].

Collins, Terence. 1978. *Line-Forms in Hebrew Poetry: A Grammatical Approach to the Stylistic Study of the Hebrew Prophets*. Rome: Pontifical Biblical Institute.

Comrie, Bernard. 1976. *Aspect*. Cambridge: Cambridge University Press.

——. 1985. *Tense*. Cambridge–New York: Cambridge University Press.

Curtius, Georg. 1863. *Erläuterungen zu meiner griechischen Schulgrammatik*. Prague: F. Tempsky.

Dahl, Östen. 1975. "On Generics." In *Formal Semantics of Natural Language*, ed. E. L. Keenan (London-New York-Melbourne: Cambridge University Press), 99-111.

Dahood, Mitchell J. 1952. "Canaanite-Phoenician Influence in Qoheleth." *Biblica* 33:30-52, 191-221.

Damourette, Jacques and Pichon, Édouard. 1932. *Des Mots à la Pensée—Essai de Grammaire de la Langue Française (Livre 5, Le Verbe)*. Paris: Collection des linguistes contemporains.

Davidson, Andrew B. 1901. *Hebrew Syntax*. 3d ed. Edinburgh: T. and T. Clark.

Deny, Jean. 1971. *Grammaire de le langue Turque*. Wiesbaden: Dr. Martin Säudig oHG.

Dietrich, Franz E. C. 1846. *Abhandlungen zur hebräischen Grammatik*. Leipzig: F. C. W. Vogel.

Dillard, Raymond B. 1987. *2 Chronicles*. Word Biblical Commentary 15. Waco, TX: Word.

Dotan, Aron. 1997. *The Dawn of Hebrew Linguistics: The Book of Elegance of the Language of the Hebrews by Saadia Gaon*. Jerusalem: World Union of Jewish Studies [Hebrew].

Driver, Godfrey R. 1936. *Problems of the Hebrew Verbal System*. Edinburgh: T. & T. Clark.

Driver, Samuel R. 1891 [1913]. *An Introduction to the Literature of the Old Testament*. 9th ed. Edinburgh: C. Scribner's Sons.

———. 1892. *A Treatise on the Use of the Tenses in Hebrew and Some Other Syntactical Questions*. 3d ed. Oxford: Oxford University Press.

Durham, John I. 1987. *Exodus*. Word Biblical Commentary 3. Waco, TX: Word.

Eskhult, Mats. 1990. *Studies in Verbal Aspect and Narrative Technique in Biblical Hebrew Prose*. Uppsala: Uppsala University Press.

———. 2000. "Verbal Syntax in Late Biblical Hebrew." In *Diggers at the Well: Proceedings of a Third International Symposium on the Hebrew of the Dead Sea Scrolls and Ben Sira*, ed. T. Muraoka and J. F. Elwolde (Leiden: Brill), 84-93.

Ewald, Heinrich. 1827. *Kritische Grammatik der hebräischen Sprache*. Leipzig: Hahn.

———. 1828. *Grammatik der hebräischen Sprache*. Leipzig: Hahn.

———. 1831. *Grammatica Critica Linguae Arabicae*, Leipzig: Hahn.

———. 1870. *Ausführliches Lehrbuch der hebräischen Sprache des Alten Bundes*, 8th ed. Göttingen: Dieterich.

Florentin, Moshe. 2000-2001. "The Distribution of Short and Long Imperfect Forms in Biblical Hebrew." *Lešonenu* 63:9-18 [Hebrew].

Garr, Randall W. 2006. "The Paragogic *nun* in Rhetorical Perspective." In *Biblical Hebrew in Its Northwest Semitic Setting*, ed. S. E. Fassberg and A. Hurvitz (Winona Lake, IN: Eisenbrauns), 65-74.

Gesenius, Wilhelm. 1815. *Geschichte der hebräischen Sprache und Schrift*. Leipzig: F. C. W. Vogel.

———, Emil Kautzsch, and Arthur Ernest Cowley. 1910. *Gesenius' Hebrew Grammar*. Oxford: Clarendon.

Givón, Talmy. 1994. "Irrealis and the Subjunctive." *Studies in Language* 18:265-337.

Goldenberg, Gideon. 1966. *The Amharic Tense-System*. PhD diss., Jerusalem: The Hebrew University [Hebrew].

———. 1977. "Imperfectly-Transformed Cleft Sentences." In *Proceedings of the Sixth World Congress of Jewish Studies*. Jerusalem: World Union of Jewish Studies, 127-133.

———. 1985. "Verbal Category and the Hebrew Verb." In *Language Studies* 1:295-348 [Hebrew].

———. 1983a. "On Syriac Sentence Structure." In *Arameans, Aramaic and the Aramaic Literary Tradition*, ed. M. Sokoloff (Ramat-Gan: Bar-Ilan University Press), 97-140.

———. 1983b. "Nominalization in Amharic and Harari: Adjectivization." In *Studies in Semitic Linguistics*, ed. G. Goldenberg (Jerusalem: Magnes Press), 343-366.

———. 1991. "Direct Speech and the Hebrew Bible." In *Studies in Hebrew and Aramaic Syntax Presented to J. Hoftijzer*, ed. K. Jongeling, H. L. Murre-van den Berg, and L. van Rompay (Leiden: Brill), 79-96.

Goldfajn, Tal. 1998. *Word Order and Time in Biblical Hebrew Narrative*. Oxford: Clarendon.

Goldingay, John E. 1989. *Daniel*. Word Biblical Commentary 30. Dallas, TX: Word.

Gordon, Cyrus H. 1949. "Azitawadd's Phoenician Inscription." *Journal of Near Eastern Studies* 8:108-115.

Greenstein, Edward L. 1988. "On the Prefixed Preterite in Biblical Hebrew." *Hebrew Studies* 39:7-17.

Gross, Walter. 1975. "Das nicht substantivierte Partizip als Prädikat im Relativsatz hebräischer Prosa." *Journal of Northwest Semitic Languages* 4:23-47.

Harris, James. 1771. *Hermes or Philosophical Inquiry Concerning Universal Grammar*. London: John Nourse & Paul Vaillant.

Harris, Zellig S. 1952. "Discourse Analysis." *Language* 28:1-30.

Hatav, Galia. 1997. *The Semantics of Aspect and Modality, Evidence from English and Biblical Hebrew*. Amsterdam–Philadelphia: John Benjamins Publishing Company.

———. 2000a. "Time Movement in Biblical Hebrew." *Hebrew Linguistics* 47: 63-84 [Hebrew].

———. 2000b. "(Free) Direct Discourse in Biblical Hebrew." *Hebrew Studies* 41:7-30.

———. 2004. "Anchoring World and Time in Biblical Hebrew." *Journal of Linguistics* 40:491-526.

Heller, Roy L. 2004. *Narrative Structure and Discourse Constellations: An Analysis of Clause Function in Biblical Hebrew Prose*. Harvard Semitic Studies, vol. 55. Winona Lake, IN: Eisenbrauns.

Heyse, Karl W. L. 1856. *System der Sprachwissenschaft*. Berlin: F. Dümmler.

Hinrichs, Erhard. 1986. "Temporal Anaphora in Discourse." *Linguistics and Philosophy* 9:63-82.

Hjelmslev, Louis. 1961. *Prolegomena to a Theory of Language*. Wisconsin: University of Wisconsin Press.

Huehnergard, John. 1987. "Stative, Predicative, Pseudo-Verb." *Journal of Near Eastern Studies* 46:215-232.

Huesman John. 1956. "Finite Uses of the Infinitive Absolute." *Biblica* 37:271-295.

Hughes, James. 1993. "Review of B. K. Waltke and M. O'Connor, *An Introduction to Biblical Hebrew Syntax*." *Journal of Jewish Studies* 44:132-137.

Hurvitz, Avi. 1972. *The Transition Period in Biblical Hebrew*, Jerusalem: Bialik Institute [Hebrew].

———. 1997. "Historical Linguistics and the Hebrew Bible—The Formation and Emergence of Late Biblical Hebrew." In *Studies in Language: Hebrew Through the Ages—In Memory of Shoshanna Bahat*, vol. 2, ed. M. Bar-Asher (Jerusalem: The Academy of the Hebrew Language), 15-28 [Hebrew].

———. 2000. "Can Biblical Texts be Dated Linguistically? Chronological Perspectives in the Historical Study of Biblical Hebrew." *Vetus Testamentum Supplement* 80:143-160.

Ibn Ezra, Abraham. 1791. *The Scales of the Holy Tongue (Ma'aznayim)*, Wolf (Benjamin) ben Samson Heidenheim Edition. Offenbach: Tzvi Hirsch Schpitz [Hebrew].

———. 1827. *The Book of Purity (Sefer Tzakhot), Adroitly Annotated by* Gabriel Hirsch Lippman. Fürth: Tzirndorfer [Hebrew].

Ibn Janah, Jonah. 1964. *The Book of Embroidery (Sefer haRikmah), in the Hebrew Translation of R. Judah ibn Tibbon*, vol 1, *The Body of the Text and Its Meaning*. Ed. M. Vilinski. Jerusalem: Hebrew Language Academy [Hebrew].

Isaksson, Bo. 1987. *Studies in the Language of Qoheleth: With a Special Emphasis on the Verbal System*. Studia Semitica Upsaliensia, vol. 10. Stockholm: Almqvist & Wiksell International.

Jakobson, Roman, Carl Gunnar Michael Fant, and Morris Halle. 1952. *Preliminaries to Speech Analysis, The Distinctive Features and Their Correlates*, Technical Report No. 8. Cambridge, MA: MIT Press.

———. 1960. "Linguistics and Poetics." In *Style in Language*, ed. T. A. Sebeok (Cambridge, MA: MIT Press), 350-377.

———.and Morris Halle. 1971. *Fundamentals of Language*. 2d ed. The Hague-Paris: Mouton.

Joosten, Jan. 1989. "The Predicative Participle in Biblical Hebrew." *Zeitschrift für Althebraistik* 2:128-159.

———. 1992. "Biblical Hebrew *weqātal* and Syriac *hwā qātel* Expressing Repetition in the Past." *Zeitschrift für Althebraistik* 5:1-14.

———. 1999. "The Long Form of the Prefix Conjugation Referring to the Past in Biblical Hebrew Prose." *Hebrew Studies* 40:15-26.

———. 2002. "Do Finite Verbal Forms in Biblical Hebrew Express Aspect?" *Journal of the Ancient Near Eastern Society* 29:49-70.

———. 2005. "The Distinction between Classical and Late Biblical Hebrew as Reflected in Syntax." *Hebrew Studies* 46:327-339.

———. "The Disappearance of Iterative WEQATAL in the Biblical Hebrew Verbal System." In *Biblical Hebrew in Its Northwest Semitic Setting*, ed. S. E. Fassberg and A. Hurvitz (Winona Lake, IN: Eisenbrauns), 135-153.

Joüon, Paul. 1923. *Grammaire de l'hébreu biblique*. Rome: Pontificio Istituto Biblico.

———, and Takamitsu Muraoka. 1996. *A Grammar of Biblical Hebrew*. Rome: Pontificio Istituto Biblico.

———, and Takamitsu Muraoka. 2006. *A Grammar of Biblical Hebrew*. 2d ed. Rome: Pontificio Istituto Biblico.

Kamp, Hans. 1979. "Events, Instants and Temporal Reference." In *Semantics from Different Points of View*, ed. R. Bäuerle, U. Egli, and A. von Stechow (Berlin: Springer Heidelberg), 376-417.

——, and Christian Rohrer. 1983. "Tense in Text." In *Meaning, Use and Interpretation in Language*, ed. R. Bäuerle (Berlin-New York: W. de Gruyter), 250-264.

——, and Uwe Reyle. 1993. *From Discourse to Logic*. Dordrecht-Boston-London: Springer.

Kesterson, John C. 1984. *Tense Usage and Verbal Syntax in Selected Qumran Documents*. PhD diss., Washington, DC: Catholic University of America.

Kiefer, Ferenc. 1987. "On Defining Modality." *Folia Linguistica* 21:67-94.

Kimhi, David. 1793. *Sefer haMikhlol*. Fürth: Itzik Zirndorf [Hebrew].

Knudtzon, Jørgen A. 1889. "Vom sogenannten Perfekt und Imperfekt im Hebräischen." In *Actes du Huitième Congrès International des Orientalistes* (Leiden: Brill). 73-83.

Kogut, Simcha. 1987. "On the Meaning and Syntactical Status of הנה in Biblical Hebrew." In *Language Studies* 2-3:245-258 [Hebrew].

König, Eduard. 1897. *Historisch—Comparative Syntax der hebräischen Sprache*, 3 vols. Leipzig: J. C. Hinrichs.

Kropat, Arno. 1909. *Die Syntax des Autors der Chronik verglichen mit der seiner Quellen*. Weimar: A. Töpelmann.

Kuryłowicz, Jerzy. 1973a. *Studies in Semitic Grammar and Metrics*. London: Curzon.

——. 1973b. "Verbal Aspect in Semitic." *Orientalia* 42:114-120.

Kutscher, Yechezkel E. 1959. *The Language and Linguistic Background of the Isaiah Scroll*. Jerusalem: Magnes Press [Hebrew].

Kuzar, Ron. 2006. "The Consecutive Modal Verb Construction in Israeli Hebrew." *Lešonenu* 68:119-138 [Hebrew].

Lacocque, André. 1979. *The Book of Daniel*. Atlanta: John Knox.

Lambert, Mayer. 1893. "Le Vav Conversif." *Revue des Études Juives* 26:47-62.

Landy, Francis. 1992. "In Defense of Jakobson." *Journal of Biblical Literature* 111:105-113.

Lazard Gilbert. 1975. "La Catégorie de l'éventuel." In *Mélanges linguistiques offerts à Èmile Benveniste*. Collection Linguistique (Société de linguistique de Paris [Louvain: Peeters]), 70.

Levita, Elias. 1767. *The Grammar of Elias*. Berlin: Speier [Hebrew].

Licht, Jacob. 1965. *The Rule Scroll: Scrolls from the Wilderness of Judea—1QS, 1QSa, 1QSb*. Jerusalem: Bialik Institute [Hebrew].

Longacre, Robert E. 1983. *The Grammar of Discourse*. New York: Plenum.

——. 1992. "Discourse Perspective on the Hebrew Verb: Affirmation and Restatement." In *Linguistics and Biblical Hebrew*, ed. W. R. Bodine (Winona Lake, IN: Eisenbrauns), 177-189.

Lyons, John. 1968. *Introduction to Theoretical Linguistics*. Cambridge: Cambridge University Press.

——. 1977. *Semantics*, 2 vols. Cambridge: Cambridge University Press.

McFall, Leslie. 1982. *The Enigma of the Hebrew Verbal System: Solutions from Ewald to the Present Day.* Sheffield: Almond.

Meillet, Antoine. 1916. "Sur le sens linguistique de l'unité latine." *Revue des Nations Latines* 1. Reprinted in Antoine Meillet, *Linguistique historique et linguistique générale* (Geneva: Slatkine, 1982), 310-322.

Meyers, Carol L., and Eric M. Meyers. 1993. *Zechariah 9-14.* Anchor Bible 25C. New York: Doubleday.

Mishor, Mordechai. 1983. *The Tense System in Tanaitic Hebrew.* PhD diss., Jerusalem: The Hebrew University [Hebrew].

Monnesland, Svein. 1984. "The Slavonic Frequentative Habitual." In *Aspect Bound,* ed. C. de Groot and H. Tommola (Dordrecht: Foris), 53-76.

Moran, William L. 1950. "The Use of the Canaanite Infinitive Absolute as a Finite Verb in the Amarna Letters from Byblos," *Journal of Cuneiform Studies* 4:169-172.

Myers, Jacob M. 1965. *2 Chronicles.* Anchor Bible 13. Garden City, NY: Doubleday.

Niccacci, Alviero. 1990. *The Syntax of the Verb in Classical Hebrew Prose.* Journal for the Study of the Old Testament Supplement Series 86. Sheffield: Sheffield Academic Press.

———. 1997. "Analyzing Biblical Hebrew Poetry." *Journal for the Study of the Old Testament* 74:77-93.

———. 2001. "Poetic Syntax and Interpretation of Malachi," *Liber Annuus* 51:55-107.

O'Connor, Michael P. 1980. *Hebrew Verse Structure.* Winona Lake, IN: Eisenbrauns.

Orlinsky, Harry M. 1940-1941. "On the Cohortative and Jussive After an Imperative or Interjection in Biblical Hebrew." *Jewish Quarterly Review N.S.* 31:371-382.

———. 1941-1942. "On the Cohortative and Jussive After an Imperative or Interjection in Biblical Hebrew." *Jewish Quarterly Review N.S.* 32:191-205, 273-277.

Palmer, Frank R. 2001. *Mood and Modality.* 2d ed. Cambridge: Cambridge University Press.

Partee, Barbara H. 1984. "Nominal and Temporal Anaphora." *Linguistics and Philosophy* 7:243-286.

Polzin, Robert. 1976. *Late Biblical Hebrew: Toward an Historical Typology of Biblical Hebrew Prose.* Missoula, MT: Scholars Press.

Prior, Arthur N. 1967. *Past, Present and Future.* Oxford: Oxford University Press.

Qimron, Elisha. 1986. *The Hebrew of the Dead Sea Scrolls.* Atlanta: Scholars Press.

———. 1988. "Observations on the History of Early Hebrew (1000 BCE-200 CE) in the Light of the Dead Sea Documents." In *The Dead Sea Scrolls: Forty Years of Research,* ed. D. Dimant and U. Rappaport (Leiden-Jerusalem: Brill and Yad Ben Zvi), 349-361.

———. 1998. "A New Approach toward Interpreting the Imperfect Verbal Forms in Early Hebrew." *Lešonenu* 61:31-43 [Hebrew].

Rainey, Anson F. 1986. "The Ancient Hebrew Prefix Conjugation in the Light of Amarnah Canaanite." *Hebrew Studies* 27:4-19.

———. 1996. *Canaanite in the Amarna Tablets*, vol. 2. Leiden–New York–Cologne: Brill.

Reichenbach, Hans. 1947. *Elements of Symbolic Logic*. New York: Macmillan.

Revell, Ernest J. 1989. "The System of the Verb in Standard Biblical Prose." *Hebrew Union College Annual* 60:1-37.

Rofé, Alexander. 1986. "The War between David and Goliath—Myth, Theology and Eschatology." *Eshel Beer Sheva*, vol. 3. Beer Sheva: Ben Gurion University, 55-89 [Hebrew].

Rooker, Mark F. 1990. *Biblical Hebrew in Transition: The Language of the Book of Ezekiel*. Journal for the Study of the Old Testament Supplement Series 90. Sheffield: Continuum International Publishing Group.

Rubinstein, A. 1952. "A Finite Verb Continued by an Infinitive Absolute in Biblical Hebrew." *Vetus Testamentum* 2:362-367.

Rundgren, Frithiof. 1959. *Intensive und Aspektkorrelation*. Uppsala: Lundequistska Bokhandeln; Wiesbaden: Otto Harrassowitz.

———. 1961. *Das althebräische Verbum: Abriss der Aspektlehre*. Stockholm: Almqvist & Wiksell.

Saussure, Ferdinand de. 1972. *Cours de linguistique générale*. Ed. Tulli D. Mauro. Paris: Payot.

Schneider, Wolfgang. 1974. *Grammatik des biblischen Hebräisch*. Munich: Claudius-Verlag.

Schröder, Nicolaus W. 1766. *Institutiones ad Fundamenta Linguae Hebraeae in usum Studiosae Juventutis*. Groningae: J. Bolt.

Segal, M. Z. 1932. "Construction of Conditional Clauses in Biblical and Mishnaic Hebrew." *Lešonenu* 4:191-211 [Hebrew].

Sharvit, Shimon. 1980. "The 'Tense' System of Mishnaic Hebrew." In *Studies in Hebrew and Semitic Languauges: Dedicated to the Memory of Prof. Eduard Yechezkel Kutscher*, ed. G. B. A. Sarfatti et al. (Ramat-Gan: Bar-Ilan University), 110-125 [Hebrew].

Skinner, John. 1930. *A Critical and Exegetical Commentary on Genesis*. 2d ed. Edinburgh: T. & T. Clark.

Smith, Mark S. 2000. "The Infinitive Absolute as Predicative Verb in Ben Sira and the Dead Sea Scrolls: A Preliminary Survey." In *Diggers at the Well: Proceedings of a Third International Symposium on the Hebrew of the Dead Sea Scrolls and Ben Sira* (Leiden-Boston-Köln: Brill), 256-267.

Solá-Solé, Josep M. 1961. *L'infinitif Sémitique*. Paris: Champion.

Sternberg, Me'ir. 1983. "Language, World, and Perspective in Biblical Narrative Art: Free Indirect Discourse and Modes of Covert Penetration." *Hasifrut/ Literature* 32:88-131 [Hebrew].

Talshir, David. 1987. "The Development of the Imperfect Consecutive Forms in Relation to the Modal System." *Tarbiz* 56:585-592 [Hebrew].

Talstra, Eep. 1978. "Text Grammar and Hebrew Bible. I: Elements of a Theory." *Bibliotheca Orientalis* 35: 169-174.

Taube, Moshe. 1997. "Echo-construction in Yiddish." *Massorot* 9-10-11:397-420 [Hebrew].

Tur-Sinai, Naftali H. 1954. *The Language and the Book, the Volume on Language.* Jerusalem: The Bialik Institute [Hebrew].

Von Humboldt, Wilhelm. 1836. *Über die Verschiedenheit des menschlichen Sprachbaues und ihren Einfluss auf die geistige Entwickelung des Menschengeschlechts.* Berlin: Königlichen Akademie der Wissenschaften.

Waltke, Bruce K., and Michael P. O'Connor. 1990. *An Introduction to Biblical Hebrew Syntax.* Winona Lake, IN: Eisenbrauns.

Washburn, David L. 1994. "Chomsky's Separation of Syntax and Semantics." *Hebrew Studies* 35:27-46.

Watson, Wilfred G. E. 1984. *Classical Hebrew Poetry.* Journal for the Study of the Old Testament Supplement Series 26. Sheffield: JSOT Press.

Weinrich, Harald. 1964. *Tempus: Besprochene und erzählte Welt.* Stuttgart: W. Kohlhammer.

Williamson, Hugh G. M. 1985. *Ezra, Nehemiah.* Word Biblical Commentary 16. Waco, TX: Word.

Zevit, Ziony. 1990. "Roman Jakobson, Psycholinguistics, and Biblical Poetry." *Journal of Biblical Literature* 109:385-401.

Zewi, Tamar. 1992. *Syntactical Modifications Reflecting the Functional Structure of the Sentence in Biblical Hebrew.* PhD diss., Jerusalem: The Hebrew University [Hebrew].

Index of Texts

LXX
Genesis

1 Samuel

2 Samuel

Samaritan Pentateuch
Deuteronomy

Dead Sea Scrolls
1QH

1QM